THE 1972 PARRAMATTA JAIL GLOSSARY

Dr Bruce Moore has published many studies of Australian English. He was chief editor of the two-volume *Australian National Dictionary: Australian Words and Their Origins* (2016). He edited Australian dictionaries for Oxford University Press, including the *Australian Oxford Dictionary*, the *Australian Concise Oxford Dictionary*, and the *Australian Pocket Oxford Dictionary*. His book *Speaking Our Language: The Story of Australian English* (2008) is the standard account of the history of Australian English. Other monographs include *What's Their Story: A History of Australian Words* (2010) and *Come in Spinner: A History of Two-up and Its Language* (2022). He was Director of the Australian National Dictionary Centre at the Australian National University from 1994 to 2011, and is currently an Honorary Associate Professor at ANU.

STUDIES IN THE HISTORY OF AUSTRALIAN ENGLISH

The Australian National Dictionary Centre (ANDC) was established in 1988 to study the history of the Australian English lexicon. Its major research project is the *Australian National Dictionary: Australian Words and Their Origins* (AND). The first edition of AND was published in 1988 by Oxford University Press and was edited by W.S. Ramson. The second edition was published in 2016 and was edited by Bruce Moore. An updated online edition will be launched in 2024. AND records words that are uniquely Australian, are used more frequently here, and/or which have special significance in Australia. It is the preeminent historical record of the Australian English lexicon.

In addition to AND, researchers at the ANDC have produced numerous lexical monographs that have focused on particular aspects of the Australian vocabulary, including historical periods such as the convict era, the gold rush era, and the world wars, as well as regional studies looking at the vocabularies of parts of Australia such as South Australia, Queensland, and Western Australia.

In this tradition, the ANDC has launched a new series of studies of the history of the Australian English vocabulary. **Studies in the History of Australian English** will include critical editions of historical glossaries, dictionaries, and wordlists. Through making these lexical resources more widely available to researchers and those interested in the history of language, we hope to further the study of the development of the English language and English-language lexicography. The series will also include dictionaries of some specialised vocabularies, and thereby help to contribute to the documentation of the Australian English lexicon.

The 1972 Parramatta Jail Glossary is the first book in the series.

AMANDA LAUGESEN
Series Editor
Director ANDC and chief editor,
Australian National Dictionary: Australian Words and Their Origins

THE 1972 PARRAMATTA JAIL GLOSSARY

AN EDITION WITH COMMENTARY

Bruce Moore

First published in 2023 by Australian Dictionary Publications.
austdictionarypublications@gmail.com

This publication is copyright. Apart from any fair dealing for the purpose of private study, research, criticism or review, as permitted under the Copyright Act 1968, no part may be reproduced by any process without written permission. Enquiries should be made to the publisher.

© Bruce Moore

Print: 978-0-6459550-0-2
e-Pub: 978-0-6459550-1-9

Design and Layout: Ampersand Duck. Cover Design by Caren Florance: includes the 1899 sketch plan for Parramatta Jail (NSW Archives).

THE 1972 PARRAMATTA JAIL GLOSSARY

AN EDITION WITH COMMENTARY

Bruce Moore

First published in 2023 by Australian Dictionary Publications.
austdictionarypublications@gmail.com

This publication is copyright. Apart from any fair dealing for the purpose of private study, research, criticism or review, as permitted under the Copyright Act 1968, no part may be reproduced by any process without written permission. Enquiries should be made to the publisher.

© Bruce Moore

Print: 978-0-6459550-0-2
e-Pub: 978-0-6459550-1-9

Design and Layout: Ampersand Duck. Cover Design by Caren Florance: includes the 1899 sketch plan for Parramatta Jail (NSW Archives).

CONTENTS

Acknowledgements   vi

Introductory Material

1   The Parramatta Jail Glossary: Background   1

2   Parramatta Jail   3

3   The Social Functions of Underworld and Prison Slang   9

4   The Words in the Glossary   12

5   Where Do the Words in the Glossary Come From?   24

6   The Editing of the Glossary   34

7   Bibliography   37

The Parramatta Jail Glossary   **41**

Appendix A: Two pages from the manuscript   223

Appendix B: Transcription of Glossary with corrections and emendations indicated in footnotes   227

Appendix C: Alphabetised Glossary with corrections and emendations included   241

ACKNOWLEDGEMENTS

My main thanks go to the group of prisoners who compiled this word list in 1972. The prisoners' names are not known, but they have certainly made an important contribution to our understanding of prison slang, and of aspects of the history of Australian English. My thanks also to the *Macquarie Dictionary* editors, Susan Butler and Vanessa Mack, who were instrumental in getting the prisoners to put the list together.

Mark Gwynn, Amanda Laugesen, Julia Robinson, and Gina Ward read the finished manuscript, and offered useful comments and critiques. Thanks also to Lorenz Daley, Mark Dapin, Sally Flynn, and Ghil'ad Zuckermann for information and advice on various matters. Currency Press gave me access to the Jim McNeil files at the National Library of Australia. The online version of *Green's Dictionary of Slang* was an invaluable resource. The staff of the National Library of Australia, especially in the Petherick Room, were always helpful. Thanks also to Caren Florance for her expertise and care in the design and typesetting.

The edition draws on the material collected for the 1988 and 2016 editions of the *Australian National Dictionary*, and on the continuing research of the Australian National Dictionary Centre at the Australian National University.

1. THE PARRAMATTA JAIL GLOSSARY: BACKGROUND

The *Parramatta Jail Glossary* was produced by prisoners at Parramatta Jail in Sydney in 1972. It consists of a typewritten and unalphabetised list of 362 words and phrases with definitions.

This glossary was used for citation evidence in the first edition of the *Australian National Dictionary* (1988). It was used extensively by Gary Simes in his *Dictionary of Australian Underworld Slang* (1993), an edition of two prison glossaries compiled by two prisoners in Sydney in 1944 and in 1950 (revised 1955). The glossary was used again as citation evidence for the second edition of the *Australian National Dictionary* (2016).

The glossary contains prison slang, but it also includes underworld slang and more general slang and colloquialisms. Many of the entries provide the earliest evidence for Australian words and phrases and for special Australian senses of more widely known words. For these reasons the material in the glossary is of great importance to the history of Australian English, and it should be in the public domain. This is the major rationale for this edition.

In order to bring the glossary into the public domain I embarked on an edition of it in the tradition of historical lexicography as exemplified by the *Oxford English Dictionary* and the *Australian National Dictionary*. Gary Simes also edited his prison glossaries in the same manner. In this tradition the edition aims to give a history of all the words, meanings, and phrases in the Glossary, and to illustrate the history of their use by quotations from other texts.

During most of the time that I was working on the edition, I knew nothing of how the Parramatta Jail Glossary had been compiled. For the Australian National Dictionary Centre the glossary existed only as an 11-page photocopied document. When cited in the *Australian National Dictionary* the bibliographical information for it reads simply: 'Unpublished typescript, ANDC archive'.

The problem of the origin of the glossary was solved for me by Pat Manser's 2021 book *More than Words: The Making of the Macquarie Dictionary*. The first edition of the *Macquarie Dictionary* appeared in 1981, but work began in late 1969, and in the early 1970s efforts were under way to collect Australian material. Two early researchers on the project, Vanessa Mack and Sue Butler, headed off to Parramatta Jail:

> Another area the dictionary was able to tap into came about as a result of Vanessa and Sue's involvement in a program initiated by the Governor of Parramatta Gaol, where some prison inmates would meet weekly with people from outside the prison community to participate in a program designed to expand the prisoners' communication skills. The

inmates were also encouraged to write stories, poetry and plays as part of their rehabilitation. This led to many opportunities for the collection of prisoners' language. After Sue and Vanessa had made clear their interest in the collection of words and expressions used by the inmates, the participants went on to create a special wider group to encourage everyone in the prison to contribute. (p. 64)

And so the 1972 Parramatta Jail Glossary came into existence. Some of the words in the glossary found their way into the first edition of the *Macquarie Dictionary*. In the list of specialists who contributed to the first edition of the *Macquarie Dictionary* we find: 'PRISON SLANG The Resurgents Debating Society, Parramatta Gaol'.

Section 2 of the introductory material provides a brief history of the Parramatta Jail, focusing especially on the state of the prison at the time the Glossary was compiled. It introduces the important figure of Jim McNeil, a prisoner in Parramatta jail, who in the period 1971 to 1974 wrote a number of plays about prison life. Whereas the Glossary is simply a list of words with definitions, McNeil's plays contextualise many of the terms and give us a sense of the prisoners' voices.

Section 3 places the contents of the Glossary within the wider history of prison-slang lexicography, and within wider explorations of the functions of language within a prison system.

Section 4 examines the range of words and phrases in the Glossary, dividing them up into semantic clusters: life in prison, including food, accommodation, and sex; the language of crime; the language of criminals' relationships with the police; and the language of the court system. Most importantly, it looks at the way prisoner values are embedded in the language of the prison system.

Section 5 examines where the words in the Glossary come from. Some of them have an origin in British slang, a tradition of criminal slang that Australia shared until late in the nineteenth century. In the first half of the twentieth century some terms are imported from American criminal slang. The vast majority of the terms and phrases, however, are Australian.

Section 6 explains the principles of editing, and gives a guide to the main features of a typical entry.

Section 7 is a bibliography of the material relevant to these introductory sections, and includes lists of Australian underworld and prison slang.

Then follows the edited Parramatta Jail Glossary.

At the end of the book there are three appendices. Appendix A is a copy of two pages from the eleven-page typed manuscript of the Parramatta Jail Glossary. Appendix B is a literal transcription of the unalphabetised glossary, with corrections and emendations indicated in footnotes. Appendix C is the alphabetised glossary with corrections and emendations included.

2. PARRAMATTA JAIL

A jail existed at Parramatta from 1796 to 2011.[1] It was initially called *Parramatta Gaol* (with the older 'gaol' spelling rather than 'jail'), and from 1992 it was called the *Parramatta Correctional Centre*. The centre was closed in 2011.

In 1788, ten months after the First Fleet arrived at Sydney, Governor Phillip began a settlement on the Parramatta River about 25 kilometres west of Sydney. It was called Rose Hill, named after a British politician, but in 1791 Phillip changed the title to its Aboriginal name Parramatta (meaning 'place' + 'eels'). In 1796 a jail, made of log and thatch, was built near the river. It was badly damaged by a fire in 1799. Work on a new building, made of stone, began in 1802 and was completed in 1804. The jail was again damaged by fire in 1807, and the building deteriorated over the following years.

A new jail was built between 1835 and 1842, and this formed the structural and design basis of the jail that existed in 1972 when the Glossary was written. A sketch plan from 1861 shows the initial three wings radiating out from the gaoler's house (see Fig. 1). Between 1870 and 1900 three more cell wings were gradually built, separate from the original three cells, and the final structure of the cell part of the prison can be seen in an 1899 plan (see Fig. 2).

From the late 1920s many of the prisoners were required to take part in the jail's manufacturing pursuits, and workshop areas were constructed for these activities. In 1972, the year when the glossary was put together, the average daily prisoner population at Parramatta was 457.[2] Of these, 138 inmates were regularly involved in the jail's manufacturing pursuits, including garment making (30), boot making (40), bread baking (17), cabinet making (14), brush making (17), and tinsmithing (20).

The prisoners' accommodation, even as late as 1972, was hardly salubrious. Over time, and in line with changes in thinking about how jails should be run, the cells were configured for single accommodation, or for more than one prisoner per cell. This was usually one or three prisoners per cell, with two per cell being avoided because of the fear that the two cell mates would engage in sex. Kerr describes the cells in 4 Wing and 5 Wing, which were constructed in the 1880s:

> The standard size cell in 5 and 4 wings was 10' x 8' although 4 wing had pairs of enlarged 13'9" x 10' cells on each level at the northern end. The

---

[1] Historical information provided from: J. Kerr, *Parramatta Gaol Central Precinct: Assessment of Cultural Significance and Recommended Heritage Requirements* (1985); J. Kerr, *Parramatta Correctional Centre: Its Past Development and Future Care* (1995); N. Sahni (compiler), *Parramatta Gaol* (2020).
[2] Parliament of New South Wales. Report of the Department of Corrective Services for the year ended 30 June, 1972.

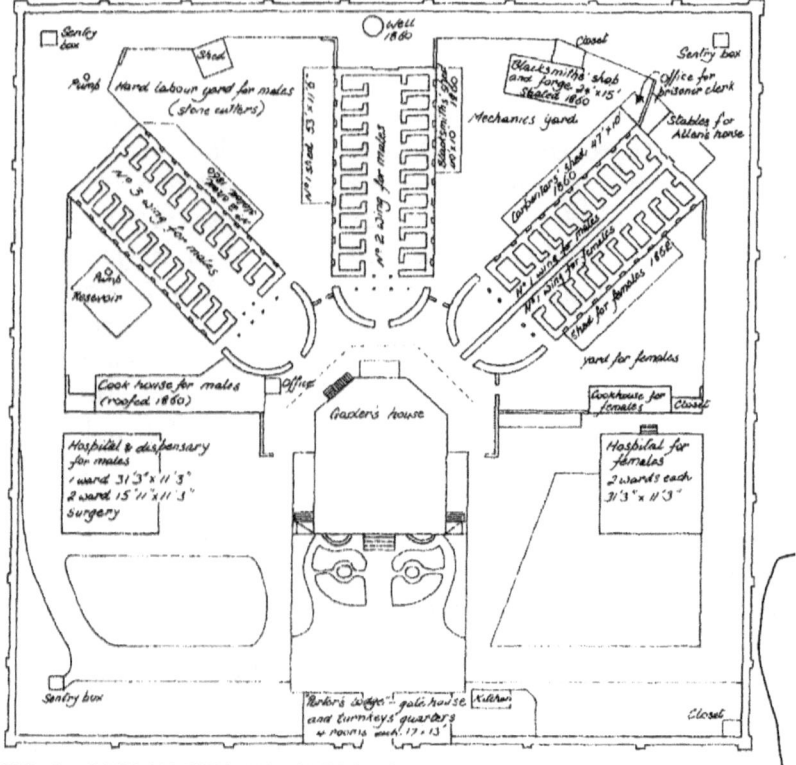

FIG. 1   PARRAMATTA JAIL SKETCH PLAN, 1861

10′ x 8′ cells were intended for single occupation but were large enough to accommodate three men if necessary. Official abhorrence of homosexual activity always prevented the placement of two men in a cell.[3]

Well into the twentieth century, the accommodation remained primitive. Kerr (1995) reports: 'In 1911 the sewerage system was completed. ... It serviced water closets throughout the gaol but not individual cells. The cells retained the traditional night buckets which were emptied into a sewer inlet beside a tub shed in the south-west corner of the gaol' (p. 35). It was not until 1969 that work began on the sewering of the cells. This was completed in 1974, and so at the time of the compiling of the Glossary, some cells were still unsewered. Jim McNeil's plays *The Chocolate Frog* and *The Old Familiar Juice* were written and performed (1970–72) while he was in Parramatta Gaol, and both are set in jail cells with buckets rather than sewered toilets. The bucket is referenced in the Glossary's phrase to describe the mood of a prisoner who is coping well with his sentence—*doing it on the shit tub*.

---

[3]   *Parramatta Correctional Centre: Its Past Development and Future Care* (1995), p. 25.

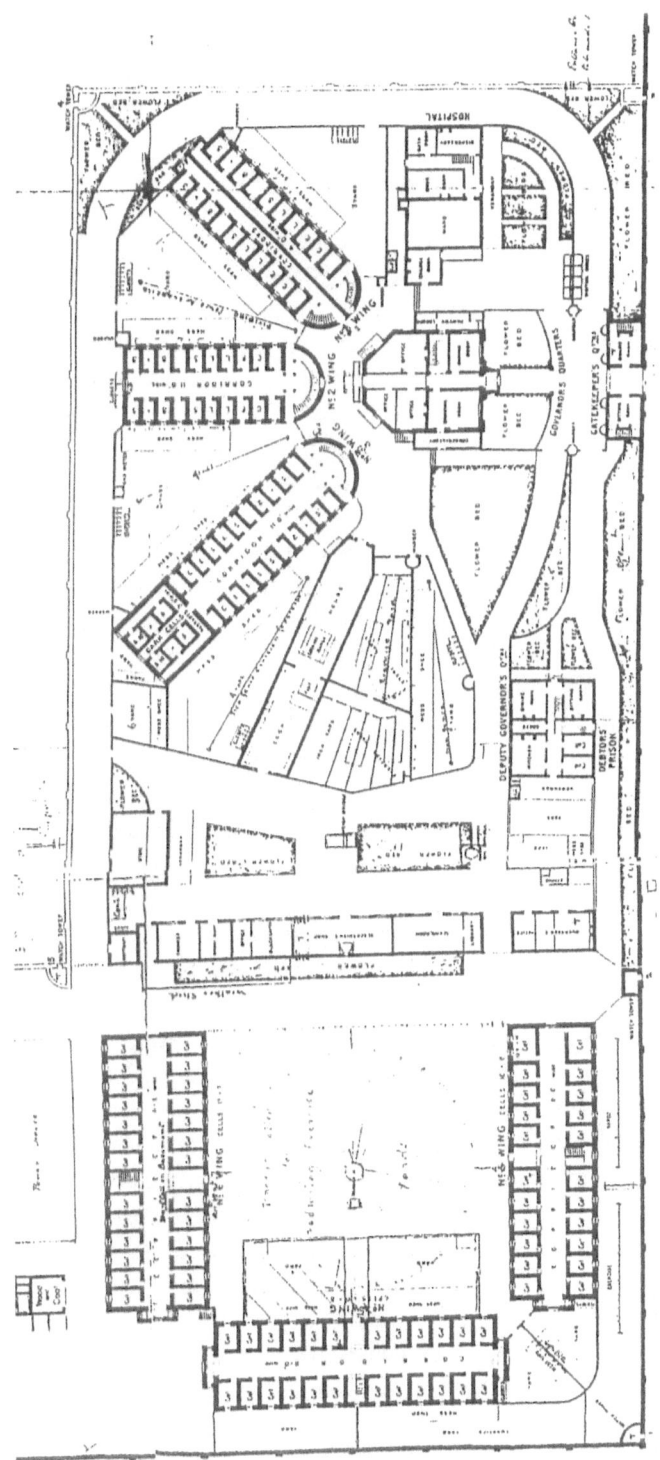

FIG. 2 PARRAMATTA JAIL SKETCH PLAN, 1899

In 1979 the television program *60 Minutes* included an episode, set in Parramatta Jail, which followed a young minor offender experiencing a day in jail: 'Reporter Ian Leslie follows a young offender through a day in Parramatta Prison in which veteran convicts undertake to show him just how hard prison life can be. The potential delinquent is warned in strong terms about the possibility of homosexual rape, of bashings and other cold facts of prison life. It's part of a plan known as the Recidivist Program in which old cons try to dissuade young people from a life of crime'. The episode includes good footage illustrating the physical environment of the prison. It is available at <youtube.com/watch?v=0zBHKiXvLzs>

At the time when the Glossary was put together, Parramatta Jail was used especially for the incarceration of long-term recidivist prisoners. Two of the main gangs in the prison in the late 1960s were controlled by Darcy Dugan (1920–91), bank robber and notorious prison escape artist, and Neddy Smith (1944–2021), murderer, rapist, and drug trafficker.

In spite of the famed toughness of the prison, the visit of the Macquarie researchers to Parramatta Jail in 1972 coincided, as Pat Manser points out, with a relatively enlightened program of cultural and artistic activities for the inmates. Some of these activities are described by ex-prisoner Max Williams in his book *Dingo! My Life on the Run* (1980). A literary discussion group, which included Darcy Dugan, examined texts ranging from *The Iliad* and *The Aeneid* to James Joyce's *Ulysses*. A debating society developed, led by a group that called themselves the Resurgents, and it took part in debating competitions both within and outside the prison. There was an art group, whose members entered their work in exhibitions and competitions. The Resurgents produced a magazine called *Contact*, and firsthand accounts of many of the cultural activities are to be found in it. The writer Rodney Hall visited the prison in 1972 to run a poetry club, and this eventually led to the publication of the book *Poems from Prison* (1973), edited by Hall, and with poems by Max Williams and others.

The potential for violence, however, was always present. There were regular concerts for the inmates, and in December 1972 a group of dancers performed for them. In the audience was Len Lawson, sentenced to life imprisonment for rape and murder: 'At the end of the performance, [Lawson] whipped out a knife and jumped to the stage, holding the blade to the throat of dancer Sharon Hamilton in what prison warders believe was an escape attempt'.[4]

Even so, the positive cultural environment of the prison in the early 1970s was a significant achievement, and it can aid our understanding of the Glossary. This is especially true of the development of a prison theatre group. The August 1970 number of the magazine *Contact* reports that Jim McNeil, at that time president of the Resurgents, had written a play about prison life called *The Last Cuppa*, which had been performed twice in the jail. McNeil had been sentenced

---

[4] *Sun-Herald* (Sydney) 30 November 2003, p. 19.

to 17 years imprisonment in 1967 for armed robbery. In December 1970 *Contact* reported that a theatre group had been created, and that another play by Jim McNeil, *The Chocolate Frog*, was in rehearsal. The August 1971 number of *Contact* gave a detailed report of the production of this play by Q Theatre at the AMP Theatre in Circular Quay. The December 1972 *Contact* reported that McNeil's *The Old Familiar Juice* (a rewriting of *The Last Cuppa*), had been performed in the jail earlier that year before moving to a number of outside theatres. Towards the end of 1972 McNeil was transferred to Bathurst Jail, and there he wrote his third prison play *How Does Your Garden Grow*. Because of his talents as a playwright, there was a campaign by the arts community for McNeil to be released from prison early, and this happened in October 1974. McNeil wrote one more prison play, *Jack*, which was performed in 1977.

McNeil's plays provide a useful supplement to the Parramatta Jail Glossary. The Glossary provides headwords with definitions, but the plays can reveal how the words are used in actual speech. When McNeil's plays were published, there was for each publication a glossary of terms used in the plays. Some fifty of the words in the glossaries to the plays also appear in the Parramatta Jail Glossary. With single- or two-word definitions there is occasionally some overlap in the wording of definitions. For example, both define *kite* as 'newspaper' and *screw* as 'prison warder'. But in most cases the definitions in the two texts are clearly quite independent of one another, and we do not know if McNeil was in any way instrumental in the compilation of the Glossary. The following examples from the glossaries are representative, with the first definition being from the Parramatta Jail Glossary (PJG), and the second from the McNeil glossaries (McN):

back a tail PJG: 'follow after someone else in sexual intercourse'
McN: 'in two up, to back a long shot, here to participate in sodomy'

cruel PJG: 'ruin chances'
McN: 'to spoil an opportunity'

drop off PJG: 'quit what you are doing or else'
McN: 'to desist from pressuring someone, to ease the pressure'

hoon PJG: 'man who lives off worker'
McN: 'pimp, one who lives off the earnings of a prostitute'

lag PJG: 'give someone up'
McN: 'to report misdemeanours'

squarehead PJG: 'honest citizen'
McN: 'one who has never been in prison, one who lives by the norms of society outside prison'

Because McNeil's use of the terms in his plays serves to contextualise them in a way the Parramatta Jail Glossary never does, I have included quotes from McNeil's plays among the illustrative quotations wherever possible (and in addition often quoting the definitions from McNeil's glossaries).

3. THE SOCIAL FUNCTIONS OF UNDERWORLD AND PRISON SLANG

A prison is what Erving Goffman in his book *Asylums* (1961) calls a 'total institution'. By the term 'total institution' Goffman means a social structure in which a group of people spend the bulk, if not all, of their time working, sleeping, and socialising within the physical and psychological boundaries of the institution. For people who live their lives outside total institutions, such day-to-day activities take place in a fairly diffuse manner, 'in different places, with different co-participants under different authorities, and without an overall rational plan' (pp. 6–7). The lives of those who live in total institutions are much more constrained by overt rules, and have severe limits placed on their physical and social freedom. As examples of such total institutions, in addition to prisons, Goffman mentions mental hospitals, monasteries and convents, concentration camps, ships, boarding schools, and army barracks.

There are, of course, important differences between the kinds of total institutions listed in the previous paragraph, and yet they all have a set of noteworthy features in common:

> First, all aspects of life are conducted in the same place and under the same single authority. Second, each phase of the member's daily activity is carried on in the immediate company of a large batch of others, all of whom are treated alike and required to do the same thing together. Third, all phases of the day's activities are tightly scheduled, with one activity leading at a prearranged time into the next, the whole sequence of activities being imposed from above by a system of explicit formal rulings and a body of officials. Finally, the various enforced activities are brought together into a single rational plan purportedly designed to fulfil the official aims of the institution. (Goffman p. 6)

One important aspect of such institutions is that they develop their own special languages: 'An "institutional lingo" develops through which inmates describe the events that are crucial in their particular world' (p. 55).

M.A.K. Halliday in *Language as Social Semiotic* (1978) expanded on the languages of such 'total institutions', calling the institutions 'antisocieties', and calling their languages 'antilanguages'. Halliday defines an 'antisociety' as 'a society that is set up within another society as a conscious alternative to it. It is a mode of resistance, resistance which may take the form either of passive symbiosis or of active hostility and even destruction' (p. 164). The 'antilanguage' is the means by which this alternative to 'normal' society is created: 'The antilanguage is a language of social conflict—of passive resistance or active opposition; but at the same time, like any other language, it is a means of expressing and maintaining the social structure—in this case, the structure of the antisociety' (p. 185).

The two worlds of 'outside the prison' and 'inside the prison', society and antisociety are dramatised in Jim McNeil's *The Chocolate Frog*. The new cellmate Kevin tries to lecture Tosser and Shirker on how they should look forward to the time when they will rejoin the society outside the prison:

> KEVIN: This place ... prison ... it's not forever, it's *not all* there *is!* But you both talk and behave as if this gaol is another world, as if you have no other place Outside, or part to play ... I mean, when you get out of here again ...
>
> (*He stops, confused.*)
>
> TOSSER: (*flatly*) This is *our* world. *They* own the other one.

Shirker later explains that in some cells you can get up on the cupboard and look out at night and see the lights of the outside world that seem to embody a realm of freedom: 'All the lights shinin' like port'oles in the dark, in the winders of their houses, and in the streets, that yer wish yer was walkin' down one of 'em to yer own light ... I just used ter hang there starin', like a kid in a lolly-shop window'. But he has come to realise that he was a fool to imagine that he could ever be part of that world:

> SHIRKER: Whose world? That's just the point, don't yer see? Out there, that's their world ... and my mistake was in fergettin' that little fact. (*Smiling*) ... What if they let me outer here ternite, right now this minute? (*Drooping*) I could walk down all the streets I liked ... wouldn't be one light in one of the windows that was shinin' fer me ... or the likes of me. (*His voice hardening*) *This here* is *my* light! And *this* is *my winder*! (*Softly*) 'N this is *my world* ... yer see?

Thus, whether the criminal is in prison or outside he is still defined as being part of the underworld/prison world. And his world is structured by his language.

In some total institutions the special language is generated almost entirely within the institution. Others have influence both from within and without. For example, the special language used by cadets at the Royal Military College Duntroon in Canberra in the early 1980s was generated largely by the special circumstances of living and training within the institution, but because the military college was part of the larger Australian Defence Force some jargon and slang from the wider military world found its way into the enclosed world of the cadets.[5]

---

[5] Bruce Moore, *A Lexicon of Cadet Language: Royal Military College Duntroon in the period 1983 to 1985* (Canberra: ANDC, 1993).

Prisoners such as the cohort that was at Parramatta in 1972 typically had a long association with the underworld and the criminal class. As teenagers they may have been sent to reform schools as a result of petty crime; many were professional criminals who had been in and out of the prison system. Such prisoners inevitably brought with them the language and attitudes of a criminal subculture that exists apart from the prison. Cressey and Irwin point out that although in all prisons there is a rigid code of behaviour, it operates by rules that are also shared with the outside criminal world: 'The "prison code"—don't inform on or exploit another inmate, don't lose your head, be weak, or be a sucker, etc.—is also part of a criminal code, existing outside prisons'.[6] Prison language does not arise only from the situation of imprisonment; it also draws heavily on the language of the underworld.

It is sometimes suggested that the function of underworld and prison language is secrecy, that it is a kind of argot used to hide or disguise criminals' intentions from the authorities. There was probably some truth in this in the extensive criminal languages recorded between the sixteenth and eighteenth centuries. But by the time we get to the twentieth century it is likely that the police and the prison authorities can decode this language as well as any prisoner. The main function of the language is, as Halliday argues, the creation and maintenance of an alternative social structure—in Shirker's words, an alternative world. This is the group solidarity to which its members aspire, even if the moral code that underlies it may often be breached. And the language that they use to create and express this alternative world is one of the few aspects of their life in prison that the prisoners have any control of.

---

[6] D.R. Cressey & J. Irwin 'Thieves, Convicts and the Inmate Culture', *Social Problems* 10:2 (1962), pp. 142–155 (p. 145).

4. THE WORDS IN THE GLOSSARY

This section examines some of the significant semantic clusters of words. The original manuscript of the Glossary is unalphabetised, but the listing is not entirely random. The compilers sometimes list together semantically related words: types of thieves; cheques and dud cheques; prostitution; sharing and not sharing the proceeds of crime; kinds of firearm; ways of warning that danger is ahead; kinds of police; the process of interrogation at a police station; informers and informing; the procedures of a court; periods of imprisonment; kinds of tobacco; kinds of prison cell; sex in prison; money terms; and so on. Such linking sometimes helps to clarify the meaning of a term whose sense is not fully evident from the brief definition provided. These clusters can be seen in the transcription of the original document, available at Appendix B.

(i) Life in Prison

Many of the terms in the Glossary refer to aspects of the everyday life of the prison. Even when seemingly neutral in denotation, they are often loaded with emotional and psychological connotations. The jail goes by such names as *boob*, *can*, *nick*, and *stir*, seemingly neutral, but compounds generated from these words indicate the ever-present challenges to the inmate's sense of self, and of the attempts of the institution to break him. An inmate who is broken by his prison experience and becomes psychologically disturbed and removed from reality is *boob happy* or *stir-crazy*. The standard cell is called a *peter*, *shovel*, or *slot*, and while it may be preferable to the darkness and complete isolation of the punishment cell called a *black peter* (from the lack of light) or *go-slow* (from the slow passing of time), all the cells are at core and purpose places of deprivation. The inmate is *sloughed up* (locked in his cell) for long periods and is at the mercy of the *screws* or prison warders in the case of a medical or other emergency, with the conflict between inmates and screws indicated by the term *knock up*—a loud banging on cell doors, carried out by many prisoners to attempt to force the authorities to act if a prisoner needs assistance. Such cell doors may be solid steel or *on the grill* ('composed of bars'). There is no privacy, and prisoners and their cells may at any time be subjected to a *ramp*, a search for prohibited goods. If a prisoner is regarded as a troublemaker in one prison, he might be rapidly transferred to another prison in an operation known as a *shanghai*, carried out by plainclothes prison officers called the *mod squad*. If the bars of the cell door indicate deprivation of freedom of movement, the *shit tub* within the cell is a marker of the deprivation of personal amenities (many of the cells at Parramatta were still unsewered in 1972). But *bars* and *shit tub* are also part of the language of absolute deprivation: the phrases *to go off the bars* or *to go off the tub* indicate suicide by hanging within the cell.

Items supplied to the prisoners by the institution are inevitably regarded by them as second-rate. Prison meals are *S.O.S.* 'the same old shit', the porridge served for breakfast is *burgoo* or *moosh*, *boob tea* is weak tea made from jail-supplied leaves, and *chew and spew* is prison stew. Prisoners were provided with a ration of two ounces of tobacco per week, known as a *double* or a *swy*, and the poor-quality tobacco provided is derided as *boob tobacco*. In the days before harder drugs took over the prison system, tobacco was one of the most important items for exchange and bartering. Illegally obtained non-prison tobacco and cigarettes were especially prized: *flat* and *grouse weed* were terms for high quality tobacco from outside the prison; *African* and *grouse cigarette* were terms for outside tailor-made cigarettes.

Indeed, the role of tobacco in the prison system is one of the means by which the prison's alternative social structure is generated. A December 1972 number of the Parramatta Jail's prisoners' magazine *Contact* explains how tobacco in the prison is the equivalent of money in the outside world:

> Tobacco in prison is wealth, it is currency, it is a balm and a curse just like money outside the walls. Prisoners trade everything from false teeth to shoe laces for it, if they need it; some will steal it if they can, in fact a full weed pouch is as much a status symbol as a full pocket of money outside.

Some of the items that are included in the Glossary might seem relatively unimportant to an outsider, but they often point to attempts to assert the continuing agency of the prisoner in a struggle against the prison system's attempt to deny any sense of agency. Thus, a *boil-up* is the making of illegal cups of tea in the cell, using the hidden *dry*, 'unmade tea(leaves)', and using some kind of illegal device to heat the water—the Glossary lists *fat wick* 'a strip of material covered with fat, rolled up, and lit for the purpose of boiling water'. In a context where privacy is almost entirely absent, and where letters to loved ones outside are censored, the *stiff* ('an uncensored letter smuggled out of prison') was an important way of reclaiming some sense of privacy and personal agency. In an era when prisoners had no access to radio or television, a *jigger* (a crystal set or crystal radio receiver) was often constructed from bits and pieces salvaged from around the prison, so that radio programs could be illegally listened to in the cells. Jim McNeil's plays show that the illegal brewing of alcohol in cells was common at Parramatta, but there are few terms relating to this process in the Glossary—there is *lunatic soup* for 'cheap potent wine', which perhaps refers to an alcoholic drink brewed in a cell, and there is the jocular term *musical milk* for 'methylated spirits mixed with milk' and drunk for alcoholic effect.

A cluster of terms (about 22 or 6% of the total) refer to homosexuality, or what we might refer to now as MSM 'men who have sex with men'. A paper about homosexuality in Victoria's Pentridge Prison, written by a long-term inmate John Price, sets out very clearly the circumstances and structure of male sex in this prison, and its main structural features are borne out by evidence from other prisons.[7] The main sex roles are *cat*, *hock*, and *queen*. The cat is a young man, typically under 23, who does not identify as homosexual outside of prison, but who accepts a passive role in sexual intercourse while in prison. It is understood that he does this for reasons of protection and for economic reasons (such as getting extra food and tobacco, good clothes, etc.), but at the same time this provides proof of his innate weakness—he needs the protection of the provider, and he is therefore judged by other inmates as being at the bottom of the social scale ('getting fucked for lollies is as about as low as you can go'). The hock is any man who performs only the active role in sexual intercourse. The hock invariably denies that he is homosexual, and he will sometimes be violent during sex in order to convince both himself and others that the intercourse is merely a matter of sexual release. The queen is a man who identifies as gay both inside and outside the prison, and is prepared to take the passive role in sexual intercourse in prison. While they are often victims of violence, their social status is generally higher than that of the cat, and they may establish a relatively stable relationship with a hock. This structural pattern is replicated in prisons in many countries.

The term *cat* appears in the Glossary, along with its synonyms *Ballarat* (rhyming slang) and *receiver of swollen goods*. The terms *mark* (rhyming slang from *Mark Foy* 'boy') and *nephew* refer to a young man acting as a cat. *Hock* similarly appears, along with the synonyms *arse bandit*, *dung puncher*, *sheriff* ('a hock who jealously guards a cat'), *shirt lifter*, and the ironic *Rudolf Vaselino*. The term *queen*, however, does not appear in the Glossary. Interestingly this term does not appear in the many glossaries of Australian prison slang, with the exception of the 1950 Glossary by a prisoner known only as 'Thirty-five', and who defines it as 'a passive homosexual',[8] a sense that is fairly standard and not suggestive of the structural significance supposed by the hock, cat, queen trinity. In Jim McNeil's play *How Does Your Garden Grow* the character Brenda is certainly a queen in the sense suggested by the John Price article, but nowhere is he called such. Thus, while *cat* and *hock* are widespread terms, the evidence suggests that while 'queen' was a role within the sex structure, the term *queen* was not widely used in the prison system.

Price argues that the cat is generally despised, and this is a common claim in accounts of male prison sex:

---

[7] Price wrote the paper 1981–83. He committed suicide in 1983, and the paper was published in 1984 by Deakin University academic Graeme Angus, who had been given the paper by Price: 'Homosexuality in a Victorian Male Prison', *Mental Health in Australia*, July 1984, pp. 3–12.

[8] 'Thirty-five', The Argot, in G. Simes *A Dictionary of Australian Underworld Slang* (1993), p. 165.

'Queens', who are generally homosexual in the outside world, and who dress as women as far as they are able, have medium to high status in prison. ... There is no indication that 'queens' are ever ostracised for their homosexuality. On the other hand, the second category of men who take a 'feminine' role in homosexual acts are *not* regarded as 'true' homosexuals (that is, homosexuals in the outside world) and are despised as 'cats' or 'punks'; they have a very low status. These men are invariably *called* homosexuals, however, from the moment of their first act of intercourse (which is often in an overtly coercive, or even rape, situation). Their ostracism is that of a despised caste.[9]

'Punk' is a common term in American prisons for what in Australia is termed a *cat*. In Goldin's 1950 study of language in an American prison 'punk' appears in a list of synonyms for 'passive pederast':

apple pie; aunt; bender; bindle boy; boy; brat; Mr. Brown; business; candy; charity stuff; chicken; coozey; drag; double-barrelled ghee; flap; floosie, fruit; fruit for the monkeys; fruit under the old system; gal-boy; gash; gazooney; ginch; girl; gonzel; gunzel; hat; hide; hump under the old system; hunk of hat; hunk of quiff; hunk of skin; hunk of snatch; kid; kife; lay; morph; morphodite; nephew; nola; one of the Brown family; piece of pratt; piece of snatch; pink pants; poger; pogie; pratt-boy; punk; quiff; receiver; ringtail; round-eye; round-heels; skin; slavey; snatch-peddler; stern-wheeler; tail; taker; one who has been tampered with; trade; twidget; two-bit hustler; two-way ghee; whiskers; Willie; works.[10]

A few of the terms on this list can refer to either the 'passive' or 'active' partner, but what is significant about the American list is the sheer number of terms. Halliday, in his study of the antilanguages of 'total institutions' argues that one of their typical features is 'over-lexicalisation', meaning that many terms are generated for particular items that are important in the structuring of the institution and its values. Goldin's 1950 American lists include 50+ for kinds of arrest, 95+ for the verb 'to inform', 20+ for prison guard, 45+ for policeman, 50+ for prostitute, 45+ for swindler. There are some minor concentrations of terms in the Australian evidence, but for some reason the overlexicalisation predicted by Halliday's model and evident in the American evidence does not occur in the Parramatta evidence. Other Australian evidence supports this. Tupper and Wortley's *Anthology of Prison Slang in Australia* (1990) brings together material from many sources, and the only synonym that it adds to the Parramatta Glossary evidence for *cat* synonyms in the Australian prison system is *girl boy*.

---

[9] K. Richmond, 'Fear of homosexuality and modes of rationalisation in male prisons', *Australian & New Zealand Journal of Sociology*, 14:1 (1978), pp. 52–53.
[10] H.E. Goldin et al, *Dictionary of American Underworld Lingo* (1950), p. 292.

The activity of anal sex as performed by the hock is indicated (in addition to the literal denotations of such names as *arse bandit*, *dung puncher*, and *shirt lifter*) by such terms as *back a tail* ('engage in anal intercourse after another person') and *seat* ('to insert one's penis in someone's anus'). The phrase *a ride there for a ride back* is a rare indication of the existence of what might now be termed 'flip-flop sex', with both partners anally penetrating one another during the one sexual encounter. Four terms for 'anus' perhaps indicate obsession or anxiety about anal intercourse—*blot, clacker, freckle, kyber*. *Roseleaf*, defined as 'tongue in bum', is what now would be termed 'rimming'. The *starter* (or means of getting anal intercourse going) is something like margarine, used as 'a substitute for vaseline' or other lubricant.

There are a few terms relating to heterosexual sex in the Glossary: *boy in the boat* 'clitoris', *leg opener* 'alcohol supplied to a woman', and *ted* 'vagina'. But almost all the sexual terms relate to men having sex with men, an indication of how important this is in the structure of prison life, and how a language needs to be created to describe and naturalise it.

Most of the terms listed in this section are specific to the prison circumstances. Some of the terms listed would be used in the outside criminal world, such as *boob* and *nick* for 'prison', but these are not great in number. Some of the terms also exist in the slang of the wider 'non-criminal' world, but they often have a new slant or significance in the prison world. In the outside world the homophobic terms *arse bandit*, *dung puncher*, and *shirt lifter* are highly pejorative, and can be applied to any homosexual. In the prison context they are applied only to the hock (no doubt in part because of the 'insertive' role he plays), but because the hock is not regarded as a 'true' homosexual the terms do not carry the equivalent pejorative and derogatory weight of their outside-prison use.

(ii) The Criminal World

Most of the terms mentioned so far, or at least the context in which they are used, are prison-specific. There are some other large categories of terms that are used by prison inmates, but which are also part of the wider language of the underworld.

a. Crimes

One very large group, making up about 22% of the terms in the Parramatta list, covers crimes, methods of performing criminal acts, weapons used in crime, and the like.

At the less serious end of the spectrum are petty crimes that even in 1972 have a slightly old-fashioned feel to them, suggestive of a criminal world that was in the process of disappearing. Here belong the *running feed* (leaving a cafe without paying for the meal), the *snow-dropper* ('a person who steals

clothes from a clothesline'), and the *dudder* ('a person who sells inferior goods claiming they are high-grade'). A bit further up the line are the crimes of shoplifting and pickpocketing. Terms associated with shoplifting include *clout* ('a method of concealing the stolen property under a coat'), *head-puller* ('a person who distracts a shop assistant's attention while an accomplice steals'), *hoister* ('shoplifter'), *nonch* (a method of concealing stolen goods by draping a coat over them). Terms associated with pickpocketing include *bin* ('pocket'), *block* ('wristwatch'), *bumper* ('person who bumps a victim off balance while an accomplice steals a wallet'), *dip* ('pickpocket'), *kick* ('pocket'), and *whippy* and *willy* ('wallet'). Any crime of theft might call in the services of a *drop* (a 'fence' or 'receiver of stolen goods'). Money crime is also represented by the *bouncer* ('dud cheque') and *paper hanger* ('a passer of dud cheques'), and the phrase *to fly a kite* means 'to pass a dud cheque'.

More serious crime is represented by the world of burglary and safe-breaking. The verb *case* 'to get the layout of a premises for a prospective robbery' could be the preparatory action for burglaries of various kinds. The *pussy-footer* is 'an opportunist sneak-thief' and the *barber* is 'a person who steals from a residential premises without forcing entry', whereas the *bustman* is 'a person who breaks into a commercial premises' and the *tankman* is 'a person who specialises in stealing from safes'. For these more serious burglaries there may be extra participants such as lookouts who are called *cockatoos* and *nit-pickers*, and a *wheelman* who is driver of a getaway car. And in this realm belong guns with names such as *cannon*, *joint*, *piece*, and *roscoe*. Prostitution, often an aspect of organised crime, is represented by *hoon* ('a man who lives off a prostitute'), and *kupie* and *worker*, both terms for 'prostitute'.

b. Criminals and the Police

Terms referring to the criminal's engagement with police account for about 8% of the Parramatta Glossary. Ordinary police are called *wallopers*, detectives are *heavies* or *jacks*, and undercover police are the *dog squad*. If you are caught *dead to rights* ('red-handed') or *sprung* in the commission of a crime you may be *buckled* ('arrested') and *lumbered* ('taken to a police station') in a *bun wagon* ('paddy wagon'). There the police will take a *mug shot*, you will be *grilled*, perhaps *under the lights*, with the possible outcomes of *come nothing* ('make no admissions') or *come yer guts* ('confess to the crime'). A common fear is that you will be *loaded* ('framed'), *verballed* ('forced to sign a fabricated confession'), or *dollied* ('loaded up with false material evidence'). There is always the possibility that one of the police officers in the arresting and charging process will be a *sugar bag* ('police officer who accepts bribes') who will respond positively to a *sling* ('bribe'). Another possibility is *ginger ale* (rhyming slang for 'bail'), even if it rests on the dubious foundation of *straw bail* ('papers signed by a sugar bag on false security').

c. Criminals and the Courts

Terms referring to the criminal's engagement with the courts and with the process of sentencing account for about 11% of the Parramatta Glossary. Two courts are listed. The *low jump* was 'the court of petty sessions' (now called a 'local court') which dealt with minor criminal and civil matters. The *high jump* was 'the court of quarter sessions', which could deal with more serious crimes (excluding those that were punishable by death). These courts were usually presided over by a magistrate who was a called a *beak*, one of the oldest slang terms in the Glossary, first appearing in England in the sixteenth century. If the person admits his guilt, this is indicated by a nod, and by the phrases *get yer head down* or *nod yer head*. Traditionally Friday was set aside for prisoners who were known to be pleading guilty and this was called *woodpeckers' day*, probably from the notion that the guilty nods proceeded as quickly as the bird pecked down into the tree. To be acquitted is to *beat it* or *get up*. To be found guilty is to *go under* or be *sunk*. In response to a guilty verdict the prisoner could decide to *kick along with it* ('accept it with equanimity') or to *hoist the flag* ('indicate that he would appeal'). Legal aid was not widely available in Australia until after 1973. Friends of the prisoner might put on a *barrel*, a benefit night centred on the drinking of beer, to raise funds to pay for defence counsel or to put up bail. Or there might simply be a collection of money, called a *Kentucky*.

A period of imprisonment was called a *lagging*, and there were many slang terms for different lengths of sentence. The Glossary includes:

bed and breakfast 7 days
sleep 7 days to three months
drag 3 months
zack 6 months
clock 12 months
swy 2 years
spin 5 years
brick 10 years
the lot life imprisonment

Within the prison the length of a prisoner's sentence can be a measure of the status afforded to him by the warders or the other prisoners. The following account refers to the system in Sydney's Darlinghurst Jail in 1880, and although it does not use the terms *sleep*, *drag*, and so on, it structures the status of the prisoners according to the lengths of stay designated by such terms:

> **1880** *Evening News* (Sydney) 10 April p. 7: When the prisoner is removed from the dock he is straightway marched back to the prison, in company with a ticket, on which is written the length of his sentence, and ticket and man are handed to the attendant warder. This ticket is left in A wing

but the convict is taken over to B wing, there to be shaved and put into a complete suit of prison garments. New? Well, that depends entirely upon the length of his sentence; the shorter the sentence the older the clothes! And here it may be as well to remark upon the various treatment to which the different sentences are subjected. The 'toe-ragger' (so called from the habit his class have of wrapping their feet in old rags in default of boots) who has come in possibly on a charge of drunkenness, or under that truly absurd and most supremely British enactment, the Vagrant Act, is treated even by the prisoners with contumely, scorn, and contempt. The larrikin who has committed an assault on the police, and has been summarily sentenced to three months, receives scant attention from his fellows, and nothing but harsh words from the warders. The Quarter Sessions convict comes next in order, generally a man sentenced from 18 months to two years for larceny, or perhaps forgery. He is much better treated, and if he be an old offender, is perhaps referred to by his comrades as an authority. Next comes the long sentence men—men who, at any rate, in the eyes of the sentencing judge, have committed heinous offences—these are the pets of the warders, and are shown and pointed out by them with pride to all, and any visitor to the gaol. But the men who receive the best treatment are the condemned men, or those who have been sentenced to death and reprieved. These last are lucky indeed! they are quite an institution, in themselves, for being, in general, 'lifers', the authorities naturally feel a certain pride in making them as comfortable as possible.

If the court declares that a criminal is a habitual offender, extra years could be added by the judge to the prison sentence, and this was referred to as *the key* or *the twist*. A criminal who regularly turns up at the prison after being sentenced for short periods of time might be described as *in and out like a honeymoon prick*.

All these terms are part of the language of the underworld as well as the language of prisoners and the prison, but within the prison system some have greater significance than outside it, because of the role they play in defining the prisoner's identity and his place within the prison structure.

(iii) Criminal Values

The values of the criminal world are shared by criminals both in and outside prison. One of the Glossary's longest definitions is for the term *crim*. This is a standard Australian term for a 'criminal', but the Glossary is at pains to stress that the abbreviation applies only to one kind of criminal. It defines *crim* as 'a professional thief' and adds that 'this term only applies to those who uphold (the) criminal code', and that 'it is a mistake to think that anyone in gaol automatically qualifies'. Thus a very common Australian abbreviation has a very precise and limiting meaning within the criminal world. Other terms in the

Glossary give an indication of what it means to 'uphold the criminal code'.

The Glossary tells us that a person who upholds the criminal code is *solid*: 'staunch to criminal code'. The earliest record of the word *solid* being an important value in criminal circles is provided in American contexts. In 1931 G. Irwin in *American Tramp and Underworld Slang* gives: '*Solid*, trustworthy; sound. To be trusted' (p. 47). Eric Partridge in his 1950 *Dictionary of the Underworld*, with reference to American sources from 1933 to 1936, gives two closely-related senses: 'taking the third degree without confessing or impeaching; completely trustable by the underworld'. In their 1962 study of American underworld and prison slang Cressey and Irwin argue that the 'right guy' (the 'trustworthy guy') in the prison system displays the same qualities that are valued in the outside criminal world, and that these qualities are encapsulated in the term *solid*:

> The core values of this subculture ... include the important notion that criminals should not betray each other to the police, should be reliable, wily, but trustworthy. ... In the thief subculture a man who is known as 'right' or 'solid' is one who can be trusted and relied upon. High status is also awarded to those who possess skill as thieves, but to be just a successful thief is not enough; there must be solidness as well. A solid guy is respected even if he is unskilled, and no matter how skilled in crime a stool pigeon may be, his status is low.[11]

Twenty years later a study of a prison in the south-eastern US showed that *solid* was still central to the values within the prison: '"A Solid convict" is an inmate who will not "snitch", "rat", or "fink" on a fellow inmate because he is committed to the inmates and against the officials. He is the most respected category of inmates by both officials and inmates'.[12]

In the American context, the definition of the 'right guy' within the prison and the 'solid' guy outside the prison is almost identical with the Parramatta Glossary's definition of *crim*. In both cases criminal expertise must go hand in hand with an adherence to the criminal code, and with loyalty to other criminals or prisoners. While the early evidence for this sense of *solid* is American, at some stage it was transferred to Australia. It appears in Australia in 1950, first in a glossary of criminal slang published by Sydney detective B.K. Doyle: '*Solid*, one who is firm, rigid, quite unmovable in his views, actions, and assertions; one who is firm in loyalty to a comrade';[13] and in the same year in a New South Wales prison glossary: '*Solid*, staunch'.[14]

---

[11] D.R. Cressey & J. Irwin, 'Thieves, Convicts and the Inmate Culture', *Social Problems* 10:2 (1962), p. 146.
[12] B. Little, 'Prison Lingo: A Style of American English Slang', *Anthropological Linguistics* 24:2 (1982), p. 238.
[13] B.K. Doyle, 'It's Not What They Say ...', *Australian Police Journal* April (1950), p. 119.
[14] 'Thirty-five', *The Argot*, in G. Simes *A Dictionary of Australian Underworld Slang* (1993), p. 189.

Of course there are many kinds of action that breach the criminal code. For example, in the outside criminal world a person might cheat someone of his proper share of the proceeds of a robbery, and this is referred to as *to lash* or *to take the knock*. Within the world of the prison it is taboo to steal from another prisoner's cell, and a person who does this is condemned as a *peter thief*. The most significant breach of the criminal code, however, is informing on another *crim* to the police or to the prison authorities. American prisons have many terms for a person who does this, such as 'fink', 'rat', and 'snitch'; Goldin's 1950 American Underworld Lingo lists 60 terms for 'informer'. The Australian system makes do with one—*dog*.

Dog is the most negative word in the underworld and prison system. The Parramatta Glossary defines it as 'informer'. The playwright Jim McNeil in a note he provided for the August 1972 Russell Street Theatre production of his play *The Chocolate Frog*, which had been written and performed in Parramatta Jail, explains:

> In prison jargon, a 'chocolate frog' denotes a dog. And a dog is one whose conduct violates, or has violated in times past the informal 'laws' of prison society. A dog in prison is a criminal in the sight of those termed criminal themselves by ordinary society. And a dog should be judged, has to be punished, deserves to be ostracised and deprived—as criminals are.

Tim Anderson, a member of Ananda Marga, was convicted of conspiracy to murder in 1979 and served time in Long Bay Gaol, Parramatta Gaol, and Parklea Prison before being pardoned in 1985. In 1989 he published a book about his prison experience, *Inside Outlaws: A Prison Diary*. The book includes a glossary of 'boobtalk', and in it he defines *dog*:

> *Dog*, informer, traitor, general enemy. ... The specific meaning of this is (usually) a police informer or former accomplice who gives (fabricated or true) evidence against you in a criminal case, and therefore may be the cause of your conviction and imprisonment. It may also refer to a person who provides incriminating 'information' but does not actually give evidence. A dog is liable to any sort of extreme sanction from any prisoner. To be declared a dog in jail means that the person's life is at risk; therefore, informers in jail usually arrange for themselves to be in solitary confinement 'on protection'.

Subsequently, in 1990, Anderson was convicted of ordering the Hilton Hotel Bombing of 1978, but was acquitted on appeal the following year. During the committal hearing for this case in 1989, one of the prosecution witnesses was the notorious criminal Raymond Denning who had spent many years in various prisons. Later in his career Denning became a police informer, and testified against former associates and others, breaching the fundamental rule of the criminal code. He testified with false evidence against Tim Anderson, but the underworld made it clear to the court what it thought of this *dog*:

> A large bone was placed on a railing in the courtroom by an ex-prisoner who then shouted out 'you forgot your lunch, Denning'.[15]

All aspects of a *crim's* past behaviour are summed up by the term *form*. The Glossary defines this as 'criminal record', although *form* includes information about a prisoner's character and his reputation in the underworld in addition to information about charges and convictions. The term comes from horseracing—you can predict how a horse will perform in the present from a detailed knowledge about how it has performed in the past.

The terms *form*, *solid*, and *dog* are important in Jim McNeil's 1971 play *The Chocolate Frog*, written and produced in Parramatta Jail. The setting is a cell in Parramatta Jail inhabited by two long-term prisoners Shirker and Tosser, who know one another very well. Tosser nostalgically laments the fact that it is now difficult to be sure about who is a *dog* (*chocolate frog* in rhyming slang, and *chocolate* in abbreviated form) and who is not: 'Trouble is, but, yer never know these days just who is a bloody chocolate, and who ain't. Yer see blokes is supposed to be good fellers, talkin' ter maggots yer *know* are bloody tail-waggers'. At the beginning of the play a new cellmate named Kevin arrives, who makes the mistake of admitting that he dobbed in a mate to the court when they were both being tried for a robbery. Shirker and Tosser immediately brand him a dog, and call him by such names as Wuffy, Baskerville, Fido, and Mr Tuckerbox.

Shirker warns the newbie Kevin that the other prisoners will be keen to know what his *form* is, especially to know if he has any taint of being an informer:

> *Our* forms is already *established*, if yer know what I mean? There's *no one* in the nick here can point the finger of scorn at me or Toss. But you're *new* ter the scene, 'n *as* such yer'll be answerin' all kinds of questions in the next few days. All the crims'll wanter know yer *form* ... 'n they'll be lookin' ter me 'n Toss fer a rundown on yer. That's why we ask yer questions ... we're *entitled* to, see? It could be that yer a bit short on credentials. Might even be a chockie frog, or somethin': in which case, a'course, we'd have ter *say so* around the place.

The play reveals that Tosser and Shirker, although they look back nostalgically to a time when there was supposedly honour among thieves, nevertheless breach the spirit and perhaps the letter of the criminal code in their own dealings. At the very beginning of the play Shirker hides a packet of tailor-made cigarettes in his bunk (although he is seen by Tosser) and in subsequent conversation claims they have only second-rate jail tobacco for their cigarettes. Later in the play Shirker

---

[15] D. Brown, 'Notes on the Culture of Prison Informing', *Current Issues in Criminal Justice* 5 (1993), p. 56.

indicates that he believes Tosser once told the police his whereabouts after a robbery, but Tosser insists that he has always been *solid*:

> TOSSER: I've always been *solid* ... all me life! (Pointing at SHIRKER) An' listen: if you're some kind of under-the-lap dog, then you just sit up on yer tucker-box ... I've been solid all me bloody life!
> SHIRKER: Is 'at so, is it? Well ... It was you started this. And yer fergettin', mate, that I've known yer as long as yer've known yerself. Don't give me all yer crap about how 'solid' yer've always been!

Passages such as these, where the terms *dog*, *form*, and *solid* appear, demonstrate how although these value terms exist both in the language of the underworld and the language of the prison, they are more commonly used within the prison system. Indeed, they are at the forefront of the prisoners' awareness. Criminals both inside and outside the prison would agree that a good man is one who upholds the criminal code, and that the worst crime is informing to the authorities on a fellow criminal. The awareness of this code, however, is much more intense within the prison, and the consequences of breaking the code are much more serious. The key terms therefore often carry more weight and consequences when used within the prison system, as distinct from their use in the wider underworld.

And this explains why the value terms occur so often, even obsessively, in the speech of Tosser and Shirker. In the world of secondary socialisation that a prison is, prison language is the cement that holds together the structure of the prisoners' alternative reality.

5. WHERE DO THE WORDS IN THE GLOSSARY COME FROM?

Studies and lists of underworld and prison slang have appeared since the seventeenth century. Gary Simes provides a very detailed and scholarly study of this history in the Introduction to his book *A Dictionary of Australian Underworld Slang* (1993). Julie Coleman includes material on these semantic areas in her wider historical study of English slang in the four-volume *History of Cant and Slang Dictionaries* (see Bibliography). The indispensable research tool for the history of English slang is *Green's Dictionary of Slang*, available online at: https://greensdictofslang.com/

There is a small group of words in the Parramatta Jail Glossary that have a long history in criminal slang.

An early British dictionary of criminal slang was *A New Dictionary of the Terms Ancient and Modern of the Canting Crew* (London 1699) put together by someone known only as 'B.E. Gent'. *Canting* in the title means 'using the dialect of thieves and vagabonds'. This dictionary contains over 4000 entries, and along with some underworld terms has much general slang and even General English terms. It includes the terms *chive* for 'a knife' (which appears in the Parramatta Glossary as *shiv*), and *darbies* 'irons, shackles or fetters' (which appears in the Parramatta Glossary defined as 'handcuffs').

Francis Grose's *A Classical Dictionary of the Vulgar Tongue* (London 1785) includes *chive* and *darbies*, and adds a few more terms that are echoed in the Parramatta Jail Glossary. Grose includes *kicks* 'breeches', which is probably the origin of the Parramatta Jail Glossary's *kick* 'pocket'. He gives *clout* 'a handkerchief', often a target of pickpockets, and this word, which can also mean more generally 'a piece of cloth', may be the ancestor of the Parramatta Glossary's *clout* 'a method used by shoplifters' which involved 'concealing stolen property under topcoat while being worn'. The Parramatta Glossary includes *lift* in the sense 'to steal'; Grose lists the word and cross-references it to *shoplifter*. Grose includes *under a cloud* 'in adversity' and the Parramatta Glossary also includes this phrase with a specific jail sense, defining it as 'under suspicion of being a dog' (that is, 'under suspicion of being an informer'). Grose's *whack* 'a share of a booty obtained by fraud' has an echo in the Parramatta Glossary's verb *whack up* 'divide into shares'.

J.S. Farmer & W.E. Henley's *Slang and Its Analogues: Past and Present* (London 1890–1904) includes about 40 terms that appear in the Parramatta Glossary with senses that are either the same or clearly related. These include the seven terms in the earlier Gent and Grose lists, as well as such terms as:

beak a magistrate
booby-hatch a police station (probably the origin of the later *boob* 'prison')
buckled arrested, taken into custody
bust a burglary
dip a pickpocket
drag three months' imprisonment
hoister a shoplifter
lagging a term of imprisonment
monkey £500
screw a turnkey[16]
snow-dropping stealing linen
square head an honest man
stiff (in prison) a clandestine letter
stir a prison

This suggests that by the end of the nineteenth century there was a cluster of terms that were shared by British and Australian underworld slang, and no doubt their transfer to Australia had something to do with the transportation of convicts to Australia. Such slang continues to be recorded in the twentieth century, especially by Eric Partridge in his various general slang dictionaries and in his *Dictionary of the Underworld* (1950), although it is often difficult to discern from Partridge's evidence exactly where and when the terms he cites were used.

More specific in their evidence are (in Britain) P. Tempest's *Lag's Lexicon: A Comprehensive Dictionary and Encyclopaedia of the English Prison To-day* (1950) and (in America) *The Dictionary of American Underworld Lingo* (1950) by H.E. Goldin, F. O'Leary, & M. Lipsius.

Tempest explains in a Preface to *Lag's Lexicon* that he was imprisoned in an English jail for five years for manslaughter, and that: 'Only those words and phrases which are in constant use to-day, and which I have actually heard during my enforced sojourn within the walls of six different prisons, have been included' (p. vii). His list shares 13 terms with the Parramatta Glossary, mostly terms that have occurred in the earlier lists, such as *darbies, dip, lagging, monkey, snow-dropping,* and *stiff*. Tempest includes *peter* in the sense 'a safe ... Also anything that can be locked', and he adds the originally Australian sense 'a prison cell', indicating that it had spread into British use. He includes *burgoo*, and notes that it was 'Australian service slang for porridge'. The Tempest evidence suggests that by the middle of the twentieth century, two decades before the Parramatta Glossary was compiled, British and Australian prison slang had diverged, and that there was not a lot of commonality between the two lexicons.

---

[16] i.e. a jailer.

The American evidence is slightly different. The Goldin dictionary was compiled from evidence collected within a major American prison that included prisoners from most of the American states. The evidence was collected mainly by two long-term prisoners and a prison chaplain. The American dictionary shares some 40 terms with the Parramatta Jail Glossary. About half of these are international, or have a clear origin in British slang, but the other half are underworld and prison terms that originated in the US. As listed in the Parramatta Glossary they include:

block wristwatch
boob gaol
bouncer dud cheque
bugged alarmed
can gaol
dodger bread
dog it squib it
give (someone) up inform on someone
grand $1000
lamp look
paper hanger passer of dud cheques
peg look
piece concealable firearm
roscoe gun
sloughed up locked in cell
under the lights questioned at C.I.B.
vag charged with vagrancy

This evidence suggests that some American underworld and prison terms found their way into Australia from the end of the nineteenth century and into the first half of the twentieth century. Even so, the overlap is not great. By the first half of the twentieth century the Australian underworld and Australian prisons had clearly developed their own distinctive lexicons.

The Development of Underworld and Prison Language in Australia

1812 JAMES HARDY VAUX A New and Comprehensive Vocabulary of the Flash Language

Vaux was an English petty criminal who was transported three times to Australia (1801, 1809, 1831). During his second time in the colony he was found guilty of receiving stolen property, and was sent to the penal settlement for secondary offenders (i.e. convicts found guilty of a second crime committed while serving time for their first crime) at Newcastle. There he compiled *A New* and *Comprehensive Vocabulary of the Flash Language*, which he dedicated to the Commandant at Newcastle, James Skottowe, no doubt to ingratiate himself into Skottowe's favour.

The dictionary appears to draw on Vaux' direct knowledge of the language of underworld London and the colony of New South Wales. It includes some 300 headwords. Some of these, which also appear in the Parramatta Glossary, are familiar from the lists discussed above, such as *beak*, *chiv*, *clout*, *darbies*, and *hoist*. Vaux also includes some other terms that appear in the Parramatta Glossary (or are closely related). Grose's 1785 dictionary included *crab* in its rowing sense in the phrase *to catch a crab* meaning 'to make a faulty stroke in rowing whereby the oar becomes jammed under water' (OED), but Vaux is the first to include an extended sense as the verb *to crab*: 'to prevent the perfection or execution of any intended matter or business'. It is this extended sense that must lie behind the Parramatta Glossary's sense 'to impede progress'. *Lagging* in the sense 'a sentence of transportation' is originally British underworld, although Vaux is the earliest to record it. In both British and Australian usage this term widens in meaning to refer to 'any prison sentence', and this is the sense recorded in the Parramatta Glossary. The Parramatta Glossary gives *lumbered* in the sense 'taken to a police station'. This goes back to a phrase *to be in lumber* and the associated verb *to lumber*, meaning 'to imprison, to arrest', both being first recorded by Vaux. This sense is chiefly Australian, although there is occasional use elsewhere. The Parramatta Glossary gives *sloughed up* 'locked in cell', and Vaux includes '*Slour*, to lock, secure, or fasten ... *Slour'd* or *slour'd up*, locked, fastened'. This word is recorded largely in the US in the nineteenth century, and is still listed in Goldin's 1950 American prison dictionary, but the earliest evidence for the term is in Vaux. In all, Vaux includes 18 of the Parramatta Glossary's 362 terms—with identical, closely related, or historically earlier senses.

1895 CORNELIUS CROWE *The Australian Slang Dictionary*

Cornelius Crowe was a Melbourne police officer. The subtitle of his dictionary promises a work 'Containing the Words and Phrases of the Thieving Fraternity', and Crowe claims that his work will enable the police and the general public to crack the local criminal code. Although many of the definitions are taken over from earlier British and American dictionaries, we can assume that the terms were current in Melbourne in the 1890s. There are about 100 Australian words that are not taken from other sources, and which are therefore important evidence for the history of Australian English. This is quite a lengthy text, with some 2574 entries.

There are about thirty underworld terms in the dictionary that are echoed in the later Parramatta Glossary. Some have been encountered in the dictionaries listed above, such as *beak*, *buckled*, *chive*, *darbies*, *drag*, *fly a kite*, *hoister*, *lumbered*, *monkey*, *screw*, *snow dropper*. Other terms he lists derive from

British and American underworld lingo: *served him out* 'punished him', *pony* '£25', *weed* 'tobacco', *whack* 'a share of plunder'. At times Crowe's terms give clues to the origins of some of the Parramatta Glossary's terms: *on the square* 'living honestly' lies behind the Parramatta Glossary's *squarehead* 'honest citizen', *sugar* 'money' helps to explain the Parramatta Glossary's *sugar bag* 'policeman who accepts bribes' (or 'sweeteners'), and a *strawman* is 'a worthless surety', of the kind that lies behind the Parramatta Glossary's *straw bail* 'bail papers signed by sugar bag on worthless surety'.

There are also a few significant additions to the originally British and American material, which give some clues about the development of an Australian underworld lexicon. Crowe includes *hotel barbers* 'thieves lodging at hotels for the purpose of robbing', which appears in the Parramatta Glossary in the abbreviated form *barber*. To *turn dog* is defined as 'to turn Queen's evidence', a specific use of the Australian phrase meaning 'to be an informer; to betray a colleague or change allegiance'. Crowe gives *fitted* 'found guilty', and the same term and definition are given in the Parramatta glossary. This is an Australian sense of the verb *fit*: 'to fix upon a person the responsibility for having committed a criminal offence by securing sufficient evidence to ensure a conviction'.

The number of terms that appear in both Crowe and the Parramatta Glossary (about 30) suggests that the Australian underworld was developing a distinctive lexicon in the late nineteenth century. This continues to develop significantly in the first half of the twentieth century.

1941 SIDNEY J. BAKER *A Popular Dictionary of Australian Slang*

Baker was a New Zealand-born Australian journalist and linguist who was an ardent collector of Australian colloquialisms. This is the first of several important books he produced on Australian English. Second and third editions of the *Popular Dictionary* appeared in 1943, and a few of the terms listed below appeared in the later editions.

About 45 terms from the Parramatta Glossary appear in the same or similar senses. These include:

barber	hock	nit keeper	spot
bumper-up	jack	on the coat	square off
clock	jerry	peter	swy
cockatoo	Kentucky	poof rorter	twist
cold biting	key	rort	toe ragger
cruel	lagging	shelf	under the lap
dodger	leg-up	silvertail	warb
dudder	lob	smother	yarra
fit	lunatic soup	snork	zack
grouse	Mark (Foy)	spin	

Since this is a dictionary of Australianisms, Baker is not interested in the international underworld terms that are also included in the Parramatta Glossary, such as *darbies* and *screw*. Baker's work is therefore a significant contribution to our understanding of the development of the terms that eventually appear in the Parramatta Glossary.

He adds more Parramatta terms in his subsequent publications, often gathered from the lists of others—for example, he gained access to the 1950 list of the prisoner known as 'Thirty-five' and printed many terms from this list in *Australia Speaks* (1953) and in later publications. Apart from these 'Thirty-five' terms, Baker's first edition of *The Australian Language* (1945) provides *blot*, *half a spot*, and *spot*; *Australia Speaks* (1953) provides *dodger* in the specific sense 'jail bread', *flat*, *mocker*, *put the knife through*, and *secko*; *The Drum* (1959) provides *African*; and the second edition of *The Australian Language* (1966) provides *shirt-lifter*.

1944 TED HARTLEY

Hartley was a conscientious objector in the Second World War, who was imprisoned for two periods in 1943 and 1944 because of his beliefs. The novelist Kylie Tennant asked Hartley to provide her with a list of prison slang to use in her novels, and Gary Simes came across the list in the Tennant Papers at the National Library of Australia. There were some pages missing from the beginning and end of the document: it starts at *bludger* and ends with *screw* (although an entry for *shelf* is signalled by a cross-reference in an earlier entry). The remaining list includes 64 of the 362 Parramatta Glossary terms. Gary Simes edited Hartley's list (along with a similar list by 'Thirty-five' as described in the next entry) in his *Dictionary of Australian Underworld Slang* (1993). These are the terms that Hartley's dictionary shares with the Parramatta Glossary (for an explanation of those marked with a dagger † see the next entry for 'Thirty-five'):

black peter	*cannon*	*do it on the shit tub*	*hock*†
bodgie†	*clock*†	*do it tough*	*hoist*†
boil-up	*clout*†	*dodger*†	*jack*
boob†	*cold*†	*drack*†	*jigger*†
boob happy†	*on the coat*	*drag*†	*the key*†
boob weed†	*come yer guts*	*fitted*†	*knock up*
brass†	*crab*†	*form*	*lagging*†
brick† ($10)	*crack it*†	*front*†	*lift*†
brick† (10 years)	*crim*	*get over*	*the lot*†
buckle†	*dip*†	*gig*†	*low jump*
bumper†	*do it*	*grand*†	*lumber*
bust†	*do it hard*	*grouse*†	*monkey*†
bustman†	*do it on my skull* (head)	*high jump*	*moosh*†

peter†	ramp† (verb)	ridge†	screw†
pony	ramp† (noun)	rort†	seine†
racehorse	red light	roseleaf†	shelf†

1950, 1955 'THIRTY-FIVE' The Argot. N.S.W. Prison Slang

The author is known only by the term 'Thirty-five', from the last two digits of his prison number. He was a long-term prisoner and a former schoolteacher, who completed a first version of his dictionary in 1950, and after his release in the early 1950s produced a revised version that was typed up in 1975 but which can be dated to 1955. Only the first half of the revision exists. 'Thirty-five's' lists include 148 of the 362 items in the Parramatta Glossary. The terms shared by 'Thirty-five' and Ted Hartley are marked in the previous entry with a dagger (†). The terms that are in 'Thirty-five' but not in Hartley are:

arsey	doing the crust	posted
backstop	dudder	pound
easy mark	elephant's trunk	put a knife through
barber	flat	roscoe
bat (= penis)	fly a kite	scarper
beak	give up	score
bin	grouse	seat
block	half spot (implicit at spot)	secko
blot	hard	shanghai
blow down the ear of	haste	shitkicker
boy in the boat	heelie	shovel
brassco	hoon	silvertail
bridge	jump the box	sleep
bring undone	khyber	slice
burgoo	kick along	sling
can	kite	smack (= cop) a blue
captain	lag	slotcase
case	lamp	slue
cat	lamping (implicit at lamp)	smoke
chaff	lash	smother
chiv	mark	sneak go
cockatoo	mocker	snooker
cold bite (noun)	nit keeper	snork
cop it sweet	nod the nut/head	snowdrop (implied at snowdropper)
cruel	(not the) full quid	solid
cunt starver	peter thief	solid
cut out	point	spin

squarehead	tank	tropical
square off (verb for noun)	take to the toe (= hit the toe)	twist
stiff	toe ragger	turn up
swy¹	toey	vag
swy²	track	warb
take the knock		

In total, the Hartley and 'Thirty-five' lists include 169 of the 362 Parramatta items.

1967 'The Whisper All Aussie Dictionary' in the *Kings Cross Whisper*

This dictionary was published over a number of issues of the satirical Sydney newspaper, established by Terry Blake and Jim Ramsay. It is an important text, providing the earliest evidence for many Australian terms. It contains 124 of the Parramatta 362, so it is close to the total of terms in Simes. 29 of these are not in Simes or in Baker. Jim Ramsay was later the compiler of the slang book *Cop it Sweet*.

a chew it and spew it	drop	heavy	spring
('a cheap cafe' cf. Parramatta	earn	joint	straw bail
chew & spew 'prison stew')	flum	knocked	turn it up
air raider	freckle	nick	twine
barley	ginger ale	optic	
break	half a slice[17]	peg	
bunch up	half inch	put through	
clacker	half pie	robert young	
dog squad	handle	sloughed up	

If we add together the Parramatta terms in Baker, Hartley, 'Thirty-five', and the *All Aussie Dictionary* the number of shared terms is about 208 of the Parramatta Glossary's 362.

In the post 1972 period (i.e. after the Parramatta Glossary was put together) various collections of Australian slang continue to include a significant number of underworld and prison terms, especially Jim Ramsay's 1977 *Cop it Sweet* (which includes about 160 of the Parramatta terms), and R. Aven-Bray's 1983 *Ridgey Didge Oz Jack Lang* (about 113). A number of prison slang glossaries appear as appendices to works that deal with the underworld and prison. Barry Ellem's 1984 *Doing Time: The Prison Experience* includes 'A Glossary of Prison Jargon' (with about 68 Parramatta terms). Tim Anderson's 1989 book *Inside Outlaws: A Prison Diary* is a series of essays written during his imprisonment in NSW jails, including Parramatta. The chapter called 'Boobtalk' includes 60 of the Parramatta terms. Bernie Matthews' 2006 *Intractable: Hell has*

---

[17] Parramatta Glossary has *slice*.

a Name, Katingal: Life inside Australia's First Super-max Prison includes a glossary that shares 56 terms with Parramatta.

While the lexicon of the Australian underworld and prison system developed largely independent of the British and American systems, it is not surprising, given the geographical closeness, and the general closeness of their colloquial languages, that there are significant overlaps between the Australian and New Zealand prison lexicons. The term *half pie* 'half-hearted' may have its origin in the Maori language, and the term *mocker* 'clothes' may have originally been borrowed from Arabic by New Zealand soldiers during the First World War (although it is not recorded until the Second World War). Both terms found their way from New Zealand to Australia.

Greg Newbold's *The Big Huey: An Inmate's Candid Account of Five Years inside New Zealand's Prisons* (1982) includes a glossary that shares about 60 terms with the Parramatta Glossary. Diana Looser's *Boobslang: A Lexicographical Study of the Argot of New Zealand Prison Inmates, in the period 1996–2000* (PhD 2001) also contains about 60 shared terms. These texts include:

back up	get buckled	roscoe
beat it	go-slow	score
bed & breakfast	go under	screw
block	grand	seat
boob	half inched	shelf
boob tobacco	he's elephants	shiv
brass	hit the toe	sling
brick¹	hock	slot
brick²	jacks	sloughed up
bugged (both have *bug* 'a burglar alarm')	jerry	snooker
	kick	solid
bust (as verb)	laggin'	spot
can	lash	sprung
case	left-handed drop	square off
cat	lot, the	stink
cockatoo	monkey	stir
come undone	nick	stir-crazy
cop it sweet	nod yer head	tank
dog	on the coat	tankman
do it hard	peg	toey
double	peter	track (as 'tracker')
easy mark	piece	trick cyclist
finger	pound	verballed
fly a kite	racehorse	Warwicks
form	ramp	weed
front	rort	whack

In total, the Newbold and Looser glossaries include 77 of the Parramatta Glossary's terms. This is a significant overlap of terminology, and indicates that there has been much interaction between the prison and underworld populations of Australia and New Zealand, and that this continued in the second half of the twentieth century. This contrasts with the British and American interaction with Australia, which had clearly ceased with Britain early in the twentieth century, and with the US by the middle of the twentieth century.

6. THE EDITING OF THE GLOSSARY

(a) Reorganisation of list

The Glossary exists as an 11-page typed document. The headwords are not alphabetised. Samples are given at Appendix A.

A transcription of the complete document is given at Appendix B. This original document is important because the terms are sometimes grouped thematically, or are listed by association—for example, there is a long list of terms referring to the court system, beginning with *front* and ending with *the lot*; there is a similar long list of terms associated with homosexuality, beginning with *hock* and ending with *starter*; twelve terms associated with money are listed beginning with *seine* and ending with *five cents in the dollar*; and so on.

There are a few obvious typographical errors in the manuscript, and some entries that need minor changes. Where I have made changes, these are footnoted in this transcribed document.

I have also made a few global changes. The manuscript capitalises head words and the first word of definitions, and also randomly capitalises other words. These have all been made lower case, in line with dictionary practice, except for proper names. For about a dozen headwords the manuscript puts an 'a' before the headword (*a double*); these have been removed for consistency. In three instances the definite article 'the' precedes the headword: *the key*; *the lot*; *the twist*. These have been alphabetised as: *key, the*; *lot, the*; *twist, the*. There is a colon before a definition in the manuscript; these have been removed in the final edited version.

Appendix C gives an alphabetised version of the corrected and emended list.

The headwords in the manuscript do not always obey the traditional rules of dictionaries. For example, *heavies* appears in the plural form whereas a dictionary would give the singular *heavy* as the headword. Phrases that begin with a preposition or other minor word, such as *on the coat*, are listed under the first word, whereas a dictionary would usually list these under the word that is most important semantically—in this case, *coat*. This edition, however, retains the headwords as listed in the manuscript, and gives cross-references in square brackets from the alphabetical position where you might expect the phrase to be. Thus, there is an entry [**coat** *see* ON THE COAT].

In my commentary, wherever small capitals are used (as with ON THE COAT), this tells the reader that they will find this term or phrase as a headword.

(b) The structure of a typical entry

The headword is given in bold, followed by the definition in plain roman. These are verbatim from the manuscript, with some very minor changes that are noted in Appendix B.

Everything that follows the headword and definition is my commentary. This commentary usually follows in the order outlined below, although at times the main areas of commentary cannot be clearly separated out one from the other. For example, the meaning of a term sometimes needs to be discussed along with information about its origin.

The first information provided concerns the regional status of the term, and whether it is underworld or prison slang. The main labels are:

General English. This is used to describe terms and senses that exist in the main countries dealt with in the commentary, especially Australia, Britain, and the US. A term marked 'General English' is used in these countries, although it may have begun its history in one of them.

Australian English. This is used to describe terms and senses that exist primarily in Australian English.

British English. This is used to describe terms and senses that exist primarily in British English.

American English. This is used to describe terms and senses that exist primarily in American English.

General Underworld Slang

Australian Underworld Slang
Australian Prison Slang

British Underworld Slang
British Prison Slang

American Underworld Slang
American Prison Slang

The description 'slang' in these labels is not a marker of register, as with the traditional register markers of 'formal', colloquial', 'slang', and so on. Rather, it indicates that a term belongs to the jargon of a particular group, with 'underworld slang' designating the special language of the criminal world, and 'prison slang' designating the special language that develops within prison systems.

At times, the definition given in the Glossary is a bit cryptic or unclear, and I have often given clarification and expansion of the meaning immediately after the regional designation.

Information is provided about the etymology of the word. The etymology follows the rubric 'Origin', although the discussion of the origin often needs to be fleshed out with historical background and other information.

There then follows a list of dated quotations that illustrate the history of the word (where these are available and useful). Such a use of illustrative quotations is at the core of the historical lexicography represented by such works as the *Oxford English Dictionary* and the *Australian National Dictionary*. I have taken these quotations from Australian sources (books, newspapers, social media, etc.), since these provide the historical and cultural contexts for the terms in the Parramatta Glossary. Sometimes it has been useful to add quotations from overseas sources, especially when these illustrate the earliest use of a term—these quotations are placed in square brackets to distinguish them from the Australian quotations. Occasionally I have added a note in square brackets at the end of a quotation, introduced by *Ed.*, to clarify something within the quotation.

Readers should be advised that the content of this book includes some material that might be considered offensive.

7. BIBLIOGRAPHY

Anderson, Tim, *Inside Outlaws: A Prison Diary*, Redfern Legal Centre Publishing: Sydney, 1989.

The Australian National Dictionary, 2nd edn, ed. Bruce Moore, OUP: Melbourne, 2016.

Aven-Bray, R., *Ridgey Didge Oz Jack Lang*, The Author: Sydney, 1983.

Baker, Sidney J., *A Popular Dictionary of Australian Slang*, Robertson & Mullens: Melbourne, 1941.

Baker, Sidney J., *A Popular Dictionary of Australian Slang*, 2nd edn, Robertson & Mullens: Melbourne, 1943.

Baker, Sidney J., *A Popular Dictionary of Australian Slang*, 3rd edn, Robertson & Mullens: Melbourne, 1943.

Baker, Sidney J., *The Australian Language*, Angus & Robertson: Sydney, 1945.

Baker, Sidney J., *Australia Speaks*, Shakespeare Head Press: Sydney, 1953.

Baker, Sidney J., *The Drum: Australian Character and Slang*, Currawong: Sydney, 1959.

Baker, Sidney J., *The Australian Language*, 2nd edn, Currawong Publishing: Sydney, 1966.

'B.E. Gent', *A New Dictionary of the Terms Ancient and Modern of the Canting Crew*, W. Hawes: London, 1699.

Bentley, W. K. & J. M. Corbett, *Prison Slang: Words and Expressions Depicting Life Behind Bars*, McFarland & Co.: Jefferson, N.C., 1992.

Brown, D., 'Notes on the Culture of Prison Informing', *Current Issues in Criminal Justice* 5 (1993), pp. 54–71.

Clemmer, D., *The Prison Community*, Rinehart: New York, 1958.

Coleman, Julie, *A History of Cant and Slang Dictionaries, Volume I: 1567–1784*. OUP: Oxford, 2004.

Coleman, Julie, *A History of Cant and Slang Dictionaries, Volume II: 1785–1858*, OUP: Oxford, 2004.

Coleman, Julie, *A History of Cant and Slang Dictionaries, Volume III: 1859–1936*, OUP: Oxford, 2009.

Coleman, Julie, *A History of Cant and Slang Dictionaries, Volume IV: 1937–1984*, OUP: Oxford, 2010.

Copspeak: A Glossary of Terms, Abbreviations and Phrases Employed by Police Officers Throughout Australasia, compiled by B. Swanton, Australian Institute of Criminology: ACT, 1988.

BIBLIOGRAPHY

Cressey, D.R. & J. Irwin, 'Thieves, Convicts and the Inmate Culture', *Social Problems* 10:2 (1962), pp. 142–155.

Crowe, Cornelius, *The Australian Slang Dictionary*, (No name of publisher): Melbourne, 1895.

Doyle, B.K., 'It's Not What They Say ...', *Australian Police Journal* April (1950), pp. 110–20.

Einat, T. & H., 'Inmate Argot as an Expression of Prison Subculture: The Israeli Case', *Prison Journal* 80:3 (2000), pp. 309–25.

Ellem, Barry, *Doing Time: The Prison Experience*, Fontana: Sydney, 1984.

Farmer, J.S. & W.E. Henley, *Slang and Its Analogues Past and Present*, London, 1890-1904.

Featherstone, L. & A. Kaladelfos, *Sex Crimes in the Fifties*, Melbourne University Press: Carlton, 2016.

Goffman, Erving, *Asylums*, Penguin: Harmondsworth, 1961.

Goldin, H.E., F. O'Leary & M. Lipsius, *Dictionary of American Underworld Lingo*, Twayne: New York, 1950.

Green, Jonathon, *Green's Dictionary of Slang*, online version: https://greensdictofslang.com/

Grose, Francis, *A Classical Dictionary of the Vulgar Tongue*, S. Hooper: London, 1785.

Hall, Rodney (ed.), *Poems from Prison: Jack Murray, Max Williams, Eric Mackenzie, Robin Thurston*, University of Queensland Press: St Lucia, 1973.

Halliday, M.A.K., *Language as Social Semiotic: The Social Interpretation of Language and Meaning*, Edward Arnold: London, 1978.

Hartley, Ted, 'Glosssary', in G. Simes, *A Dictionary of Australian Underworld Slang*.

Heilpern, D., *Fear or Favour: Sexual Assault of Young Prisoners*, Southern Cross University Press: Lismore, 1990.

Honeywill, R., *Wasted: The True Story of Jim McNeil—Violent Criminal and Brilliant Playwright*, Viking: Melbourne, 2010.

Ibrahim, N. & M. Quinney, *Glossary of Gaol Slang: Pentridge Gaol*, Unpublished Typescript, ANDC, 1995.

Irwin, G., *American Tramp and Underworld Slang*, Scholaris: London, 1931.

Kaladelfos, A. & Y. Smaal, 'Sexual Violence and Male Prisons: An Australian Queer Genealogy', *Current Issues in Criminal Justice* 31:3 (2019), pp. 349–64.

Kerr, J.S., *Parramatta Gaol Central Precinct: Assessment of Cultural Significance and Recommended Heritage Requirements*, NSW Public Works for the Department of Corrective Services: Sydney, 1985.

Kerr, J.S., *Parramatta Correctional Centre: Its Past Development and Future Care*,

Department of Corrective Services: Sydney, 1995.

Knight, J., *The Dictionary of Victorian Prison Slang*, online: 2018.

Little, B., 'Prison Lingo: A Style of American English Slang', *Anthropological Linguistics* 24:2 (1982), pp. 206–44.

Looser, Diana, *Boobslang: A Lexicographical Study of the Argot of New Zealand Prison Inmates, in the Period 1996–2000*, PhD thesis, University of Canterbury, Christchurch, 2001.

The Macquarie Dictionary, Macquarie Library: St Leonards, 1981.

Manser, P., *More than Words: The Making of the Macquarie Dictionary*, Macquarie Dictionary: Sydney, 2021.

Matthews, Bernie, *Intractable: Hell has a Name, Katingal: Life inside Australia's First Super-max Prison*, Pan Macmillan: Sydney, 2006.

Mayr, A., *Prison Discourse: Language as a Means of Control and Resistance*, Palgrave Macmillan: Basingstoke & New York, 2004.

Mayr, A., 'Prison Language', in *Encyclopedia of Applied Linguistics*, ed. C.A. Chapelle, Wiley-Blackwell: Hoboken, N.J., 2012.

McNeil, Jim, *The Chocolate Frog, The Old Familiar Juice: Two Plays*, Currency Press: Sydney, 1973.

McNeil, Jim, *How Does Your Garden Grow*, Currency Press: Sydney, 1974.

McNeil, Jim, *Collected Plays*, Currency Press: Sydney, 1987.

Meredith, J., *Learn to Talk Old Jack Lang: A Handbook of Australian Rhyming Slang*, Kangaroo Press: Kenthurst NSW, 1984.

Moore, Bruce, *A Lexicon of Cadet Language: Royal Military College Duntroon in the Period 1983 to 1985*, ANDC: Canberra, 1993.

Newbold, Greg, *The Big Huey: An Inmate's Candid Account of Five Years Inside New Zealand's Prisons*, Collins: Auckland, 1982.

The Oxford English Dictionary, online version: https://www.oed.com/

Parliament of New South Wales, *Report of the Department of Corrective Services for the year ended 30 June, 1972*.

Partridge, Eric, *A Dictionary of the Underworld*, Routledge & Kegan Paul: London, 1950.

Price, J., 'Homosexuality in a Victorian Male Prison', *Mental Health in Australia* July (1984), pp. 3–12.

Prison & Drug Slang, New South Wales Corrective Services, 2001.

Ramsay, Jim, *Cop It Sweet: A Dictionary of Australian Slang and Common Usage*, Allegheney News Service: Sydney, 1977.

Richmond, K., 'Fear of Homosexuality and Modes of Rationalisation in Male Prisons', *Australian and New Zealand Journal of Sociology* 14:1 (1978), pp. 51–57.

Roth, M.P., *Prisons and Prison Systems: A Global Encyclopedia*, Greenwood Press: Westport, Conn., 2006.

Sahni, N. (compiler), *Parramatta Gaol*, City of Parramatta Research & Collection Services: Parramatta, 2020.

Simes, Gary, *A Dictionary of Australian Underworld Slang*, OUP: Melbourne, 1993.

Tempest, P., *Lag's Lexicon: A Comprehensive Dictionary and Encyclopaedia of the English Prison To-day*, Routledge & Kegan Paul: London, 1950.

'Thirty-five', 'The Argot. N.S.W. Prison Slang', in G. Simes, *A Dictionary of Australian Underworld Slang*.

Tupper, V., 'Colloquial Language in New South Wales Prisons', *Journal of Studies in Justice* 1:1 (1987), pp. 71-83.

Tupper V. & R. Wortley, *Anthology of Prison Slang in Australia* (1990), National Library of Australia, Pandora Archive: https://webarchive.nla.gov.au/tep/135962

Vaux, James Hardy, *A New and Comprehensive Vocabulary of the Flash Language*, 1812, published in *Memoirs of James Hardy Vaux*, London, 1819.

Whisper All Aussie Dictionary, in *Kings Cross Whisper* issues 32-43 (1967).

Williams, Max, *Dingo! My Life on the Run*, Fontana: Sydney, 1980.

Withnel, E., 'Doing Time: The Temporal Reality of the Criminal's Existential World', *Australian Journal of Cultural Studies* 1 (May) (1983), pp. 80-91.

Withnel, E., 'Stone Walls ... The Spacial Determinations of the Criminal's Existential World', *Australian Journal of Cultural Studies* 2 (November) (1984), pp. 61-89.

THE 1972 PARRAMATTA JAIL GLOSSARY

ABBREVIATIONS USED:

AND: *Australian National Dictionary*
GDS: *Green's Dictionary of Slang*
OED: *Oxford English Dictionary*

African cigarette.

Australian English.

The term refers to a manufactured or tailor-made cigarette with an in-built filter, as distinct from a roll-your own cigarette that is made from loose tobacco and a cigarette paper.

Origin: Shortening of *African nigger*, rhyming slang for *cigger* 'cigarette'.

In prison, cigarettes were typically rolled from prison-supplied inferior tobacco (called BOOB TOBACCO), and the tailor-made cigarette was a luxury item. The tailor-made cigarette was also called a GROUSE CIGARETTE.

1959 S.J. BAKER *The Drum* p. 83: *African*, a tailor-made cigarette.

1983 R. AVEN-BRAY *Ridgey Didge Oz Jack Lang* p. 11: Lighting up an African he gargled on slowly.

1984 J. MEREDITH *Learn to Talk Old Jack Lang* p. 19: *African nigger*: cigger, cigarette.

1990 V. TUPPER & R. WORTLEY *Anthology of Prison Slang in Australia* (National Library of Australia, Pandora Archive): *African nigger*. Rhyming slang for 'cigger', i.e. cigarette. Cigarettes are an important element in prison life. Sometimes just 'African'.

2001 *Prison & Drug Slang: NSW Corrective Services*: *African*, (abbreviation) African nigger: Cigarette.

[aim up see CAN'T AIM UP.**]**

air raider nagging sheila.

Australian English.

The term refers to 'a loud and incessant talker'. The Glossary associates it with a stereotypical 'carping woman'. The earliest evidence attributes the term to the female voice, but later evidence, including prison slang (as in the 1990 quote below) is not gender specific, and the term means 'a person who talks incessantly'.

Origin: From the sound of an air raid in wartime or the siren that warns of it.

The 1990 quote indicates that the form *air raid* is also used as a noun meaning 'incessant talk'. The 1984, 1994, 1995, and 2011 quotes show the form *air raid* being used as a verb meaning 'to talk incessantly'.

1967 *Whisper All Aussie Dictionary* in *Kings Cross Whisper* 32 p. 7: *Air raider*: The worst type of female. An arguer, sometimes a screamer, but always a pest.

1983 R. AVEN-BRAY *Ridgey Didge Oz Jack Lang* p. 17: *Air raider*, argumentative female.

1984 B. ELLEM *Doing Time: The Prison Experience* p. 186: *Air raid*, to talk in an obsessive, overbearing, or loud-mouthed way.

1990 V. Tupper & R. Wortley *Anthology of Prison Slang in Australia* (National Library of Australia, Pandora Archive): *Air raid*, incessant talk. An 'air raider' is someone given over to excessive locution.

1994 M.B. Read *Chopper 4: For the Term of His Unnatural Life* p. 54: Harry the Greek spends most of his day muttering and mumbling and air raiding about bloody two-headed Tasmanians.

1995 N. Ibrahim & M. Quinney *Glossary of Gaol Slang: Pentridge Gaol* (Unpublished Typescript ANDC): *Air raid*, sound off loudly, usually complaining.

2011 J. Kerr & R. Mooney *A Pack of Bloody Animals* p. 167: Did you say, 'It was air raiding, mouthing off a bit'? —'I can't remember'.

arse bandit person prepared to rape a male if need be.

Australian Prison Slang.

In General English use this is a term for 'a gay man'. It is usually derogatory and offensive (although see the gay use in the 1999 quote). In the prison system it has a very specific meaning, and it is a synonym for HOCK, a man who takes the penetrative role in male to male sex. In the prison system the other male in this sexual act may be an unwilling participant, thus the definition noting that the hock may be prepared to use violence against another man to do this. In prison contexts, where situational homosexuality is common, the *arse bandit* (who is called a HOCK) generally does not identify as gay, and the kind of sexual activity designated by the literal sense of the term is therefore to the fore in its application to him. See also DUNG PUNCHER, SHIRT LIFTER. The 2015 British quote in square brackets suggests that *arse bandit* now has a similar sense in the British prison system.

It is not clear where the term originated. The earliest evidence for the standard sense is from 1961 in the 5th edition of Partridge's slang dictionary (see below), but Partridge gives no source. Partridge says that *arse bandit* is a synonym for *arse king*, and defines *arse king* as 'a notorious sodomite'. The term appears in Australian, British, and American sources between 1971 and 1977.

[**1961** E. Partridge *Dictionary of Slang and Unconventional English* 5th edn, vol. 2 p. 893: *Arse bandit*, synonym of arse king.]

1971 J. McNeil *The Chocolate Frog* in *The Chocolate Frog, The Old Familiar Juice: Two Plays* (1973) p. 31: You'll find in the Old Testament that a dog was what was called a sodomite—an arse-bandit, yer see? (*Shrugging*) Yeah, 'n so it's always been the word us blokes use, ter say that some swine is a swine.

1977 J. Ramsay *Cop It Sweet* p. 8: *Arse bandit*, homosexual.

1983 R. Aven-Bray *Ridgey Didge Oz Jack Lang* p. 17: *Arse bandit*, aggressive male homosexual.

1988 C. Galea *Slipper!* p. 86: Neither of us fell for the 'arse-bandit' routine, being both ugly enough and tough enough to not have to worry about any hocks fancying us.

1990 V. Tupper & R. Wortley *Anthology of Prison Slang in Australia* (National Library of Australia, Pandora Archive): *Arse-bandit*, a sexually-active homosexual male who associates with passive gays mainly for sex.

1999 *Capital Q Weekly* (Sydney) 5 November p. 38: (personal advertisement): Versatile, mature arse bandit wants top and bottom men for all in uninhibited arse play.

[**2015** N. 'Razor' Smith *The Criminal Alphabet: An A-Z of Prison Slang* p. 144: *Arse bandit*, a predatory homosexual who will take what he wants, by force if necessary.]

arsey lucky.
Australian English.
The term also appears with the spellings *arsie* and *arsy*.
Origin: An alteration of the Australian term *tin-arsed* 'very lucky' (AND; first recorded 1941), which in turn derives from *tin arse* 'an unusually lucky person' (AND; first recorded 1898). The term *tinny* 'lucky' appeared by 1918, and this may have influenced the form of *arsey*. The 'lucky' element in the meanings of *tin arse* and *tin-arsed* derives from the fact that *tin* had developed the sense 'money, cash'.

1950 'Thirty-five' in G. Simes *Dictionary of Australian Underworld Slang* (1993) p. 3: *Arsey*, lucky.

1953 S.J. Baker *Australia Speaks* p. 104: *Arsey*, lucky.

1960 J. Walker *No Sunlight Singing* p. 23: I was real arsy to pick up a job here.

1977 R. Beilby *Gunner* p. 87: She's apples. Now you just lie back an' take it easy. Ya got a homer, mate, you arsey bastard.

1987 R.G. Barrett *Boys from Binjiwunyawunya* p. 156: A dubbo like you would be arsey enough to fluke something like this. ... They're as rare as rocking-horse shit.

2017 *Daily Telegraph* (Sydney) 12 May p. 82: Cowboys skipper Gavin Cooper described some of Canterbury's tries as 'arsey'.

back a tail follow after someone else in sexual intercourse.
Australian Prison Slang.
Evidence for this term exists only in the Parramatta Jail Glossary and in J. McNeil's play *The Chocolate Frog*. McNeil was an inmate at Parramatta at the time the Parramatta Jail Glossary was compiled, but his definition of the term differs in emphasis. In his glossary to the plays, McNeil says *back a tail* means 'to participate in sodomy'. In the play the prisoner Shirker equates *backing a tail* with a *turnabout*, meaning that it involves reciprocal anal sex. The Parramatta Glossary definition 'follow after someone else in sexual intercourse' initially might seem to mean 'for a second person to perform (anal) sex on a person immediately after another', but it is possible that it is in keeping with McNeil's definition, and means 'for each of the men to engage in anal sex'.
The 1977 quote (as with many examples in Ramsay's book) has been taken verbatim by Ramsay from McNeil's glossary; it is not evidence of use of the term outside the prison context.

1971 J. McNeil *The Chocolate Frog* in *The Chocolate Frog, The Old Familiar Juice: Two Plays* (1973) p. 31: Tosser: Yer wanner drop off sayin' that, about backin' a tail... SHIRKER: Ahh, don't worry mate ... they reckon turnabout's fair play. (*Chuckling*) I nearly fainted the first time.

1973 J. MCNEIL *The Chocolate Frog, The Old Familiar Juice: Two Plays* p. 118 (Glossary): *Back a tail*, to participate in sodomy.

1977 J. RAMSAY *Cop It Sweet* p. 88: *Back a tail*, participate in sodomy.

backdown decline to fight.

General English.

This is a specific use of the verb *back down* 'to withdraw a claim or assertion in the face of opposition; to retreat or yield'. The specific use refers to stepping back from an arrangement or invitation to fight. As a verb this term usually appears as two words: *back down*.

Backdown appears in the typescript a few entries after *back up* 'to seek revenge'. The compiler associates the two terms, and this is because they represent the two possible responses to a perceived slight—ignore it ('decline to fight') or try to rectify it ('seek revenge').

The specific sense 'decline to fight' is long established, and the 1896 and 1904 quotes below provide early evidence for it. Even so, as the bringing together of *backdown* and *back up* in the typed Parramatta Glossary indicates, physical violence is one of the important ways in which hierarchies are established among a prison population, and these terms have a greater significance within the prison than they would without.

1896 *Referee* (Sydney) 15 April p. 6: Ted Pritchard's grandiloquent challenge to Tom Duggan upon the hitter's arrival in England came to nought. Tom was prepared to box for the National Sporting Club's purse and £200, or the purse alone; but the whilom English champion middle-weight backed down, much to Duggan's chagrin.

1904 *Malcolm Chronicle and Leonora Advertiser* 24 June p. 3: 'Battler' Thompson, who made himself notorious in the Gwalia-Malcolm football match, at which he issued a verbal challenge to fight any Malcolm resident for £60, quietly backed down when the amount was put up to back J. Kleish against him.

1993 M.B. READ *Chopper 3: How to Shoot Friends and Influence People* p. 83: Some people who learn karate do it because, deep down, they are the worst combination, cowards with a violent streak. No matter how good they get, they will always back down against a man they fear may be their equal. They just use their fistic skills to frighten and beat up people physically inferior to themselves. Funny, isn't it, but I never seem to have that much trouble with those sorts of characters.

back stop someone prepared to support you in fight.

Australian English.

This is a specific use of the more general Australian sense of the term: 'anyone or anything that is a help or support, and can be relied on; a second line of defence, a back-up'.

Origin: Figurative use of the cricket term *backstop*—a fielding position directly behind the wicketkeeper, with the player designated to field any balls that the wicketkeeper fails to stop; thus, a second line of defence. The term also appears in baseball, where it means 'a fence behind the catcher to stop the ball; also, the catcher himself or his position' (OED), but this is unlikely to be the direct source of the Australian sense.

Quotes 1922 and 1950 refer to fights, and quotes 1950 and 1984 are in prison contexts.

> **1893** *Illustrated Sydney News* 11 March p. 17: Ted had always been first with her from the time he was 11, and she, a light quick child of 5, had been invaluable to him as a backstop.
>
> **1922** *Daily Examiner* (Grafton) 11 March p. 2: Mr Pollack: You didn't hit back at Berry? Witness (assuming surprise): 'At the young fellow?' [Mr Pollack:] 'Didn't you hit him?' Witness: What! Hit the young fellow, with the old fellow as a backstop to give me a hiding? (Laughter).
>
> **1950** 'Thirty-five' in G. SIMES *Dictionary of Australian Underworld Slang* (1993) p. 4: *Backstop*, a person looked to for support. 'He's a good backstop in a blue'.
>
> **1984** E. WITHNEL *Australian Journal of Cultural Studies* 2 (November) p. 71: A crim's ... china (china plate) is an integral part of his territorial claims. Where one is, so shall the other be. One acts as a 'backstop' (loyal supporter in times of crisis) for the other—fall out with one and you fall out with both.
>
> **2018** *Bowen Independent* 16 May p. 44: This evolved to Burnie becoming not only a valued, reliable caring neighbour but her backstop. As Laurel's mobility failed her over the more recent years, a kind hearted Burnie once again stepped up, taking her to do her shopping, the paying of her bills and the grocery shopping.

back up seek revenge.

Australian Underworld and Prison Slang.

Origin: The term *back up* in General English can be used as a noun meaning 'support or help; something or someone that can be called on if necessary', and as a verb meaning 'to provide support'. In these senses, the term is synonymous with Australian *back stop* (the entry above). The Australian prison and underworld sense derives from the term's role as an opposite to *back down*—in a dispute, if you 'back down' you do not seek to assert your rights or correct a perceived wrong or slight (and therefore risk losing face), but if you 'back up' you seek to do the opposite.

Writing in 1990, Tupper and Wortley state that the 'revenge' sense does not appear in Australia:

> **1990** V. TUPPER & R. WORTLEY *Anthology of Prison Slang in Australia* (National Library of Australia, Pandora Archive): Back-up. Another prisoner who can be called up for support, especially in a fight. This contrasts with New Zealand usage where the term refers to revenge. (Newbold).

Newbold and Looser provide evidence of New Zealand prison usage:

> **1982** G. NEWBOLD *The Big Huey* p. 244: *Back up*: retaliation, revenge.
>
> **2001** D. LOOSER *Lexicon of Boobslang in the Period 1996–2000* (thesis) p. 10: *Back up*, to get even, to take revenge upon one who has done one wrong, even over reasonably trivial matters (a face-saving exercise).

However, the Parramatta Jail Glossary and the quotations below indicate that the sense is also Australian.

1993 A.S. Smith & T. Noble *Neddy* p. 178: At the time, he didn't have a clue who had attempted to shoot him. He was blaming a group of guys from Melbourne and was all set to go down there and back-up on them.

2005 J. Pring *Abo: A Treacherous Life: the Graham Henry Story* p. 14: I'd heard all the news about Barry McCann taking a shot at Ned while I was in jail, which is a great place for underworld gossip. So the first thing I did was ask Ned why he hadn't backed up (taken revenge) over this attempt on his life.

2006 B. Matthews *Intractable ... Life inside Australia's First Super-max Prison* p. 147: 'Back up mate. You've got to back up on each one of them. Take them out altogether or take them out one at a time. Whichever way, you've got to back up on them, Peter', I told him. 'You have to show them, and the rest of the jail, that you can't be stood over, otherwise you are going to have trouble whatever jail you are in'.

bad mug person who makes mountain out of molehill.
Australian Underworld Slang.

The term means 'a great idiot', and can be applied to a person whose foolish behaviour causes difficulties for others.

A *mug* in underworld parlance is anyone who doesn't belong to the underworld and is therefore 'a gullible person'. *Bad mug* is an intensified form meaning 'an absolute fool' (as in the early quote 1894 which refers to a country 'mug's' relief at escaping the attempts of some female criminals to fleece him at the races), and can also be applied to someone within the underworld or prison system who behaves inappropriately, someone who 'puts on a turn' and causes problems for others. The term is sometimes used in non-underworld contexts (see quote 2004).

The Australian use does not have the 'evil' connotations of the New Zealand use of the term (see the 1982 NZ quote in square brackets).

1894 *Herald* (Melbourne) 6 November p. 1: I was in pocket from the day's business, and had had a good lunch for nothing. I don't think I was such a very bad mug, after all.

1950 'Thirty-five' in G. Simes *Dictionary of Australian Underworld Slang* (1993) p. 222: The criminal thinks that he has a moral right to plunder society ('No one is exempt') and that people who assist in his detection and arrest are morally depraved. Those who work for a living are *mugs* and *squareheads*, whilst those who live by robbing the *mugs* are *smarties* and *shrewdies*. The victim who complains *bellers* (bellows) like a *bad mug*.

1967 *Whisper All Aussie Dictionary* in *Kings Cross Whisper* 39 p. 4: *Shanghai*, term used when a prisoner is transferred from one prison to another. Usually after the crim has been playing up like a bad mug.

[**1982** G. Newbold *The Big Huey* p. 251: *Bad mug*, sinister or evil character.]

2004 *Daily Telegraph* (Sydney) 15 December p. 97: Ricky Barnes, take a bow. Sure, you might have carried on like a pork chop at last weekend's Masters. You might have lost the plot and putted like a guy who left his medication back in his hotel drawer. But hey, you proved yourself to be human. You blew it big-time. You did what tennis players do every time they throw a racquet or cuss. You behaved like a bad mug.

bad trot lean time.
Australian English.

The term means 'a run of bad luck, a miserable time'.

Origin: The ultimate source of this term is horse training and horseracing, where a horse goes for a training run (a 'trot') and might have a 'good trot', a 'bad trot', etc. A *bad trot* became synonymous with the phrase 'a spell (or run) of bad luck'. The formulations *trot, good trot, bad trot*, etc., also appear in two-up gambling contexts to describe a good or bad run of luck in playing the game, and this association probably served to popularise the terms.

> **1916** *Newcastle Morning Herald* 9 February p. 9: The leading boats got a big advantage while the three back markers had a bad trot, losing 5 minutes to the second buoy, Newcastle getting the worst.
>
> **1943** *War Drum* (Brisbane) October p. 2: Our battalion ... was having a pretty bad trot.
>
> **1974** J. McNeil *How Does Your Garden Grow* p. 109: Sweeper: I reckon I've done about twenty-three years in the nick—a bit at a time. ... Mick: You have had a bad trot.
>
> **2014** *Ayr Advocate* 27 June p. 20: Xanthe has had a bad trot, first with a thumb injury and then tearing his hamstring at training, but I believe he could be right.

Ballarat cat.
Australian Prison Slang.

Within the prison system a *cat* is 'a young passive male sexual partner'. The system that enables sex between men in the prison is explained in section 4 of the Introductory material. See the entry for CAT.

Origin: Rhyming slang. As with most examples of rhyming slang, the rhyme is arbitrary, and there is no special significance in the choice of the name of the Victorian city.

> **1983** R. Aven-Bray *Ridgey Didge Oz Jack Lang* p. 19: Ballarat, passive male homosexual.
>
> **1984** E. Withnel *Australian Journal of Cultural Studies* 2 (November) p. 72: When a crim comes to jail he may be resisting certain homosexual tendencies, thus he teams up with a 'cat' (catamite, an admitted homosexual), able to dismiss the relationship, initially, on the grounds of simple sexual release—getting 'a drain' or 'an empty' from a 'ballarat' (cat), which being a legacy from boys' homes, thus quasi permissible.
>
> **1990** V. Tupper & R. Wortley *Anthology of Prison Slang in Australia* (National Library of Australia, Pandora Archive): Ballarat, homosexual. Rhyming slang for 'cat'.
>
> **2001** *Prison & Drug Slang: NSW Corrective Services: Ballarat,* homosexual, as in *cat* (rhyming slang).

barber one who steals from residential premises without forcing entry. *Australian Underworld Slang.*

The term is an abbreviation of the fuller term *hotel barber* or *pub barber*, referring to a thief who robs hotel guests.

Origin: The term plays on the notion that such a thief 'barbers' or 'trims' the guests (AND).

The Parramatta Jail Glossary refers to theft from 'residential premises' and indicates that this theft is carried out 'without forcing entry'. In most evidence for this term the thefts take place in hotels, and they are typically carried out when rooms are left open and unattended while guests are using bathrooms, or having dinner, or when guests are asleep. It is likely that 'residential premises' in the definition refers to places such as hotels 'that provide accommodation in addition to other services' rather than referring to 'private houses', and therefore thefts from 'residential premises' stand in contrast with thefts from commercial premises.

The word *barber* in association with thieving first appears in the phrase *to play the barber*, meaning 'to work as a pickpocket', recorded in Sydney:

1855 *Bell's Life in Sydney* 12 May p. 3: A city prowler, who called himself doubleyou Johnson, was introduced as a reputed thief, and charged with trying to come the double over Mr Norris, a very useful young officer in the detective police. Mr Norris said—'There was a large assemblage of people in York-street; I have seen the prisoner before ... and I saw he would shun me; not liking to be cut by an old acquaintance, I entered into conversation with him, and he proffered to give me "regulars", or "a score of pounds", if I'd let him perform certain peculiar operations on the pockets of the mob; he asked me to let him "work the pig" and "come the barber" meaning to pick pockets'.

A decade later, a verb *to barber* appears in the 1865 anonymous British (though published in the US) *Leaves from the Diary of a Celebrated Burglar and Pickpocket*. A group of petty criminals spend the night in a communal bedroom of a hotel, and in the morning one of them claims to 'have been "barbered" while ... asleep' (p. 7) and his money stolen. This suggests that the thieving sense of 'barber' might have its origin in British Underworld Slang, but all other evidence is Australian. Two years after the *Diary*, the verb is also recorded in Australia:

1867 *Bell's Life in Sydney* 27 April p. 6: I know well enough that it is quite common for a well-dressed thief to take apartments in an hotel and 'barber' all the inmates; in other words, to get up in the night, visit all the rooms, and steal as much as possible.

The earliest records for the noun use the compound *hotel barber* (see below quote 1871), and the abbreviated form (as it is given in the Parramatta Glossary) first appears in 1884 (see below).

1871 *Ballarat Star* 28 August p. 2: At the Melbourne City Court, on Friday, George William Harrington was committed for trial on two charges of robbery from hotels. The prisoner, it appears, is respectably connected in England, and is described by the detectives as being about the cleverest 'hotel barber' ever known in the city.

1884 *Queensland Figaro* (Brisbane) 12 July p. 40: 'Hotel barbering' seems to be coming into fashion in Queensland. Brisbane recently had a big robbery at the Grand Hotel. The thieves went systematically through every bedroom in the House and barbered every pocket they came across, shaving each victim clean. They are believed to have collared over £100. On charges of being the barbers in this 'poll'-ing affair, a solicitor new to Brisbane and named S. Vokes Dudgeon, and his friend Heyde, are now enduring the *hades* of awaiting in Brisbane gaol their trial.

1902 *Truth* (Brisbane) 29 January p. 2: In thieves' slang 'a barber' is a man who takes up his residence at an hotel or lodging-house with a portmanteau apparently filled with valuables, but stuffed with old papers or worthless clothing. In the night time, or by day, if it suits him better, he 'goes through' the rooms and annexes what portable property he can, and takes his departure unostentatiously.

1932 *Sunday Mail* (Brisbane) 13 November p. 20: For greater security the 'Barbers' are frequently themselves guests, carefully observing their fellow-guests, and getting the general lay-out of the rooms fixed in their minds before commencing operations.

1972 *Meanjin* p. 149: A barber is a person who clips the rooms of motels and hotels, and during dinner hour ... a barber clipped the rooms. ... By nine o'clock that night many of the residents of the motel ... complained that some of their personal effects ... had been stolen.

barley cut it out; stop it.

Australian English.

In general Australian use, the term is a call for a truce in children's games (see quote 1992), and therefore means 'stop the game for the time being'. The underworld use is a specific use of this sense, but it is a firmer call for some activity to cease. There are variants (often regional) such as: *bar, barleys, barlies, bars*.

Origin: The term came into Australian English from British dialect, and is probably a variant of *parley* 'a meeting between opposing sides in a dispute'.

1918 *Ross's Monthly* (Melbourne) November p. 21: Ross's' Satirical Dictionary ... Barley—what the belligerents ought to say.

1967 *Whisper All Aussie Dictionary* in *Kings Cross Whisper* 32 p. 6: *Barley*, desist from doing something at the request of another.

1971 F. Hardy *Outcasts of Foolgarah* p. 91: 'Hey, barley', the Red Dean cautioned, 'slowly, slowly, catchee monkey, don't let us create a big stink in the whole city yet awhile'.

1992 *Canberra Times* 27 December p. 32: Take, for example, the childhood idea of 'barley'. You are in the middle of a game, but something intervenes—a quick trip to the loo, an untied shoelace or a dropped chewy—and you call 'barley'. Immediately, all the rules are suspended and the status quo is meticulously upheld until a resumption is called.

2017 R. Mann *Pentridge: Voices from the Other Side* p. 77: 'You're supposed to be breaking that rock up'. 'I'm not breaking any rocks ... I never once touched a rock. I cried barley on that'.

barrel benefit night, proceeds going towards payment of bail or defence counsel of crim arrested.

Australian Underworld Slang.

The term refers to a fundraising event, with beer sold from a barrel, to help a person charged with a crime who cannot afford the cost of bail or legal support.

This is a specific use of a term that is used to describe a party or function with beer or wine served from a barrel, and in those contexts (as in most of the quotes below) called a *barrel night, barrel party, beer barrel party, keg, keg night, keg party*. Typically, such parties are held to celebrate a birthday or to farewell someone, or to raise funds for a local sporting club. See also quote 2005 where donated money is also collected in a barrel.

1922 *Chronicle* (Adelaide) 12 August p. 40: A Beer Barrel Party. ... In answer to a telephone message from a resident of Alfred-crescent, North Fitzroy, stating that eight men were standing round a barrel of beer, Constable Field hurried to the Edinburgh Gardens at 12.30 a.m. on Saturday.

1954 *Murrumbidgee Irrigator* (Leeton) 13 April p. 3: Old Yanconians to Meet in Sydney. The Sydney Sub-branch is holding a 'Barbecue and Barrel Night', at Terry Hills, Sydney on Easter Saturday (April 17). This date has been chosen to enable country chaps down for the Easter Show to be able to meet their old school mates.

1986 *Western Tiers* (Tasmania) 20 August p. 21: A very enjoyable time was had by many of our members, just recently, when Mike Trouselot put on a barrel, prior to his leaving for his new appointment as Manager of the SBT Bank in Glenorchy.

2001 *Prison & Drug Slang: NSW Corrective Services*: *Barrel, a*, a party (usually on Sunday) with kegs containing beer.

2005 J. Pring *Abo: A Treacherous Life: the Graham Henry Story* (in extra chapter included in electronic version): We had one tradition for blokes who were trying to raise funds for their defense in court cases. We held fundraisers which we nicknamed barrels. Throughout the day of drinking and gathering, everyone would donate. Whatever came out of the barrel, which of course was cold hard cash, then this money went to pay for the criminal's defense, and also to the family to see them through the hard years if the defense wasn't so good.

2021 *Standard* (Warrnambool) 29 May p. 63: Just a note regarding the barrel night which was due to be held here at the Tackle Shack on Friday night. The event obviously had to be postponed due to the latest COVID-19 statewide lockdown. Once things become clearer, we will be able to announce a rescheduled date for the event and get it all happening again—as big as before with talks, food, giveaways, specials and more.

bat material pornographic material (Masturbation).

Australian English.

The term refers to a pornographic book or magazine that is used to facilitate masturbation. The term *bat material* is not otherwise recorded, but the online *Urban Dictionary* has the synonymous *batting material* (see quote 2004), indicating that the term is now associated with masturbation internationally, although the Australian evidence in the Parramatta Glossary is significantly earlier.

Origin: *Bat* in the sense 'penis' is recorded in American English from the 1930s (GDS), although there is one very early British example from 1779 (GDS). This is one of a number of terms that associate the penis with a stick or rod (*joystick, staff, sword, wand*, etc.). The verb phrase *to go off the bat* 'to masturbate' (see quotes 1950, 1990) is Australian. The verb phrase *to bat oneself off* (see quote 1986) is also Australian.

1950 'Thirty-five' in G. Simes *Dictionary of Australian Underworld Slang* (1993) p. 4: *Bat*, the penis; so *to go off the bat*, masturbate.

1985 'Thommo' *Dictionary of Australian Swearing and Sex Sayings* p. 15 (cited from T. Dalzell & T. Victor *New Partridge Dictionary of Slang* 2006): *Bat*, male masturbation.

1986 R.G. Barrett *The Real Thing* p. 189: But he's got a Thai wife who's the best cook you've ever seen. ... Some of the dishes she serves up'll make you want to start batting yourself off up against the table.

1990 V. Tupper & R. Wortley *Anthology of Prison Slang in Australia* (National Library of Australia, Pandora Archive): *Bat*, masturbate. As in 'to go off the bat' or 'to go to bat'.

1990 V. Tupper & R. Wortley *Anthology of Prison Slang in Australia* (National Library of Australia, Pandora Archive): *Bat material*, erotic literature used for masturbation. From 'go off the bat' ... masturbate.

[**2004** *Urban Dictionary* 17 May: *Batting material* is another word for pornography or eye candy.]

2006 B. Matthews *Intractable ... Life inside Australia's First Super-max Prison* p. 393: *Batted*, attacked with a wooden paddle tennis bat. It is also slang for masturbation.

beak magistrate.

General English.

This is a very old term, with records going back to the sixteenth century, and it has been used to refer to a constable and a schoolmaster as well as a magistrate or judge.

Origin: The origin of the term is unknown, although many theories have been put forward, including the notion that it may be from *beak* (as in the bird's appendage) applied humorously to the human nose to refer to someone who noses around with evidence etc., or an alteration of Old English *beag* 'ring' used to refer to an official chain of office. In the Australian records it first appears in Vaux (quote 1812).

1812 J.H. Vaux *New Vocabulary of the Flash Language* in *Memoirs* (1819) II p. 155: *Beak*, magistrate.

1895 C. Crowe *Australian Slang Dictionary* p. 7: *Beak*, a magistrate; the nose.

1950 B.K. Doyle *Australian Police Journal* April p. 111: *Beak*, Stipendiary or Police Magistrate on the Bench.

1989 T. Anderson *Inside Outlaws: A Prison Diary* p. 142: *Beak*, magistrate.

1990 V. Tupper & R. Wortley *Anthology of Prison Slang in Australia* (National

Library of Australia, Pandora Archive): *Beak*, judge or magistrate. Despite an extended history (Grose) this term is still widely used.

1992 M.B. READ *Chopper 2: Hits and Memories* p. 57: When asked by the beak if he had anything to say before sentence was passed, he said he suffered from a multiple personality disorder and the doctors had told him that he had as many as seven different personalities. The magistrate, who must have been in good humor, replied, 'multiple personalities: well, I sentence you to seven days jail, but the rest of you can go free'.

beat it be acquitted.
Australian Underworld and Prison Slang.

The term means 'to be found not guilty of a charge and therefore acquitted'. The verb *beat* is used elsewhere with a specific transitive object, especially as *beat the case*, but the formulation *beat it* seems to be Australian.

Origin: This is a specific use of *beat* in the sense 'to defeat, overcome', applied to the courtroom as a place of battle, where victory for the defendant is acquittal.

In the 1950 quote the *beat it* formulation is in the illustrative sentence.

1950 'Thirty-five' in G. SIMES *Dictionary of Australian Underworld Slang* (1993) p. 10: *Beat*, to be found not guilty on a count. 'He fronted for the bust but beat it'.

1953 *Truth* (Brisbane) 28 December p. 26: In Brisbane Police Court last Monday, James Le Roy McCune, 48, cook was charged before Mr. A.E. George, S.M., that on October 3, 1952, he unlawfully took an unmarried girl out of the custody of her father. Plainclothes-constable Sergio Giuseppe Peluchetti said in evidence that he brought McCune by air from Adelaide to Brisbane. McCune is alleged to have told Peluchetti: 'I'll beat this "blue". Clarke, the magistrate in Adelaide and the prosecutor, told me I would beat it'.

1971 J. McNEIL *The Chocolate Frog* in *The Chocolate Frog, The Old Familiar Juice: Two Plays* (1973) p. 23: TOSSER: Why didn' yer get 'im orf? SHIRKER: Yeah! Why didn't yer help him beat it, hey?

1973 J. McNEIL *The Chocolate Frog, The Old Familiar Juice: Two Plays* p. 114 (Glossary): *Beat it*, (prison slang), to defeat an indictment.

1984 B. ELLEM *Doing Time: The Prison Experience* p. 186: *Beat it*, to defeat an indictment, to be found not guilty.

1990 V. TUPPER & R. WORTLEY *Anthology of Prison Slang in Australia* (National Library of Australia, Pandora Archive): *Beat*, to defeat an indictment. As in 'to beat it'.

1995 N. IBRAHIM & M. QUINNEY *Glossary of Gaol Slang: Pentridge Gaol* (Unpublished Typescript ANDC): *Beat it*, found not guilty.

2007 M.B. READ *Chopper 11: Last Man Standing* p. 206: Read was charged with the murder of Sammy the Turk Ozerkam. He beat it on self-defence.

bed & breakfast seven days imprisonment.
British and Australian Underworld and Prison Slang.

The term means 'a very short prison stay, especially an overnight one'. The Parramatta Glossary is the only Australian evidence for this term.

Origin: Jocular use of the standard accommodation sense: 'the provision of a bed for a night and breakfast the following morning: an arrangement offered by hotels, boarding houses, etc.' (OED). Although the Parramatta Glossary specifies seven days (rather than overnight), this is in keeping with some later British evidence specifying a sentence of short duration (see 1996 quote). The 2015 British quote has the overnight sense.

[**1996** A. Devlin *Prison Patter* p. 26: *Bed and breakfast*, very short sentence.]

[**2015** N. 'Razor' Smith *The Criminal Alphabet: An A-Z of Prison Slang* p. 154: A night in the punishment block before appearing in front of the governor for adjudication is known as bed and breakfast, as is an overnight stay in any prison while en route to another one.]

being grilled being interrogated.

General English.

The verb *grill* 'to subject to severe questioning' (OED) is recorded from the late nineteenth century.

Origin: Transferred from *grill* 'to cook on a gridiron or similar heating apparatus', probably a variant of *roast* with the same meaning.

1925 *Smith's Weekly* (Sydney) 10 January p. 22: A few days later, the plain clothes man met the boy in the street, and 'grilled' him. The boy, however, remained sulkily silent.

1968 J. Alard *He Who Shoots Last* p. 151: That afternoon when returned to their cages Penitentiary Red was quick to open the conversation. 'Da stroke sez Ragged wuz beat up and chucked in da hole (*footnote*: a solitary confinement cell). Dose two jacks grilled him fer hours'.

2005 *Cairns Post* 9 November p. 1: Cairns criminals are being grilled, searched and arrested in a series of concentrated police stings to stop random bashings and robberies.

be read up have criminal record read aloud in court.

Australian Underworld Slang.

This is the occasion when an accused or convicted person has their prior convictions put to them ('read up' or 'read out'), often during a cross-examination or during sentencing. Later usage tends to be *read out* rather than *read up* (see quotes 1956 and 2003).

The 1894 quote is reporting on a South African case, but the writer is Australian.

1892 *Daily Telegraph* (Sydney) 18 November p. 3: At the Water Police Court Kirk was charged with larceny as a bailee, and several previous convictions being read up against him he was sentenced to four months in gaol.

1894 *Truth* (Sydney) 9 December p. 1: In another case, police-constable was sentenced to six years hard labor for kicking a woman to death. Before sentence was imposed, the following previous convictions were read up against him — eighteen months for theft, four years for manslaughter, and five years for an aggravated assault on a woman.

1914 *Truth* (Brisbane) 7 June p. 10: When his record was read up, Butler admitted that his sentences totalled 63 years, but, of course some were concurrent and all reducible by good behavior in prison.

1956 *Argus* (Melbourne) 7 July p. 9: And he certainly was sick of hearing his list of prior convictions read out. 'I'm sick of hearing them', he said. 'I think I have lived in gaol more than anywhere else. I'm ashamed of it, too. I've got about four sheets of convictions. About 50 convictions, and I don't wish to hear them again'.

2003 *Herald Sun* (Melbourne) 29 March p. 2: But yesterday the hurdles at which he had stumbled were apparent as he humbly admitted in Warrnambool Magistrates' Court to a number of prior convictions read out by prosecutor Boris Kayser.

bin pocket.

British and Australian Underworld Slang.

There is one early example in the British evidence from 1864, but the main British evidence begins in the 1930s. The early evidence appears in the context of thieving and pickpocketing, although in later use it appears in non-criminal contexts.

Origin: Specific use of *bin* 'a receptacle'.

1950 B.K. DOYLE *Australian Police Journal* April p. 111: *In the Bin*, in the pocket.

1954 E. LAMBERT *Veterans* p. 15: Lasher's hand grabbed up his beer and he sank it in three gulps. Tully finished his slowly, but with the glass still at his lips he reached out and gave Lasher's elbow a swift pat. 'Touch your bin', said Lasher, and Tully produced the money for the next drink.

1955 'Thirty-five' in G. SIMES *Dictionary of Australian Underworld Slang* (1993) p. 11: *Bin*, a pocket in the coat or waistcoat (English).

1967 *Whisper All Aussie Dictionary* in *Kings Cross Whisper* 32 p. 7: *Bin*, pocket.

1983 R. AVEN-BRAY *Ridgey Didge Oz Jack Lang* p. 19: *Bin*, pocket.

black peter punishment cell devoid of light and furniture.

Australian Prison Slang.

The term means a prison cell devoid of light that is used to punish a prisoner for infractions of the prison rules.

Origin: See PETER. The 'black' refers to the darkness of a solitary confinement cell.

The 1945 quotation is from an article by the Australian novelist Kylie Tennant who managed to get herself imprisoned in Long Bay Jail in Sydney as part of the research for her novel *Tell Morning This* (which was published in 1953 as *The Joyful Condemned*). In the article she describes her prison experience, and then uses it in her novel (see quote 1953). Note that Tennant also uses the term as a verb.

1931 *Worker's Weekly* (Sydney) 23 October p. 4: I was creditably informed by eye-witnesses that as a result of his punching a 'Screw' on the jaw that a muster was called subsequent to the act of eight 'Screws' who proceeded to a cell and called Eldridge out, when he was seized, portered to the Black Peter accompanied by the kicking and punching of several of them.

1945 *Sun* (Sydney) 25 February p. 3: The Black Peter in Long Bay is a black cell where you can sit and be eaten by mosquitoes. You have no other entertainment. Girls have been in that black cell as long as four days at a time. One girl was 'black-petered' a night and a day for saying 'Hello' to the doctor as he passed.

1953 K. TENNANT *The Joyful Condemned* p. 259: The prison doctor was walking down from the gate. He had once got a girl two days in the black peter for saying good-day to him.

1968 J. ALARD *He Who Shoots Last* p. 151: It makes me shudder ta think of him slaued up in da Black Peter. ... Dey chuck ya in a black cooler by yerself. No mat, not even a blanket, alive as dey is. Dey frisk ya fer weed and wotever else ya got, den dey take yer shoes and socks.

1974 R. ADAMSON & B. HANFORD *Zimmer's Essay* p. 18: During roll-call in the exercise yard he might grow bored with company, fall down and go to sleep; when he went this far the screws were duty-bound to carry him off to black peter.

1984 P. READ *Down There With Me On Cowra Mission* p. 109: They put you in the Black Peter. They take your shoes off ... Take your belt off you. You're put in this 'ere cell, you can't even see your hand in front of you.

2006 B. MATTHEWS *Intractable ... Life inside Australia's First Super-max Prison* p. 80: When I came to I was laying on my back in the 'Black Peter' [solitary confinement cell] with strips of raw flesh flapping from my neck, arms and hands.

block wristwatch.

Australian and American Underworld Slang.

The earliest recorded evidence is Australian (see 1895 and 1910 quotes), and the first American evidence appears in 1914.

Origin: In the 1895 quote the *block and tackle* is 'a watch and chain'. It is likely that *block and tackle* is the original term, from a similarity between a watch and its chain and the lifting device of a pulley with ropes running along that is called 'a block and tackle', and that *block* is an abbreviated form of this. The 1922 quote uses both *block and tackle* and *block*.

1895 C. CROWE *Australian Slang Dictionary* p. 9: *Block and tackle*, watch and chain.

1910 *Register* (Adelaide) 4 May p. 10: A choice sample of the 'slang' vocabulary was presented to the Adelaide Police Court on Tuesday. ... 'I'm here to thieve and you know it. I'll take a "leather", but I won't touch "reds", or a "block"'. ... Subsequent enquiries disclosed that 'leather' or 'pogue' meant, in slang dictionary, purse; 'reds' was the term for jewellery, 'block' for a watch.

1922 *Argus* (Melbourne) 23 March p. 6: 'Get any "pogues" to-day?' is the usual greeting of one pickpocket—or 'dip and hook' as he calls himself—to another. If he has had a successful day the other 'dip' would reply in these terms, 'I got two "presents", a "pogue", a red "block", two white "blocks", a "slang", a "block and tackle", and two "props"'. Translated, this means, 'I obtained two sums of money from men's hip-pockets, a wallet containing a considerable sum of money, a gold watch, two silver watches, a watch chain, a watch and chain, and two scarf pins'.

1967 *Whisper All Aussie Dictionary* in *Kings Cross Whisper* 32 p. 7: *Block*, a dud watch. They look like gold but would turn the wrist green after a very short while.

1975 *Bulletin* (Sydney) 26 April p. 45 (article on underworld slang): He had been charged with dudding; that is, misrepresenting the origin, quality and value of goods he sold. In this case they were watches (blocks).

blonk idiot.

Australian English.

The term means 'a fool, an idiot'.

Origin: Of unknown origin. Green speculates: '? echoic of a solid object, i.e. the fool's head, hitting something hard' (GDS). There is some post-2010 non-Australian evidence for *blonk* meaning 'a well-built male of the club bouncer type' but this is probably unrelated. A Northern Territory motorcycle gang was called *the blonks*, an acronym from *Bike Lovers Only Need Kick Starts*, but the early date of the Parramatta Jail Glossary indicates that there is no connection. Perhaps an alteration of *blank* (GDS has American evidence from the 1950s and 1960s for *blank* meaning a 'bad or insignificant, worthless person').

1984 B. ELLEM *Doing Time: The Prison Experience* p. 187: *Blonk*, a fool or a dill.

1985 'THOMMO' *Dictionary of Australian Swearing and Sex Sayings* p. 16 (cited from T. Dalzell & T. Victor *New Partridge Dictionary of Slang* 2006): *Blonk*, an incompetent, inept, boring person.

1986 R. SPICER *Mud and Stars* p. 7: Right be-fucking-hind you, you stupid blonk.

1989 *Sydney Morning Herald* 18 May p. 3: Mr Beale, the new Opposition spokesman on employment and training, said tens of millions of dollars were being lost every year because many waterside workers could not use machinery because of alcohol problems. 'Some of these are known in the industry as "blonks". Severe cases are called "double blonks" by their workmates', he said.

1990 V. TUPPER & R. WORTLEY *Anthology of Prison Slang in Australia* (National Library of Australia, Pandora Archive): *Blonk*, a foolish person.

1995 N. IBRAHIM & M. QUINNEY *Glossary of Gaol Slang: Pentridge Gaol* (Unpublished Typescript ANDC): *Blonk*, a fool or a dill.

2010 *Brisbane News* 26 May p. 3: That's not to say that you need a degree to be a critical thinker—Albert Einstein said, information is not knowledge, and I'm sure we all know university graduates who are, as my father would say, blonks.

blot anus.

Australian English.

Origin: Transferred use of *blot* 'dark patch' (AND).

1945 S.J. BAKER *Australian Language* p. 156: *Blot*, the posterior or anus.

1965 W. DICK *Bunch of Ratbags* p. 262: He pushed me away and he gave me a kick up the blot.

1974 D. IRELAND *Burn* p. 146: Maybe he'll grab this last chance for some action after sitting on his blot all these years.

2006 *Australian* (Sydney) 14 August p. 10: In the age of *Big Brother*, millions of people sit around on their blots watching other people on TV, and they're still not sick of it.

blow down their lug ear bash.

Australian English.

The Glossary's definition for *blow down someone's lug* uses the Australian term *earbash*, which means 'to subject someone to a torrent of words; to harangue'. *Lug* is an old-fashioned General English word for 'ear'.

Origin: The phrase is similar in form to General English *blow down someone's ear* (also *blow down someone's earhole, blow in someone's ear*), which is widely recorded from the 1930s onwards. But this phrase means 'to whisper' rather than 'to earbash'. This 'whisper' sense for *blow down someone's ear* existed in Australia, and it is illustrated in the 1949 quote below. The same whispering sense existed in Australia for the variant *blow down someone's lug*, as illustrated by the 1931 quote.

The Parramatta Glossary entry and the 1953 entry below do not have the whispering element, and the emphasis is on 'talking incessantly' i.e. 'earbashing'. This indicates that the original whispering sense for the phrase *blow down someone's lug* was varied in Australia to also refer to loud and incessant talking. The similar mainly Australian phrase *to chew someone's ear* means 'to talk incessantly', and this phrase sometimes appears as *to chew someone's lug* (see quote 1901). See also GOT THEIR LUG.

> **1901** H. LAWSON 'A Bush Publican's Lament': He hooks me with his finger ter the far end o' the bar—as if he was goin' ter tell me that the world was ended—an' he hangs over the bar an' chews me lug, an' tries to speak, an' breaks off inter a sort o' low shriek, like a terrified woman, an' he says, 'For Mother o' Christ's sake, giv' me a drink!'

> **1931** *Truth* (Sydney) 11 January p. 2: Anyone who missed Desert Lily in the early stages of yesterday's third heat of the Maiden Welter must have been concentrating on the tail-enders or had sand in their eyes. For those that did miss her, however, let us blow down your lug that she's on the right road to being one of the fastest things this side of the lighthouse, and keep a sharp look-out for the next time she's entered in a similar affair.

> **1949** L. GLASSOP *Lucky Palmer* p. 34: He was called 'Lolly' because he was always whispering about winning hundreds and thousands of pounds. ... 'Lucky' had been talking about him to Max only that morning. 'This "Lolly's" a beauty', he had said. 'He comes up here one night and blows down my ear about all the mazooma he's won'.

> **1953** K. TENNANT *The Joyful Condemned* p. 101: 'And while I'm taking her to the station', the sergeant continued with morose deliberation, 'she nearly had me sobbing with pity, she blows down my lug to that extent. All about her old drunken grandma chasing her with an axe, and the matron of the home she was in twisting her arm, and how at a convent she'd been in they beat her with leather belts, and when we get to the station she accused me of raping her!'

blue bit five dollars.

Australian English.

In the typed-up original Parramatta Glossary this appears as a synonym for SPIN at the 'spin' entry, and does not have its own separate entry: 'Spin (or Blue Bit): Five Dollars'.

Origin: The Glossary points out that *blue bit* is a synonym for *spin*. The original banknote called a *spin* was worth £5 and was coloured blue. With decimalisation (1966), the new $5 note was mauve, and it was the $10 note that was blue. It is possible that for a time $5 continued to be called a *blue bit*, but later evidence suggests this changed to the $10 (see the quotes). Although the reference is to a banknote rather than a coin, the *bit* element probably derives from the use of this term for small silver coins.

1984 B. ELLEM *Doing Time: The Prison Experience* p. 187: *Blue bit*, ten dollars ($10.00).

1990 V. TUPPER & R. WORTLEY *Anthology of Prison Slang in Australia* (National Library of Australia, Pandora Archive): *Blue bit*, ten dollar note.

bodgie false.

Australian English.

The term means 'fake, false, worthless' (AND) and first appeared in Australian English in the 1940s. In the form *bodgie* or *bodger* it was also used as a noun to mean 'something or someone that is fake, false, or worthless'. Some Australian male youths of the 1950s were called *bodgies* because they attempted, in a manner regarded as 'fake', to imitate American fashions and styles.

Origin: An alteration of the term *bodger*, a British dialect word for 'a clumsy, unskilful worker'. The British dialect word *bodge* as a verb meant 'to repair awkwardly ... to work clumsily or roughly' and as a noun 'a clumsy piece of workmanship' (*English Dialect Dictionary*).

1944 T. Hartley in G. SIMES *Dictionary of Australian Underworld Slang* (1993) p. 17: *Bodgy*, anything that is faulty, no good or sham—in the sense that it is not fair dinkum. ... If a prisoner thinks that a story or poem which another prisoner claims to have written is really copied, he says 'It's a bodgy'. Similarly 'bodgy weed' was the name given to an issue of tobacco which when opened was found to be mildewed. ... The origin probably goes back to the days when prisoners were expected to submit a fixed task of work daily—work slummed over to make the quota often being rejected as 'botchy'; i.e. botched.

1978 O. WHITE *Silent Reach* p. 173: This heap is hot—else why did they give it a one-coat spray job over the original white duco and fix it with bodgie number plates?

1981 *Telegraph* (Brisbane) 7 April p. 8: So I wrote out a few bodgie cheques, and did a bit of stealing.

2010 *Gold Coast Bulletin* 16 September p. 28: The only reason Mr Abbott delayed his frontbench reshuffle until this week was to present a bodgie impression of Coalition unity for the election.

bodgie address false address.

Australian English.

Origin: See BODGIE.

1965 *Victorian Hansard* 13 p. 4168: Some 'bodgie' address would be given by buyers.

1986 P. Corris *Deal Me Out* p. 5: I checked on the first two—Majors and Stanford, both Holdens. Phoney as a three dollar note—bodgie addresses, crook licences, no money in the bloody accounts. That's about twenty thousand bucks worth of car gone west.

2012 *Whirlpool Forum* (online) 9 March: Probably find that they have deliberately put a bodgie address on their website so that irate 'customers' don't come around and hassle them.

boil up   make illegal cup of tea in cell.

Australian Prison Slang.

The verb *boil up* in General English means 'to bring to boiling point'. In Australia, New Zealand, and Canada it has the specific meaning of making tea, especially when outdoors. The Australian prison use is in this tradition, with the additional specifics of being illegal and involving some ingenious methods of creating heat. Also used as a noun to describe the process of making tea, or the tea itself.

1944 T. Hartley in G. Simes *Dictionary of Australian Underworld Slang* (1993) p. 17: *Boil-up*, a hot drink prepared surrepticiously [*sic*] in one's cell. One method is to make a tiny fire of thinly sliced sticks and, if you have it, some bees wax from the boot shop, and this is lit on the lid of your cell tub. ... A safer and more popular method is to remove the light bulb and then suspend your mug from the conduit with string so that the light socket is immersed in the water. The current heats the water ... Also *to boil-up*.

1974 J. McNeil *How Does Your Garden Grow* p. 33: Second officer: Oh come on! I know a boiling-up wire when I see one ... like this one.

1983 R. Aven-Bray *Ridgey Didge Oz Jack Lang* p. 21: *Boil up*, illegal tea making in prison.

1990 V. Tupper & R. Wortley *Anthology of Prison Slang in Australia* (National Library of Australia, Pandora Archive): *Boil up*, to prepare boiling water for tea or coffee utilising a boil-up kit.

boob   gaol.

Australian English.

The term is used mainly for 'a prison' but also for 'military detention cells'. It is recorded earliest in this sense in Australia, and although (especially in the earlier period) sometimes used in the US, it has continued longer in Australia. The term is also used in compounds to designate things made in the prison or supplied by the prison, with the implication that such things are second-rate or inferior—see BOOB TEA, BOOB TOBACCO.

Origin: From American *booby hatch* 'a lock-up or gaol; a home for the insane' (OED). This American term probably derives from the nautical term *booby-hatch*: 'On the deck of a vessel: a removable cover ... over a hatchway which allows people access to a lower deck or compartment but which is not large enough to be used for cargo; (hence) a hatchway of this type' (OED).

1904 *Sunday Times* (Perth) 6 March p. 10 (headline): Pampered Prisoners. Banquets in Bunbury Boob.

1941 *Argus* (Melbourne) 15 November (Weekend Magazine Supplement) p. 1: *Boob*, detention barracks.

1950 B.K. Doyle *Australian Police Journal* April p. 111: *Boob*, gaol.

1968 J. Alard *He Who Shoots Last* p. 28: But how ya gonna get inta da boob?

1978 D. Stuart *Wedgetail View* p. 44: Poor bugger, he'd been in an' out o' boob for years; couldn't keep his hands orf anything once he got a bit o' grog in.

1989 T. Anderson *Inside Outlaws: A Prison Diary* p. 142: *Boob*, jail, second-rate. If something is put together in jail with makeshift equipment and the result is second-rate (eg, a tattoo, craftwork, repair work), the explanation may be: 'It's a boob-job'.

1990 V. Tupper & R. Wortley *Anthology of Prison Slang in Australia* (National Library of Australia, Pandora Archive): *Boob*, prison. Term also employed as adjective to describe things associated with prison, usually denoting inferior quality, eg 'boob clothes', 'boob tea', 'boob talk', etc.

2010 *Herald Sun* (Melbourne) 20 April p. 25: My thoughts on Carl are just a fat rat that was eventually going to get his right whack in the boob.

boob happy eccentric. Divorced from reality. Brought about by the strain of gaol routine. Similar to battle fatigue.

Australian Prison Slang.

The term means 'psychologically disturbed as a result of imprisonment' (AND). See also STIR-CRAZY.

Origin: See BOOB. For the *happy* element, the OED notes: 'As the second element in compound adjectives (particularly common during and following the Second World War (1939–45)) relating to (temporary) mental instability associated with the first element'.

1944 T. Hartley in G. Simes *Dictionary of Australian Underworld Slang* (1993) p. 19: *Boob happy*, mentally unbalanced because of imprisonment.

1950 'Thirty-five' in G. Simes *Dictionary of Australian Underworld Slang* (1993) p. 19: 'He's a boob rat', or 'he's boob happy', i.e. imprisonment has sent him off balance.

1968 J. Alard *He Who Shoots Last* p. 122: They approached the forbidding grey walls, which strike terror into the hearts of first offenders, which bring despair to the revisitors and which are home to the boob-happy or stir-crazy.

1977 J. McNeil *Jack* in *Collected Plays* (1987) p. 208: He's been pretty strange lately, probably goin' boob-happy.

1980 J. Simmonds & A. Gollan *For Simmo* p. 147: One day while I was walking up and down my cell. ... I was almost shouting as I talked to myself. ... I realized I was starting to go 'Boob happy' or in the words of the Department 'institutionalised'.

1990 V. Tupper & R. Wortley *Anthology of Prison Slang in Australia* (National Library of Australia, Pandora Archive): *Boob happy*, used to describe an institutionalised prisoner. Someone who has done too much prison, who has given up, who cannot survive outside.

boob tea weak gaol made tea.

Australian Prison Slang.
Prison-supplied tea-leaves were regarded as inferior.
Origin: See BOOB.

1972 J. McNEIL *The Old Familiar Juice* in *The Chocolate Frog, The Old Familiar Juice: Two Plays* (1973) p. 79 (after trying an alcoholic drink brewed in the prison cell): *(winking)* Better 'n boob *tea*.

1990 V. TUPPER & R. WORTLEY *Anthology of Prison Slang in Australia* (National Library of Australia, Pandora Archive): *Boob*, prison. Term also employed as adjective to describe things associated with prison, usually denoting inferior quality, eg 'boob clothes', 'boob tea', 'boob talk', etc.

boob tobacco low grade gaol issued tobacco.

Australian Prison Slang.
Prison-supplied tobacco was regarded as inferior.
Origin: See BOOB. An earlier form is *boob weed* (see quotes 1944 and 1967).

1944 T. Hartley in G. SIMES *Dictionary of Australian Underworld Slang* (1993) p. 19: *Boob weed*, tobacco issued in gaol.

1967 *Whisper All Aussie Dictionary* in *Kings Cross Whisper* 32 p. 7: *Boob weed*, poor quality prison issue tobacco.

1972 J. McNEIL *The Old Familiar Juice* in *The Chocolate Frog, The Old Familiar Juice: Two Plays* (1973) p. 69: Wouldn't give yer two bob a ton fer their boob terbaccer.

1980 B. JEWSON *Stir* p. 15: I'll take one a yer smokes ... Otherwise I'll cough meself t' death ... It's the fucken boob terbacca, y'see.

bouncer dud cheque.

American and Australian Underworld Slang.
The term means 'a bad cheque'. It appears in the US from the 1920s onwards, and is occasionally encountered in Australia. The corresponding verb has been very common in Australia, as in 'the cheque bounced'.
Origin: The bank 'bounces' the cheque back to the account holder if there are insufficient funds in the account to honour it.

1944 *Sun* (Sydney) 5 November p. 2: The Gaming and Betting Act, Section 16 of which says clearly that any contract or agreement arising from betting or gambling is void. But it does seem fair that bookmakers should be given protection from valueless cheques. The man who proffers a 'bouncer' to his butcher or his grocer or his publican is liable to a long term of imprisonment. Yet a racing debtor who passes a valueless cheque to his bookie has only to plead that it was an illegal transaction and he goes scot-free.

1954 *Advocate* (Burnie) 15 July p. 7: Be warned! Don't accept a 'bouncer'. Police yesterday warned that valueless cheques were being passed on the North-West Coast, and that already 'a considerable sum of money' had been obtained by fraudulent means.

box on with it contest court case.
Australian Underworld and Prison Slang.
   This is a specific use of Australian *box on* meaning 'to fight on, to persevere' (AND), especially in adverse circumstances. The Parramatta Glossary's court-case sense is a specific use of the wider sense.
   Origin: From the literal sense of 'to continue to box or fight'.
   The quotations illustrate the wider Australian sense, although the 2007 quote is close to the Parramatta Glossary specific sense.

> **1913** *Geelong Advertiser* 17 July p. 4: Mr Mottram said they would 'box on'. Notwithstanding the economic pressure brought upon them, and the lash of starvation that hung over the homes of thousands of men because of the immigration policy of the Murray-Watt Government, he did not believe many men would offer their services to Stone and Siddeley to scab.
>
> **1916** *Astra* (Melbourne) September p. 13: The gong has sounded, you take your stand / In the midst of the ring of life, / 'Box on' is your first and your last command, / As you enter the worldly strife.
>
> **1962** V.C. HALL *Dreamtime Justice* p. 109: The party had crossed the first nightmare salt-arm with surprising ease and then had boxed on with varying fortunes.
>
> **1980** M. WILLIAMS *Dingo!* p. 76: I got five years' hard labour. Five years! ... The big shots said I was lucky. Box on with it, they said.
>
> **2007** M.B. READ *Chopper 11: Last Man Standing* p. 5: I was the one voted most likely to die. But I'm still here after all these years, boxing on, still pleading not guilty.

boy in the boat clitoris.
General English.
   The term was first recorded in the US in 1916.

> **1950** 'Thirty-five' in G. SIMES *Dictionary of Australian Underworld Slang* (1993) p. 23: *Boy in the boat*, the clitoris.
>
> **1990** V. TUPPER & R. WORTLEY *Anthology of Prison Slang in Australia* (National Library of Australia, Pandora Archive): *Boy in the boat*, clitoris.

brasco shithouse. (Toilet)
Australian English.
   Spelling variants include *brascoe*, *brassco*, and *brasker*.
   Origin: Of unknown origin. There is no evidence for the popular etymology that toilets were manufactured by a firm with a name such as 'Brass Co.' The suggested etymology in the 1967 quotation, a play on 'where the *brass* (k)nobs go', is unlikely.

> **1950** 'Thirty-five' in G. SIMES *Dictionary of Australian Underworld Slang* (1993) p. 24: *Brassco*, the dunny at a showground.
>
> **1967** *Whisper All Aussie Dictionary* in *Kings Cross Whisper* 32 p. 7: *Brasco*, toilet. A play on words, 'where the brass nobs go'.

1984 B. Ellem *Doing Time: The Prison Experience* p. 187: *Brasko*, toilet, lavatory.

1984 G. Carey *Just Us* p. 62: We locked the screw in the brassco one night. ... You'd have to be pretty thick to let a crowd of kids lock you in a brassco.

1995 N. Ibrahim & M. Quinney *Glossary of Gaol Slang: Pentridge Gaol* (Unpublished Typescript ANDC): Brassco, toilet. From the words Brass Co., on the bowl.

2006 *Newcastle Herald* 13 May (Weekender Supplement) p. 34: While flicking through a desk calendar during a lazy afternoon on the brascoe, I came across a nugget of wisdom which ... changed my life evermore.

2017 news.com.au (online) 28 April: Your complete guide to prison slang. ... The last place you'd want to spend those years is in the 'bone yard', which is where 'protected' inmates such as sex offenders and informants are housed. End up there and you'd want to be careful going to the brasco with your date roll, if you know what I mean.

brass not pay your debts.

Australian Underworld Slang.

The term means 'to leave (a person or place) without paying a debt; to defraud of money' (AND).

Origin: From General English *brass* 'money', from the metal used to make some coins (OED).

1939 K. Tennant *Foveaux* p. 312: 'I brassed a mug yesterday', he told her, 'and everything's sweet again'. He flashed a roll of notes as big as his fist.

1944 T. Hartley in G. Simes *Dictionary of Australian Underworld Slang* (1993) p. 23: *Brass*, money. Hence *to brass*—to rob, or to trick a person into parting with his money.

1968 J. Alard *He Who Shoots Last* p. 87: At da meetin' he brassed (*footnote*: to leave, owing money) all the bookies.

1975 *Bulletin* (Sydney) 26 April p. 46 (article on underworld slang): He wouldn't give you up (inform to the police) and never brass you (steal from a thief or mate).

1988 C. Galea *Slipper!* p. 223: I never did like the low mongrel anyway Joe. From the first time he tried to brass me and treat me like a dog.

1990 V. Tupper & R. Wortley *Anthology of Prison Slang in Australia* (National Library of Australia, Pandora Archive): *Brass*, to defraud or cheat another prisoner. 'You're brassed' is a declaration employed by a prisoner to indicate that he has no intention of repaying a debt.

2001 *Prison & Drug Slang: NSW Corrective Services*: *Brass*, swindle, refuse to pay debts.

2002 R.G. Barrett *Mystery Bay Blues* p. 18: 'What are you doing in Bondi? You low life, little piece of shit'. 'Hey. That's not very nice, Les'. 'No. And neither's brassing me for two hundred dollars. You prick of a thing'.

break an excuse.

Not otherwise recorded, except in the phrase *go for breaks* in New Zealand (see quote 1982). Perhaps loosely related to the General English phrase *give someone a break* 'give someone a chance, to let off, to excuse, to give an opportunity' (GDS).

[**1982** G. Newbold *The Big Huey* p. 245: *Go for break(s)*, lie, make excuses.]

brick¹ ten dollars.

Australian English.

Originally (and most commonly) for £10, and after the introduction of decimal currency (1966) sometimes used for $10 and occasionally for $20 (the approximate equivalent value of the former £10).

Origin: From the reddish-brown colour of the ten-pound note (AND).

1914 A.B. Paterson in C. Semmler *The World of Banjo Paterson* (1967) p. 324: Pop it down, gents, if you don't put down a brick you can't pick up a castle!

1944 T. Hartley in G. Simes *Dictionary of Australian Underworld Slang* (1993) p. 25: *Brick*, £10.

1950 B.K. Doyle *Australian Police Journal* April p. 111: *Brick*, £10; or ten years' imprisonment.

1967 *Whisper All Aussie Dictionary* in *Kings Cross Whisper* 32 p. 7: *Brick*, twenty dollars or ten pounds.

1984 B. Ellem *Doing Time: The Prison Experience* p. 187: *Brick*, ten years, or ten dollars.

brick² ten years.

Australian Underworld and Prison Slang.

The term means 'a sentence of ten years' imprisonment'.

Origin: Transfer of the number 10 from *brick* in the sense 'ten pounds' (later 'ten dollars'). See previous entry.

1944 T. Hartley in G. Simes *Dictionary of Australian Underworld Slang* (1993) p. 25: *Brick*, £10, a sentence of ten years. It will be noted that many prison sentences are derived from equivalent slang for money.

1968 J. Alard *He Who Shoots Last* p. 124: 'So you got five years again, Red'. ... 'It mighta been worse; I coulda got a brick'.

1973 *Contact: Parramatta Jail Resurgents Magazine* June n.p.: Now Billy, he's a real character. For him ... the ten years he's just done is a brick.

1984 B. Ellem *Doing Time: The Prison Experience* p. 132: There was a crim killed when some bricks from a building construction in the jail fell on him. Well, the joke that went around was, 'did you hear about the bloke who got a brick and couldn't handle it?'

1995 N. Ibrahim & M. Quinney *Glossary of Gaol Slang: Pentridge Gaol* (Unpublished Typescript ANDC): *A brick*, ten years.

2006 B. Matthews *Intractable ... Life inside Australia's First Super-max Prison* p. 393: *Brick of years*, a ten-year sentence.

2017 news.com.au (online) 28 April: Your complete guide to prison slang. ... You might encounter some of these types while 'doing a brick' (10 years).

bridge exposing sensuous parts of body.

Australian English.

The compiler probably means this as a verb: 'to expose the sensuous parts of the body', and the verb probably therefore means 'to pose is such a way as to emphasise one's attractive physical features'.

Origin: Of unknown origin. The quotes fall into three groups, and they all have an element of physical display, giving some hints about where the Parramatta Glossary sense comes from. The 1923 and 1985 quotes have *bridge* as a verb meaning 'to display'. The 1955 and 1982 quotes have *bridge* as a noun in a verb phrase that means something like 'to display sexually'. The final five quotes have the verb phrase *bridge up*. All five have a sense of 'showing off', including showing the body off, and standing with a boxer's pose to elicit admiration (2018).

> **1923** *Smith's Weekly* (Sydney) 11 August p. 15: Me, Robbo, Darkie and Adelaide Jack was sittin' in the bar when the possum blew in: 'arf molo. He was well clobbered an' wore a slang big enough to tow the Makura, with a locket like a meat safe 'anging to it. The ugma shouted fer the mob and bridges a roll thick enough to choke Big Mouth Annie. ... Glossary: *possum* 'fool' ... *arf molo* 'half drunk' ... *clobbered* 'clothed' ... *slang* 'watchchain' ... *ugma* 'mug'.
>
> **1955** 'Thirty-five' in G. SIMES *Dictionary of Australian Underworld Slang* (1993) p. 25: *Put on a bridge*, (of a girl) to flaunt her charms.
>
> **1982** N. KEESING *Lily on a Dustbin* p. 176: A girl who 'chucks a bridge' sits with her underpants visible.
>
> **1983** R. AVEN-BRAY *Ridgey Didge Oz Jack Lang* p. 19: *Bridge*, display something.
>
> **1986** R.G. BARRETT *The Real Thing* p. 37: In fact, why don't you both take the rest of the night off, get a couple of sheilas and go and have a blow out somewhere? Take the Rolls and bridge up a bit. Charge it all to me.
>
> **1990** V. TUPPER & R. WORTLEY *Anthology of Prison Slang in Australia* (National Library of Australia, Pandora Archive): *Bridge up*, show off (physically) or shape up as if to fight.
>
> **2005** J. PRING *Abo: A Treacherous Life: the Graham Henry Story* p. 294: Again the Clone was out to get rid of me. He made out to everyone around him that he was this big underworld figure, a hitman, always bridging up about the people he'd killed.
>
> **2017** news.com.au (online) 28 April: 'Your complete guide to prison slang'. ... Bridge up — to fight or show off.
>
> **2018** J. KNIGHT *Dictionary of Victorian Prison Slang* (online) p. 6: *Bridge up*, to ostentatiously stand erect for the purpose of presenting a well-built physique. Example: 'He bridges up every time someone looks at him in the gym'.

bring undone cause someone to be found out.

Australian Underworld Slang.

Specific use of General English *undone* 'brought to decay or ruin; ruined, destroyed' and *to come undone* 'to come to grief' (OED). The Parramatta Glossary use is specific in that it refers to the exposure or failure of a criminal activity.

> **1950** 'Thirty-five' in G. SIMES *Dictionary of Australian Underworld Slang* (1993)

p. 92: '*Rorts* are always *brought undone* by gigs'.

1950 'Thirty-five' in G. Simes *Dictionary of Australian Underworld Slang* (1993) p. 209: *Undone*, ruined, brought to naught.

1990 V. Tupper & R. Wortley *Anthology of Prison Slang in Australia* (National Library of Australia, Pandora Archive): *Bring undone*, to discover or frustrate someone's plans. To have been 'brought undone' is every prisoner's lament.

1995 N. Ibrahim & M. Quinney *Glossary of Gaol Slang: Pentridge Gaol* (Unpublished Typescript ANDC): *Brought undone*, caught.

2021 *Cairns Post* 4 February p. 20: A woman with a history of dangerous drug offending since 2012 has been sentenced to jail after her criminal activities were brought undone by undercover police.

[**buckled** *see* GET BUCKLED.]

bugged alarmed.

American and Australian English.

From the verb *bug* 'to fit with a burglar alarm' (OED).

The early American evidence is illustrated in quotes 1927 and 1950. This sense of *bug* does not appear elsewhere in the Australian evidence, and *bug* is generally used in Australian criminal contexts to mean 'to tap a telephone or to install any form of electronic surveillance' (GDS). This surveillance sense was originally American, but is now General English (and is illustrated below by the Australian quotes 1972 and 2007). Even so, two glossaries of New Zealand Prison Slang include the burglar alarm sense (see quotes 1982 and 2001), suggesting that this sense is likely to have been present in Australia, as its presence in the Parramatta Glossary suggests.

[**1927** *Dialect Notes* (American Dialect Society) vol. 5, x, p. 440: *Bug* ... to protect a safe with electric alarm devices.]

[**1950** H.E. Goldin *Dictionary of American Underworld Lingo* p. 35: *Bug*, to wire for burglary protection.]

1972 *Canberra Times* 22 March p. 1: An allegation that the Australian Government had 'bugged' a room occupied by the Malaysian delegation to the five-power talks in Canberra in 1969 was strongly denied by the Minister for Foreign Affairs, Mr Bowen, last night.

[**1982** G. Newbold *The Big Huey* p. 246: *Bug*, burglar alarm.]

[**2001** D. Looser *Lexicon of Boobslang in the Period 1996–2000* (thesis) p. 32: *Bug*, a burglar alarm.]

2007 M.B. Read *Chopper 11: Last Man Standing* p. 29: Police also had his house bugged, so when he rang his victim's brother to demand a ransom, police recorded the lot.

bumper dip's accomplice. Bumps into victim while dip removes whippy.

Australian Underworld Slang.

A *dip* is a 'pickpocket' and a *whippy* is a 'wallet'. See entries for DIP and WHIPPY.

Origin: From the fact that this accomplice physically bumps an intended victim to unsettle him, while the pickpocket steals from the victim's pocket.

The term appears elsewhere (and in the citations below) as *bumper-up*.

> **1941** S.J. Baker *A Popular Dictionary of Australian Slang* p. 15: *Bumper-up*, a pickpocket's confederate.
>
> **1944** T. Hartley in G. Simes *Dictionary of Australian Underworld Slang* (1993) p. 31: *Bumper-up*, a special meaning used by pickpockets denotes a confederate who bumps an intended victim so that his attention is distracted enabling the pickpocket to rob him.
>
> **1953** *Argus* (Melbourne) 31 October p. 9: The dip or rip and tear man (pickpocket): Years of training go into the perfection of his art. He's the complete specialist and very rarely turns his hand to anything else. ... The 'rip-and-tear man' usually works with a 'bumper-up'—someone who bumps the victim off balance and distracts his attention while the pickpocket 'lifts' the 'willy' (wallet). Most pickpockets begin as 'bumpers-up'.

bunch up put someone in impossible position.

Australian Underworld Slang.

Most of the evidence points to this being the kind of thieving activity described in the entry for BUMPER. But this is not entirely in keeping with the Parramatta Glossary's definition, which is closer to the sense given by 'Thirty-five' in his 1950 entry, which is cross-referenced from *bunch up* to *bump up* and defined 'to urge someone to take a particular course of action'. In his 1955 version, 'Thirty-five' again cross-references *bunch up* to *bump up*, and this time defines 'to act as an accomplice to a thief by bumping a victim, and so distracting his attention'.

Origin: Probably from the notion of a group of people bunching together and putting pressure on another (the Parramatta and first 'Thirty-five' definition), or (in the thieving sense) for a group to work together to steal from another.

> **1950** 'Thirty-five' in G. Simes *Dictionary of Australian Underworld Slang* (1993) p. 31: *Bump up*, to urge someone to take a particular course of action.
>
> **1955** 'Thirty-five' in G. Simes *Dictionary of Australian Underworld Slang* (1993) p. 31: *Bump up*, to act as an accomplice to a thief by bumping a victim, and so distracting his attention.
>
> **1950, 1955** 'Thirty-five' in G. Simes *Dictionary of Australian Underworld Slang* (1993) p. 31: *Bunch up*, to BUMP UP in company.
>
> **1967** *Whisper All Aussie Dictionary* in *Kings Cross Whisper* 32 p. 7: *Bunch up*, a confidence trick played by one or more persons against an unsuspecting person.
>
> **1983** R. Aven-Bray *Ridgey Didge Oz Jack Lang* p. 19: *Bunch up*, trick by confusing the victim.

bung it pass contraband on to someone else to avoid being buckled with it.

Australian Underworld Slang.

The phrase means 'to pass on illegal goods to someone else to avoid being arrested in possession of them'. See the entry GET BUCKLED.

Origin: This is a specific use of senses of the verb *bung* that are well attested in General (especially British) English from the 1820s: 'to pass, to throw, usually energetically or aggressively' (GDS), 'to hand over, to give quickly; especially in imperative. e.g. *bung this round to Fred*' (GDS). In the Parramatta Glossary definition the emphasis is on the contraband being passed quickly and secretly to an accomplice.

1944 T. Hartley in G. SIMES *Dictionary of Australian Underworld Slang* (1993) p. 32: *Bung*, give quickly without hesitation. Generally used in the imperative mood. The note of urgency about this expression may also denote the need for speed so that the transfer will not be observed. Thus 'Bung this around to Mick' means 'Take this around to Mick, quickly and give it to him but careful no one else sees it'.

bun wagon police paddy wagon.
Australian Underworld Slang.

Origin: The origin of *bun* is not entirely clear, but the synonymous *bum van* (see quote 1989) suggests that it is from *buns* = 'buttocks'. The variation *bun truck* also appears (see quote 2001). There is some Canadian evidence of the term also being used for a 'paddy wagon' from the 1990s and later, and this is probably an independent development, perhaps with reference to a bread delivery van or a hamburger van (see quote 2014 in square brackets).

1983 R. AVEN-BRAY *Ridgey Didge Oz Jack Lang* p. 21: *Bun wagon*, police trawler.

1989 T. ANDERSON *Inside Outlaws: A Prison Diary* p. 143: *Bum van*, small police or prison 'escort van' or 'paddy wagon' with wooden bench-seats and covered with wire and rubber-coated canvas. Hold 4 to 6 (or more) prisoners.

1990 V. TUPPER & R. WORTLEY *Anthology of Prison Slang in Australia* (National Library of Australia, Pandora Archive): *Bun wagon*, police or prison van used for transporting prisoners. … *Bum van*, a prison escort van, variant of 'bun wagon'.

2001 *Prison & Drug Slang: NSW Corrective Services*: *Bun truck*, prison caged escort vehicle.

[**2014** B. SHARP *Forty-Three Years in The Royal Canadian Mounted Police* p. 52: I walked over to Huget, who was standing by the provost van, sometimes called a paddy wagon, but for reasons unknown to me, more commonly called the *bun wagon*. We managed to cram twelve of the fifteen prisoners into the back of the *bun* wagon.]

burgoo hominy (gaol breakfast).
Australian Prison Slang.

The term refers to the porridge served at breakfast. While this term is occasionally used in British prison contexts (e.g. in the 1930s), the prison use is mainly Australian. The Parramatta Glossary gives MOOSH as a synonym.

Origin: The word is from Arabic *burgul* meaning 'cooked, parched, and crushed wheat' (OED). In English it came to be used to describe 'a thick oatmeal gruel or porridge', originally as used by seamen, but later in many contexts including (in

Australia) in the outback and in the army. In the United States it refers to 'a soup or stew made with a variety of meat and vegetables, used especially at outdoor feasts' (OED).

1948 *Sunday Times* (Perth) 30 May p. 3: I doubt whether your dog would stomach prison fare. A dixie of bergoo (the colloquial expression for porridge), a cup of black tea and half a loaf of dry bread, are deposited ceremoniously upon the floor.

1950 'Thirty-five' in G. SIMES *Dictionary of Australian Underworld Slang* (1993) p. 33: *Burgoo*, the porridge served in gaol: wheatmeal, oatmeal, and even cornmeal (a nautical, bush, and military term for porridge or oatmeal gruel).

1967 *Whisper All Aussie Dictionary* in *Kings Cross Whisper* 32 p. 7: *Burgoo*, same as mush, prison porridge.

1984 B. ELLEM *Doing Time: The Prison Experience* p. 38: I then had to make a decision as to where I would use the sugar and condensed milk mixture. I opted to use it on the burgoo and to drink the tea as it had been served. The porridge was thick and sticky and barely palatable.

1990 V. TUPPER & R. WORTLEY *Anthology of Prison Slang in Australia* (National Library of Australia, Pandora Archive): *Burgoo*, prison porridge.

1995 N. IBRAHIM & M. QUINNEY *Glossary of Gaol Slang: Pentridge Gaol* (Unpublished Typescript ANDC): *Burgoo*, porridge.

2017 R. MANN *Pentridge: Voices from the Other Side* p. 99: And this awful burgoo, stuff that Hannibal was supposed to have conquered the Alps on—some type of porridge. We didn't even have real milk; we'd have powered milk.

bust breaking & entering (commercial premises).
British and Australian Underworld Slang.

The term is used for a break-in and burglary, especially of a commercial premises such as a shop, a factory, etc. (and this is the emphasis in the Parramatta Glossary definition), although it is also used in Australian English of a burglary of a residential premises. It is first recorded as *burst* in an 1857 British glossary of underworld terms, then as *bust* in an 1859 American glossary of underworld terms. In the same period it also appears as a verb meaning 'to break into'. The verb is used in the US in the twentieth century, as elsewhere, but the noun is mainly used in Britain and Australia in this period.

1931 *Sun* (Sydney) 17 August p. 7: At the police station Kinman said, 'I'll take what is coming to me as far as the "bust" is concerned, but don't go too hot on the gun stuff'.

1944 T. Hartley in G. SIMES *Dictionary of Australian Underworld Slang* (1993) p. 34: *Bust*, breaking and entering a factory or dwelling.

1950 B.K. DOYLE *Australian Police Journal* April p. 111: *Bust*, to break in. 'Do a bust' usually means to rob a house, shop, or factory.

1967 *Whisper All Aussie Dictionary* in *Kings Cross Whisper* 32 p. 7: *Bust*, the act of breaking and entering premises.

1968 J. ALARD *He Who Shoots Last* p. 35: I believe Eyebrows O'Leary is doing a stretch over some bust he pulled with the Broadway Monkey.

1981 *Telegraph* (Brisbane) 7 April p. 8: 'Busts' are breakings and enterings, in underworld slang.

1990 V. Tupper & R. Wortley *Anthology of Prison Slang in Australia* (National Library of Australia, Pandora Archive): *Bust*, break and enter. As in to 'do a bust'.

1996 M.B. Read *Chopper 6: No Tears for a Tough Guy* p. 125: One night, a chemist's shop in Victoria Street got busted into and a modest quantity of pethidine vials went missing, along with a large tin of morphine tablets and two bottles of methadone. It was just another chemist's shop bust, no big news.

bustman one who specializes in busts.
Australian Underworld Slang.
The term means 'a burglar; a person who breaks and enters (a dwelling etc.)' (AND). See BUST.

1944 T. Hartley in G. Simes *Dictionary of Australian Underworld Slang* (1993) p. 34: *Bust*, breaking and entering a factory or dwelling. Hence *a busman* [sic]—a thief who commits this form of robbery.

1953 K. Tennant *The Joyful Condemned* p. 39: Mort, who was a fair mechanic and a most incompetent burglar, had been bored by his job. ... Jake, who was much more intelligent, and therefore a better 'bustman', could plan.

1975 B. Latch & B. Hitchings *Mr X, Police Informer* p. 224: The dumps where the bust men snooker their stuff.

1983 R. Aven-Bray *Ridgey Didge Oz Jack Lang* p. 21: *Bust man*, house breaker.

1990 V. Tupper & R. Wortley *Anthology of Prison Slang in Australia* (National Library of Australia, Pandora Archive): *Bustman*, a criminal whose main activity is break and enter.

1993 A.S. Smith *Neddy* p. 234: There were shoplifters, armed robbers, bust men [*professional burglars*]—there was someone from nearly every type of crime drinking there.

2006 B. Matthews *Intractable ... Life inside Australia's First Super-max Prison* p. 101: Then there were the professional armed robbers, the rapists, the bust men and the car thieves who all had their individual rungs on the prison social ladder as well.

butter up use flattery as means to exploit.
General English.
The term is first recorded in Britain in the late eighteenth century.

1885 *Bulletin* (Sydney) 9 May p. 14: We most decidedly think it would be misplaced kindness if, when we see glaring matters inimical to the furtherance of amateur rowing, we buttered them up in the 'everything-passed-off-satisfactorily' style of the daily Press.

1994 M.B. Read *Chopper 4: For the Term of His Unnatural Life* p. 12: How come whenever you need to butter someone up I end up becoming the butter.

can gaol.
General English.

Originally American (first recorded 1912), and although now used in General English it remains chiefly an American term.

Origin: Extended sense of *can* 'container', used from the late nineteenth century for a small room, a lavatory etc. It was then variously used to describe places of imprisonment, such as at a police station, thence to a prison.

1932 *Sunday Mail* (Brisbane) 13 November p. 20: Argot of Crime ... The watch house is the 'can'.

1950 B.K. DOYLE *Australian Police Journal* April p. 111: *Can*, gaol or cell.

1967 *Whisper All Aussie Dictionary* in *Kings Cross Whisper* 33 p. 4: *Can*, prison.

1995 N. IBRAHIM & M. QUINNEY *Glossary of Gaol Slang: Pentridge Gaol* (Unpublished Typescript ANDC): *The can*, prison.

2022 *Border Mail* (Albury-Wodonga) 23 March p. 3: Career crook is in the can, yet again, after sentence for police pursuits.

cannon concealable firearm.

American and Australian Underworld Slang.

The term is used for 'a pistol, a revolver, esp. a large one' (OED). Evidence for use is almost exclusively US, but the Parramatta Glossary entry and quote 1944 indicate that it is one of those terms that found its way from the US into Australian Underworld Slang, and had some limited use there.

Origin: Transferred from the General English sense of *cannon*: 'a large, heavy piece of artillery formerly used in warfare, typically one requiring to be mounted for firing, usually on a wheeled carriage; now chiefly used for signalling, ceremonies, or re-enactment'. The transfer was made to pistols or revolvers that were larger than the standard kind.

1944 T. Hartley in G. SIMES *Dictionary of Australian Underworld Slang* (1993) p. 38: *Cannon*, revolver.

can't aim up no ability.

General English.

The phrase means that a person lacks skill, is incompetent, etc.

In the typed-up glossary this phrase appears immediately after CAN'T FIRE and immediately before CANNON, JOINT, and PIECE, all terms for 'concealable firearm'. The terms *aim up* and *aim down* appear in instructions for firing guns in particular circumstances (see quote 1914). Both *can't aim up* and *can't fire* allude literally to an inability to fire a gun accurately, and therefore indicate incompetence and inaptitude.

At a later date the term *aim up* is used in the reporting of team sport, and refers to a team's need to play competently and well (see quote 1994). A team that 'aims up' demonstrates good ability, and this is probably another transfer from the 'firing' sense, a transfer also evident in the Parramatta Glossary entry.

1914 *Kalgoorlie Western Argus* 14 April p. 14: Military Encampment. Goldfields Regiment at Work. Field Firing Day. ... The men work in pairs against each other.

The pairs lie down extended to three paces some fifty yards in rear of the fire position. Rifles loaded with four rounds in the magazine. Targets to appear anywhere, within 600 yards of the fire position. Sights not to be altered after the first shot, but aiming up and down must be employed. On service, men would not alter their sights under a close fire, and therefore they must learn to aim up and down.

1994 *Canberra Times* 16 September p. 33: It has been four years since we tasted grand final success so make no mistake, we are dead-set hungry. And don't believe the rot that we won't be able to aim up after the gruelling Canterbury game. We will bounce back. We are too good a team not to.

can't be educated won't be told.
General English.
The phrase means that a person will not take advice.
The 1971 citation is not the exact form of the headword, but it is from McNeil's play set in Parramatta Jail, and gives a context for the usage.

1971 J. McNeil *The Chocolate Frog* in *The Chocolate Frog, The Old Familiar Juice: Two Plays* (1973) p. 28: Kevin: I don't want any tea. Tosser: (*enraged*) Shuddup! Yer'll drink what yer told. Time yer started gettin' educated, I reckon.

can't fire no ability.
General English.
The phrase means that a person lacks skill, is incompetent, etc. A variant of can't aim up.
Origin: In the typed-up glossary this phrase appears immediately before can't aim up and before cannon, joint, and piece, all terms for 'concealable firearm'. It therefore appears in a cluster of terms describing weapons and their uses, and the compilers of the Glossary clearly believe that *can't fire* refers to an inability to use a gun properly, thereby designating incompetence.

It is possible, however, that the ultimate origin of this phrase lies in combustion engines rather than guns. Since the early twentieth century the phrase *to function* (or *operate, fire,* etc.) *on all* (or *four,* or *six,* etc.) *cylinders* has meant '(of an internal-combustion engine) to be working at full power; hence *figurative*, to function properly, to be in good form' (OED). Quote 1932 shows the figurative transfer to a sporting context. The later use of the verb *fire* to mean 'to perform well' may be an abbreviation of the longer phrase (see quote 1975).

1932 *Truth* (Sydney) 17 April p. 17: They say 'Smacker' Blair has his Armidale hopefuls firing on all cylinders. He tries them out in the first real game of the season. Sunday next, against Glen Innes.

1975 *Canberra Times* 10 June p. 16: South Canberra continues to run hot and cold and will need to fire with two tough games against Lakes United and South Woden in the next three rounds.

captain person who foots the bill.
Australian English.

The term means 'a person with money to spend, especially one who buys drinks for an assembled company' (AND).

Origin: The OED points to the use of *captain* as 'a term of address (without implying any office or rank)' and compares with the similar use of *governor*. Two early examples are from American tramp slang (see quotes 1926 and 1931) but these may be formulations that are independent of the Australian usage.

[**1926** 'Hobo Lingo' in *American Speech* I p. 650: *Captain*, one off the job and free with his money.]

[**1931** G. IRWIN *American Tramp and Underworld Slang* p. 47: Captain, one free with his money, and so able to command respect and enforce orders. ... Use probably comes from the negro's delight in bestowing titles on anyone in authority, whether that person is entitled to the rank or not.]

1944 T. Hartley in G. SIMES *Dictionary of Australian Underworld Slang* (1993) p. 38: *Captain*, the member of a group who has recently 'inherited' funds, and is therefore paying exes, especially shouting drinks.

1967 *Whisper All Aussie Dictionary* in *Kings Cross Whisper* 33 p. 4: *Captain*, a person buying all the drinks.

1973 J. POWERS *Last of the Knucklemen* p. 63: (*Standing and heading for the fridge*) I'll be the captain for a round of beers.

1983 R. AVEN-BRAY *Ridgey Didge Oz Jack Lang* p. 22: *Captain*, one who buys the drinks.

carve him up pull all his money off him.
British and Australian Underworld Slang.

The phrase is recorded in Britain from the 1930s onwards. See E. Partridge, *Dictionary of the Underworld* (1950) where he defines *carve up* 'to swindle a confederate out of (part of) his share, of loot' (p. 107). See quotes below for the British evidence. There is, however, a slight difference of emphasis in the Parramatta Glossary definition, where it seems to refer to someone being robbed of his money rather than being deprived of a share in loot. Not otherwise recorded in the Australian evidence.

[**1933** C.E. LEACH *On Top of the Underworld* p. 138 (Glossary of Crooks' Argot): *Carve up*, swindle accomplice out of share.]

[**1936** J. CURTIS *The Gilt Kid* (1947) p. 141: The cash-box had two lids which opened up from a central hinge. There was no lock on it. All it held was a sheet of postage stamps and a load of silver coins. 'We'd better divvy up here', said Scaley, 'so as we don't have to carry these bloody cash-boxes around'. 'Sure we'll divvy up here. What's up with you? Think I'm going to carve you up?']

case get layout of premises for prospective robbery.
General English.

The term means 'to examine, inspect, or study; to size up. Frequently in *to case the joint, gaff, job*, etc.: to reconnoitre a place in anticipation of committing a robbery or some other crime there' (OED). Originally American Underworld Slang from the early twentieth century.

Origin: GDS suggests an origin in the jargon of the card gambling game Faro, where *case* meant 'to watch carefully'.

1944 T. Hartley in G. Simes *Dictionary of Australian Underworld Slang* (1993) p. 39: *Case*, to look over premises with a view to robbery.

1950 B.K. Doyle *Australian Police Journal* April p. 112: *Case a joint over*, survey a place prior to robbing it.

1984 B. Ellem *Doing Time: The Prison Experience* p. 132: I'd had my eyes on this fancy house for a while. I'd cased the joint and it looked good, easy pickings.

1990 V. Tupper & R. Wortley *Anthology of Prison Slang in Australia* (National Library of Australia, Pandora Archive): *Case*, to survey an establishment for the purposes of potential burglary. Thus, 'to case the joint'.

cat passive homosexual.
Australian English. Chiefly as *Prison Slang*.

In prison use, it refers to a young male, usually not homosexual, who is forced or coerced into passive sexual relationships with other male prisoners, or forced or coerced into performing fellatio on other male prisoners. Also used in prison more generally for 'homosexual person', usually with an emphasis on effeminacy (see quote 1984). Occasionally used in non-prison contexts (see quotes 1973 and 1987). See discussion of the term in section 4 of the introductory material. See also HOCK.

There is an American example from 1953 (see quote in square brackets), but the wide range of meanings given for the term suggests that this is a version of *cat* meaning 'prostitute' (American English also has *pussy* 'a male homosexual') combined with American *cat* 'a person'. The sense 'male homosexual' for *cat* is not otherwise attested in the American evidence.

Origin: From *cat(amite)* 'a boy kept for homosexual practices; the passive partner in anal intercourse' (OED), enforced by *cat* 'female prostitute'.

1950 'Thirty-five' in G. Simes *Dictionary of Australian Underworld Slang* (1993) p. 39: *Cat*, a passive homosexual. (Possibly from 'cat', a spiteful woman, more probably abbreviation of catamite.)

[**1953** W. Brown *Monkey on My Back* p. 99: The word *cat*, for example, was used to mean another boy, or a prostitute, or a man looking for a woman, or a homosexual.]

1967 *Whisper All Aussie Dictionary* in *Kings Cross Whisper* 33 p. 4: *Cat*, an effeminate homosexual.

1967 B.K. Burton *Teach Them No More* p. 49: Terry was amazed at first to find that his friend was a homosexual, a cat. He had expected that they would be strange, queer animals, very different from other men. But here he was, quite a decent sort of chap to talk to.

1971 J. McNeil *The Chocolate Frog* in *The Chocolate Frog, The Old Familiar Juice: Two Plays* (1973) p. 45: I believe you about the boys' homes, about gaols, about cats and dogs and chocolate frogs!

1973 *Digger* (Melbourne) 13 January p. 6: The two things sharpies hate most are longhairs and poofters, which places some of us in double jeopardy. It can get a bit heavy down in the station standing alone and feeling a little vulnerable because you know that they know, and they jostle you, making miaowing sounds and muttering 'Cat! Cat!'

1974 R. ADAMSON & B. HANFORD *Zimmer's Essay* p. 31: The big losers in the prison sexual politik are the 'cats', who will not accept feminine status, but who are weak and so are raped, or coerced into cock-sucking.

1984 B. ELLEM *Doing Time: The Prison Experience* p. 105: What we call a cat, a guy who wears make-up and plucks his eyebrows. They usually are not promiscuous and will have a relationship with only one guy at a time.

1987 G. Simes in *Outrage* (Melbourne) December p. 19: For the most part prisoners engaging in sex conform to well-defined behavioral roles that mimic traditional, pre-feminist male-female relations on the outside. The *hock* fucks or is sucked off by the *queen* or the *cat*, the two distinct types who take the female role. Of these the *cat* is a young, good-looking or pretty male, often straight (at least to begin with), who is pressured or forced into sex. Unable to defend himself, he falls victim to the hock. His initiation (*breaking in* or *turning out*) may take the form of outright rape or it may be a more subtle form of seduction or pressure whereby he comes to a realization that a relationship with a hock is preferable to the alternative, rape or pack-rape repeated continually and unpredictably. Or he may unwittingly be got into debt by a hock who will graciously agree to accept repayment in the form of sexual favors. The cat may revert to heterosexuality on release or he may remain gay.

1987 *Sydney Morning Herald* 12 January p. 2: They did exist. We knew a sergeant-major who was a cat. He had a lieutenant for a friend and we all knew what was going on, but it was kept quiet.

1989 T. ANDERSON *Inside Outlaws: A Prison Diary* p. 144: *Cat*, male homosexual generally; more specifically, a male homosexual who acts as a 'passive' partner. Also refers to 'drag-queens', transsexuals.

1990 V. TUPPER & R. WORTLEY *Anthology of Prison Slang in Australia* (National Library of Australia, Pandora Archive): *Cat*, a male person who takes the passive role in a homosexual relationship. A person who openly admits he is gay and submissive. An effeminate person. A probable contraction of catamite. Note that Partridge uses the term to denote a female harlot with no reference to homosexuality.

2006 B. MATTHEWS *Intractable ... Life inside Australia's First Super-max Prison* p. 393: *Cat*, effeminate homosexual or one who takes the female role in a homosexual relationship.

2016 J. PHELPS *Australia's Toughest Prisons: Inmates* p. 4: You want a suck? We have a cat down there giving all the boys head-jobs.

chaff money.

Australian English.

Origin: An earlier Australian version of this term is *chaff money*, used in horseracing parlance to designate paltry winnings—enough money only to buy chaff for the horse (see 1907 quote for this form). At a later date the chaff element comes to be used just for 'money'.

1907 *Sunday Times* (Perth) 2 June p. 10: Anyway, the stake was only worth 25 sovs. to the winner—just chaff money for a few weeks, as it were.

1939 K. Tennant *Foveaux* p. 352: He would describe the police as 'sweating on them like a mob of vultures' and he gave money its rightful designation of 'chaff', 'sugar' or 'hay'.

1950 'Thirty-five' in G. Simes *Dictionary of Australian Underworld Slang* (1993) p. 41: *Chaff*, money.

1966 *Kings Cross Whisper* July p. 8: But here in Kings Cross cabbage means money, and so does ... chaff, brass, bread.

1968 J. Alard *He Who Shoots Last* p. 87: 'Too bad we didn't git da bookie's chaff', lamented the Wrecker.

chew & spew   prison stew.
Australian Prison Slang.

This prison sense is a specific use of the Australian term that is usually used of a place that sells cheap food (often takeaway) and for the food itself (often not very appetising). The Parramatta Jail term is a specific use to refer to a typically unappetising prison meal, enforced by the extra rhyme on *stew*.

With the exception of the Tupper & Wortley 1990 quote, the quotes illustrate the standard Australian sense.

1967 *Whisper All Aussie Dictionary* in *Kings Cross Whisper* 32 p. 7: *A chew it and spew it*, a very cheap sleazy cafe.

1979 *Sun-Herald* (Sydney) 3 June p. 103: You've got to live on take-away greasies from the local 'chew and spew' restaurants.

1988 L. Johansen *The Dinkum Dictionary* p. 64: Chew and spew, 1. Any cheap cafe or restaurant serving take-away or fast-foods: e.g. We're eating at the local chew and spew tonight. 2. Take-away food; fast-food; junk food.

1990 V. Tupper & R. Wortley *Anthology of Prison Slang in Australia* (National Library of Australia, Pandora Archive): *Chew 'n spew*, prison food.

2020 *Sunday Telegraph* (Sydney) 23 February p. 86: One night I went to a chew-and-spew and found I'd forgotten my wallet. It was chopsticks at midnight over an $18 pad thai.

clacker   arsehole.
Australian English.

The term means 'the anus, the backside' (AND).

Origin: Specific use of *clacker* 'that which clacks', with reference to emitting wind (AND). Cf. *clack* 'to make a sound intermediate between a clap and a crack' (OED). It is unlikely to be an alteration of *cloaca* 'sewer or drain'; 'in birds, reptiles, most fishes, and the monotreme mammals: the common chamber or cavity into which the digestive, urinary, and reproductive tracts discharge their contents' (OED, from Latin *cloaca* 'underground drain, sewer').

1960 J.E. Macdonnell *Don't Gimme the Ships* p. 135: From beneath them a familiar voice floated up in angelic tones: 'Come on then up there, off your clackers! Keep those hammers moving!'

1967 *Whisper All Aussie Dictionary* in *Kings Cross Whisper* 33 p. 4: *Clacker*, posterior.

1989 *Farmer's Weekly* (Perth) 5 July p. 5: And as far as I'm concerned you can stick your thumb up your clacker.

1999 *Tracks* March p. 30: Surfers paddled their clackers off to get into the good-sized peaks.

2013 T. Winton *Eyrie* p. 99: Talks about you, now. Day and bloody night. Thinks the sun shines out yer clacker.

clean the books up confess to numerous unsolved crimes.

Australian Underworld Slang.

The implication is that you confess to a number of crimes that you probably did not commit as part of a deal to get a lesser penalty for the crime you have been charged with. The police are satisfied because it looks as if they have solved the crimes.

Origin: From the phrase *on the books* referring to a police list of unsolved crimes (see quotes 1924 and 1942 for this formulation). American Underworld Slang has the synonymous phrase *clean up the calendar* (see quote 1950 in square brackets).

1924 *Herald* (Melbourne) 14 April p. 6: There are on the police books many unsolved crimes.

1942 *Morning Bulletin* (Rockhampton) 27 August p. 2: It would be interesting to know how many of these thefts have been reported to the authorities and have remained on the books as unsolved crimes.

[**1950** H.E. Goldin *Dictionary of American Underworld Lingo* p. 45: *Clean up the calendar*, to plead guilty to a number of charges, including those of which one is innocent. This 'solution' of open cases for the police brings from them a promise of leniency in court.]

1961 *Tribune* (Sydney) 23 August p. 7: Snakes had cantered off on his own, muttering to himself incoherently, wondering which charity refuge he might doss in. Originally the slum product of a broken home, he was of very limited intelligence and had never known how to fend for himself. Born gaol-bait as they put it. Snakes was never 'out' more than a fortnight at most and his nervous disposition was deteriorating every year. According to the Crims, the harmless sub-human Snakes is regularly used by the Wallopers to 'clean up the books'. The Crims claim that when this nervous wreck is dragged into a station, he may readily be induced to confess to a number of petty thefts or breakings in an area which would otherwise have to stand listed as unsolved.

2018 *Courier Mail* (Brisbane) 13 December p. 29: Justice may still be served for cold-case murder victims. … 2018 has been the year of the cold case. So much so that the number of cases being reworked could be interpreted as expressing a collective urgency to clean up the books.

cliner dud.

Australian English.

In Australia *cliner* meant 'a girl, a girlfriend' (current from the 1890s to the 1940s), a borrowing from German *kleine* 'little'. The sense 'dud' is otherwise

80 **clock**

unknown, except for the adjectival definition 'dodgy' in the 1983 quote below.

1983 R. Aven-Bray *Ridgey Didge Oz Jack Lang* p. 33: *Kliner*, dodgy.

clock twelve months.

Australian Underworld and Prison Slang.
  The term means 'a prison sentence of twelve months' (AND).
  Origin: From the number of hours on a clock face.

  1941 S.J. Baker *A Popular Dictionary of Australian Slang* p. 18: *Clock*, 12 months' gaol sentence.

  1950 B.K. Doyle *Australian Police Journal* April p. 112: *The Clock*, 12 months' imprisonment.

  1968 J. Alard *He Who Shoots Last* p. 2: If I get picked up I'll at least get the clock.

  1977 J. Ramsay *Cop It Sweet* p. 23: *Clock*, twelve month's jail sentence.

  1988 *Copspeak* (Australian Institute of Criminology) p. 13: *Clock*, a 12 months sentence.

  1990 V. Tupper & R. Wortley *Anthology of Prison Slang in Australia* (National Library of Australia, Pandora Archive): *Clock*, a twelve month sentence.

clout method used by shoplifters: concealing stolen property under topcoat while being worn.

Australian Underworld Slang.
  Origin: The usual sense of *clout* in General Underworld Slang (originally British) is 'to steal'. *Clout* was a word for 'a piece of cloth, handkerchief' (and more generally 'clothing'), and *clouting* was originally the stealing of handkerchiefs, and then used of any kind of theft (see quote 1941 for an Australian usage). The Parramatta Glossary definition, although dealing with theft, is different in emphasis and uses *clout* in the sense 'to hide'. The OED lists *clouted* meaning 'covered with, or wrapped in, a clout or cloth', and this must be the sense, for in the definition the stolen property is concealed by a topcoat. This sense of 'hidden' is given by 'Thirty-five' in the 1955 quote.

  1941 S.J. Baker *A Popular Dictionary of Australian Slang* p. 18: *Clout*, to steal (something).

  1955 'Thirty-five' in G. Simes *Dictionary of Australian Underworld Slang* (1993) p. 47: *Clouted*, hidden.

[**coat** *see* on the coat.]

cockatoo lookout.

Australian English.
  The term means 'a lookout posted by those engaged in an illegal activity (often gambling activities such as the playing of two-up) to give warning of any threat of interruption; any lookout' (AND).
  Origin: From the fact that one or more birds act as lookouts for a flock of

feeding cockatoos. The term first appeared in convict contexts in the early years of the New South Wales colony (see quote 1827).

> **1827** P. Cunningham *Two Years in New South Wales* (rev. ed.) vol. 2 p. 288: It being a common trick to station a sentinel on a commanding eminence to give the alarm, while all the others divert themselves, or go to sleep. Such are known here by the name of 'cockatoo-gangs', from following the example of that wary bird.
>
> **1934** *Bulletin* (Sydney) 1 August p. 36: For years those betting on the outers had to employ one or more 'cockatoos' to give warning when a John Hop was spotted.
>
> **1950** 'Thirty-five' in G. Simes *Dictionary of Australian Underworld Slang* (1993) p. 48: *Cockatoo*, person posted to watch for police or warders while illegal doings are afoot; also person posted by hotel licensee trading after hours, or two-up school operator to watch for police.
>
> **1950** B.K. Doyle *Australian Police Journal* April p. 112: *Cockatoo*, a tout whose duty it is to inform of the approach of the Police.
>
> **1988** *Copspeak* (Australian Institute of Criminology) p. 13: *Cockatoo*, lookout posted to warn principal(s) of approaching police presence.
>
> **1995** N. Ibrahim & M. Quinney *Glossary of Gaol Slang: Pentridge Gaol* (Unpublished Typescript ANDC): *Cockatoo*, some-one on watch for the authorities.
>
> **2013** *Herald Sun* (Melbourne) 5 October p. 98: The trainer and his assistant, their eyes darting about, disappeared into the stable as a 'cockatoo', who was also the truck driver, locked the gate and stood watch.

cold innocent of charge laid against you.

Australian Underworld Slang.

The term means 'not guilty of an offence; innocent'. The Australian phrase *to do it cold* means 'to serve a prison sentence for a crime one did not commit; to be wrongly convicted' (AND).

Origin: This probably derives from *cold* as the opposite of *hot* in a common underworld sense. The term *hot* is used in various senses related to illegality and criminality: 'of stolen property: easily identifiable and so difficult to dispose of; (hence) stolen. Also of a person: wanted by the police' (OED).

> **1929** *Advocate* (Burnie) 8 July p. 2: It had to be explained that 'doing it cold' meant suffering for a crime that one had not committed.
>
> **1944** T. Hartley in G. Simes *Dictionary of Australian Underworld Slang* (1993) p. 66: 'Doing it cold' means that you are serving a sentence for a crime of which you are innocent.
>
> **1950** 'Thirty-five' in G. Simes *Dictionary of Australian Underworld Slang* (1993) p. 49: *Cold*, not guilty of an offence. 'I'm cold', or 'I'm doing it cold'.
>
> **1967** *Whisper All Aussie Dictionary* in *Kings Cross Whisper* 33 p. 4: *Cold as a maggot*, an expression used when describing how innocent one is of police charges.
>
> **1973** *Contact: Parramatta Jail Resurgents Magazine* June n.p.: He reckons he was cold on his blue but he's copped it sweet.
>
> **1989** T. Anderson *Inside Outlaws: A Prison Diary* p. 144: *Cold*, not guilty or innocent of a charge or allegation. A person in jail who's not guilty is said to be 'cold on a blue'.

cold bite ask a stranger for money.

Australian English.

The phrase means 'to beg for money; to ask a stranger for money'. A variant is *cold fang* (see quote 1967). Often as verbal noun *cold-biting*. In the 1950 quote *cold bite* is a noun.

Origin: From the adverbial sense of *cold* 'unprepared, unannounced' (GDS) + *bite* 'to solicit money from' (AND).

> **1941** S.J. BAKER *A Popular Dictionary of Australian Slang* p. 19: *Cold biting*, a straight-out request by a down-and-out for money.
>
> **1950** 'Thirty-five' in G. SIMES *Dictionary of Australian Underworld Slang* (1993) p. 49: *Cold*, without excuse, shameless—'a cold bite', i.e. a shameless piece of begging.
>
> **1967** *Whisper All Aussie Dictionary* in *Kings Cross Whisper* 33 p. 4: *Cold fang*, to ask strangers for money.
>
> **1973** H. HUELIN *Keep Moving* p. 126: I resorted to cold-biting round the wealthier houses. This effort yielded five shillings—enough to buy food and tobacco for several days.
>
> **1979** G. STEWART *The Leveller: The Story of a Violent Australian* p. 126: The 'drunken bums and alkies' were dirty, and had no gear and hung around pubs, 'cold biting' — begging money.
>
> **1997** *Age* (Melbourne) 3 July (Metro Section) p. 1: But welfare agencies and the police are unanimous—do not give money to beggars. Asking passers-by directly for money, 'cold-biting', is unpleasant for everyone involved.

come nothing make no admissions.

This appears to be the opposite of the phrase COME YER GUTS 'confess' (listed below). Not otherwise recorded.

come out of the woodwork appear from nowhere.

General English.

The phrase *to come* (or *crawl*) *out of the woodwork* means 'to come out of hiding; to emerge from obscurity' (OED).

Origin: The 'crawl' variant gives the clue to an original phrase that referred to insects appearing from the woodwork of a building.

> **1966** *Tribune* (Sydney) 4 May p. 2: Out of the woodwork. The sudden recent appearance of a gaggle of 'ultra Right' shout-and-bash groups is no accident. Such groups thrive in the atmosphere of war jingoism being deliberately cultivated by the Holt regime and its press supporters.
>
> **1973** *Current Affairs Bulletin* (Sydney) August p. 31: They are the new Australian playwrights and they are coming out of the woodwork everywhere.
>
> **1992** M.B. READ *Chopper 2: Hits and Memories* p. 75: Receiving mail in prison can be one of the great delights. It really helps break the loneliness. ... When I say the book brought some whackos out of the woodwork, I must admit that not all the letters come from mental patients.

2005 J. Pring *Abo: A Treacherous Life: the Graham Henry Story* p. 277: During Ned's murder trial it was amazing to see all the sly crooks and all the cops come out of the woodwork to put the boot in.

2018 G. Plunkett *The Whiskey Au Go Go Massacre* p. 238: Finch left Australia on the day of his release, with the newspaper headline greeting him at his destination reading 'Welcome Back Killer'. With Finch gone, a number of informants came out of the woodwork.

come undone be found out.

General English.

This phrase means 'being caught in the committing of a crime', and is a specific use of General English *undone* 'brought to decay or ruin; ruined, destroyed' (OED) and *to come undone* 'to come to grief' (OED), 'to fail, to come to disaster'. See also BRING UNDONE.

1984 B. Ellem *Doing Time: The Prison Experience* p. 199: *Undone*, to get found out, to get caught; for example, he came undone.

1981 *Telegraph* (Brisbane) 7 April p. 8: I got two years there, for breaking and entering. I did it to help a relative. He told me where the money was in a house. I copped the blue when we came undone. He shared the money, but not the jail. I served it at Long Bay.

2005 J. Pring *Abo: A Treacherous Life: the Graham Henry Story* p. 290: Now the police don't need informers as much as they used to. The phones crooks carry around with them do all the hard work for the cops. They can locate you within ten metres of where you are while you're carrying one. The number of crooks who have come undone through talking on a mobile phone, or openly in a coffee shop, is just unbelievable.

come yer guts confess.

General English.

This phrase was originally British, and in the form *come one's guts* 'to give information' (GDS) it is recorded from the 1930s, and is loosely synonymous with the originally American *spill one's guts*. Australia had an earlier similar phrase *give one's guts* (see quote 1914).

1914 *Truth* (Melbourne) 24 January p. 11: I told this fool to hold his tongue, but he gave the police his guts, and blew the gaff.

1944 T. Hartley in G. Simes *Dictionary of Australian Underworld Slang* (1993) p. 51: *Come* (*his, your etc*) *gutz*, to confess.

1953 K. Tennant *The Joyful Condemned* p. 49: 'You needn't say anything', Sergeant Bluall told Jake . . . 'We've got it on you. Your cobber's come his guts'.

1953 K. Tennant *The Joyful Condemned* p. 295: The sullen, big oaf, baited and jeered at by everyone, a man who had 'come his guts to the coppers', was almost driven desperate.

1966 E.J. Wallace *Sydney and the Bush* p. 141: 'The police are outside'. Bill thought: 'A pinch? Me? Come me guts? A top-off? Strike! I'll tell 'em it was a stranger, like'.

cop it sweet don't retaliate.

Australian English.

The phrase means 'to accept something unpleasant without complaint; to accept a set-back with equanimity' (AND). In early underworld use, the phrase is a way of stressing that incriminating evidence about someone else would not be passed on to the police.

> **1951** *Argus* (Melbourne) 10 October p. 5: 'After I identified the two men in the line-up I went back to St. Kilda. I had people come to me and say, "You had better do the right thing. Cop it sweet"'. Mr Burke: 'What does that mean?' 'Don't squeal. They said: "Cop it sweet. The same thing might happen to you"'.
>
> **1953** *Advertiser* (Adelaide) 12 June p. 1: A gunman fired six shots at him as he answered the door of his father's home in Frederick street, Windsor, at 1.10 a.m. When police interviewed him on that occasion he refused to talk and said, 'I will cop it sweet' (Underworld jargon for 'I won't talk').
>
> **1967** *Whisper All Aussie Dictionary* in *Kings Cross Whisper* 33 p. 4: *Cop it sweet*, never divulging information to the police. Take the blame rightly or wrongly.
>
> **1974** J. McNeil *How Does Your Garden Grow* p. 39: And don't worry about the way yer knocked me about before, I'll cop it sweet, no chance of me saying anything or making any complaints.
>
> **1984** B. Ellem *Doing Time: The Prison Experience* p. 188: *Cop it sweet*, accept what comes.
>
> **1988** *Copspeak* (Australian Institute of Criminology) p. 15: *Cop it sweet*, accept adverse circumstances without complaint.
>
> **1992** R. Hay *Catch Me if You Can: The Life and Times of Darcy Dugan* p. 378: There was also a new culture and pecking order in the gaols. It had been developing through the seventies and had now arrived with a vengeance. The old school of prisoners convicted of standard offences like armed robbery, violence and petty crime had been replaced by the drug culture syndrome. Addicts and pushers were dictating events. Solidarity amongst prisoners was traded for a needle. Individuals would sell their mother for a fix. Nobody trusted anybody, as informants were everywhere. Solitary was no longer a punishment determined by the administration, but a protection demanded by the prisoners. Characters like Darcy, who hated drugs and all those associated with the trade, were relics of the past. Their values, discarded like a used syringe. The idea of 'copping it sweet', a forgotten principle.
>
> **2006** B. Matthews *Intractable ... Life inside Australia's First Super-max Prison* p. 119: As more and more conscientious objectors and Vietnam War protesters became imprisoned, they introduced a new mentality of 'stand up and be counted' that ran contrary to the old crims' philosophy of copping it sweet and doing their time as easily and quietly as possible.

cop the blue take the blame.

Australian English. Chiefly as *Underworld Slang.*

Origin: Perhaps from *blue* in the Australian sense 'a summons' (the legal documents were originally printed on blue paper). Probably influenced by *blue* in the sense 'disturbance, trouble', thus 'accept the blame and the consequent punishment'.

1932 *Telegraph* (Brisbane) 27 September p. 1: 'I can tell you an easy way to get a car—money from home—all you got to do is to hire a car', suggested the defendant. 'They deliver it to you in the street ... send it to Sydney and sell it ... I'll "cop the blue", and there'll be no risk'.

1940 *Truth* (Brisbane) 17 November p. 2: One of the worst knock-'em-down-and-drag-'em-out affairs ever seen on a Brisbane racecourse was the Third Division at Albion Park yesterday. It ended in a protest, and disqualification for two jockeys, who, however, couldn't be blamed for all that 'Truth' saw. The riders who 'copped the blue' were the two Dwyers, Ron and Tommy.

1945 *Guinea Gold* (Papua New Guinea: Australian Edition) 8 February p. 2: 'I got it nowhere. It's just my bad luck, but I'll cop the blue', said Cecil Horan Brady, 42, builders' labourer, to Detective-Sergeant Cronau when he was found in possession of 12 bottles of wine.

1953 *Newcastle Sun* 6 October p. 1: Addressing him, Judge Amsberg said: 'You say in your statement to the police that one of three men rang up the shopkeeper and claimed you had some cigarettes for sale. You then say, "I fronted. I've been tipped off and copped the blue", which, in underworld jargon, means that someone informed on you and you would have to take the consequences'.

1966 *Hansard House of Representatives* 29 September p. 1510: He is letting them cop the blue, as is commonly said in criminal circles. If he is so low that he is prepared to allow others to take the consequences of his actions, he is unworthy to be called an Australian and a member of this Parliament.

1981 *Telegraph* (Brisbane) 7 April p. 8: I got two years there, for breaking and entering. I did it to help a relative. He told me where the money was in a house. I copped the blue when we came undone. He shared the money, but not the jail. I served it at Long Bay.

crab impede progress.
General English.

Origin: Probably a form of British *crab* meaning 'to spoil, to upset, to ruin' (GDS). This sense is first recorded in Britain in 1829. It appears slightly earlier in the dictionary of the Australian convict Vaux (see quote 1812), but of course Vaux gathered much of his material from the British underworld. Cf. American *crab someone's act* 'to spoil someone's plans, to interfere' (GDS). All senses derive in some way from perceptions about the crustacean, but it is possible that direct influence is from 'catching a crab' in rowing ('to make a faulty stroke ... whereby the oar becomes jammed under water'), which in turn probably derives from the humorous notion that an oar has been caught by a crab.

1812 J.H. VAUX *New Vocabulary of the Flash Language* in *Memoirs* (1819) II p. 164: *Crab*, to prevent the perfection or execution of any intended matter or business.

1944 T. Hartley in G. SIMES *Dictionary of Australian Underworld Slang* (1993) p. 56: *Crab*, to impede, spoil, prevent, hinder. Derived from 'to catch a crab' in rowing a boat.

86   **crack it**

> **1950** 'Thirty-five' in G. SIMES *Dictionary of Australian Underworld Slang* (1993) p. 56: *Crab*, to bring an enterprise to failure, as inept accomplice or informer.
>
> **1989** T. ANDERSON *Inside Outlaws: A Prison Diary* p. 145: *Crab*, one who wrecks things for everyone. 'Crabbing it' means stuffing-up things for others. This is actually the result of a rather successful scheme by boys' homes administrators, where there is collective punishment for the petty offence of one person. The person is then put 'on the crab' and may be bashed; the result of a 'divide and rule' tactic.

crack it have an earn.
Australian Underworld Slang.

The phrase means 'carry out a successful and profitable robbery'. An EARN is 'the proceeds of a robbery', so the Parramatta Glossary's sense of *crack it* is 'to make money from a successful robbery', although even in underworld contexts the sense is sometimes the more general 'have a good win'.

Origin: Specific use of Australian English *crack it* 'to succeed in an enterprise' (AND). A related Australian sense of the phrase is 'to succeed in finding a sexual partner'.

The 1936 quote is an example of *crack it* meaning 'to make money from an enterprise', in this case from goldmining. Other uses of the phrase occur more typically in the phrase *crack it for (something)*, as in the 1981 quote, and this formulation also occurs in later British use. In the 1974 quote from Jim McNeil's prison play Sam asks 'Brenda' how he managed to get hold of some good 'outside' tea rather than the usual prison tea. The request in the 1968 quote is addressed to the prison doctor by a prisoner.

> **1936** W. HATFIELD *Australia through the Windscreen* p. 199: They had worked alongside men who had 'cracked it' on this field in the early days and kept finds to themselves.
>
> **1968** J. ALARD *He Who Shoots Last* p. 131: Lend us five until I crack it (*footnote*: have a win at gambling).
>
> **1974** J. MCNEIL *How Does Your Garden Grow* p. 127: How'd yer crack it for this?
>
> **1981** A. WILKINSON *Up Country* p. 105: Everyone agrees it is splendid to see the 'cocky' (farmer) crack it for a quid for once.

crim professional thief. This term only applies to those who uphold criminal code. It is a mistake to think that anyone in gaol automatically qualifies.

Australian Underworld and Prison Slang.

In general Australian use *crim* means 'a criminal', but in Australian Underworld and Prison use it has the narrower and more specific sense of 'a person who has a significant criminal record and who is loyal to the criminal code'.

The abbreviation of *criminal* to *crim* appears earliest in Australia, and while occasionally found in Britain and the US, it is chiefly used in Australia and New Zealand. The quotes below include the general 'criminal sense' as well as the narrower 'underworld/prison sense'.

1903 *Examiner* (Launceston) 5 September p. 5: His head was split open with an axe. Robbery is supposed to be the motive of the crims.

1953 K. Tennant *The Joyful Condemned* p. 293: David's bewilderment increased when the redoubtable Chigger Harris, the king of the jail, made conversation with him and addressed him as 'mate'. When Chigger honoured any crim in the gaol, that was the accolade.

1971 J. McNeil *The Chocolate Frog* in *The Chocolate Frog, The Old Familiar Juice: Two Plays* (1973) p. 30: See, in the old days, the crims never had nothin' ter read: no magazines, no papers, or nothin'. The Bible was the only thing in yer cell, see? Yer had to use it fer cigarette papers and keep a few chapters fer readin' now and again.

1973 J. McNeil *The Chocolate Frog, The Old Familiar Juice: Two Plays* p. 115 (Glossary): *Crim*, (colloquial), criminal, a person with a substantial criminal record.

1984 B. Ellem *Doing Time: The Prison Experience* p. 188: *Crim*, a prisoner, especially one with several convictions.

1995 N. Ibrahim & M. Quinney *Glossary of Gaol Slang: Pentridge Gaol* (Unpublished Typescript ANDC): *Crims*, inmates.

2021 *Daily Telegraph* (Sydney) 11 November p. 52: Cops are spitting chips. They spend months gathering evidence and then see these crims waltz straight back on to the streets.

cruel ruin chances.

Australian English.

The term means 'to spoil (an opportunity etc.); to ruin (the chances of a person or enterprise succeeding)' (AND).

Origin: From the adjective *cruel* 'causing or characterised by great suffering; extremely painful or distressing'. The Australian sense of the verb sometimes appears as the phrase *to cruel the* (or *someone's*) *pitch* (see 1920 quote), suggesting some influence from the phrase *to queer the pitch* 'to interfere with or spoil the business in hand' (OED).

1879 *Melbourne Punch* 4 December p. 222: The poet's wife waits for his coming in vain, / Bewailing the fate that has 'cruelled' him.

1920 *Cootamundra Herald* 11 June p. 8: Great disappointment for Wallendbeen and the district! The Prince's visit had to be cut out. Melbourne overdid the business, and 'crooled the pitch' for many other places which wanted to honour the royal visitor.

1950 'Thirty-five' in G. Simes *Dictionary of Australian Underworld Slang* (1993) p. 60: *Cruel*, to spoil a scheme, to bring it to nought. 'Trust Bill to cruel it'.

1967 *Whisper All Aussie Dictionary* in *Kings Cross Whisper* 33 p. 4: *Cruel*, to make a mess of something as in 'I've cruelled myself with the bookie'.

1972 J. McNeil *The Old Familiar Juice* in *The Chocolate Frog, The Old Familiar Juice: Two Plays* (1973) p. 89: Ahhh! Will you shut yer gob? Wodder you have to *cruel* a man for?

1973 J. McNeil *The Chocolate Frog, The Old Familiar Juice: Two Plays* p. 115

(Glossary): *Cruel*, to spoil; *to cruel someone*, to spoil or frustrate his scheme or plan.

1990 V. Tupper & R. Wortley *Anthology of Prison Slang in Australia* (National Library of Australia, Pandora Archive): *Cruel*, as in 'to cruel someone's chance', thus to spoil or frustrate their plans.

2003 *Australian* (Sydney) 28 June p. 3: Strong real estate activity, which has seen a rebound in prices for units, could cruel chances of an interest rate cut when the Reserve Bank meets on Tuesday.

[**crust** see DOING THE CRUST.]

crusted charged with vagrancy.

Australian English.

This is the past participle of the Australian verb *crust* meaning 'to charge a person with vagrancy' (AND). The verb appears in the early twentieth century (see quote 1910). See also VAG.

Origin: From *crust* 'a vagrancy charge; a vagrant' (AND), from the fact that such a person has little or no money or means of subsistence, and therefore 'lives on a crust'. See DOING THE CRUST.

1910 *Advertiser* (Adelaide) 4 May p. 13: He told him to get work and warned him that if he was in the city without work by Monday he would arrest him. Bromley replied, 'I don't work. I don't intend to work and all the police in Adelaide won't make me work. I am here to thieve, and you know I am. Catch me square dinkum and I will plead guilty. You don't want to crust me. Crusting is no good to you'. ... It was afterwards found that ... in the slang dictionary ... 'crusting' meant charging a man with vagrancy.

1967 *Whisper All Aussie Dictionary* in *Kings Cross Whisper* 33 p. 4: *Crust*, a vagrant. To be crusted is to be vagged. From the proposal that a person has not enough money to purchase a crust of bread.

1968 J. Alard *He Who Shoots Last* p. 214: Ya should be crusted fer talkin' rot at a time like dis.

1983 R. Aven-Bray *Ridgey Didge Oz Jack Lang* p. 22: *Crusted*, arrested for vagrancy.

cunning kick undeclared money.

Australian English.

The term literally means 'a secret pocket' and thence 'hidden money'.

Origin: *Cunning* here means 'guileful, sly, secret' and *kick* means 'pocket'. See KICK.

1952 *Truth* (Brisbane) p. 22: For the benefit of women readers we just have to betray the secret of the Cunning Kick. 'Kick', ladies, is slang for pocket. And the 'Cunning Kick' is a secret back pocket that married tailors put into every pair of pants they build for married customers. It defies any woman's search. And into the Cunning Kick go all the extras *he* gets for overtime, or basic-wage increase, or bonus, and so on, that you don't know anything about.

1972 K. Clift *The Saga of a Sig: The Wartime Memories of Six Years Service in the*

Second A.I.F. p. 99: Ned was an original, full of Irish wit, generous as he would never hesitate to lend us a quid if needed and he always seemed to have a cunning 'kick'.

2019 *Sydney Morning Herald* 31 July p. 21: A mate had some cash hidden in the garage. He called it his 'cunning kick'.

cunt starver in gaol for maintenance. (not supporting wife)

Australian English.

The term means 'a husband who defaults on the payment of maintenance to a wife or ex-wife' (AND). This term also appears in the milder form *wife starver* in the 1930s (see quote 1933).

1933 *Australian Women's Weekly* (Sydney) 28 October p. 2: One of the most astonishing bodies in Australia has come into existence as a result of the marriage and maintenance laws of the various States. Vulgarly dubbed 'The Wife Starvers' Association', the official title of the organisation is the Maintenance and Alimony Reform Association.

1950 'Thirty-five' in G. SIMES *Dictionary of Australian Underworld Slang* (1993) p. 60: *C-nt starver*, person imprisoned as in previous entry. [*Ed.* The previous entry in Simes from 'Thirty-five' is for *the C-nt Act*, the Deserted Wives and Children Act, 1901-6.]

1974 R. ADAMSON & B. HANFORD *Zimmer's Essay* p. 30: Maintenance prisoners, by the way, get good jobs—on the farm just outside the prison—and real crims, who are never allowed outside the brick walls, despise them, and call them 'cunt-starvers'.

1988 *Copspeak* (Australian Institute of Criminology) p. 17: *Cunt starver*, male who refuses to pay maintenance to separated or former spouse. [archaic]

1990 V. TUPPER & R. WORTLEY *Anthology of Prison Slang in Australia* (National Library of Australia, Pandora Archive): *Cunt starver*, the sentence served by a male maintenance defaulter.

cut it out do gaol rather than pay fine.

Australian English. Chiefly as *Underworld and Prison Slang.*

The verb *cut out* means 'to erase (a fine) by serving a term in prison' (AND). In the Parramatta Glossary formulation the 'it' refers to the fine.

1931 *Mirror* (Perth) 8 August p. 6: 'Well, at present I'm cutting out a fine for stealing', the witness retorted.

1939 K. TENNANT *Foveaux* p. 350: 'Only a week! I thought it would have taken a couple of years to work out the summonses'. 'They're concurrent', Herb said simply. 'That's the idea of getting as many as you can before you go in. I've known fellers cut out thirty in one week'.

1950 'Thirty-five' in G. SIMES *Dictionary of Australian Underworld Slang* (1993) p. 61: *Cut out*, to serve a term of imprisonment instead of paying a fine.

1987 R.G. BARRETT *The Boys from Binjiwunyawunya* p. 164: You reckon I wouldn't be game to cut out that fine in Long Bay do you?

1989 T. Anderson *Inside Outlaws: A Prison Diary* p. 145: *Cutting it out*, doing time in jail to 'cut out' fines. Many truck drivers, for instance, accumulate road fines and then cut them out by going to jail for the period of the largest fine (where $50 = 1 day), as all the smaller fines are cut out concurrently.

1990 V. Tupper & R. Wortley *Anthology of Prison Slang in Australia* (National Library of Australia, Pandora Archive): *Cut-out*, to discharge fines while in prison. A day in prison is equivalent to a certain amount. Many prisoners choose this option.

1991 J. Wright *The Angel of Death* p. 14: She was a 'cracker'—a King's Cross prostitute who was cutting out her latest fine in gaol.

darbies handcuffs.

General English.

The term means 'handcuffs, fetters' (OED), and is first recorded in Britain in the seventeenth century.

Origin: Probably from an earlier phrase *Darby's bands* (or *Father Darby's bands*) 'some rigid form of bond by which a debtor was bound and put within the power of a moneylender' (OED). The OED adds: 'It has been suggested that the term was derived from the name of some noted usurer of the 16th cent.'

1849 *Melbourne Daily News* 20 August p. 2: Upon examining the handcuffs it was perfectly clear that another blow would have severed 'the darbies', the blows which had been levelled at them having cracked them in several places.

1899 *Clarence and Richmond Examiner* (Grafton) 24 January p. 6: He opened his eyes and said dosily, 'I'm done; you can put the darbies on me'. Then he rose to his feet and extended his wrists as if to receive the handcuffs.

1950 B.K. Doyle *Australian Police Journal* April p. 112: *Darbies*, handcuffs.

1988 *Copspeak* (Australian Institute of Criminology) p. 19: *Darbies*, handcuffs, manacles. [archaic]

deadset no doubt.

Australian English.

As an adjective the term means 'genuine, absolute' and as an adverb it means 'truly; really; absolutely' (AND). It can be written as one word (*deadset*) or as two (*dead set*).

Origin: From *dead set* 'an absolute stop' (OED), in the sense of being completely brought to a stop, and hence expressing certainty (originally, in proceeding no further).

1953 *Argus* (Melbourne) 11 September p. 14: I think Advocate is a 'dead set' Cup horse, and a hard race now could flatten him.

1977 J. Ramsay *Cop It Sweet* p. 28: *Dead set*, absolutely sure; indisputable.

1979 G. Carey & K. Lette *Puberty Blues* p. 9: Deadset, I'm not hungry, I just had a curried chop in Home Science.

1984 B. Ellem *Doing Time: The Prison Experience* p. 188: *Dead set*, true, I mean it.

2006 *Newcastle Herald* 25 January p. 43: With Australia Day tomorrow, *Good*

Taste did some digging for a day's diet chock-a-block full of tucker you can dead-set bog into.

dead to rights caught red handed.

General English.

The phrase means 'completely, certainly'; 'red-handed, in the act' (OED). It was originally American English where it is recorded from the 1850s.

Origin: *Dead* has the sense 'unequivocally, utterly' as in phrases such as *dead certain*, *dead drunk*. *To rights* means 'properly'. The 'caught redhanded' sense derives from the notion that if someone is caught in the act of committing a crime the evidence is certain and unequivocal.

> **1890** *Horsham Times* 28 November p. 2: Why, there was our old sergeant, he railroaded Bob, got him dead to rights, give him the collar, and up he went. What was the consequence? Bob got two years. Two years and one day from that day the sergeant was killed, struck from behind at night with a sand club. We arrested, but he had covered his tracks well, and as we could prove nothing against him he was discharged.

> **2016** *Courier Mail* (Brisbane) 23 May p. 22: Let me see if I've got this right. Labor, having been caught dead to rights with their grubby political hands in the NBN commercial-in-confidence documents cookie jar, have launched a foaming-mouthed attack on 'the integrity' of the AFP, who were simply doing their job.

[deal see DO A DEAL.]

Dear John goodbye letter from lover.

General English.

The term means 'a letter, usually from a woman to a man, ending a romantic or sexual relationship' (OED). Primarily used in the context of the armed services and prisons, where situational separation can put strains on relationships. It appeared originally in American English during the Second World War. The 1945 quote, in square brackets, is an early American example.

> [**1945** *Democrat & Chronicle* (Rochester, New York State) 17 August p. 17: 'Dear John', the letter began. 'I have found someone else whom I think the world of. I think the only way out is for us to get a divorce', it said. They usually began like that, those letters that told of infidelity on the part of the wives of servicemen. ... The men called them 'Dear Johns'.]

> **1972** *Contact: Parramatta Jail Resurgents Magazine* December n.p.: Men in prison look forward to letters. When they get them, most look at the first page to see if it starts out, 'Dear John ...'

> **1983** E. WITHNELL *Australian Journal of Cultural Studies* 1 (May) p. 84: Then, finally, the dislocation completes itself with a 'dear john'—a letter at mail call, from his wife or lover, telling him that their relationship is over.

> **1995** N. IBRAHIM & M. QUINNEY *Glossary of Gaol Slang: Pentridge Gaol* (Unpublished Typescript ANDC): *Dear John letter*, when your wife writes to tell you she's leaving you.

2006 B. Matthews *Intractable ... Life inside Australia's First Super-max Prison* p. 104: It was 'Marmite' over in 4 Wing who opened the door to another escape plot when he got a Dear John letter.

dip   pickpocket.

General Underworld Slang.

The term first appeared in the US in the mid nineteenth century.

Origin: From the earlier verb *dip* 'to pick pockets', from the notion of the thief 'dipping' into the victim's pocket.

1924 *Macleay Argus* (Kempsey) 11 April p. 4: May Walsh, the cleverest pickpocket in Australia, who received 18 months the other day at Darlinghurst Sessions, is one of the few outstanding figures of Sydney's underworld. ... Unlike most other 'dips' she believed in exchange. In the place of filched notes, she would leave a roll of brown notes similar in shape and size of the genuine articles.

1941 K. Tennant *Battlers* p. 264: 'So you're a dip'. He ruefully placed his possessions in his pocket. ... It was humiliating to have his pocket picked.

1944 T. Hartley in G. Simes *Dictionary of Australian Underworld Slang* (1993) p. 64: *Dip*, a pickpocket.

1977 J. Ramsay *Cop It Sweet* p. 29: *Dip*, orig. Eng. Pickpocket

1989 T. Anderson *Inside Outlaws: A Prison Diary* p. 145: *Dip*, pickpocket. A dying profession.

1996 J. Byrell *Lairs, Urgers and Coat-Tuggers* p. 51: There was ... a slick local dip and coat-tugger named George 'Georgie Boy' Griffin.

2010 A. Shand *King of Thieves* p. 4: Like most criminal activities, thieving is a vocation, a specialised trade even. A tank man cannot be a hoister, no more than a dip (pickpocket) can be a gunnie or a bust man (burglar).

do a deal   plead guilty for pre-arranged sentence.

General English.

This is a specific use of the standard phrase *do a deal* '(of two or more parties) to enter into an agreement for their mutual benefit'.

1991 M.B. Read *Chopper 1: From the Inside* p. 94: The game of let's make a deal is played in every court house in Australia, always has been and always will be. Maybe a little cash is handed to the lawyer to encourage him to get in there and see what he can do but the system is based on 'Can we do a deal, can we make this go away?'

2015 *Herald Sun* (Melbourne) 29 June p. 24: Granata was originally charged with 62 counts of rape, 94 counts of assault and 10 counts of threatening to kill but did a deal with prosecutors pleading guilty to 16 charges including nine counts of rape, one count of intentionally causing serious injury and two counts of making threats to kill.

dodger   bread.

Australian English.

Origin: Transferred use of American *dodger* 'a small cake, usually hard baked, of corn meal', perhaps ultimately from British dialect *dodge* 'a large cut or slice of food'.

> **1897** *Bulletin* (Sydney) 7 August (Red Page): Loaf of bread—'Dodger'.
>
> **1919** W.H. Downing *Digger Dialects* p. 19: *Dodger*, bread.
>
> **1944** T. Hartley in G. Simes *Dictionary of Australian Underworld Slang* (1993) p. 67: *Dodger*, a very thick slice of bread. Hence 'bread'.
>
> **1950** B.K. Doyle *Australian Police Journal* April p. 112: *Dodger*, gaol bread.
>
> **1968** S. Gore *Holy Smoke* p. 9: Take the troops a few loaves of home-baked dodger.
>
> **1980** J. Hepworth & J. Hindle *Boozing Out in Melbourne Pubs* p. 141: None of your sliced bread here, but proper hunks of dodger.
>
> **1990** V. Tupper & R. Wortley *Anthology of Prison Slang in Australia* (National Library of Australia, Pandora Archive): *Dodger*, baked bread.

dog informer.

Australian English. Especially as Underworld and Prison Slang.

The term means 'an informer; a person who betrays colleagues or changes allegiance. Chiefly in the phrase *to turn dog (on)*' (AND). While it is often used in prison and underworld contexts, the term is sometimes used more widely in Australian English. There is some occasional use of the term in the US.

Origin: Specific use of *dog* 'a worthless or contemptible person' (OED).

Jim McNeil uses the rhyming slang synonym *chocolate frog* in his plays (see quote 1971) that were written in Parramatta Jail at about the time the Glossary was produced, but it does not appear in the Parramatta Glossary.

> **1848** J. Syme *Nine Years in Van Diemen's Land* p. 273: A man known to give officers information is designated by the epithet 'Dog'.
>
> **1877** *Vagabond Annual* p. 138: 'A dog' is the name given to a prisoner who spies on his comrades, or to a warder who is obnoxiously active in searching and reporting every petty case.
>
> **1922** *Telegraph* (Brisbane) 9 November p. 12: Did you hear what Cooky said. He practically accused me of hitting Billy. He is going to turn dog on me after all that I have done for him.
>
> **1967** *Whisper All Aussie Dictionary* in *Kings Cross Whisper* 34 p. 4: *Dog*, a prison informer.
>
> **1971** J. McNeil *The Chocolate Frog* in *The Chocolate Frog, The Old Familiar Juice: Two Plays* (1973) p. 45: I believe you about the boys' homes, about gaols, about cats and dogs and chocolate frogs!
>
> **1973** J. McNeil *The Chocolate Frog, The Old Familiar Juice: Two Plays* p. 10: A dog is one whose conduct violates, or has violated in times past the informal 'laws' of prison society. A dog in prison is a criminal in the sight of those termed criminal themselves by ordinary society. And a dog should be judged, has to be punished, deserves to be ostracised and deprived—as criminals are.
>
> **1984** B. Ellem *Doing Time: The Prison Experience* p. 104: If someone is found to be an informer among the prisoners he is branded as a 'dog'. This is the worst thing a prisoner can be called. ... The threat of this label is a powerful form of control within the prison environment.

1989 T. Anderson *Inside Outlaws: A Prison Diary* p. 146: *Dog*, informer, traitor, general enemy. ... The specific meaning of this is (usually) a police informer or former accomplice who gives (fabricated or true) evidence against you in a criminal case. ... It may also refer to a person who provides incriminating 'information' but does not actually give evidence. A dog is liable to any sort of extreme sanction from any prisoner. To be declared a dog in jail means that the person's life is at risk; therefore, informers in jail usually arrange for themselves to be in solitary confinement 'on protection'.

1993 D. Brown 'Notes on the Culture of Prison Informing' *Current Issues in Criminal Justice* 5 p. 56: Most of the US literature on prison informing seems to use the term 'rat' or 'snitch'. 'Dog' is the well established Australian term, directly or through rhyming slang derivatives such as 'chocolate frog'. ... The persistence of the notion can be seen in the incident during the Tim Anderson committal in Sydney in 1989 when former prison folk hero Ray Denning was giving evidence. A large bone was placed on a railing in the courtroom by an ex-prisoner who then shouted out 'you forgot your lunch, Denning'.

1995 N. Ibrahim & M. Quinney *Glossary of Gaol Slang: Pentridge Gaol* (Unpublished Typescript ANDC): *Dog*, informer; child molester.

2006 B. Matthews *Intractable ... Life inside Australia's First Super-max Prison* p. 19: The term originated from an incident in Charles Dickens' *Oliver Twist*. Sykes, the villain in the book, was being chased through London streets but eluded the pursuing Bobbies by hiding in a chimney. Sykes had a faithful mongrel dog. The police let the dog run free and it led them to its master hiding in the chimney. From that literary beginning Australian crims have always used the word 'dog' to describe an informer or somebody who gives people up.

dog it squib it.

General English.

The phrase means 'to act lazily or half-heartedly; to slack, idle; (also) to hold back through fear or unwillingness to take a risk' (OED). It was originally an American term and appeared in the early twentieth century.

Origin: It is not clear how these particular negative meanings came to be attached to the behaviour of dogs.

1938 *Daily News* (Perth) 19 February p. 10: Old English ... Equal favorite. Had every chance and looked winner on turn, but he 'dogged' it again.

1993 *Canberra Times* 13 February p. 6: The Opposition's spokesman on industrial relations, John Howard, was accused yesterday of 'dogging it' after he failed to show up to a planned protest by building workers.

dog squad undercover police.

Australian Underworld Slang.

In later use (see quote 1996) the term refers to a police squad that uses dogs in their work.

Origin: From *dog* in the Australian sense 'a prison warder; a police officer, detective, undercover police officer, etc.' (AND).

1967 *Whisper All Aussie Dictionary* in *Kings Cross Whisper* 34 p. 4: *Dog squad*, under cover wallopers. They live as criminals with criminals and molls. They never appear in court. They rely entirely on the stupidity and trust of the crims to gather information.

1983 R. AVEN-BRAY *Ridgey Didge Oz Jack Lang* p. 25: *Dog squad*, undercover police squad.

1988 *Copspeak* (Australian Institute of Criminology) p. 22: *Dog Squad*, undercover police officer grouping. [archaic]

1996 *Daily Telegraph* (Sydney) 24 October p. 13: Welcoming yet another officer into the witness box, Justice Wood offered to suppress his name upon learning he was from the 'dog squad'. Dog squad is slang for the undercover Physical Surveillance Branch, whose members' identities are kept secret. Justice Wood then was informed that this officer was from the real Dog Squad—a dog handler.

doing the crust serving a sentence for vagrancy.

Australian Underworld Slang.

Origin: From Australian *crust* 'a vagrancy charge; a vagrant', which derives from the fact a person so charged has little or no money or means of subsistence, and therefore 'lives on a crust'. See CRUSTED. See also VAG.

The 1910 and 1922 quotes have slightly different formulations, but are synonymous with the headword *doing the crust*.

1910 L. ESSON *Three Short Plays* (1911) p. 14: *Constable*: You're qualifying for a stiff for the crust. ... You're likely to bring a Sixer, I'm warning you. [*Ed.* A *stiff* is 'a summons', and a *sixer* is 'a sentence of six months'.]

1922 *Goulburn Evening Penny Post* 18 April p. 2: In the vernacular of the police courts to be locked up on a vagrancy charge is to be 'put in under the crust'.

1950 'Thirty-five' in G. SIMES *Dictionary of Australian Underworld Slang* (1993) p. 60: *Doing the crust*, of prisoners convicted under the Vagrancy Act.

do it hard let sentence get you down.

General Prison Slang.

This use of the verb *do* was originally British, meaning 'to serve out (a term of punishment)' (OED). The verb can be followed by various adverbs and phrases that designate how the prisoner is serving his term. Partridge in *Dictionary of the Underworld* lists *do it tough* and *do it easy* as general prison slang. Of course, one can 'do it hard' in various aspects of life, but the phrase has its specific prison sense.

The Glossary bunches together a number of similar idioms (beginning with 'do') that indicate how a prisoner is dealing with a sentence: DO IT ON YER HEAD, DO IT ON THE SHIT TUB, DO IT TOUGH, DO IT HARD.

1944 T. Hartley in G. SIMES *Dictionary of Australian Underworld Slang* (1993) p. 65: *Do it, Doing it*, a prisoner does not serve but *does* a sentence. The accepted courtesy greeting in jail is 'How are you doing it?' The usual replies are 'Doing it easy' or 'Doing it tough'. The latter expression has a wide application. Anyone who paces his cell is agitated (*sic*), depressed etc. is said to be 'doing it tough' or else 'doing it hard' (less common).

1950 B.K. Doyle *Australian Police Journal* April p. 114: *Do it hard*, usually refers to an unhappy gaol prisoner who has difficulty in serving his sentence; one whose morale is broken by his incarceration.

1953 K. Tennant *The Joyful Condemned* p. 294: Mort Clipman was the one who was 'doing it hard'.

1974 J. McNeil *How Does Your Garden Grow* p. 126: Sam: Doing it hard, mate? Mick: (*tersely*) I reckon I am.

1984 B. Ellem *Doing Time: The Prison Experience* p. 189: *Doing it hard*, someone who can't settle into or accept his sentence; for example, he's 'doing it hard'.

1989 T. Anderson *Inside Outlaws: A Prison Diary* p. 146: *Doing it*, doing your sentence in jail. That is, you might be doing it hard, or doing it 'on your head' (easily); depending on the length of your sentence, the conditions of the jail, and your state of mind.

1990 V. Tupper & R. Wortley *Anthology of Prison Slang in Australia* (National Library of Australia, Pandora Archive): *Doing it easy/hard*, descriptive of the pains of imprisonment. Thus, 'doing it hard' means a prisoner can not settle into or accept his sentence.

1995 N. Ibrahim & M. Quinney *Glossary of Gaol Slang: Pentridge Gaol* (Unpublished Typescript ANDC): *Doing it hard*, having difficulty adjusting to prison.

2001 *Prison & Drug Slang: NSW Corrective Services*: *Doing it hard*, an inmate who is depressed is said to be doing it hard.

do it on the shit tub serve sentence as easy as possible.
Australian Prison Slang.

Origin: For the origin of formulations of this kind after the verb *do* see DO IT HARD. The *shit tub* is the sanitary bucket used in a cell (see quotes 1974 and 2010). Even as late as 1972, not all cells at Parramatta Jail were sewered.

This phrase is synonymous with DO IT ON YER HEAD. Quote 1967 has the milder *seated on the can*. Quote 2010 describes the standard Parramatta Jail *shit tub*.

1944 T. Hartley in G. Simes *Dictionary of Australian Underworld Slang* (1993) p. 65: *Do it, Doing it*, a prisoner does not serve but *does* a sentence. The accepted courtesy greeting in jail is 'How are you doing it?' The usual replies are 'Doing it easy' or 'Doing it tough'. ... A contemptuous rejoinder to anyone who dolefully tells you that they have only a comparatively short time to go is 'Could do it on my skull', or less delicately 'Could do it on my sh-t tub'.

1967 K. Tennant *Tell Morning This* p. 156: 'How long are you doing?' 'Six months'. The Sailor indicated that he could do this sentence while seated on the can provided in every cell for the satisfaction of the inmate's private functions.

2010 R. Honeywell *Wasted: The True Story of Jim McNeil, Violent Criminal and Brilliant Playwright* p. 72: There was no sewerage at Parramatta Jail, so the cells had no toilets. Instead prisoners had to make do with what was universally known as a shit tub: a bucket with a handle and lid that was put outside the cell door in the morning and replaced with a clean one during lunch. Nothing had changed in 200 years.

do it on yer head serve sentence as easy as possible.

General Prison Slang.

The phrase *do it on one's head* or *do it standing on one's head* means 'to do something with consummate ease' (OED). The OED points out that in early use this phrase typically referred to the serving out of a prison sentence, and this continues to be a specific prison use of the more general sense. See DO IT HARD.

The quotes use the variants *do it standing on one's head* and *do it on one's skull*. The phrase is synonymous with DO IT ON THE SHIT TUB.

> **1877** *Launceston Examiner* 6 January p. 5: Thos. Brody, a prisoner under sentence in the House of Correction, pleaded guilty to a charge of disobeying one of the prison regulations. It appears he would not salute the warders and officers, and cursed and swore at them. He was now sentenced to seven days' solitary confinement, which he said he could do standing on his head.
>
> **1944** T. Hartley in G. SIMES *Dictionary of Australian Underworld Slang* (1993) p. 65: A contemptuous rejoinder to anyone who dolefully tells you that they have only a comparatively short time to go is 'Could do it on my skull'.
>
> **1989** T. ANDERSON *Inside Outlaws: A Prison Diary* p. 146: *Doing it*, doing your sentence in jail. That is, you might be doing it hard, or doing it 'on your head' (easily); depending on the length of your sentence, the conditions of the jail, and your state of mind.
>
> **1990** V. TUPPER & R. WORTLEY *Anthology of Prison Slang in Australia* (National Library of Australia, Pandora Archive): *Doing it standing on one's head*, to serve a prison sentence without undue worry.
>
> **1995** N. IBRAHIM & M. QUINNEY *Glossary of Gaol Slang: Pentridge Gaol* (Unpublished Typescript ANDC): *Doing it standing on me head*, easy.

do it tough let sentence get you down.

General Prison Slang.

See the synonymous DO IT HARD. E. Partridge in *Dictionary of the Underworld* (1950) lists *do it tough* as general prison slang. Of course, one can 'do it tough' in various aspects of life, but the phrase has its specific prison sense.

> **1944** T. Hartley in G. SIMES *Dictionary of Australian Underworld Slang* (1993) p. 65: The accepted courtesy greeting in jail is 'How are you doing it?' The usual replies are 'Doing it easy' or 'Doing it tough'.
>
> **1950** 'Thirty-five' in G. SIMES *Dictionary of Australian Underworld Slang* (1993) p. 205: 'Jack does it tough' ... i.e. gaol depresses him.
>
> **2011** F. HARARI *A Tragedy in Two Acts* p. 163: Marcus has a good reason for being in protection. He is an ex-judge. ... Having a profile in jail is tantamount to having the worst life in jail. So he is doing it tough in there.

dollied loaded with false material evidence.

Australian Underworld Slang.

As the verb *dolly* the term means '(of a police officer) to introduce fabricated material evidence to attempt to bring about a conviction'. The headword is the past participle, used as an adjective.

Origin: The verb *dolly* meaning 'to prettify; to doll up' has existed in General English since the 1950s, and the 'loaded with false evidence' sense possibly comes from this. In the *Bulletin* article quoted below it sounds as if the consorting officer falsified evidence about a role in a break and enter crime.

> **1975** *Bulletin* (Sydney) 26 April p. 44 (article on underworld slang): 'That arse—you know, the consorter what dollied you on the bust last year—what's his name?' 'Taylor'.

don't be a gig mind your own business.
Australian Underworld and Prison Slang.
  The phrase means 'don't be a stickybeak, don't interfere'.
  Origin: In Australian English a *gig* is 'one who pries; a busybody; a stickybeak' and in criminal contexts it can also be 'an informer' (AND). The two senses have different origins, but they become blurred in criminal contexts, and therefore in the prison the accusation of being a gig carries more negative connotations than the term's general use. See GIG for a complete account of the term.

> **1944** T. Hartley in G. SIMES *Dictionary of Australian Underworld Slang* (1993) p. 92: *Gig*, a stickybeak, a person who looks at others working.... The most frequent use is in the expression 'Don't be a gig'. The reply to most questions.

> **1984** B. ELLEM *Doing Time: The Prison Experience* p. 105: *Michael, what are some of the rules that prisoners live by?* Well don't be a gig, in other words if you see something going on you mind your own business. If I see something I shouldn't see, I don't see it. It's none of my business.

dook pass something secretly.
General English.
  Dook (or *duke*) is General English for 'hand' (first recorded mid nineteenth century). The corresponding verb is used in the sense 'to shake hands', and then 'to pass with the hands, to give out, to hand over', and this action is sometimes done secretly, sometimes with the suggestion of illegality or bribery. These senses all exist in General English.
  Origin: Some argue that the 'hand' sense may have developed from rhyming slang, and the explanation for this possibility is quite complicated: (1) the term *fork* in the plural form *forks* was used in slang to refer to the fingers (with reference to the tines of a fork), and therefore to the hand; (2) *Duke of York* is rhyming slang for *fork*, and therefore for *fork* in the sense 'hand'; (3) *Duke of York* was abbreviated to *duke*. The problem with this rhyming slang theory is that the early evidence for *duke* comes from the United States, where rhyming slang is rare, and where such a complex example therefore seems unlikely. The Romany word *dukking* meaning 'palmistry, palm-reading' has also been suggested. But the origin of the international sense 'hand' is uncertain.

> [**1950** H.E. GOLDIN *Dictionary of American Underworld Lingo* p. 63: *Duke*, to hand, usually surreptitiously. 'Duke me the swag (loot), and I'll screw (leave)'.]

> **1967** K. TENNANT *Tell Morning This* p. 219: Certainly I have a share of this and

that, but I'm dooking all the higher-ups just to keep in sweet so I don't have some honest copper winning promotion on me.

1978 H.C. Baker *I Was Listening* p. 41: 'It was pretty poor light in the kitchen and when the jackpot built up a bit. You' (another cunning smirk) 'just dooks yerself a good hand from the bottom of the pack'.

double two ounces of tobacco.

Australian Prison Slang.

The term is not otherwise recorded in the Australian evidence. It is also used in NZ (see quote 1962 in square brackets). It is synonymous with swy¹, which is the usual term in Australia.

The standard ration of two ounces of tobacco per week was established by the end of the nineteenth century (see quote 1888) and was still the standard ration at the end of the twentieth century (see quote 2006).

1888 *Australian Star* (Sydney) 30 October p. 3: After the first year of a prisoner's sentence has expired, he is allowed a portion of tea, sugar, and two ounces of tobacco weekly. When two years are passed, vinegar is added to the list of indulgences.

[**1982** G. Newbold *The Big Huey* p. 247: *Double*, two-ounce packet of prison tobacco.]

2006 B. Matthews *Intractable ... Life inside Australia's First Super-max Prison* p. 92: Innovation was the mother of creation inside Parramatta *Jail*. Match-splitting was another weekly ritual for smokers inside the *jail*. Each prisoner was issued *two ounces of tobacco* each week and a box of 50 matches, making them a precious commodity.

drack ugly.

Australian English.

The term means 'unattractive, dreary, unprepossessing', with spelling variants *drack, drac, drak*. It first appeared in the 1940s, and has now largely disappeared.

Origin: Perhaps from *Dracula*, popularised by the 1931 film, and the 1936 film *Dracula's Daughter*. Less likely is an origin in *dreck* 'rubbish, trash' from Yiddish *drek*. In 1900 a 'mock-Yiddish' passage appeared in the *Sydney Sportsman*, and it included the phrase *drac stuff* to describe some inferior jewellery (3 October p. 1). This is likely to be an alteration of *dreck*, here meaning 'trashy', and it is interesting evidence of the currency of the word in Sydney at that time; but Australian *drack* appears much later.

1944 T. Hartley in G. Simes *Dictionary of Australian Underworld Slang* (1993) p. 70: *Drak, the drak*, unpleasant, rotten, no good. Thus 'It was a drak concert'. 'This gaol is the drak'. A recent word derived from Dracula.

1946 *Woman* (Sydney) 27 May p. 27: 'If you're left with the drac sort', (from Dracula—a girl who had no looks) said the short boy.

1953 T.A.G. Hungerford *Riverslake* p. 94: The Causeway's all right—a damned sight better than the turns up at the Albert Hall. Anyway, it's a football dance, not just one of those drac turns they slap on for the locals.

1972 A. Chipper *Aussie Swearers Guide* p. 38: *Drack sort*, opposite of *good sort*. ... A *drack sort* often has a mind of her own, refuses to be segregated at parties, and complains bitterly when asked to polish a car, scrape a boat, or watch footie in the rain.

2013 *Sydney Morning Herald* 5 January (News Review Section) p. 14: Agapanthus ... They're great when in first bloom, but then they start to wilt, and droop and fall over and generally look very drack.

drag three months.
Australian Underworld and Prison Slang.

The term means 'a period of imprisonment of three months'. It was originally British Prison Slang, recorded from the 1830s, but in the post Second World War period it has been primarily Australian.

Origin: From the standard figurative senses of *drag*, such as 'an obstruction to progress, an annoyance, a bore' (OED). See quotes 1944 and 1968 for the likely origin.

1851 *Empire* (Sydney) 1 December p. 419: Sabbath fighting. ... Rooney was dealt with by their worships on Monday morning, and in addition to a penalty of £2, he was ordered off the Turon in 12 hours, otherwise, drunk or sober, orderly or disorderly, Bathurst Gaol was to 'hould' him for '*a drag*'.

1877 T.E. Argles *Pilgrim* I p. 6: He expected to receive at the hands of the magistrates a term of imprisonment which he designated as a '*drag*' (three months), his offence being that of ... assaulting a constable.

1882 *Sydney Slang Dictionary* p. 3: *Drag*, three months in prison.

1919 V. Marshall *The World of the Living Dead* p. 85: O, no more I'll slip the toe-raggers and rag-timers the chews / Just ter brighten up their stretches, sleeps an' drags.

1944 T. Hartley in G. Simes *Dictionary of Australian Underworld Slang* (1993) p. 71: *Drag*, a sentence of three months imprisonment. It's probably derived from the fact that as all prisoners are agreed the time drags the most on this sentence.

1950 B.K. Doyle *Australian Police Journal* April p. 112: *Drag*, 3 months' imprisonment.

1968 J. Alard *He Who Shoots Last* p. 259: Drag, three months, referred to as such for it is considered in prison circles to be such a drag. With long terms one settles down. A year or so is mediocre but three months is an in-between and most unpalatable.

1975 *Bulletin* (Sydney) 26 April p. 44 (article on underworld slang): 'What yer get?' 'A drag'.

1990 V. Tupper & R. Wortley *Anthology of Prison Slang in Australia* (National Library of Australia, Pandora Archive): *Drag*, a three month prison sentence.

drop a fence; receiver of stolen goods.
General English.

This term was originally British and American Underworld Slang from the early twentieth century. In addition to meaning 'a receiver of stolen goods', *drop* is also used to mean 'a delivery of stolen goods' and 'a place where stolen goods are delivered' (GDS).

Origin: From the notion of stolen goods being 'dropped off' or 'delivered'.

1967 *Whisper All Aussie Dictionary* in *Kings Cross Whisper* 34 p. 4: *Drop*, a receiver of purloined property.

1983 R. AVEN-BRAY *Ridgey Didge Oz Jack Lang* p. 24: *Drop*, stolen goods, receiver, informer.

drop from the ceiling suddenly appear beside you.

General English.

A commonplace formulation to indicate a surprise appearance.

Origin: Probably originating with the example of a spider dropping down from the ceiling (see quote 1914).

The 1922 quote is from an American crime novel, widely serialised in Australian newspapers.

1914 *Journal* (Adelaide) 31 January p. 6: We heard of one elderly lady who ran out and rang up the fire brigade when a black spider dropped from the ceiling on her neck.

1922 *Gnowangerup Star* 18 November p. 4: However, the fact remains that the fortune is now mine, that Emily is alive and knows about it, and that she appeared before me in my sleeping room last night, as mysteriously as if she had dropped from the ceiling, and demanded it all.

drop off quit what you're doing or else.

Australian English.

The term means 'to desist, stop'.

Origin: From one of the standard senses of the verb *drop*: 'To cease to keep up, or have to do with; to have done with; to leave off or let alone' (OED).

1971 J. MCNEIL *The Chocolate Frog* in *The Chocolate Frog, The Old Familiar Juice: Two Plays* (1973) p. 31: TOSSER: Yer wanner drop off sayin' that, about backin' a tail... SHIRKER: Ahh, don't worry mate ... they reckon turnabout's fair play. (*Chuckling*) I nearly fainted the first time.

1973 J. MCNEIL *The Chocolate Frog, The Old Familiar Juice: Two Plays* p. 115 (Glossary): *Drop off*, (colloquial), to desist from hectoring or otherwise pressuring someone, to ease the pressure.

1985 R.G. BARRETT *You Wouldn't Be Dead for Quids* p. 153: He ... head butted him across the bridge of his nose, not hard enough to knock him out but enough to give him the drum to drop off.

2010 A. SHAND *King of Thieves* p. 23: And if a copper began to get too interested, they would just slip him 'a monkey' (500 quid) and he would soon drop off.

2010 A. SHAND *King of Thieves* p. 193 (Glossary): *Drop off*, to desist in an inquiry or endeavour.

dropped informed on.

Australian Underworld Slang.

Past tense or past participle of a verb *drop* 'to inform on'.

Origin: Quote 1967 gives *drop* as a noun (also quote 1983), but if this entry is by Jim Ramsay (see comments on the *Whisper All Aussie Dictionary* in section 5 of the introductory material), in his 1977 book Ramsay removes the 'informer' sense at *drop* and includes it in the fuller entry at the verb phrase *drop the bucket* (see quote 1977). It seems likely that the Parramatta Glossary's *dropped* is from the verb *drop* that is a shortening of the phrase *drop the bucket (on)*.

>**1950** B.K. DOYLE *Australian Police Journal* April p. 112: *Drop the bucket*, drop the responsibility suddenly on to someone else.
>
>**1967** *Whisper All Aussie Dictionary* in *Kings Cross Whisper* 34 p. 4: *Drop*, a receiver of purloined property. Also used to refer to an informer.
>
>**1977** J. RAMSAY *Cop It Sweet* p. 32: *Drop the bucket*, to throw responsibility for an offence on to someone else; Inform on.
>
>**1983** R. AVEN-BRAY *Ridgey Didge Oz Jack Lang* p. 24: *Drop*, Stolen goods, receiver, informer.

dry unmade tea(leaves).

Australian Prison Slang.

Elsewhere recorded only in the 1990 quote below.

>**1990** V. TUPPER & R. WORTLEY *Anthology of Prison Slang in Australia* (National Library of Australia, Pandora Archive): *Dry leaves*, tea leaves. Sometimes just 'dry'.

dubbo imbecile.

Australian English.

The term means 'a country bumpkin, a fool' (AND).

Origin: From *Dubbo*, the name of a country town in New South Wales, with the implication that this is a site of rustic simplicity and thickheadedness.

>**1973** D. FOSTER *North, South, West* p. 17: You've only got to look at all the bushwacking, nestfeathering dubbos we get for Education ministers.
>
>**1980** B. HORNADGE *The Australian Slanguage* p. 172: In Sydney these days a person (particularly if from the country) who is a bit dense or otherwise considered objectionable is branded a *dubbo*.
>
>**1990** V. TUPPER & R. WORTLEY *Anthology of Prison Slang in Australia* (National Library of Australia, Pandora Archive): *Dubbo*, a simple countrified prisoner.
>
>**1999** *Daily Telegraph* (Sydney) 27 February p. 12: When will these sporting dubbos fall into line with the discipline and respect displayed by most footballers of other codes?

dudder person who sells inferior quality goods and presents them as high grade merchandise.

Australian Underworld Slang.

This is a very old criminal term for a seller of shoddy goods, going back to Britain in the eighteenth century: 'A dishonest trader or pedlar, esp. of clothes or handkerchiefs; *specifically,* one who dupes others into buying inferior goods for a high price' (OED). Although the term was originally British, its use died out in Britain by the early twentieth century, and it became mainly Australian. Australia also has the verb *dud* 'to trick, defraud, deceive'.

Origin: From *dud* 'an article of clothing, esp. a cloak, made from rough, coarse cloth' (GDS).

1941 S.J. Baker *A Popular Dictionary of Australian Slang* p. 26: *Dudder,* a swindler, a cheat.

1967 *Whisper All Aussie Dictionary* in *Kings Cross Whisper* 34 p. 4: *Dudder,* a seller of shoddy goods.

1972 *Telegraph* (Brisbane) 30 August p. 24: Criminals and con men were running mock auctions in Queensland which were fleecing the public. The operators were known as dudders and professional shoddy-droppers.

1983 R. Aven-Bray *Ridgey Didge Oz Jack Lang* p. 24: *Dudder,* seller of phoney goods.

dung puncher another name for a hock.
Australian Prison Slang.

In General English use this is a term for 'a gay man'. It is usually derogatory and offensive. In the prison system it has a very specific meaning, and it is used of a HOCK, a man who takes the penetrative role in male to male sex. In prison contexts, where situational homosexuality is common, the *dung puncher* (who is called a HOCK) generally does not identify as gay, and the kind of sexual activity designated by the literal sense of the term is therefore to the fore in its application to him. See also ARSE BANDIT, SHIRT LIFTER.

This term is recorded earliest in Australia (in this Parramatta Glossary), although it is now used more widely.

1988 L. Johansen *The Dinkum Dictionary* p. 112: *Dung-puncher,* a homosexual man.

1996 P. West *Fathers, Sons and Lovers* p. 149 (the speaker is referring to the time of his upbringing in the 1930s): No—I didn't know anyone who did it. I suppose there were many of them around. The common name for them was windjammers or dung-punchers.

2007 P. Mitchell *Dodging the Bull* p. 137: 'Seeya later, Harry', half the men in the pub called out as we left. And because our father picked wild flowers on our property for a living, some men yelled out, 'Watch out those flowers don't turn you into a dung puncher!' I didn't know what that meant then, but my father responded by saying, 'No worries about that fellas' and pushing his hips back and forward.

earn proceeds of robbery.
Australian Underworld Slang.

104 easy mark

This noun means in Australian English 'that which is earned', either legally, as a 'salary, profit', or by various other means. The Parramatta Glossary sense is a specific underworld use of the term to refer to the 'earnings' from a robbery.

Origin: Australian creation of a noun from the General English verb: 'to do work or render service in return for (wages); to receive or be entitled to (money, a livelihood, or some other material advantage) through work or another activity' (OED).

1967 *Whisper All Aussie Dictionary* in *Kings Cross Whisper* 34 p. 4: Earn, any money earned by using the wits.

1975 *Bulletin* (Sydney) 26 April p. 45 (article on underworld slang): The police had asked him for a monkey ($500) in return for not opposing bail in the magistrate's court. The Pig replied, 'no bail, then no earn for you', meaning that if he were not released on bail he wouldn't be able to steal. If he couldn't steal then obviously he wouldn't be able to pay the police.

2006 B. MATTHEWS *Intractable ... Life inside Australia's First Super-max Prison* p. 19: My stepbrother had just got out of jail after doing a stint for safe-cracking. He was looking for an earn.

easy mark soft touch.

General English.

The term means 'someone or something overcome, mastered or persuaded without difficulty, anything achieved with ease' (GDS), and is recorded from the late nineteenth century.

Origin: *Easy* in the sense 'designating someone or something able to be captured, overcome, exploited, or persuaded without difficulty' (OED) has been used since the sixteenth century in similar compounds, such as *easy game, easy prey, easy target, easy touch*.

1949 L. GLASSOP *Lucky Palmer* p. 240: He picked an easy mark, 'Lucky', when he picked you.

1950 'Thirty-five' in G. SIMES *Dictionary of Australian Underworld Slang* (1993) p. 138: *Easy mark*: an easily gulled person.

1992 M.B. READ *Chopper 2: Hits and Memories* p. 23: As I have maintained from the beginning in this shooting case, it was a set-up. Not the police, mind you. Too many people owed me big money, and I was a bloody easy mark—a scapegoat.

1999 'How to Survive in Prison' in *Ralph* March p. 21: If someone stands over you for your shoes or clothes, stand up for yourself, otherwise everyone will know you're an easy mark.

[educated *see* CAN'T BE EDUCATED.**]**

[elephants *see* HE'S ELEPHANTS.**]**

fat wick strip of sheeting or like material spread with fat, rolled up, and lit for purposes of boiling up.

Australian Prison Slang.

This is an improvised method of heating water, on a principle similar to the traditional slush lamp made from a wick and a container of fat. Not otherwise recorded.

finger point out, accuse.
General English.
The OED defines: 'to identify (an offender) to the police; (more generally) to inform on or betray (a person)'. This was originally American Underworld Slang, first recorded 1930 (see quote in square brackets), and now widespread.

> [**1930** *Flynn's* (also called *Flynn's Weekly*, *Flynn's Weekly Detective Fiction*) (New York) 13 December p. 194: Frank Lee … had 'fingered' many, many dealers to the Feds.]
>
> **1984** B. Ellem *Doing Time: The Prison Experience* p. 189: *Finger*, to finger a person means to inform.
>
> **1988** *Copspeak* (Australian Institute of Criminology) p. 27: *Finger*, to inform upon or otherwise identify a person to police.
>
> **1990** V. Tupper & R. Wortley *Anthology of Prison Slang in Australia* (National Library of Australia, Pandora Archive): *Finger*, to accuse, identify or inform upon. An abbreviated form of the original phrase 'to put the finger on'.
>
> **2013** D. Whish-Wilson *Zero at the Bone* p. 214: Louise described the same young male fingered by the neighbour.

[**fire** *see* CAN'T FIRE.]

[**fire** *see* ON FIRE.]

fitted found guilty.
Australian English.
In this Australian use, *fit* has had two related senses: (1) 'to fix upon a person the responsibility for having committed a criminal offence by securing sufficient evidence to ensure a conviction'; (2) 'to fix upon a person the responsibility for having committed a criminal offence by contriving sufficient evidence to ensure a conviction' (AND). Especially in the second sense the verb sometimes appears as *fit up*.

The early evidence has the neutral sense, and this is represented by the Parramatta Glossary's 'found guilty'. The 1944 and 1950 quotations below from NSW prison glossaries are similarly neutral. Later uses stress the manipulation of evidence and are often synonymous with the term *frame*.

> **1882** 'Rolf Boldrewood' *Robbery Under Arms* in *Sydney Mail* 2 September p. 374: When he gets in with men like his old pals he loses his head, I believe. … He'll get 'fitted' quite simple some day if he doesn't keep a better look-out.
>
> **1919** V. Marshall *The World of the Living Dead* p. 12: Three charges agin' me—righteous, vag, an resistin'. Fitted on first two.
>
> **1944** T. Hartley in G. Simes *Dictionary of Australian Underworld Slang* (1993) p.

83: *Fitted*, found guilty (and sentenced) on a charge. Thus 'I got fitted on the break & entering but I beat all the other charges'.

1950 'Thirty-five' in G. SIMES *Dictionary of Australian Underworld Slang* (1993) p. 83: *Fit*, to convict. 'He fronted on seven busts, and was fitted on four and beat the rest' i.e. appeared charged on seven counts of break and enter; was convicted on four, and acquitted on the rest.

1971 J. McNEIL *The Chocolate Frog* in *The Chocolate Frog, The Old Familiar Juice: Two Plays* (1973) p. 23: He wouldn't have been fitted at all, most likely, if you hadn't gone and jumped in the box, and give 'im up!

1973 J. McNEIL *The Chocolate Frog, The Old Familiar Juice: Two Plays* p. 115 (Glossary): *Fit*, (colloquial), to convict, with a suggestion of manipulation; to fit the facts to the indictment.

1984 B. ELLEM *Doing Time: The Prison Experience* p. 189: *Fit*, to convict, with a suggestion of a manipulation of the facts.

1989 T. ANDERSON *Inside Outlaws: A Prison Diary* p. 146: *Fitted*, framed with material evidence or with a false charge. If you are 'fitted' on a charge, it is most likely that police are fabricating evidence.

1990 V. TUPPER & R. WORTLEY *Anthology of Prison Slang in Australia* (National Library of Australia, Pandora Archive): *Fit*, to be wrongfully incriminated with spurious evidence. As in 'to be fitted' or 'to be fitted up'. Presumably from the idea of fitting the facts to suit the situation. Equivalent to U.S. term frame.

five cents in the dollar insane.

Not otherwise recorded, but this phrase follows the pattern of similar currency-based phrases suggesting that a person is not very intelligent or sane, as *nineteen and six in the pound*, *not the full shilling*, *not the full quid*, and *two cents short of a buck*.

flap blank cheque leaf.

Australian English.

E. Partridge in his *Dictionary of Slang and Unconventional English* (ed. 2, 1938) lists *flap* 'a cheque' but without any source or information about where it was used. Subsequent evidence is Australian.

Origin: Of uncertain origin, probably related to *flap* in the sense 'something hanging broad and flat, as a shutter'. Perhaps influenced by *kite* in the sense 'a cheque'—see FLY A KITE.

1935 *Labor Daily* (Sydney) 26 September p. 4: During a trial before Judge Thomson this week it was stated that a man had been 'fluttering kites'. This was crookdom's slang for passing valueless cheques. Ten years ago this offence was known among criminals as 'passing off flaps', while 'a kite' was a term for a newspaper surreptitiously smuggled into a gaol. The term 'kite' was derived from the fact that schoolboys formerly made kites out of newspapers.

1950 *Argus* (Melbourne) 7 June p. 2: Today the 'tank man' (safe breaker to you), the 'flap man' (worthless cheque operator to you), and the smart 'hook' (pickpocket to you) are the best dressed men in the Court.

1953 *Sydney Morning Herald* 3 January p. 6: *False flap*, a bad cheque.

1955 'Thirty-five' in G. SIMES *Dictionary of Australian Underworld Slang* (1993) p. 83: *Flap man*, one who passes dud cheques.

1983 R. AVEN-BRAY *Ridgey Didge Oz Jack Lang* p. 28: *Flaps*, cheques.

flat grouse tobacco.
Australian English.

The term means 'good quality, fine-cut, tobacco'. See GROUSE CIGARETTE.

Origin: From the fact that is finely cut and therefore sits 'flat'. For the origin of *grouse* see GROUSE CIGARETTE.

1902 *Bulletin* (Sydney) 31 March p. 31: A half plug of 'flat' ... mysteriously disappeared.

1950 B.K. DOYLE *Australian Police Journal* April p. 112: *Flat*, fine cut flake tobacco.

1955 'Thirty-five' in G. SIMES *Dictionary of Australian Underworld Slang* (1993) p. 83: *Flat*, tobacco other than that issued by the Department. 'Jack copped two oz of flat'.

flum fluke it.
Australian English.

This verb means 'to fluke something, to achieve by a fluke' (AND). The Parramatta Glossary contains the earliest evidence for the verb. The corresponding noun meaning 'a fluke, a chance win; luck' (AND) appears slightly earlier (see quote 1967).

Origin: Perhaps from *flummox* 'to confound, bewilder, nonplus' (OED).

1967 *Whisper All Aussie Dictionary* in *Kings Cross Whisper* 34 p. 4: *Flum*, a fluke, a lucky chance.

1993 *Daily Telegraph Mirror* (Sydney) 11 September p. 108: FootyTAB's betting on the premiership winner closed after five rounds but if you're a keen student of reserve-grade teams you might flum Pick the Margins.

2005 *Daily Telegraph* (Sydney) 28 May p. 80: First scoring play options are little more than a lottery, no matter what the match, so again it falls to punters to try to find the right option in margin betting or, for the high flyers, to flum the half/fulltime double.

fly a kite pass dud cheque.
General English.

The term *kite* was used for 'a cheque' and then for 'a dud cheque' in Britain and the US from the 1830s. The phrase to *fly a kite* came to mean 'to pass a dud cheque'.

Origin: *Kite* has been General English for various kinds of bills of exchange from the early nineteenth century, and then for cheques, blank cheques, and dud cheques. The phrase *fly a kite* referred to the process of raising money on bills of exchange (from the early nineteenth century), and when the 'cheque' sense shifted to include 'dud cheques' the phrase was used to refer to the illegal raising of money by means of dud cheques. The papers used in all these transactions were called 'kites' probably with jocular allusion to a toy kite made of paper. GDS has a good collection of quotes for all these meanings.

1895 C. Crowe *Australian Slang Dictionary* p. 42: *Flying kites*, passing valueless cheques.

1950 B.K. Doyle *Australian Police Journal* April p. 114: *Fly a kite*, present a valueless cheque.

1977 J. Ramsay *Cop It Sweet* p. 36: *Fly a kite*, cash a cheque, orig. cash a dud cheque.

1983 R. Aven-Bray *Ridgey Didge Oz Jack Lang* p. 28: *Fly a kite*, cash a dud cheque.

2006 B. Matthews *Intractable ... Life inside Australia's First Super-max Prison* p. 394: Flying kites and paper hanging, cheque frauds.

form criminal record.
Australian and British Underworld and Prison Slang.

The term means 'a list of previous convictions'. The British evidence appears in the 1950s, so the Australian is slightly earlier. Some of the Australian quotes below indicate that *form* in an Australian underworld and prison context also can include a judgement about a person's adherence to the criminals' code of conduct.

Origin: Transferred from horseracing terminology for the previous racing and training performance of a horse.

1944 T. Hartley in G. Simes *Dictionary of Australian Underworld Slang* (1993) p. 85: *Form*, character. Habitual behaviour whether good or bad. Derived from a horseracing expression. It is usually employed in an ironical sense thus: 'You showed nice form—spilling your guts to the cops'. 'Don't talk to me. I know your form'. 'He's a wake up to your form'.

1967 *Whisper All Aussie Dictionary* in *Kings Cross Whisper* 34 p. 4: *Form*, criminal record, as in racehorse form.

1971 J. McNeil *The Chocolate Frog* in *Two Plays* (1973) p. 37: But you're *new* ter the scene, 'n *as* such yer'll be answerin' all kinds of questions in the next few days. All the crims'll wanter know yer *form*... 'n they'll be lookin' ter me 'n Toss for a rundown on yer ... It could be that yer a bit short on credentials. Might be even a chockie frog or somethin'; in which case, a'course, we'd have ter *say so* around the place. Just so the good fellers wouldn't be seen talkin' to yer.

1983 R. Aven-Bray *Ridgey Didge Oz Jack Lang* p. 28: *Form sheet*, prison record.

1984 B. Ellem *Doing Time: The Prison Experience* p. 189: *Form*, a person's criminal or prison record.

1989 T. Anderson *Inside Outlaws: A Prison Diary* p. 145: *Form*, criminal or police record; list of previous convictions or charges. Example: 'What sort of form have you got?'

2006 B. Matthews *Intractable ... Life inside Australia's First Super-max Prison* p. 394: *Form*, record, usually criminal record, or character.

freckle anus.
Australian English.

The term means 'arse, anus'.

Origin: Transferred use of *freckle* 'a yellowish or light-brown spot in the skin' (OED).

1967 *Whisper All Aussie Dictionary* in *Kings Cross Whisper* 34 p. 4: *Freckle*, anus.

1977 B. Humphries in *Tharunka* 13 June p. 14 (from 'Mr Les Patterson's Historic Address to the British'): If I run into any of my fellow Australians rubbishing their homeland and knocking our famous finesse and refinement I'll kick his teeth so far down his throat he'll have to stick his toothbrush up his freckle to clean them.

1986 C. Bowles *G'Day* p. 83: Jeez, you're really passé sometimes Shane. Bein gay's all the go these days. Shane: I'll still keep me freckle to the wall, thanks.

2011 *Newcastle Herald* 11 June (Drive Section) p. 4: It was a compressed driving experience, a place to flog the freckle out of Audi's latest performance hottie in relative safety while staying immune to the long arm of the law.

front appear in court.
Australian English.

The term means 'to appear before (a court etc.)' (AND).

Origin: From 'appear in front of (a magistrate, a court, etc.)'

1941 *Argus* (Melbourne) 15 November (Supplement) p. 1: I have knocked out a rough glossary of Australian Army slang terms. ... *Fronting the Bull*, facing a charge.

1950 B.K. Doyle *Australian Police Journal* April p. 112: *To front*, to appear before. 'Front' the court.

1967 *Whisper All Aussie Dictionary* in *Kings Cross Whisper* 34 p. 4: *Front up*, go to court, more broadly to appear anywhere.

1968 J. Alard *He Who Shoots Last* p. 3: Look like doin a drag wen I front tomorrow.

1984 B. Ellem *Doing Time: The Prison Experience* p. 189: *Front*, to turn up; for example, 'he fronted for his trial'.

1990 V. Tupper & R. Wortley *Anthology of Prison Slang in Australia* (National Library of Australia, Pandora Archive): *Front*, to appear before some legal body. As in 'to front the court' or 'to front the superintendent'.

1995 N. Ibrahim & M. Quinney *Glossary of Gaol Slang: Pentridge Gaol* (Unpublished Typescript ANDC): *Front up*, go to court.

2011 *Geelong Advertiser* 10 November p. 4: Mr Wilson said Smith had also fronted court on a dangerous driving charge in January this year.

[full quid see NOT THE FULL QUID.]

get buckled be arrested.
Australian Underworld Slang.

The usual form is *be buckled* and means 'to be arrested or imprisoned'. This was originally British Underworld Slang in the second half of the nineteenth century, but became mainly Australian in the twentieth century.

Origin: Extension of *buckle* 'to fasten', with allusion to fetters and restraints.

1895 C. Crowe *Australian Slang Dictionary* p. 12: *Buckled*, married or taken into custody.

1932 *Sunday Mail* (Brisbane) 13 November p. 20: Joe was buckled last night. He was all keyed up with angie and tried to take a twist out of a demon, he dug his heels in and it took three of them to lumber him. [*Ed*. Angie is 'angel's food i.e. cocaine', and *demon* means 'detective, police officer'.]

1944 T. Hartley in G. Simes *Dictionary of Australian Underworld Slang* (1993) p. 29: *Buckled*, arrested.

1950 'Thirty-five' in G. Simes *Dictionary of Australian Underworld Slang* (1993) p. 29: *Buckle*, to arrest. 'The coppers buckled him and lumbered him to Central'.

1967 *Whisper All Aussie Dictionary* in *Kings Cross Whisper* 32 p. 7: *Buckled*, to be caught out and arrested by the police.

1968 J. Alard *He Who Shoots Last* p. 140: I keeps tellin' dem I didn't do it, but it wuz no use, dey buckles me.

1975 *Bulletin* (Sydney) 26 April p. 44 (article on underworld slang): When I got buckled they asked for two spot. [*Ed.* A *spot* is '$100'. See HALF SPOT.]

1988 *Copspeak* (Australian Institute of Criminology) p. 8: *Buckle*, to arrest and charge an offender; alternatively, *buckled* is to be arrested.

2006 B. Matthews *Intractable … Life inside Australia's First Super-max Prison* p. 395: *Get buckled*, get caught; 'to buckle' is prison slang for surrendering or giving up; getting caught or being arrested.

get over intimidate someone.

Australian English.

Origin: Probably a variant of Australian *stand over* 'to intimidate or threaten; to extort money from someone' (AND).

1944 T. Hartley in G. Simes *Dictionary of Australian Underworld Slang* (1993) p. 92: *Get over (someone)*, to intimidate, to crush someone's spirit, to enforce deference. Thus 'Don't try & get over me or I'll roof your face in'. 'The screws will try and get over you, unless you stand up to them'.

1953 T.A.G. Hungerford *Riverslake* p. 121: The bastard backed up three times on the goulash. … I knocked him back on the fourth, and he bucked. So I went crook—you let them animals get over you once, and you're a goner.

1953 *Newcastle Sun* 23 November p. 9: At last he was arrested. There was no point in sending him back to his home, so a magistrate with good intentions — which were to backfire — sent Tommy to a 'school'. 'We'll come and see you often, love', said mum between sobs. 'Don't let the mugs get over you', said dad.

get up be acquitted.

Australian English.

Specific use of Australian *get up* meaning '(originally of a racehorse) to be successful in an endeavour, to win'. See the 1904 quote for the horseracing sense, and the 1983 quote for the more general sense. The prison sense derives from the fact that if you win the case you are acquitted.

Synonymous with BEAT IT (the phrases appear one after the other in the typed-up Parramatta Glossary).

1904 H. Fletcher *Dads Wayback* p. 100: When ther public fancies yer nag's chance, an' puts ther beans on, ther books gives yer ther office, an' that prad don't quite get up that time; though he runs close.

1983 *Sun-Herald* (Sydney) 9 October p. 9: 'I can't think of one confronting feature film that has criticised our society and got up', he says.

get yer head down plead guilty.
Australian Underworld Slang.
See NOD YER HEAD.
Origin: From the action of nodding the head to indicate a guilty plea in court.

1975 *Bulletin* (Sydney) 26 April p. 44: Let's eavesdrop on the Pig as he returns to his cell and talks to a friend, Gulcher, who is curious about Pig's fate at the hands of the enemy. 'Nod your nut, Pig?' 'No chance. The jacks gave me a nice load and tidied me up with verbal for desert. No way I'll get my head down to a load'.

gig witness; someone who is watching.
Australian English.

In the typed-up Parramatta Glossary the definition reads 'witness someone who is watching'. There is an Australian verb *gig* meaning 'to stare; to mock or make fun of a person; to stare mockingly at a person', and although the Parramatta Glossary entry has the appearance of being a verb, it is a very clumsy formulation and doesn't make much sense. It seems likely that there is a missing comma or semicolon after 'witness', and that this is an entry for a noun: 'witness; someone who is watching'.

In Australian English the noun *gig* means 'an inquisitive look; a person who pries, a busybody' (AND), and this is in keeping with the Parramatta Glossary's definition. In the prison context, the term *gig* may also apply to someone who is visiting the prison and who examines or 'stares' at the inmates. It can also apply to the way one prisoner 'looks at' the business of another prisoner, resulting in the accusation that he is a busybody and interferer.

Origin: The verb and the noun derive from British dialect (Scots, Irish, and northern English) *gig* 'to laugh in a suppressed manner, giggle; to quiz, laugh at, taunt' (OED), perhaps also influenced by Scots *keek* (also *geek*) 'to peep, peer, glance; to look sharply, inquisitively' (*Scottish National Dictionary*).

There is another *gig* word used in prisons. In Australian English a *fizgig* (a word of unknown origin) is a 'police informer' (AND), and this term is sometimes abbreviated to *gig*. (See especially the *Bulletin* quote from 1984 and quote 2003.) In prison contexts the two different *gigs*, the stickybeak and the police informer, can become blurred—the prisoner who is too concerned about the private affairs of another prisoner is a stickybeak who may well also be an informer. Thus 'don't be a gig' can mean 'mind your own business'. See the entry DON'T BE A GIG.

1944 T. Hartley in G. SIMES *Dictionary of Australian Underworld Slang* (1993) p. 92: *Gig*, a stickybeak, a person who looks at others working. Hence *gigs*—visitors. It is slightly derogatory because visitors have a habit of looking at prisoners as if they were curiosities in some sort of zoo.... The most frequent use is in the expression 'Don't be a gig'. The reply to most questions.

1950 'Thirty-five' in G. SIMES *Dictionary of Australian Underworld Slang* (1993) p. 92: *Gig*, (One who) unwarrantably attend(s) to, or meddle(s) in, the affairs of others; by extension ... a witness who lays on information. '*Rorts* are always *brought undone* by gigs'... (probably a corruption of *fizgig*).

1967 *Whisper All Aussie Dictionary* in *Kings Cross Whisper* 35 p. 6: *Gig*, stickybeak.

1968 J. ALARD *He Who Shoots Last* p. 2: 'Anythin' else ya wanta know?' 'No disrespect Bricky, I ain't a gig'.

1971 J. McNEIL *The Chocolate Frog* in *The Chocolate Frog, The Old Familiar Juice: Two Plays* (1973) p. 37: As soon as I set foot in the bloody *door* ... you were at me with questions! (*Shrugging*) I ask you one ... just one ... and I'm a gig!

1973 J. McNEIL *The Chocolate Frog, The Old Familiar Juice: Two Plays* p. 115 (Glossary): *Gig*, (colloquial), a person of intrusive curiosity.

1984 B. ELLEM *Doing Time: The Prison Experience* p. 190: *Gig*, a person from outside who comes in to have a look at the prison and prisoners. A prisoner who doesn't mind his own business can also be called a 'gig'.

1984 *Bulletin* (Sydney) 19 June p. 69: Fifty percent of the Drug Squad's arrests are based on information received and woebetide a user, supplier or anyone else who becomes a dog, a gig or as the police term it, a Moreton Bay. [*Ed. Moreton Bay* is short for *Moreton Bay fig*, rhyming slang for *fizgig* 'informer'.]

1990 V. TUPPER & R. WORTLEY *Anthology of Prison Slang in Australia* (National Library of Australia, Pandora Archive): *Gig*, to look. Thus a person who comes from outside to view prison and prisoners, or a prisoner who does not mind his own business.

2003 J. CLEARY *Degrees of Connection* p. 161: I'm not a gig you know—I never informed on anyone.

ginger ale bail.

Australian Underworld Slang.
   Origin: Rhyming slang.

1967 *Whisper All Aussie Dictionary* in *Kings Cross Whisper* 35 p. 6: *Ginger ale*, bail.

1995 N. IBRAHIM & M. QUINNEY *Glossary of Gaol Slang: Pentridge Gaol* (Unpublished Typescript ANDC): *Ginger ale*, bail.

give a bodgie give an alias.

Australian English.

As a noun *bodgie* can mean 'anything that is fake, false, or worthless' (AND). In the phrase *give a bodgie*, *bodgie* is short for *bodgie name* (see 1954 and 1992 quotes). See quote 1955 for the variant *pulling a bodgie*.
   Origin: See BODGIE, BODGIE ADDRESS.

1954 *Herald* (Melbourne) 22 January p. 10: In a written statement produced in the City Court today a man was alleged to have said that he worked on the Melbourne wharves for eight months under 'bodgie' names.

1955 'Thirty-five' in G. SIMES *Dictionary of Australian Underworld Slang* (1993) p. 17: *Pulling a bodgie* i.e. pretending to be what one is not, for gain.

1992 *Sun Herald* (Sydney) 28 January p. 111: During one boozy night at the Rocks, [Prince] Philip was arrested by legendary cop Frank (Bumper) Farrell for urinating in the street. Philip gave a bodgie name and it wasn't until years later when Farrell saw a photo of Philip, who had become engaged to Princess Elizabeth, did he realise who he had nabbed.

give (someone) up inform on someone.
American and Australian Underworld Slang.

The term means 'to betray, to inform against' (GDS). It was originally US, recorded from the early twentieth century.

Origin: From *give up* in the sense 'to deliver (a fugitive, oneself) into the hands of an officer of justice, an enemy' and 'to forsake, abandon' (OED).

1950 'Thirty-five' in G. SIMES *Dictionary of Australian Underworld Slang* (1993) p. 94: *Give up*, to inform against.

1968 J. ALARD *He Who Shoots Last* p. 26: I ain't ever give no one up in me life Jack.

1971 J. MCNEIL *The Chocolate Frog* in *The Chocolate Frog, The Old Familiar Juice: Two Plays* (1973) p. 23: Ah, bullshit! He wouldn't have been fitted at all, most likely, if you hadn't gone and jumped in the box and give 'im up! Why didn't yer get 'im orf?

1985 T. PRIOR *A Knockabout Priest* p. 71: There have been senior screws had a go at him [Father Brosnan], governors even, but he's still stood up. When he thinks he is right, he will never back down and he has never 'given up' (betrayed) anyone.

1990 V. TUPPER & R. WORTLEY *Anthology of Prison Slang in Australia* (National Library of Australia, Pandora Archive): *Give-up*, to inform on or betray.

go right time to strike.
Australian Underworld Slang.

The term means 'the time to put a plan into action; the time to act'. This is a specific use of General English *go* 'a try or attempt (*at* doing something); a "shot"; an occasion when something is done or attempted' (OED).

1977 J. RAMSAY *Cop It Sweet* p. 40: *Go*, chance to put one's point of view or take one's part; agreement, settled decision.

1989 T. ANDERSON *Inside Outlaws: A Prison Diary* p. 147: *A Go*, an escape, a chance, a plan or purpose.

going bad not having any success.
Australian English.

The Australian verbal phrase *go bad* means 'to be suffering economically' (GDS). If you are 'going bad' you are likely to be short of money.

Common adverbial use of *bad* for the more standard *badly*.

1987 R.G. BARRETT *Boys from Binjiwunyawunya* p. 167: 'What do you mean—you're not going to pay it?' 'I'm not paying it. I'm gonna cut it out'. ... 'Look, if you're going bad I'll pay it and you can fix me up'.

2005 *Geelong Advertiser* 4 November p. 2: 'My father was in prison when I was a kid, so he didn't teach me to go out and rob', Faure told the Geelong Advertiser in an interview in 1998. 'But . . . when mum was going bad for money, the first thing I did was go and do over a factory'.

go off the bars commit suicide by hanging.
Australian Prison Slang.

The reference is to the iron bars in the cell.

1992 D. Biles & D. McDonald *Deaths in Custody, Australia, 1980–1989* p. 381: Alone in the cell and no other prisoners in custody. ... When checked ... was found hanging by the neck with his shirt tied around his neck and to a bar of the cell grill.

2016 *Trends and Issues in Crime and Criminal Justice* (online), Australian Institute of Criminology, no. 513: Across both non-Indigenous and Indigenous prisoners, a range of fittings and materials were used in hanging deaths. Hanging points included 'other fitting in cell' (35%), cell bars (32%), shower fixtures (13%), and bunk beds (12%).

go off the tub commit suicide by hanging.
Australian Prison Slang.

The reference is to the sanitary bucket in the cell. Also called *night tub, sanitary tub, shit tub.* See also DO IT ON THE SHIT TUB. McNeil, in one of his Parramatta Jail plays, refers to both *sanitary tub* and *tub* in the stage directions (see quote 1972). An early reference to the tub in an unsewered jail cell occurs in a Henry Lawson poem (see quote 1909).

1909 H. Lawson in *Bulletin* (Sydney) 23 December p. 43: We empty the tubs and muster, with the prison slouch and tread, /And we take to the cells our breakfast of hominy and of bread.

1972 J. McNeil *The Old Familiar Juice* in *The Chocolate Frog, The Old Familiar Juice: Two Plays* (1973) p. 94: He shrugs again, then picks up the sanitary tub and carries it over to where his book is lying on the floor. He sits on the tub and begins idly turning the book's pages.

go-slow punishment cell.
Australian Prison Slang.

Origin: From the fact that time passes especially slowly in a punishment cell, because of the limited lighting and the absence of other prisoners, reading material, radios, and the like.

1972 *Contact: Parramatta Jail Resurgents Magazine* December n.p.: In my pocket is a gun that will bring me a gift-wrapped five years in the go-slow.

1989 T. Anderson *Inside Outlaws: A Prison Diary* p. 147: *Go-Slow*, the Go Slow is all trac sections (for solitary confinement), but also the Nick/Jail in general.

1998 P. Doyle *Amaze Your Friends* p. 176: I phoned Dick's lawyer. He reported that Dick was in fact out of the go-slow.

2018 J. Knight *Dictionary of Victorian Prison Slang* (online) p. 15: *Go-slow*, a punishment unit. So-called because time in a punishment unit is said to go slow.

go to press write statement incriminating self or others.
Australian Underworld Slang.

Use of General English *go to press* '(of a newspaper, book, etc.) go to be printed'; (of a person) to have work printed or published' (OED). Perhaps influenced by the stock phrases indicating an intent to make an issue public: *threaten to go to the press, threaten to go to the paper*. Not otherwise recorded in this form and sense.

go to water weaken under pressure.
Australian English.

The phrase means 'to weaken one's resolve; to lose courage in the face of opposition; to capitulate'.

Origin: Perhaps from the melting of ice as a result of heat. There is probably no reference to urination as a result of fright etc.

> **1950** 'Thirty-five' in G. SIMES *Dictionary of Australian Underworld Slang* (1993) p. 210: *Go to water*, to 'weaken', to betray one's fellow. 'He goes to water under pressure'.
>
> **1988** *Sun* (Melbourne) 6 May p. 79: Fair dinkum, the moment the West Coasters cross the Victorian border they go to water quicker than an ice cube in the Simpson Desert.
>
> **2004** H. GARNER *Joe Cinque's Consolation* p. 159: I saw how a Crown witness of what seemed to me transparent sincerity and desire to do right—the only person who had made any real attempt to break through the ghastly, paralysing spell that hung around Anu Singh and her plan to kill Joe Cinque—could go to water under the sustained onslaught of a defence cross-examination.
>
> **2007** M.B. READ *Chopper 11: Last Man Standing* p. 54: Now Gatto was arrested at the scene and was locked up in solitary confinement for 14 months. I reckon you can tell a lot about someone on how they do jail time. Most of the plastic gangsters go to water once inside, but Mick just got on with it.
>
> **2014** K. LETTE *Courting Trouble* p. 85: 'Do you really think Chantelle will go to water in the witness box?' the Countess asked, reappearing from the tiny kitchen with three wine glasses. 'Courts are bloody scary places', Roxy sighed. 'The defence barrister will portray the poor kid as "delinquent" and "manipulative". He'll say it was consensual sex that got a little rough'.

got their lug have someone listening to you.
Australian English.

Lug is an old-fashioned General English word for 'ear'. The phrase *got/have a person's lug* is a variant of General English *to have the ear of a person* 'to have the favourable attention of a person' (OED). See also BLOW DOWN THEIR LUG.

> **1916** *Northern Miner* (Charters Towers) 16 February p. 7: But I have been unable to get his lug for particulars.

go under be found guilty by jury.
Australian Underworld Slang.

grand

The phrase means 'to be found guilty and imprisoned'.

Origin: The original sense of the General English phrase *go under* is 'to go underwater, to submerge' and there are many figurative uses, including 'to succumb or be overwhelmed in the struggle for survival', 'to go bankrupt', 'to lose' (OED). The Glossary's 'being found guilty' is part of this figurative pattern. See the New Zealand quote 2001 in square brackets for a different suggestion.

1968 J. Alard *He Who Shoots Last* p. 22: 'If you blast this informer you'll go under. You can depend on that', threatened the inspector.

1984 B. Ellem *Doing Time: The Prison Experience* p. 190: *Go under*, refers to the possibility of being caught or found guilty.

1990 V. Tupper & R. Wortley *Anthology of Prison Slang in Australia* (National Library of Australia, Pandora Archive): *Go under*, to be found guilty. Opposite to 'walk'.

1992 M.B. Read *Chopper 2: Hits and Memories* p. 208: One way or the other I reckon I will receive the jury's answer today. ... This is the most important legal battle of my life, as it will in many ways decide my life. If I go under it will draw the curtain on my relationship with Margaret.

1995 N. Ibrahim & M. Quinney *Glossary of Gaol Slang: Pentridge Gaol* (Unpublished Typescript ANDC): *Go under*, found guilty.

[**2001** D. Looser *Lexicon of Boobslang in the Period 1996–2000* (thesis) p. 79: *Go under*, to be convicted ... orig. from courtroom procedure. After a sentence was passed in the courtroom, the convicted criminal would 'go under' to the police cells below.]

2001 *Prison & Drug Slang: NSW Corrective Services*: *Go under*, to be convicted of an offence.

grand $1000.

General English.

This term was originally American English, from the beginning of the twentieth century. In Australia it originally meant £1000, and after decimalisation (1966) it became $1000 (and occasionally $2000, the approximate equivalent value of the former £1000).

Origin: So called because it is a 'large' sum of money.

1930 *Telegraph* (Brisbane) 25 August p. 5: American Slang Terms of the Talkies ... A thousand dollar bill is 'one grand'.

1950 B.K. Doyle *Australian Police Journal* April p. 114: *Grand*, £1,000.

1967 *Whisper All Aussie Dictionary* in *Kings Cross Whisper* 35 p. 6: *Grand*, $2000 or £1000.

2021 *Inverell Times* 5 August p. 5: She reckons she's helped raised over 10 grand for the Inverell branch over the course of her tenure.

[**grill** see ON THE GRILL.]

[**grilled** see BEING GRILLED.]

grouse cigarette tailor made.

Australian Prison Slang.

The term means 'a good quality cigarette'. *Grouse* is an Australian term meaning 'very good of its kind, highly desirable' (AND). In prison contexts a *grouse cigarette* is one not made from the kind of cheap tobacco supplied in prison rations and used in roll-your-owns, but refers to a factory-made (or tailor-made) cigarette. The 1944 quote uses the formulation *the grouse* to refer to tobacco, tea, etc., that is of good quality.

Origin: *Grouse* is probably from British dialect *crouse* 'bold, courageous', 'pleased, happy', 'lively, cheerful, merry', with evidence from Scotland and Northern England.

> **1944** T. Hartley in G. Simes *Dictionary of Australian Underworld Slang* (1993) p. 98: *The grouse*, extra special. ... Takes on a special meaning in gaol where tobacco, tea etc is of rather poor quality so that anything smuggled in from outside is automatically knows as 'the Grouse'.
>
> **1971** J. McNeil *The Chocolate Frog* in *The Chocolate Frog, The Old Familiar Juice: Two Plays* (1973) p. 17: I was kind of hopin' somebody might lob from court with a grouse cigga ... Like, a tailor made.
>
> **1973** J. McNeil *The Chocolate Frog, The Old Familiar Juice: Two Plays* p. 116 (Glossary): *Grouse*, (colloquial), good, very good ... (prison slang) most commonly used in reference to 'outside' tobacco.

grouse weed outside tobacco high quality.

Australian Prison Slang.

The term means 'good quality tobacco'. See GROUSE CIGARETTE and WEED. In prison contexts *grouse weed* is superior to the second-rate tobacco supplied in prison rations and known as *boob weed*.

The 2013 quote refers to a boys' home for young offenders in the later 1950s, indicating how prison terminology made its way into the language of young offenders and the institutions that held them.

> **1967** B.K. Burton *Teach Them No More* p. 209: I'm going to collect all the empty packets of grouse weed I can find in the next few days, and fill them up with boob weed.
>
> **1968** J. Alard *He Who Shoots Last* p. 125: Gee, thanks, Ragged. Da stuff's like gold in here ... gees, it's da grouse weed too—we gits a coupla ounces a week, but boob weed is like smokin' horse dung.
>
> **2013** B. Campbell *Giants Leap: An Activist Folksinger's Memoir* (ebook): On the first night, I also learnt the importance of tobacco, which was the currency of boys' homes and gaols and could purchase anything within reason. There was a sliding scale of value beginning with tailor-made cigarettes that could only be obtained from visitors or in parcels from home. Then came tobacco that came from the same source as cigarettes and was called 'grouse weed'. Third down the scale was 'boob weed', a poor quality tobacco said to be the sweepings from the floor of a tobacco factory. An ounce of this was issued each week to every boy over sixteen.

half inched stolen.

General English.

From the verb *half-inch* meaning 'to steal'. This was originally British, recorded from the first decade of the twentieth century.

Origin: *Half-inch*, rhyming slang for *pinch* 'to steal'.

1908 *Sunday Times* (Perth) 21 October p. 4: Last week burglars broke into the premises of Mr. Solicitor Penny, —and stole nine fancy waistcoats, the property of that gentleman. ... But not content with taking one, / Another those poachers pinched, / And swift (in the words of the slangful gun) / My 'East and West' 'half-inched'. [*Ed. East and west* is rhyming slang for 'vest'.]

1950 B.K. DOYLE *Australian Police Journal* April p. 117: *Pinch*, or *half-inch*, steal.

1963 L. GLASSOP *The Rats in New Guinea* p. 123: Eddie bent down, took a wristlet watch from a dead Jap and read aloud the inscription on its back: 'To Reg with love from Judy'. 'He half-inched it from one of our blokes', he said.

1967 *Whisper All Aussie Dictionary* in *Kings Cross Whisper* 35 p. 6: *Half inch*, steal.

1983 R. AVEN-BRAY *Ridgey Didge Oz Jack Lang* p. 31: *Half inched*, pinched (arrested).

1984 J. MEREDITH *Learn to Talk Old Jack Lang* p. 26: *Half inch*, to pinch, to steal.

1990 V. TUPPER & R. WORTLEY *Anthology of Prison Slang in Australia* (National Library of Australia, Pandora Archive): *Half inch*, rhyming slang for 'pinch', ie to steal or arrest.

half pie half hearted.

Australian English.

Also as *half-pied*. The term also appears in New Zealand, and the earliest evidence is from New Zealand. The adjective *half-pie* means 'halfway towards, imperfect, mediocre' (OED). In addition to this adjectival use, the term appears as an adverb meaning 'not fully, partially'.

Origin: Perhaps from Maori *pai* 'good'.

1967 *Whisper All Aussie Dictionary* in *Kings Cross Whisper* 35 p. 6: *Half pie*, anything or anyone who is half hearted in his pursuits, e.g. half pie mug.

1973 J. MCNEIL *The Chocolate Frog, The Old Familiar Juice: Two Plays* p. 116 (Glossary): *Half-pie(d)*, (colloquial), half-baked, dilettante.

1974 J. MCNEIL *How Does Your Garden Grow* p. 27: RADIO: I wonder who's kissing her now ... I wonder who's looking into her eyes. / Breathing sighs, telling lies. SAM: *(joining in)* Listening to her half-pied lies.

1990 V. TUPPER & R. WORTLEY *Anthology of Prison Slang in Australia* (National Library of Australia, Pandora Archive): *Half-pie*, half-hearted or equivocal. A half-pie attempt is one to which full commitment is not given.

2006 B. MATTHEWS *Intractable ... Life inside Australia's First Super-max Prison* p. 395: *Half-pied*, half-baked or shoddy.

2021 *Morning Bulletin* (Rockhampton) 1 April (online): Mr Steinberger said 'no one would want a half-pie explanation' at the coming meeting. 'If they haven't got the information, get back to us in two months' time with a proper analysis', he said.

half spot $50.

Australian English.

The term means literally 'one half of $100' (formerly £100). See SPOT.

1939 *Sydney Sportsman* 1 May p. 20: As Byrne's selections ran first and third he hadn't much cause for concern. He'd clean up more than one and a half spot on the race.

1945 S.J. BAKER *Australian Language* p. 109: £50, half a spot.

handle con someone.

Australian Underworld Slang.

The term means 'to subject someone to a confidence trick; to con'. This verb is not otherwise attested.

Origin: J.S. Farmer & W.E. Henley in *Slang and Its Analogues* (1890-1904) give *handle* 'to conceal cards in the palm of the hand, or up the sleeves; to palm'. This trick is probably the tradition reflected in the 1967 Australian quote (where the term is a noun), and probably lies behind the Parramatta Glossary verb.

1967 *Whisper All Aussie Dictionary* in *Kings Cross Whisper* 35 p. 6: Handle, a confidence trick.

handrush bustle someone into decision.

Australian English.

The term means 'to make an eager rush for' (see quote 1906), 'to urge someone to make a decision, to seal an agreement, etc., urgently'.

Origin: A variant of standard senses of *rush*, such as 'to make a rush for, to go for'.

1906 *Mt Leonora Miner* 10 January p. 2: The denizens from the shores of the Mediterranean are entering this State at the rate of 87 per month. ... Lucca oil, macaroni, and dungarees will be hand-rushed by the new arrivals.

1924 *Sydney Sportsman* 29 July p. 3 (The owner of a harness-racing horse that performs well in training but fails in races attempts to sell the horse off): A Tasmanian seeker after pacers was selected as a good scrap-heap on which to drop the failure. So a trial was arranged. After the stipulated mile had been thrown behind in better than 'twenty-five' the visitor was hand-rushed for his cheque.

1937 *Sun* (Sydney) 24 October p. 4: Such short odds are accepted because of the huge army of Australians who contract Gambling Fever at Cup time. They know little of horses and less of sane turf investment. With a huge volume of cash coming in from all over the continent bookmakers hand-rush them with prices so false that they amount to robbery.

hand up brief open and shut case.

Australian English.

This term refers to the process of a committal hearing in a magistrate's court, before a matter is passed on to a higher court. The process is explained thus:

2010 *Australian Law Dictionary* ed. T. Mann p. 281: *Hand-up brief* A brief of evidence in a matter that is proceeding by way of committal. If the defendant does not call for the witnesses to attend and give evidence, the defendant is committed (or discharged) on the basis of the written material in the brief, which is tendered ('handed up') to the magistrate. A hand-up brief must be served on the defence and supplied to the court before any form of committal can proceed. Hand-up briefs include signed statements of all prosecution witnesses, transcripts of records of interview, copies of photographs and details of exhibits, reports and any other evidence the prosecution intends to rely on at trial.

If there is no challenge, it is likely that the case, on the evidence of the prosecution's hand-up brief, will proceed directly to the higher court.

1970 *Canberra Times* 27 June p. 8: A tyre fitter ... was committed to the Supreme Court of the ACT on charges relating to the stealing of two cheque forms, and the forging and uttering of a cheque. A plea of guilty from Seed was accepted by Mr Dobson, after he read a hand-up brief relating to the offences.

2020 *Bendigo Advertiser* 22 October p. 5: Magistrate Patrick Southey found there was enough evidence in the hand-up briefs for their matters to be sent to the County Court.

haste stop immediately or you'll be sprung.

Australian Underworld Slang.

The term means 'stop, desist'.

Origin: Probably (see quote 1950) originating as a call to act quickly in order to avoid danger, and then becoming a call indicating danger.

1950 'Thirty-five' in G. SIMES *Dictionary of Australian Underworld Slang* (1993) p. 102: *Haste*, desist! (an urgent warning to cease illegal activity because danger threatens; originally it was probably an injunction by the *cockatoo* to hasten away at the approach of the law...).

1959 S.J. BAKER *The Drum* p. 118: *Haste!*, look out! Mainly used in criminal jargon. Whence, *haste it!* To cease some activity, equivalent of *Stop it!*

1977 J. RAMSAY *Cop It Sweet* p. 44: *Haste up*, desist.

head-puller a person who directs shop assistant's attention elsewhere while accomplice steals.

Australian Underworld Slang.

2005 R. & S. SADLER *Move into English* 2 p. 133 (online; in list of synonyms for 'thief'): Head-puller, hoister ... robber, shoplifter, sneakthief [etc.].

2010 A. SHAND *King of Thieves* p. 193 (Glossary): *Head-puller*, a team member who distracts shop assistants during a hoist.

healy trick to it.

Australian English.

The term means 'perform a confidence trick'. There are spelling variants for the term, falling into two groups: those with an initial *h-* (*heelie, healy*) and those without (*illy, eelie*).

The basic sense of this term as a noun is 'a confidence trick, a confidence trickster' (AND). The Parramatta Glossary's definition suggests a verb, but such a verb is not elsewhere recorded. There is some evidence of a phrasal verb *to whack the illy* meaning 'to carry out a confidence trick'. From these words comes the term *illywhacker* 'a small-time confidence trickster' (AND), a word that gained new life in Australian English when Peter Carey used it as the title of a 1985 novel (see quotes 1985 and 2013).

Origin: The term also appears in the expanded form *eeler-spee/eeler-spieler*, forms that probably derive from the Australian word *spieler* 'a person who engages in sharp practice; a swindler', with transposition of the two syllables. The word *spieler* comes to Australia via the US, and ultimately derives from German *Spieler* 'player, gambler, gangster'.

1941 K. Tennant *Battlers* p. 183: An illy-wacker is someone who is putting a confidence trick over, selling imitation diamond pins, new-style patent razors or infallible 'tonics', altering cheques by fraud from, say, £10 to £100. ... A man who 'wacks the illy' can be almost anything, but two of these particular illy-wackers were equipped with a dart game. The board had a steel back, so that the dart would drop off, unless it struck one of three or four holes, which had been liberally provided.

1943 S.J. Baker *A Popular Dictionary of Australian Slang* (ed. 3) p. 88: *Whack the illy*, to trick or take a person down.

1955 'Thirty-five' in G. Simes *Dictionary of Australian Underworld Slang* (1993) p. 104: *Heelie* (Corresponds to *eelie* recorded by both Baker and Partridge, but I heard it only as *heelie*), the ballast in loaded dice, the brake on the crooked roulette wheel, the pea in the thimble game; any contrivance geared to 'give a pat result'.

1967 *Whisper All Aussie Dictionary* in *Kings Cross Whisper* 35 p. 6: *Healy*, a confidence trick.

1983 R. Aven-Bray *Ridgey Didge Oz Jack Lang* p. 27: *Eely*, slippery confidence trick.

1985 P. Carey *Illywhacker* p. 245: 'What's an illywhacker?' ... 'A spieler ... a trickster. A quandong. A ripperty man. A con-man'.

2013 *Australian Financial Review* (Sydney) 25 January (Review Supplement) p. 7: To be a successful Australian is to be an illywhacker, diddling inexpert people out of their cash, charging them fortunes for routine services, from tooth-pulling to banking, forever inventing new ways to fleece them.

heavies detectives.
Australian English.

In the singular *heavy* the term means 'a detective'.

Origin: Either from *heavy* in the sense 'an important or powerful person' (GDS) or 'a person of the thuggish "bouncer" type'.

1967 *Whisper All Aussie Dictionary* in *Kings Cross Whisper* 35 p. 6: *Heavy*, a detective because they are usually built that way.

1983 R. Aven-Bray *Ridgey Didge Oz Jack Lang* p. 31: *Heavies*, detectives, tough criminals.

heavy peg close scrutiny.

Australian English.

The term means 'a very intent look, a close examination'.

Origin: See PEG for the origin of this Australian noun meaning 'a look'. *Heavy* is used here in the sense 'very serious, very intent'.

> **1972** *Contact: Parramatta Jail Resurgents Magazine* December n.p.: We gave all the cars a heavy peg as we progressed. ... A car parked in front of an alnight [*sic*] chemist was standing door open and key in the ignition, waiting patiently for an industrious thief like me.
>
> **1973** *Contact: Parramatta Jail Resurgents Magazine* March n.p.: The three lairs gathered at the foot of Bruce's bed and gave the sleeping Goldisocks a heavy peg.

he's elephants he's drunk.

General English.

The term *elephant's* means 'drunk'. This was originally British, recorded from the middle of the nineteenth century.

Origin: Shortened form of *elephant's trunk*, rhyming slang for 'drunk' (see quote 1912).

> **1912** *Sport* (Adelaide) 30 November p. 13: 'Stony' was elephant's trunk down Henley Beach the other night, and woke up next morning with a 'dark brown' taste in his mouth.
>
> **1948** *Smith's Weekly* (Sydney) 25 December p. 6: Crow had recently been sipping a few quarts of fourpenny dark, and was disgustingly elephant's.
>
> **1967** *Whisper All Aussie Dictionary* in *Kings Cross Whisper* 34 p. 4: Elephants, drunk. From elephant's trunk.
>
> **1984** J. MEREDITH *Learn to Talk Old Jack Lang* p. 24: Elephant's trunk, elephants, drunk.

high jump Quarter Sessions.

Australian Underworld Slang.

The term refers to a criminal court with powers higher than a magistrate's or local court but usually not as great as the Supreme Court (though see quote 1948). Compare with LOW JUMP. The term 'court of quarter sessions' is originally British and referred to 'a court of limited criminal and civil jurisdiction and of appeal, held quarterly before justices of the peace in counties' (OED). Cf. LOW JUMP.

Origin: Because the court deals with serious matters—more serious than the matters dealt with in the court called the LOW JUMP, and therefore likely to result in a more serious sentence if found guilty.

> **1944** T. Hartley in G. SIMES *Dictionary of Australian Underworld Slang* (1993) p. 118: *The high jump*, the High Court.
>
> **1948** *Sunday Times* (Perth) 30 May p. 3: Success of passing phony cheques lay in having some place to cash them. ... Small sums only bring false pretences charge. You miss the high jump—pardon—Supreme Court.

1950 B.K. Doyle *Australian Police Journal* April p. 114: *High jump*, Sydney Quarter Sessions. The higher court.

1968 J. Alard *He Who Shoots Last* p. 123: 'Did youse front da high jump?' 'Sorry to disappoint you, Red, but ours was only a minor offence'.

1973 *Contact: Parramatta Jail Resurgents Magazine* December p. 35: He had been committed to the 'high jump' because he had refused to 'nod the head' to the filthy 'load'.

1983 R. Aven-Bray *Ridgey Didge Oz Jack Lang* p. 31: *High jump*, criminal court.

1990 V. Tupper & R. Wortley *Anthology of Prison Slang in Australia* (National Library of Australia, Pandora Archive): *High jump*, court. Thus 'to face the high jump' is to go to trial.

history in dire straits.

General English.

The term, first used in the mid twentieth century, often appears in such formulations as 'he's history', and refers to 'a person or thing that is without a future, finished, or defunct' (OED), or 'in great trouble'.

1988 *Sydney Morning Herald* 10 February p. 1: If the Coalition parties can cite a Labor betrayal on the privatisation of public assets to prove the point that the ALP is no more than a right-wing Liberal Party wearing a Labor label, then the Hawke Government will be history.

2020 *Daily Telegraph* (Sydney) 18 May p. 16: A young man climbs scaffolding to gain entry into the Australian Museum in the early hours of the morning. ... While in there he takes selfies, one with his head in the jaws of a T-Rex skeleton. ... I wonder if he will resist the urge to post his pictures on Facebook and if his friends will dob him in. If so the police will pay him a visit and he'll be history.

hit the toe run, try to escape.

Australian English.

The phrase means 'to depart' (AND), 'to depart quickly, to escape'.

1967 *Whisper All Aussie Dictionary* in *Kings Cross Whisper* 35 p. 6: *Hit the toe*, to depart.

1979 *Bulletin* (Sydney) 28 August p. 64: We know who you are and what you are, we know where your family lives and where your girl friend lives. It wouldn't be a good idea to hit the toe.

1988 *Copspeak* (Australian Institute of Criminology) p. 34: *Hit the toe*, to escape, to run away.

1995 N. Ibrahim & M. Quinney *Glossary of Gaol Slang: Pentridge Gaol* (Unpublished Typescript ANDC): *Hit the toe*, run away

1997 *Herald Sun* (Melbourne) 14 November p. 36: Ronnie hit the toe, as they say, a step ahead of the police.

2016 A. Blunt *Wool Away, Boy!* p. 261: She made up lovey-doveys with me that night, and the next day she collared the loot from the cheque account and they hit the toe together.

hit yer kick your turn to shout.

Australian English.

The term means literally 'hit your pocket' and so 'it's your turn to pay (for a round of drinks etc.); pay up'.

Origin: See KICK for the meaning 'pocket'.

1955 *Jerilderie Herald* 1 September p. 3: Secretary, Harry Doyle would like to see all those chaps who have not, as yet, 'hit the kick' for the financial year. It costs you £1 per year, and I am sure you will all agree that it is 20/- worth well spent.

1972 J. O'GRADY *It's Your Shout, Mate!* p. 36: 'Listen Jim. Are you gunna stand there all bloody day lettin' us die of thirst? Hit the kick'. It was my turn to 'shout', so I 'hit the kick'.

1977 J. RAMSAY *Cop It Sweet* p. 45: *Hit the kick*, pay up; pick up the tab.

1996 J. BYRELL *Lairs, Urgers and Coat-Tuggers* p. xviii: He always was lightning quick to hit the kick when his shout came up.

2014 *Thirsty Work North* (Gladstone) 24 February p. 11: Rule 5—If somebody buys pork crackling, chips or beer nuts and you partake, you need to hit the kick for these too when your turn comes.

hock active homosexual.

Australian Prison Slang.

The term 'active' in the Glossary's definition refers to a man who performs the 'insertive' role in a sex act. AND defines *hock* as 'the active partner in a homosexual act or relationship'. Cf. CAT. While there is some early non-Australian use (see quotes 1961, 1972), recent use seems to be exclusively within the Australian prison system.

The Australian prison sense is distinctive because it is part of the construction of male sexuality within the prison system. It is usually assumed that the hock is not homosexual, or does not view himself as such, and that his masculinity is not under threat because he performs the active role in a sexual relationship. The role of the hock is explained in quote 1993, and in section 4 of the introductory material.

Origin: The origin may be in rhyming slang for 'cock' (see quotes 1961, 1972), and thence to 'homosexual', but that development is not entirely clear. Outside the prison system, and especially in early use, the term hock can apply to any homosexual—see quote 1953 where the emphasis is on effeminacy and the term is synonymous with 'queen'.

The 1906 quote, from a text dealing with crime in London, is very early, but it is not by any means certain that the terms *hock* and *dead bent* have sexual connotations. The text says that they are synonyms for 'common thief'. The term *bent* (usually as adjective) does not acquire the sense 'sexually unusual, homosexual' until the late 1950s. In the earlier period it means 'criminal'.

[**1906** O.C. MALVERY *Soul Market* p. 242: From her I learned much of the habits of our neighbours. Of course many things that she told me would be utterly impossible to relate, and can only here be hinted at. From her I learned that most of the men in the house were 'hocks' or 'dead bents', as she called common thieves. Nearly all of them had at some period of their lives 'done time'—that is, been in prison. ... Crimes of the very worst description were openly and sympathetically discussed, and one cannot help wondering why the authorities allow such a hotbed of sin to exist.]

[**1938** E. PARTRIDGE *Dictionary of Slang and Unconventional English* p. 1003: *Hock*, a man that goes with 'poufs'.]

1953 T.A.G. HUNGERFORD *Riverslake* p. 23: 'Used to call you what?' Murdoch demanded. 'Randy', Charlesworth said. 'I don't know why—my name's Mildred!' He simpered at them and minced down to the other end of the bench, a hand on one skinny hip. 'You flaming hock!' Murdoch scoffed.

[**1961** J. FRANKLYN *A Dictionary of Rhyming Slang* p. 152: *Hock*, cock, 20 C. usage is largely confined to the underworld. The reference is to the active member in a homosexual relationship.]

1967 B.K. BURTON *Teach Them No More* p. 85: 'Is that bloke a bloody hock?' Terry asked. 'As large as life, and red-hot too. ... He has already given me quite a lot of goodies that will supplement my disgraceful diet'. 'You mean he pays you for it?' 'At the moment, he is paying me for the hope of it'.

1967 *Whisper All Aussie Dictionary* in *Kings Cross Whisper* 35 p. 6: *Hock*, a masculine homosexual.

[**1972** B. RODGERS *Queens' Vernacular* p. 168: Hock, (*from* Cockney rhyming sl = cock) the homosexual man.]

1983 R. AVEN-BRAY *Ridgey Didge Oz Jack Lang* p. 31: *Hock*, aggressive homosexual.

1984 B. ELLEM *Doing Time: The Prison Experience* p. 20: And especially if you're a young bloke you notice the old hocks eyeing you up and down. In fact the second day I was here a bloke grabbed me in the cell and tried to rape me.

1984 B. ELLEM *Doing Time: The Prison Experience* p. 191: *Hock*, the person who takes the male role in a homosexual relationship; butch.

1993 G. SIMES *Dictionary of Australian Underworld Slang* (1993) p. 105: A *hock* is a prisoner who takes the active or insertor role in homosexual relations, i.e. fucks a *cat* or *queen* anally or is fellated by a *cat* or *queen*. The role of the hock is not seen by prisoners or guards as implying homosexuality in the person who assumes it, even though some hocks are undoubtedly homosexual; the prison ideology is that the hock engages in homosexual activity *faute de mieux* and because the behaviour is viewed as 'active' and so 'male', it does not involve the sacrifice of his masculinity. [*Ed.* The phrase *faute de mieux* means 'for want of a better alternative'.]

2003 J. KERR *Wanted: John & Lucy: Rescue by Force, Silverwater Prison, 25 March 1999* p. 58: Each night Killick's 'non-homosexual' hock cellmate would sodomise his 'homosexual' cat cellmate until the day the cat squealed and was transferred.

2006 B. MATTHEWS *Intractable ... Life inside Australia's First Super-max Prison* p. 395: *Hock*, the male role in a homosexual relationship in prison.

2010 R. HONEYWELL *Wasted: The True Story of Jim McNeil, Violent Criminal and Brilliant Playwright* p. 93: Known as hocks, the men playing the dominant role in the sexual relationship rarely consider themselves homosexual, at least not at the outset. Many were heterosexual on the outside but, as hocks in prison, were always scanning the exercise yard for an attractive young prisoner.

hoister shoplifter.
General Underworld Slang.
   The term was originally British, recorded in the eighteenth century, and used of various acts of stealing including shoplifting. See 1708 quote for the earliest British evidence, where the 'hoist' is the literal process of lifting someone up to break into a house through a window. Now used more widely.
   Origin: From the verb *hoist* 'to lift', 'to steal, rob' (OED).

   [**1708** *Memoirs of the Right Villainous John Hall* (ed. 4) p. 5: Hoisters, such as help one another upon their Backs in the Night-time to get into Windows.]

   1895 C. Crowe *Australian Slang Dictionary* p. 36: *Hoister*, shop-lifter.

   1967 *Whisper All Aussie Dictionary* in *Kings Cross Whisper* 35 p. 6: *Hoister*, shop-lifter.

   1983 R. Aven-Bray *Ridgey Didge Oz Jack Lang* p. 31: *Hoister*, shop lifter.

   1989 T. Anderson *Inside Outlaws: A Prison Diary* p. 148: *Hoister*, person who's a shoplifter or warehouse thief.

hoist the flag appeal against conviction or severity of sentence.
Australian Underworld and Prison Slang.
   See 1989 and 1990 quotes for the variant *raise the flag*.
   Origin: Probably a variant of the originally nautical phrase *keep the flag flying* 'to refuse to haul down one's flag and surrender; to carry on the fight; chiefly figurative' (OED).

   1975 *Bulletin* (Sydney) 26 April p. 45 (article on underworld slang): Now Pig, always the pragmatist, asks Gulcher why he doesn't fly the flag, that is, appeal to a higher court in the hope of having the sentence reduced.

   1989 T. Anderson *Inside Outlaws: A Prison Diary* p. 146: *Flag*, appeal. To 'raise the flag' means to lodge an appeal against conviction and/or sentence.

   1990 V. Tupper & R. Wortley *Anthology of Prison Slang in Australia* (National Library of Australia, Pandora Archive): *Flag*, as in 'to raise the flag', ie to appeal one's sentence.

hoon man who lives off worker.
Australian English.
   The term means 'a man who manages a prostitute; a pimp' (AND). See WORKER.
   The word *hoon* has developed other senses in Australian English, including 'a lout, an exhibitionist' and 'a young hooligan, especially one who drives a car dangerously or at reckless speed' (AND). The earliest sense, however, is 'pimp'. In the 1915 quote Mrs Potter is accusing Leahy of being a pimp, and this was one of the common meanings of the Australian term *bludger* (used in the quote as a parallel to *hoon*) at this time.
   Origin: Of unknown origin. Suggestions have included: alteration of *hooer* 'prostitute'; alteration of *poon* 'a fool'; contraction of *hooligan*.

   1915 *Truth* (Perth) 23 January p. 2: In his defence, Leahy said he was a cab-driver, and he did not live with Rosa. He just called in that evening to see her as he was going to get his cab. Mrs. Potter saw him and called him a bludger and a 'hoon'.

1967 *Whisper All Aussie Dictionary* in *Kings Cross Whisper* 35 p. 6: *Hoon*, a male living partly or fully on the earnings of prostitution.

1971 J. McNeil *The Chocolate Frog* in *The Chocolate Frog, The Old Familiar Juice: Two Plays* (1973) p. 48: 'E's a hoon! A weak mug that bludges beer money off weak molls!!! ... The right name is egg-and-spoon, ain't it, Shirk? Yer a terry-toon, a blue-moon ... anythin' that rhymes with weak-bludger-hoon!

1973 J. McNeil *The Chocolate Frog, The Old Familiar Juice: Two Plays* p. 116 (Glossary): *Hoon*, (colloquial), pimp, one who lives off the earnings of prostitutes.

1980 M. Williams *Dingo!* p. 59: The Yanks were still there but the girls had a whisper that the American Army was shifting to Brisbane. The brothels would go with them. Bill thought we should follow the girls. 'We can be hoons, mate!' he laughed. 'A couple of Terry toons!' I didn't say much, there was a stigma to being a bludger, living off the proceeds.

1984 B. Ellem *Doing Time: The Prison Experience* p. 191: *Hoon*, a general term of insult; means the same as pimp or ponce.

1990 V. Tupper & R. Wortley *Anthology of Prison Slang in Australia* (National Library of Australia, Pandora Archive): *Hoon*, technically a pimp, but now a general expression of insult denoting a loutish person or yahoo.

1995 A.S. Smith *Catch and Kill Your Own* p. 19: He was a hoon or a bludger, call it what you like. No name could change the stigma that goes with being a person who lives off the earnings of prostitution.

hotpoint put something over someone.

Australian English.

This is a variant of Australian *point* 'to take unfair advantage of a person, situation, etc.; to do this by not carrying out one's share of work, by being lazy, etc.' (AND).

Origin: Probably from such phrases as *to get points on* 'to gain an advantage over (a rival)' (OED 1880) and *to score a point* (or *points*) *off* 'to gain a triumph over, to make a point at the expense of' (OED 1884), although these are attested later than the first Australian evidence for *point*. *Hot* has been added to the original *point* and probably acts as an intensifier.

Hotpoint is listed in the jail glossary at quote 1950 as a variant of *point*. The 1853 and 1941 quotes show early uses of *point* in Australian English.

1853 H.B. Jones *Adventures in Australia* p. 216: Doubtless, as the colony advances, this spirit of 'pointing' will disappear, and a fair legitimate system of trading and commerce will be introduced.

1941 S.J. Baker *A Popular Dictionary of Australian Slang* p. 55: *Point*, to take an unfair advantage of a person, to loaf, to impose on.

1950 'Thirty-five' in G. Simes *Dictionary of Australian Underworld Slang* (1993) p. 156: *Point*, to take another by trickery: to *hot point*, a *pointer*, or *hot pointer*, *pointing* or *hot pointing*.

howya travellin'? how are you fixed for money.

Australian English.

Origin: A variant of the phrase *how are you faring*, and more specifically of the Australian phrase *how are you holding* meaning 'are you in possession of funds/money'.

> **1926** *Dungog Chronicle* 4 June p. 5: I once heard of a scientist who also was bent on attaining a lofty vision, and with this purport in view, was known to have ascended to the top of a New York skyscraper, bent on getting a better view of things, but in his eagerness to do so, toppled over the parapet, and began his long fall to the ground — during his flight, a young man on one of the lower stories called out 'How are you travelling?' 'Goodo' replied the scientist — but then what a sorry mess he presented when he had struck rock bottom, and so with the WEA's local meetings; up to the present they appear to be travelling well, but possibly, if they decide to permit Mr Martin to meet me in debate they, too, will strike rock bottom in the shape of truth extant in and culled from the Bible. [*Ed.* The abbreviation *WEA* stands for 'Workers' Educational Association'.]
>
> **2014** T. Penna *Rich Man's Justice* p. 83: Max poured him a beer and stretched out his hand. 'G'day Darcy. How ya' travellin', mate?' Stapleton smiled and shook his hand. 'Good, Maxxy, yourself?'

in & out like a honeymoon prick said of short termer who repeatedly comes to gaol.

Australian Prison Slang.

GDS cites *in and out like a fiddler's elbow* for rapid and enthusiastic copulation. With the honeymoon prick, the most common collocation is *stiffer than a honeymoon prick*. Other variants include *up and down like a honeymoon prick* and *in there like a honeymoon prick*. A variant of the Glossary's formulation, *in and out like a honeymoon dick*, appears on an Australian Twitter site (see quote 2018).

> **2018** @peppers_ghost in *twitter.com* 25 August: Telstra signal is in and out like a honeymoon dick tonight!!

in smoke hiding from police.

Australian Underworld Slang.

Specific use (i.e. in application to police) of Australian *in smoke* meaning 'in hiding' (AND). It is also used in Britain (OED records 1938), but it is recorded earliest in Australia and is chiefly used in Australia.

> **1907** *Sunday Times* (Perth) 13 January p. 1: They say ... That a wanted embezzler isn't far away from Perth. That he is 'in smoke' at a well known chateau d'amour.
>
> **1962** *Northern Territory News* (Darwin) 9 January p. 1: Gone into hiding. He remained 'in smoke' until late this morning.
>
> **1968** F. Rose *Australia Revisited* p. 269: *Smoke* (*in smoke*), to disappear from surveillance, usually from police surveillance.
>
> **1983** R. Aven-Bray *Ridgey Didge Oz Jack Lang* p. 32: *In smoke*, hiding out.

jacks detectives.
General English.
Jack means 'a policeman or detective' (OED). Originally British but now used widely.

Origin: Perhaps a specific use of 'the male forename *Jack* ... applied in a wide range of general and specific contexts' including 'a representative of the common or ordinary people' (OED).

> **1919** W.H. Downing *Digger Dialects* p. 29: *Jack*, a military policeman.
>
> **1944** T. Hartley in G. Simes *Dictionary of Australian Underworld Slang* (1993) p. 113: *The Jacks*, the police.
>
> **1967** *Whisper All Aussie Dictionary* in *Kings Cross Whisper* 35 p. 6: *Jack*, a detective.
>
> **1968** J. Alard *He Who Shoots Last* p. 139: A carload of jacks picked me up one day as I wuz walkin' down da street.
>
> **1989** T. Anderson *Inside Outlaws: A Prison Diary* p. 148: *Jack*, police-detective; plain clothes cop.
>
> **1995** N. Ibrahim & M. Quinney *Glossary of Gaol Slang: Pentridge Gaol* (Unpublished Typescript ANDC): *Jacks*, police.
>
> **2006** B. Matthews *Intractable ... Life inside Australia's First Super-max Prison* p. 395: *Jacks*, detectives.

jerry realize.
Australian English.
The term means 'to understand, to realise' (AND). A phrase *to be jerry to* (containing an adjectival *jerry*) meaning 'to be aware of, to understand' is the earliest Australian evidence (see quotes 1893 and 1894), and this also appears in the US from 1894 (see quote 1894 in square brackets). The first Australian evidence for *jerry* by itself is 1919. In all, the American evidence is primarily *jerry to*, while the Australian evidence is primarily *jerry*. It is not clear if the term originated in Australia or America.

Origin: Of unknown origin.

> **1893** *Ballarat Star* 11 May p. 4: A horse which has been running at the unregistereds was rung into a race at Bacchus Marsh under another monica. He was artistically painted, but the 'gaff' was blown, and several of the 'heads' who had 'jerried' to the 'ring' were ready and waiting to have a bit on the second.
>
> **1894** J.W. Longford *Under Lock and Key* p. 12: The bearer of this stiff has been a good kobber of mine in stir, and as he jerrys to the lingo in this stiff, he will be able to explain everything.
>
> [**1894** T.A. Doring in L. Zwilling *TAD Lexicon* (1993) p. 50 (cited from GDS): He pulled off a ball in New York a little while ago and oney the big guys dere was 'jerry' to it.]
>
> **1919** *Aussie: Australian Soldiers' Magazine* February p. 15: As for decorations ... he was heard to remark that if his pals heard of his getting one they were to jerry that there had been a comb-out and that he had been unlucky.
>
> **1950** B.K. Doyle *Australian Police Journal* April p. 116: *Jerry*, to be awake to.

1967 *Whisper All Aussie Dictionary* in *Kings Cross Whisper* 35 p. 6: *Jerry*, to be awake up. From the prophet Jeremiah who knew all.

1972 J. McNeil *The Old Familiar Juice* in *The Chocolate Frog, The Old Familiar Juice: Two Plays* (1973) p. 71: Yer must be a nice *dunce* if yer can't jerry what we're talking about.

1989 T. Anderson *Inside Outlaws: A Prison Diary* p. 148: *Jerry*, to twig, to catch on, to understand.

1995 N. Ibrahim & M. Quinney *Glossary of Gaol Slang: Pentridge Gaol* (Unpublished Typescript ANDC): *Gerry to it*, understand.

2006 B. Matthews *Intractable ... Life inside Australia's First Super-max Prison* p. 121: By the time The Foot jerried that the gate wasn't open, it was too late. He bounced off the steel gate with one almighty groan.

jigger gaol made crystal set (illegal).
Australian Prison Slang.

The term means 'an improvised radio receiver' (AND).

Origin: Specific use of *jigger/jig* as used in General English for a variety of mechanical devices, all probably deriving ultimately from the dance called the *jig*, and its related movements. OED comments on *jig*: 'A name variously applied in different trades to mechanical contrivances and simple machines for performing acts or processes'.

1944 T. Hartley in G. Simes *Dictionary of Australian Underworld Slang* (1993) p. 115: *Jigger*, a crystal set. Although strictly prohibited there are many jiggers in the gaols. They are prison made from odd scraps of wire, wood & so on that are found within the institution & are very compact so that they can be concealed in the false bottom of a syrup tin, loaf of bread, the heel of a boot, camphorated chalk tin and so on. The crystal set is made from lead (pinched from the damp coursing on the buildings) & sulphur (from the hospital) fused by melting them together.

1953 K. Tennant *The Joyful Condemned* p. 293: He was offered ... a wireless concealed in the false bottom of a treacle tin, a beautiful job, the coil wire being part of an old scrubbing-brush, and most of the rest stolen from the fuse-box outside the cell. A complete jigger such as this was worth at least five pounds money, or forty-eight ounces of tobacco.

1967 B.K. Burton *Teach Them No More* p. 155: We could make jiggers right under the noses of the screws.

1983 R. Aven-Bray *Ridgey Didge Oz Jack Lang* p. 32: *Jigger*, illegal gaol radio.

1990 V. Tupper & R. Wortley *Anthology of Prison Slang in Australia* (National Library of Australia, Pandora Archive): *Jigger*, an illicit prison-built radio. A dated term since prisoners are now generally permitted to purchase radios and televisions.

joint concealable firearm.
General Underworld Slang.

The term was originally American English for 'a pistol' from the 1940s.

Origin: Of unknown origin. From the 1930s *joint* is variously used in the US for such objects as the penis, a syringe, and a marijuana cigarette.

1967 *Whisper All Aussie Dictionary* in *Kings Cross Whisper* 35 p. 6: *Joint*, a revolver or a hand gun.

jump shop-counter.

Australian English.

The earliest sense is 'the bar of a hotel' (see quote 1901), and soon after it refers to any counter in a shop or other commercial premises such as a bank. From the 1970s onwards it is also recorded in Britain.

In the 1983 quote the term has been transferred to the person who works behind the counter.

Origin: Of unknown origin.

1901 *Reporter* (Box Hill) 15 November p. 2: On Monday evening at Ringwood a band of larrikins from Collingwood and Richmond, who had had a good old time at the races in the afternoon, proceeded to enjoy themselves by painting the town red, being apparently under the impression that they were outside the range of police interference. The unwelcome visitors, upon being refused drink at one of the hotels, thought they would take advantage of the fact that only ladies were in charge of the place, and got behind 'the jump' and proceeded to pull beer for themselves.

1912 *Sun* (Kalgoorlie) 4 February p. 7: There was a strong flavour of mulga humor about an incident that occurred in an up-country drapery recently. 'Gimme a pair of socks', demanded a tattered battler advancing boldly to the grave assistant behind the jump. 'Y' needn't roll 'em up', he continued, staying the tying up of the parcel, 'I'll put 'em on straight away'.

1943 *Mudgee Guardian* 1 March p. 3: Preserved pig, as far as Mudgee is concerned, is off the menu. Ask for bacon or ham at the shop, and you receive a wondering sort of look from the man behind the 'jump'. The story is that our American cousins are consuming all available supplies. We don't begrudge them their feed, but we do hope that their passion for pig will show a falling off.

1983 R. Aven-Bray *Ridgey Didge Oz Jack Lang* p. 32: *Jump*, one who works behind a counter.

1985 R.G. Barrett *You Wouldn't Be Dead for Quids* p. 185: The girl behind the jump knew who Les was and ... he had a fresh beer in front of him in about ten seconds.

1990 V. Tupper & R. Wortley *Anthology of Prison Slang in Australia* (National Library of Australia, Pandora Archive): *Jump*, the counter at which an armed robbery occurs.

jump the box give sworn evidence.

Australian Underworld Slang.

The phrase means 'to give evidence in court'. Some of the citation evidence below suggests that this refers to a person giving 'Queen's evidence', which is an accomplice giving evidence for the Crown (i.e. the prosecution) against his or her former associates in crime (see quotes 1973 and 1990), but others just refer to the giving of evidence, and one says it is giving evidence in favour of the accused.

Origin: The *box* refers to a 'witness box', and the phrase derives from the fact that one 'jumps' into the witness box.

1950 'Thirty-five' in G. SIMES *Dictionary of Australian Underworld Slang* (1993) p. 118: *Jump the box*, to give evidence (in the witness box).

1967 *Whisper All Aussie Dictionary* in *Kings Cross Whisper* 35 p. 6: *Jump the box*, to give evidence in favour of a charged person.

1971 J. MCNEIL *The Chocolate Frog* in *The Chocolate Frog, The Old Familiar Juice: Two Plays* (1973) p. 31: Yer lagged yer own mate, when yer jumped box 'n give evidence.

1973 J. MCNEIL *The Chocolate Frog, The Old Familiar Juice: Two Plays* p. 114 (Glossary): *To jump in the box*, to give Queen's evidence.

1990 V. TUPPER & R. WORTLEY *Anthology of Prison Slang in Australia* (National Library of Australia, Pandora Archive): *Jump the box*, to go queen's evidence.

1991 M.B. READ *Chopper 1: From the Inside* p. 112: A well-known criminal, Shane Goodfellow, gave evidence against me at my murder trial. Farrell and Pettingill and the one they call 'Bubble Brain' thought it was funny that he jumped the box against me.

Kate Lee tea.

Australian Prison Slang.

Origin: Rhyming slang. From the name of Kate Leigh (1881-1964), a Sydney brothel owner and drug trafficker. Not otherwise recorded as rhyming slang.

The *Australian Dictionary of Biography* (1986) summarises:

> In 1919–55 Leigh's main enterprise was the lucrative 'sly-grog' trade, induced by six o'clock closing. ... From her Surry Hills home she became an organized crime entrepreneur, supplying at extortionate prices the fullest available range of illicit goods and services, including after-hours drinking venues, sly-grog, prostitution, illegal betting, gambling and, from the mid-1920s, cocaine. Acquiring the title 'Queen of the Underworld', Leigh obtained loyalty and protection from a male network of gangsters, but often had to protect them and was adept with a rifle. ... Much of the press, ignoring her connection with organized crime, treated her as the kindly provider of a social service in a repressive era, against whom no real 'wrong-doing' was convincingly proved, and pointed to her wartime patriotism and generosity to the unemployed.

keep yer guard up be careful.

General English.

The phrase *keep* (or *have*) *one's guard up* means 'be careful; be alert to possible danger'.

Origin: Transferred from sports such as fencing and boxing, where *guard* means 'a posture of defence; hence, the weapons or arms in such a posture' (OED).

2000 M.B. Read *Chopper 9: The Final Cut* p. 32: Because of her warning I was able to keep my guard up with Charlie. If she hadn't I probably would have been led to my death by a man I considered my mate.

2011 L.J. MAULE *Treatment Needs of Violent Sex Offenders* (Uni. of WA thesis)

p. 181: The following quotes explain participants' current management strategies or feelings about prison officers. ... 'I don't have a problem with them all the time. They try to help you but you still keep your guard up. Some you trust more than others'.

Kentucky collection taken up, proceeds going towards payment of bail or defence counsel of crim arrested.
Australian Underworld Slang.
Specific use of an Australian term that means 'a collection of money for alcoholic drinks for a group, or for a good cause'.

Origin: The American term *Kentucky treat* (first recorded in 1879) is ironic as it usually refers to someone who drinks alone and therefore pays for his own drinks; in later use it is synonymous with the General English *Dutch treat* (again ironic: there is no 'treat' since the costs are shared equally). In Australia, a *Kentucky* (also *Kentucky shout*) could be money collected for drinks to be bought for a group (see quote 1944), but it could also be a collection towards a cause (quote 1943 lists both senses).

> **1922** *Cumberland Argus and Fruitgrowers Advocate* (Parramatta) 1 July p. 8: There is still an indebtedness of £24 15s, and, as the Progress Association was practically the responsible body in the movement, it is expected to liquidate the accounts. The secretary ... emphasised the point that something should be done. He stated that there was a sum of £12 15s in hand with which to meet the liabilities. After much discussion, the meeting decided to make a collection in the room. Mr Harold Watson characterised it as a 'Kentucky'. Members present each gave a couple of shillings, and by this means something in the vicinity of £5 was raised.
>
> **1943** S.J. BAKER *A Popular Dictionary of Australian Slang* (ed. 3) p. 45: *Kentucky*, a collection of money to buy drinks or to aid a person.
>
> **1944** P.C. NEASBEY *Blokes I Knew* p. 73: It was agreed that this should be the occasion for a celebration so we had a 'kentucky' (each man contributing to a general collection) and two of our number were commissioned to spend it buying beer at the canteen.
>
> **1948** *Daily Telegraph* (Sydney) 9 March p. 15: Women athletes Betty McKinnon and June Maston yesterday collected only £37 on the first day of their Olympic Games appeal. They are attempting to raise £1100 to enable them to compete at the Games in London. ... Mrs. E.F. Magee, team chaperon, said she was disappointed at yesterday's response. She added: 'I had hoped for an opening day's subscription of £150'. City Tattersall's Club members will have a 'Kentucky' on Monday to assist the drive.

key, the being declared an habitual criminal.
Australian Underworld Slang.
The key refers to 'a person given an extra period of imprisonment (in addition to the sentence for a specific crime) as a result of being declared a habitual criminal; a habitual criminal; the state of being a habitual criminal' (AND). Also as *key man* (see quote 1931).

Origin: With allusion to the phrase *to lock a person up and throw away the key* 'to commit a person to prison, esp. for life' (OED). In New South Wales, the Habitual Criminals Act (1905 and revisions) allowed an extra period of imprisonment to be added to the sentence of a person designated a habitual prisoner under the Act. See quote 1989.

1931 *Daily News* (Perth) 15 August p. 2: Another 'key' man ... Thomas Forbes an elderly man with an interstate police record was today declared an habitual criminal by the Acting Chief Justice.

1941 S.J. BAKER *A Popular Dictionary of Australian Slang* p. 41: *Key*, an habitual criminal.

1946 *Singleton Argus* 14 April p. 4: The 'key' is a well-known underworld description for an habitual criminal (other fancy underworld terms for the same thing are 'the twirl', and 'the gate', and 'the twist').

1950 B.K. DOYLE *Australian Police Journal* April p. 116: *The Key*, to be declared an habitual criminal.

1967 *Whisper All Aussie Dictionary* in *Kings Cross Whisper* 35 p. 6: *Key man*, a habitual criminal. From throwing away the key.

1989 T. ANDERSON *Inside Outlaws: A Prison Diary* p. 149: *The Key*, habitual criminal's sentence. Under the NSW Crimes Act, this may be imposed if a person is convicted three times or more of the same type of offence. It carries an additional sentence of up to seven years, with minimum remission, to be served consecutive to the sentence for the actual crime.

1990 V. TUPPER & R. WORTLEY *Anthology of Prison Slang in Australia* (National Library of Australia, Pandora Archive): *The key*, a sentence given to an habitual criminal or 'H.C.', usually seven years. Thus a keyman is an habitual criminal. This categorization is becoming obsolete.

[khyber see KYBER.]

kick pocket.

General English.

Originally British, and thereafter widely used elsewhere, especially in Australia.

Origin: Of unknown origin. In the plural, *kicks* was an early slang term for 'trousers' (first recorded 1699). This may be related to *kickseys*, a word for 'trousers' in the early nineteenth century (see quote 1812).

1812 J.H. VAUX *New Vocabulary of the Flash Language* in *Memoirs* (1819) II p. 183: *Kickseys*, breeches. ... Speaking of a purse, etc., taken from the breeches pocket they say, it was *got from the kickseys*. ... To *turn out* a man's *kickseys*, means to pick the pockets of them.

1847 *Bell's Life in Sydney* 20 March p. 2: About early hour, on Monday morning, the locality of the aforesaid crib, presented the usual scene of bustle and excitement compatible with all great sporting events, and the roudy land-lord was as busy as we could wish to see him extracting the loose pewter from the *kicks* of the heterogenious assembly of ball-em-offs, that crowded every apartment of the domicile, and who were taking the necessary stimulus to clear the gills for a good shout for their favorite candidate.

1892 *Evening News* (Sydney) 3 November p. 6: A young man named Samuel Benjamin was charged before Mr. C. Delohery, S.M., at the Central P. Court yesterday, with having stolen £5 in the dwelling of Sem Ting Ching, the money of Ah Man. When arrested by Detective Keating and Constable Rae he said, 'I've got it in my "kick"'. The officers found over £6 and a Newcastle steamer ticket on accused. In reply to Mr. Kempthorne, who defended accused, the detective stated that the prisoner did not say that the money in his 'kick' was his own.

1921 *Armidale Express* 18 October p. 8: In reply to Constable Arentz, defendant said he 'had a few pounds in his kick'.

1968 J. ALARD *He Who Shoots Last* p. 260: *Kick*, pocket.

1972 *Contact: Parramatta Jail Resurgents Magazine* April n.p.: Anyone lucky enough to leave here with $30 in his kick ... usually will be found at the florists, and the lolly shop, buying a bunch of flowers and some sweets to take home to his missus and kids.

1990 V. TUPPER & R. WORTLEY *Anthology of Prison Slang in Australia* (National Library of Australia, Pandora Archive): *Kick*, pocket. Thus, 'to have something in your kick' means to have some financial resources.

2015 P. DOYLE *The Big Whatever* p. 24: She pointed at the body on the floor. 'Mel, check his pockets'. There were three fat rolls of twenties in his kick.

kick a goal be successful.

Australian English.

The phrase means 'to succeed, to have a win'.
Origin: Figurative use of the sporting term.

1973 *Contact: Parramatta Jail Resurgents Magazine* June n.p.: However, with only thirteen dollars and twenty three cents to your sullied name finding a place of abode is no cinch. ... At last Billy kicks a goal.

1984 B. ELLEM *Doing Time: The Prison Experience* p. 191: *Kicked a goal*, gained something of advantage; something good has happened to the person.

1990 V. TUPPER & R. WORTLEY *Anthology of Prison Slang in Australia* (National Library of Australia, Pandora Archive): *Kick a goal*, to succeed or win some advantage. A prisoner who has gained parole is said to have 'kicked a goal'.

1994 M.B. READ *Chopper 4: For the Term of His Unnatural Life* p. 87: My legal team and I had a good chat in the cells. ... Even if I lose this it ain't over yet but, knock on wood, I might kick a goal this time around. Still, for some strange reason I am unable to properly explain, I believe that I will walk free again. I still do not believe that all is lost.

1999 M. PINKNEY *Great Aussie Slang* p. 135: *Kick a goal*, to have sexual intercourse.

2006 B. MATTHEWS *Intractable ... Life inside Australia's First Super-max Prison* p. 336: Brenton kicked a big goal on Works Release when he secured a job as a car salesman for Fury Ford at Ryde. Part of his job allowed him to drive home in one of the second-hand cars.

kick along with it not going to appeal.

Australian Underworld and Prison Slang.

The Parramatta Glossary sense (accepting one's sentence from the court) is a specific use of the more general Australian meaning of the phrase 'to accept adverse circumstances with equanimity; to put up with a situation'.

In the quotes below, all with prison contexts, the sense is the more general 'put up with the situation', although there is emphasis on accepting the sentence given by the court and making the best of the situation.

1950 'Thirty-five' in G. SIMES *Dictionary of Australian Underworld Slang* (1993) p. 121: *Kick along*, to get along nicely, especially under discouraging circumstances.

1980 *Woroni* 2 October p. 7: When I first got here I went on a hunger strike for six days. I was refusing to wear the overalls etc. etc. and protested my being here. However I spoke to prisoners here and they advised me that the best course of action would be to kick along with it for three months no matter how barbaric and brutal the conditions, and I'd get out. I was told this was the best course of action to take and I've been trying my hardest to keep a cool head here for three months. I've heard prisoners being flogged on a number of occasions.

1989 T. ANDERSON *Inside Outlaws: A Prison Diary* p. 149: *To Kick On*, to go along with. For example, 'He's kicking along with his lagging'.

1990 V. TUPPER & R. WORTLEY *Anthology of Prison Slang in Australia* (National Library of Australia, Pandora Archive): *Kick along with it*, accept the decision and make the best of it. Thus, 'to kick along with one's sentence'.

kick on better yourself financially.

Australian English.

The phrase *kick on* has two main meanings in Australian English: (1) 'To continue (esp. in spite of hardships); to maintain or gain momentum'; (2) '(Of a party etc.) to maintain or gain momentum; (of people) to continue drinking, partying, etc.' (AND). The Parramatta Glossary's 'better yourself financially' belongs to sense 1.

Some of the Australian uses of this phrase, in the emphasis on continuing in spite of adversity, are close in sense to the previous entry *kick along with it*. But the phrase can mean 'to move past adversity and be successful'.

1977 J. RAMSAY *Cop It Sweet* p. 52: *Kick on*, improve; keep going.

1983 R. AVEN-BRAY *Ridgey Didge Oz Jack Lang* p. 33: *Kick on*, have a bit of luck.

1986 R.G. BARRETT *The Real Thing* p. 116: Reg noticed a brand new BMW. 'Hey not a bad car you've got, Les. Shit, you've kicked on'. 'It's not mine, it's my boss's'.

1992 *Victorian Reports* (Supreme Court) vol. II p. xliii: A prisoner working in the cook-house was an old acquaintance of your immediate predecessor in the office of Chief Justice, Sir Henry Winneke. Addressing the minister, the prisoner asked, 'Who's this joker you've got with you?' 'Well, that is the Chief Justice', said Mr Houghton. 'No, he's not', said the prisoner. 'Winneke's the Chief Justice. I know him well'. 'This is the new Chief Justice'. 'Yeah? Well, what happened to Winneke?' 'Well, said Houghton, 'he's the Governor of Victoria now'. 'Struth', responded the prisoner, 'he has kicked on a bit, hasn't he?'

2002 *Australian Book Review* August p. 26: When Grant discusses his own life and his own family, it is clear to me that he, too, knows his place; and that he values his life as an Aboriginal person. Any question that he may be a 'traitor' just because he has kicked on is unnecessary.

2006 B. Matthews *Intractable ... Life inside Australia's First Super-max Prison* p. 396: *Kick on*, having enough money to make a new start.

kite newspaper.

Australian English.

In General Underworld Slang a *kite* is a 'dud cheque', and this sense is reflected in the Parramatta Glossary's entry for FLY A KITE. In Australia the term *kite* was also used for 'a newspaper' (AND).

Origin: Perhaps (see quote 1998) from the notion that a *kite* is a 'skyscraper i.e. something that scrapes the sky', with *skyscraper* as rhyming slang for 'paper'. Or perhaps, as with the suggested origin for the 'bad cheque' sense, that it is made of paper (and, of course, kites were often constructed from sheets of newspaper)—and, as GDS suggests, these are all things that might 'fly away'.

> **1919** V. Marshall *The World of the Living Dead* p. 36: The thick-set hold-up man hadn't seen a kite for close on three years, and didn't know nothing about what happened of late.
>
> **1932** *Sunday Mail* (Brisbane) 13 November p. 20: Some 'crook' wandering casually in might say, 'Piped anything in the kites?' The underworldly are diligent readers of the newspapers, and no activity in their environs is allowed to escape their notice. Such is termed 'piping the kites'.
>
> **1950** 'Thirty-five' in G. Simes *Dictionary of Australian Underworld Slang* (1993) p. 122: *Kite*, a newspaper. 'The Truth's a *hot* kite', i.e. its possession is dangerous because it's forbidden.
>
> **1950** B.K. Doyle *Australian Police Journal* April p. 116: *Kite*, normally, kite means a cheque, but in gaol a kite is a newspaper.
>
> **1972** *Contact: Parramatta Jail Resurgents Magazine* April n.p.: I've been reading the latest in today's kite.
>
> **1972** J. McNeil *The Old Familiar Juice* in *The Chocolate Frog, The Old Familiar Juice: Two Plays* (1973) p. 96: (*Pointing to where a paper is lying on Bulla's bed*) You can pass me up the kite if yer like.
>
> **1990** V. Tupper & R. Wortley *Anthology of Prison Slang in Australia* (National Library of Australia, Pandora Archive): *Kite*, a newspaper or racing guide.
>
> **1998** B. Thorpe *Most People I Know* p. 114: 'I saw in the kite that you got done? ... Sydney street slang was not only rhyming but sometimes double-rhyming. Such as the word 'kite'. A kite touches and scrapes the sky and is therefore a skyscraper, which rhymes with paper. So when Brendan saw it in the kite he read it in the newspaper.

[**kite** *see* FLY A KITE.]

knock murder.

Australian English.

In both Australian and American English *knock* earlier in the twentieth century could simply mean 'kill' (see Australian evidence in quote 1920, referring to the First World War). From about the middle of the century in Australian

English *knock* was often used in the narrower sense 'to murder'. American *knock off* followed a similar path, with earlier uses meaning 'to kill', and later narrowing to murder.

Origin: From specific General English physical senses of *knock*, especially *knock out* 'to stun or kill by a blow' (OED).

> **1920** W.H. Downing *To the Last Ridge* p. 177: 'Eat, drink and be merry as possible, for tomorrow we may get knocked', was the prevailing faith.
>
> **1967** *Whisper All Aussie Dictionary* in *Kings Cross Whisper* 35 p. 6: *Knocked*, to be murdered. Shortened from the American to be knocked off.
>
> **1974** *Sydney Morning Herald* 14 February p. 12: Sergeant Aldridge said McCafferty, while being taken to police cells on a holding charge had said: 'All right, I knocked the bloke at Canterbury. I knocked the bloke at Leppington and I knocked the bloke at Merrylands. I knocked all three of them'.
>
> **2020** D. Whish-Wilson *Shore Leave* p. 169: The idea that Tremain might be knocked because of his sudden wealth didn't appear to surprise him.

knock up bang loudly on cell door when in need of medical attention.

Australian Prison Slang.

The reason for the *knock up* is usually medical, but it may be prompted by other problems.

Origin: Specific use of General English *knock up* 'to arouse by knocking at the door' (OED).

> **1944** T. Hartley in G. Simes *Dictionary of Australian Underworld Slang* (1993) p. 125: *Knock up*, to hammer on the door of your cell in order to attract the attention of the warder on duty.
>
> **1978** R.J. Denning *Diary* p. 52: In this jail you've got to knock up for about an hour before a screw comes to your cell.
>
> **1989** T. Anderson *Inside Outlaws: A Prison Diary* p. 18: I recognised some of them from the Armed Hold Up Squad, here to add injury to injury by bashing and gassing those they'd already bashed and verballed. ... Drago downstairs, who has a heart condition, was gassed for knocking up to tell them to turn the urn off, as it had boiled dry.
>
> **2006** B. Matthews *Intractable ... Life inside Australia's First Super-max Prison* p. 9: That night a crim knocked up for the male nurse, claiming sickness.
>
> **2016** J. Phelps *Australia's Toughest Prisons: Inmates* p. 257: *Knock-up*, calling a guard to a prison cell by using an intercom system.
>
> **2017** R. Mann *Pentridge* p. 200: Slashing up was probably the favourite form of self-abuse, really common. Jeez, they made messes of themselves, shocking. You know, like most of the time, it was done in the cell. It wasn't done in front of people. They'd pill out [take a heap of pills], slash up, and knock up [bang on the cell door] to be taken to hospital.

kupie prostitute.

Australian English.

The usual spelling is *kewpie*.

Origin: Shortened form of *kewpie doll*, rhyming slang for 'moll i.e. prostitute'.

A *kewpie doll* is 'a chubby doll with a curl or topknot on its head, from a design by American R.C. O'Neill (1874–1944)' (OED), and the term appeared in the first decade of the twentieth century. In Australia the term was especially associated with fairs and shows, where kewpie dolls could be bought or won as prizes in sideshow alley. The Australian version of the American kewpie doll was often a fairy-like doll, surrounded by decorative fabric and attached to a long stick. This is the object referred to by the Australian writer Kylie Tennant in the 1943 quote, and referred to in the title of Ray Lawler's play *The Summer of the Seventeenth Doll* (see quote 1955).

1943 K. TENNANT *Ride on Stranger* p. 59: Outside the turnstiles, vendors vie for custom, waving gilded kewpie dolls on canes, dolls with skirts of tinsel or teased bright wool.

1955 R. LAWLER *Summer of the Seventeenth Doll* (1957) p. 7 (stage direction): The main decorative features are the souvenirs brought down by Roo on past visits. The most notable of these are sixteen kewpie dolls, wearing tinsel headdresses and elaborately fuzzy skirts, attached to thin black canes shaped like walking sticks.

1988 'BLIND FREDDY' *Australian Dictionary of Insults & Vulgarities* n.p.: Kewpie, rhyming slang; kewpie doll; moll, prostitute.

1990 T. THORNE *Dictionary of Contemporary Slang* p. 290: Kewpie doll, an excessively cute and/or overdressed or over made-up girl or woman. The original American Kewpie Doll (a trademark name based on Cupid) is a fairy-like baby. In Australia the name is used as rhyming slang for *moll* in the sense of a prostitute.

kyber arse.

General English.

The standard spelling is *khyber*, but the form without -*h*- is common. Originally British for 'the buttocks, arse, anus' in the form *Khyber Pass* (early twentieth century) and then often abbreviated to *Khyber* (from the 1940s). It was very common in Australia in the second half of the twentieth century.

Origin: Rhyming slang *Khyber Pass* for 'arse', abbreviated to *Khyber*. From the name of a pass between Afghanistan and Pakistan.

1967 *Whisper All Aussie Dictionary* in *Kings Cross Whisper* 35 p. 6: Khyber pass, posterior.

1971 B. HUMPHRIES *Bazza Pulls It Off*: I'm as dry as a kookaburras's kyber too.

1984 J. MEREDITH *Learn to Talk Old Jack Lang* p. 29: Khyber Pass, Khyber, the arse.

1985 R.G. BARRETT *You Wouldn't Be Dead for Quids* p. 108: Fair dinkum, Les ... I'd like to go over and shove that pool cue fair up that Pommy's fat kyber.

lag give someone up.

Australian English. Especially in Underworld and Prison Slang.

The term means 'to inform against (a person) with the object of securing arrest and imprisonment' (AND; see quote 1832 for the earliest evidence). In prison contexts in Australia it means 'to inform against (a fellow prisoner)' (AND). Both senses are included in the Parramatta Glossary's definition 'give someone up'.

Origin: The verb *lag* in the early nineteenth century meant 'to transport or send to penal servitude', and although the earliest evidence is from the Australian convict Vaux (see quote 1812), he is probably recording an established British sense. In Australia it then developed the extended senses noted above. The ultimate origin of *lag* in the sense 'to transport or send to penal servitude' is uncertain. In the sixteenth century there is some minor evidence of a verb *lag* meaning 'to carry off, to steal' (OED), but there is a gap of two centuries to the 1812 Vaux evidence below.

> **1812** J.H. VAUX *New Vocabulary of the Flash Language* in *Memoirs* (1819) II p. 185: *Lag*, to transport for seven years or upwards.
>
> **1832** *Currency Lad* (Sydney) 10 November p. 3: Morrison had uttered threats that 'if his master turned him in, he would turn *him* in, and lag him'; if he could not *lag* him right, he would do it wrong.
>
> **1911** L. STONE *Jonah* p. 48: I niver lagged 'im; s'elp me Gawd, I niver put nobody away to the cops.
>
> **1968** L.H. EVERS *Fall Among Thieves* p. 177: The rights and wrongs of 'lagging' (reporting fellow prisoners to the authorities) formed the sole topic of debate.
>
> **1971** J. MCNEIL *The Chocolate Frog* in *The Chocolate Frog, The Old Familiar Juice: Two Plays* (1973) p. 32: It ain't just any sort of maggot gets to be a dog ... only those that lag other people ... who co-operate with bastards in uniform ... see?
>
> **1974** R. ADAMSON & B. HANFORD *Zimmer's Essay* p. 31: Maitland also houses ... the laggers who would be killed if they were left among crims they had lagged upon.
>
> **1984** B. ELLEM *Doing Time: The Prison Experience* p. 103: Other prisoners ... asked ... whether I lagged this guy with the knife.
>
> **2001** W. DODSON *Sharp End* p. 82: They all talked the talk about not lagging on one another and refusing to give up their mates, but in 99 per cent of cases it was all bullshit.
>
> **2005** J. PRING *Abo: A Treacherous Life: the Graham Henry Story* p. 36: As I was starting the motorbike the police arrived to arrest me. I was taken to the station where I saw all my so-called mates, who had lagged me to the cops.

laggin' prison sentence.

British and Australian English. Especially in Underworld and Prison Slang.

Originally the term referred to a sentence of transportation, and then any prison sentence.

Origin: See LAG.

> **1812** J.H. VAUX *New Vocabulary of the Flash Language* in *Memoirs* (1819) II p. 185: *Lagging matter*, any species of crime for which a person is liable on conviction to be transported.
>
> **1871** J. BAIRD *Emigrant's Guide to Australasia* p. 33: I am not certain that every individual in two English Houses of Parliament would be the worse for a seven years' 'lagging'.

1950 B.K. Doyle *Australian Police Journal* April p. 116: *Lagging*, a stretch of imprisonment.

1967 B.K. Burton *Teach Them No More* p. 48: Back in the cells, Terry received the condolences of his fellow prisoners, who all thought that was a fairly long lagging for a first offence.

1979 L. Newcombe *Inside Out* p. 106: About six more prisoners made up the van load, some with brand-new 'laggings' (prison slang for sentences) and others remanded to a later date.

1984 E. Withnel *Australian Journal of Cultural Studies* 2 (November) p. 74: He learns early that the only way to survive is to become invisible, give the screws, psychologists, whoever, what they want, so that they will take their pet theories somewhere else, practise on some other poor bastard and let him get on with his 'lagging' (sentence—not to be confused with 'lagging' which means to inform).

2006 B. Matthews *Intractable ... Life inside Australia's First Super-max Prison* p. 142: My next-door neighbour in B Wing was Peter Macari who had achieved notoriety as 'Mr Brown' in the 1971 Qantas bomb hoax. It netted Peter $500 000 and a twenty-year lagging.

2018 P. Kennedy *Long Bay* p. 215: He had been on parole but had slipped up again on the outside and been locked away for a further 'lagging'.

lamp look.

General English.

The term means 'to look (at), to observe, to watch'. It was originally American English in the late nineteenth century.

Origin: From *lamp* in the sense 'an eye', recorded from the late sixteenth century.

1904 *Sydney Sportsman* 11 May p. 1: Looking him straight in the eyes, I said, 'What ruddy rot; here's your own card, and there's not even half a share shown on her in the May [Stakes]'. ... The principal looked rattled a bit, but came back with the answer 'Oh, that's a printer's error'. ... Still lamping him I said, 'What a memory you must have. I suppose you know how many shares were on each horse'.

1937 *Chronicle* (Adelaide) 14 January p. 61: She was a gem from the city bright lights. Life had got too garish, and she had taken a job up north. In fact, she was working for Baldock, at old Shenanikin station. Toby was a gonner from the minute he had lamped her. Love! It had struck the fool deaf, dumb, and blind.

1967 *Whisper All Aussie Dictionary* in *Kings Cross Whisper* 35 p. 6: *Lamp*, to look, to observe, to watch.

1971 J. McNeil *The Chocolate Frog* in *The Chocolate Frog, The Old Familiar Juice: Two Plays* (1973) p. 35: We've seen more'n you'll ever lamp.

1983 R. Aven-Bray *Ridgey Didge Oz Jack Lang* p. 35: *Lamped*, observed.

2002 R.G. Barrett *Mystery Bay Blues* p. 56: The bloke seemed friendly enough and he hadn't lamped Les from the fight at the hotel.

lampin watching.

General English.

See previous entry LAMP.

As late as 1930 this was reported in the Australian newspapers as a new Americanism:

1930 *News* (Adelaide) 19 November p. 6: American 'Slanguage' ... When a Bowery kitchen man can tell whether an onion should be skinned in the open or under water (to prevent tears) he is said to be 'a wise guy', because he 'knows his onions' and can tell their brand without 'lamping' (looking at) them.

lash to take the knock.
Australian Underworld Slang.

See TAKE THE KNOCK, which is defined: 'to cheat someone of his share, in part or whole'. The term can also mean more generally 'to fail to honour a debt; to fail to fulfil an obligation' (GDS). Often as *lash on*.

Origin: Perhaps from the legal term *laches*: 'Delay in asserting a right, claiming a privilege, or making an application for remedy, such as to bar its being granted. Also (in early use): negligence in the performance of a legal obligation' (OED).

1923 *Smith's Weekly* (Sydney) 2 June p. 21: It hurt me to cut up, even, with such a bungler, but he was working with me, and, as I thought, doing his best, so l never 'lashed' him.

1967 *Whisper All Aussie Dictionary* in *Kings Cross Whisper* 36 p. 4: *Lash*, to renege on paying a debt.

1973 *Contact: Parramatta Jail Resurgents Magazine* June n.p.: Billy would never lash on a debt.

1983 E. WITHNEL *Australian Journal of Cultural Studies* 1 (May) p. 85: How a crim gambles, loses, 'lashes' (refuses to pay) or pays, all tell something significant about him in the enclosed environment of the nick.

1989 T. ANDERSON *Inside Outlaws: A Prison Diary* p. 149: *Lash*, to welch on a debt, not to pay up.

1993 A.S. SMITH & T. NOBLE *Neddy: The Life and Crimes of Arthur Stanley Smith* p. 136: They didn't like my refusal, but I couldn't give a fuck one way or another. They didn't give up there. They conned my partner into doing it and he just lashed on them cold [*didn't pay police their share of the proceeds*]. So they charged him with armed robbery.

1997 M.B. READ *Chopper 7: The Singing Defective* p. 109: 'I just want me money. That slut Brown lashed on a three hundred quid bet.

2005 J. PRING *Abo: A Treacherous Life: the Graham Henry Story* p. 173: Cole was also involved in the Sydney drug scene in a large way. Cole had apparently got into debt with Sayers and then lashed on the money. This caused Sayers to hire Flannery, and I heard they killed him as he drove into his home.

2006 B. MATTHEWS *Intractable ... Life inside Australia's First Super-max Prison* p. 72: Earl was nineteen when he was sentenced to life for the gangland slaying of 22-year-old Robert Francis Dunn in a Granville carpark after Dunn lashed on the proceeds of a robbery.

leave posted stand someone up. Also not bail friend out.
Australian English.

The verb *post* means 'to leave someone in the lurch' (AND). It often appears as the past participial adjective *posted*.

Origin: Of unknown origin. Perhaps related to the phrase *left at the post* 'to be beaten from the start of a race or competition' (OED).

1967 *Whisper All Aussie Dictionary* in *Kings Cross Whisper* 36 p. 4: *Posted*, to be left waiting.

1973 *Kings Cross Whisper* 47 p. 3: Soon as his back's turned, Stalky does a bunk with the wife and leaves her old man posted.

1975 *Bulletin* (Sydney) 26 April p. 45 (article on underworld slang): There's no way he'll post you on the job.

1984 E. WITHNEL *Australian Journal of Cultural Studies* 2 (November) p. 70: Greetings and farewells are used whenever crims meet and separate, even if they are likely to meet minutes later, even when they work in the same workshops; to fail in this ritual would be to leave someone 'posted' (deserted, left behind without being told what is happening), leaving him to feel abandoned, treated with disrespect.

1993 M.B. READ *Chopper 3: How to Shoot Friends and Influence People* p. 169: I got pulled into several crazy ploys and plans, and got left posted, resulting in blood hitting the footpath.

2005 J. PRING *Abo: A Treacherous Life: the Graham Henry Story* p. 15: As I approached the main culprits with a gun in my hand held down beside my leg, Ned chickened out and took off, leaving me posted.

left for dead abandoned by friends.

General English.

The phrase *leave for dead* originally and literally means 'to leave someone behind because they are assumed to be dead or are going to die'. More generally it means 'to abandon or ignore someone or something'.

1953 S.J. BAKER *Australia Speaks* p. 171: *Left for dead*, a man who was ignored or sent to Coventry by his fellows was *left for dead*.

1999 *Hansard, House of Representatives* 18 October, vol. 230, p. 11,723: If ever there was a group of young Australians who were left for dead by the Australian Labor Party, it was those people who wanted blue-collar trades and apprenticeships. You left them for dead. You were meant to represent them in the parliament but, when it actually came to the allocation of the dollars and the policy vision, the sons and daughters of the working people of Australia were left for dead by the Australian Labor Party.

left handed drop giving information to a dog knowing full well the authorities will be told thereby reducing the chance of blame.

Australian Prison Slang.

The phrase appears in the evidence as both noun and verb. In the Glossary's use of the term the *left-handed drop* is a roundabout way of alerting authorities to an issue by using a known informer (a DOG), and thereby eliminating the possibility that you yourself might be accused of informing.

Origin: Probably, as suggested in the New Zealand quote 2001, from the traditional associations of the left hand with qualities such as 'sinister, underhand, devious'. The OED comments: 'Widespread historical cultural assumptions that the left hand was weaker and therefore inferior, and that use of the left hand as the dominant hand was to be disfavoured (or even regarded as unnatural), have informed many uses of the word *left*'.

1968 J. ALARD *He Who Shoots Last* p. 260: To drop a person is to inform on him. A left handed drop is to do so in a roundabout way.

[**2001** D. LOOSER *Lexicon of Boobslang in the Period 1996–2000* (thesis) p. 106: *Left hand drop*, to secretly pass information to prison authorities in an attempt to curry favour and get through one's sentence more easily. *Left hand dropper*, an inmate who gives the impression that he is a staunch and trustworthy member of the prison community, but secretly passes information to the prison authorities in an attempt to get through his sentence more easily (e.g. to gain perks, or to be considered for early release). As one inmate explains: 'On one hand they're making out that they're one of the boys, and on the other, they're quietly talking to the screws, dropping people in it'. (poss. an allusion to the left hand as associated with secrecy, deviousness and dishonesty.)]

2018 J. KNIGHT *Dictionary of Victorian Prison Slang* (online) p. 19: *Left-hand drop*, to intentionally, recklessly or negligently get another prisoner into trouble or alert the prison staff to something untoward happening but to appear to do so unintentionally. Example; 'Did he lag on him or was it a left-hand drop?'

leg-opener alcohol supplied to woman.

Australian English.

The term means 'an alcoholic drink given to a woman in the hope that it will assist in seducing her'.

1945 R.S. CLOSE *Love Me Sailor* p. 21: Ah ha! So de old man he giff her some leg opener, eh?

1965 L. HAYLEN *Big Red* p. 133: Shearers had been known to buy a bottle of Charlie's 'leg-opener' to knock off a sheila.

1979 *Age* (Melbourne) 23 November p. 20: My mother had told me that Pimms No. 1 cup was 'what they called a leg-opener'. I only dimly visualised what this could mean.

2015 *Weekly Times* (Melbourne) 6 May (Farm Magazine) p. 12: It started back in the 1980s when then emerging wine guru Wolf Blass released a cheeky sparkling drop for Yalumba with the perplexing name Rene Pogel. While it gained early praise, it was quickly whipped from the market when news got out the name spelled backwards read Leg Opener.

leg up assistance.

General English.

Origin: The OED points out that originally the term referred to 'an act of helping a rider to mount a horse, esp. by holding and lifting one of the rider's legs as he or she swings the other over the saddle. Subsequently also: an act of helping someone to climb up, into, or over a high object'. In this sense of 'climbing', the term often appears in newspaper accounts of robberies and prison escapes. In a transferred sense the term comes to mean 'an act of assistance or aid given in order to help a person improve his or her circumstances; a means of improvement or advancement' (OED).

The 1830 quote is an early Australian example of a literal 'leg-up' being used in a robbery. The 1869 quote is an early transferred use in the sense 'any kind of assistance'. The 1950 quote plays on the literal and transferred senses.

> **1830** *Sydney Monitor* 9 June p. 2: Horam got on a shed that joins the big store, and I handed the iron to him, which he put on the wall, the other part resting on the shed; this was put for Randall to get; I then went round and found Randall still lying down; I said have you got it; he said no, he had not seen it; I said it is on the top of the wall; he replied, I cannot reach it; he then gave me a leg up and I handed one bundle down.
>
> **1869** *Ballarat Star* 28 May p. 1: There are many rumors as to who is to be appointed Commissioner of Customs. It is thought that the first offer will be made to Mr Francis, who will refuse and give Mr Wilson a leg up.
>
> **1950** *Labor Call* (Melbourne) 7 September p. 3: It's really a big laugh the way people give you a leg up, the burglars say. There's almost always a ladder somewhere around the house. And once out of every few tries, you run onto someone who actually lets you in by forgetting to lock the doors and windows. Then, once you're inside, people make it almost too easy.

lemon   anus.

Australian English.

The term means 'arse, buttocks'.

Origin: Abbreviation of *lemon and sars* (or *lemonade and sars*), rhyming slang for 'arse'. 'Sars' is an abbreviation of 'sarsaparilla'.

The 1966 and 1995 quotes have the unabbreviated forms.

> **1966** P. Mathers *Trap* p. 238: Which left Rolf on his pat malone. Given, as it were, the lemonade and sars of the business mask.
>
> **1995** J. Blackman *Best of Aussie Slang* p. 120: *Lemon and sarse*, rhyming slang for arse ... you can be either sitting on it—or given it.
>
> **1996** B. Thorpe *Sex and Thugs and Rock 'n' Roll* p. 9: 'Her lemon! ... Her lemon and sarse my son! Her arse!', he said shaking his head and smiling, not taking his eyes off her.

lice ladders   sideburns.

General English.

The earliest evidence is Australian (see quote 1937). The 1967 Partridge quote is not given the regional marking 'Australian', and the 2017 quote is from an American text. The 1937 and 2018 quotes suggest that the term has been common in Australia, though social media evidence such as Twitter indicates it is used widely elsewhere.

Origin: *Louse ladder* has been a term for 'a dropped stitch in knitting or in a stocking' since the eighteenth century, from the jocular notion that it provides a ladder for lice. The sideburns sense (*louse ladders* or *lice ladders*) arose in the twentieth century, and derives from a similar jocular perception.

> **1937** *Bulletin* (Sydney) 17 November p. 8: Thither he strides, a geranium in his buttonhole, his left arm embracing an acre or so of chrysanthemums, his face decorated with tufty louse-ladders and the smile of the smitten.
>
> [**1967** E. PARTRIDGE *Dictionary of Slang and Unconventional English* ed. 6, p. 1232: *Louse-ladders*, side-whiskers: since ca. 1920.].
>
> [**2017** D. GUILLEN *In the Summer of My Life* (online): Carol's dad wore his hair quite full, with long, full sideburns in the style of the seventies. The British call them 'sideboards'. Carol's dad called them 'lice ladders'.]
>
> **2018** *Wordwizard* (online) 13 May: An interesting Aussie turn of phrase. When I worked at the silos we had a mate affectionately known as Louse Ladders. This described his sideburns perfectly.

lift steal.

General English.

The term was originally British (recorded from the sixteenth century), and is now widespread.

Origin: From the notion 'to take up (an object) ... with dishonest intentions' (OED). Cf. *shoplifter*.

> **1827** *Sydney Gazette* 21 December p. 3: While walking in the vicinity of Sydney, in 1822, I encountered a genteel dressed man ... who stared hard at me, as I did at him, each having some recollection of the other; till at last I remembered his working his passage home as a sailor only the year previous, in the ship wherein I had returned to England, with the view, as he had told me, of 'lifting a legacy'. He had in fact 'lifted the legacy',—been tried, convicted, and transported for it.
>
> **1898** *Daily Telegraph* (Sydney) 29 October p. 13: Poultry 'lifting' seems to be a nourishing and rapidly-growing business just now. Its votaries evidently find it more lucrative and less laborious than poultry-raising.
>
> **1948** I.L. IDRIESS *The Opium Smugglers* p. 2: 'I'll bet it's not his own horse he's riding', said Dick, laughing. 'You bet it's not', drawled a tin-scratcher. 'He's lifted it from some cattleman up north'.
>
> **1954** *Land* (Sydney) 24 December p. 18: The nightwatchman at Parkes Bros.' woolshed, near Tingha, one night last week disturbed two thieves trying to lift bags of wool from the woolshed.
>
> **1990** V. TUPPER & R. WORTLEY *Anthology of Prison Slang in Australia* (National Library of Australia, Pandora Archive): *Lift*, to steal.
>
> **2015** G. DISHER *The Heat* p. 41: Wyatt's only interest in sport was that he'd once lifted the gate takings at the MCG.

loaded framed.

Australian English. Especially in Underworld Slang.

From *load* (or *load up*) 'to frame (someone); to plant false evidence on (someone)' (AND). The Parramatta Glossary is the earliest evidence for the sense. The citations often use the *load up* formulation.

Origin: From *load* 'add weight to'.

1973 *Contact: Parramatta Jail Resurgents Magazine* December p. 35: Dawn broke … the trial today. … He fell to thinking about the 'Blue' … run of the mill, except—this time he had been *loaded*. And with a gun of all things!

1983 R. Aven-Bray *Ridgey Didge Oz Jack Lang* p. 35: *Loaded up*, evidence planted by police.

1988 *Copspeak* (Australian Institute of Criminology) p. 44: *Load*, to place false incriminating evidence upon or in the vicinity of suspect(s) in order to substantiate a criminal charge. Alternatively 'Load up'.

1989 T. Anderson *Inside Outlaws: A Prison Diary* p. 149: *Loaded-up*, framed with material evidence; for example, NSW Police regularly plant or (more commonly) simply produce drugs and other illegal items, in order to arrest and successfully prosecute suspects. So a person may say that evidence in his/her case is a load-up or that he/she has been loaded up.

1990 V. Tupper & R. Wortley *Anthology of Prison Slang in Australia* (National Library of Australia, Pandora Archive): *Load*, to falsely incriminate. Thus 'to be loaded up' is to be framed.

1993 A.S. Smith & T. Noble *Neddy* p. 104, 205: I took very little notice of them as I was assured that they would not load me [*plant evidence such as drugs*] by two friendly police. … The cunt will spear one of the younger guys in to load you.

1994 M.B. Read *Chopper 4: For the Term of His Unnatural Life* p. 96: I find it impossible to believe that Lockwood and Avon were incapable, due to lack of connections, of laying their hands on a real handgun or sawn-off shotgun to load up Abdallah, had they wanted to do so.

2005 J. Pring *Abo: A Treacherous Life: the Graham Henry Story* p. 224: As hard as they tried, these task force cops had no luck at all in trapping me and this made them get filthy on me. This was when they started to use dirty tactics to try and trap me, but every time they did, another cop who was on my payroll would tell me about it. Then I would go to the Internal Affairs police and make a complaint about what the cops wanted to do to me and this got them in the shit. It also saved my arse many times from being loaded up with fabricated evidence.

2006 B. Matthews *Intractable … Life inside Australia's First Super-max Prison* p. 65: Darcy was transferred to Grafton after the screws at Parramatta loaded him up with contraband: a ten-dollar note.

lob arrive.

Australian English.

The term means 'to arrive, especially without ceremony; to turn up' (AND). Often as *lob in*, *lob on*, *lob up*, etc.

Origin: Transferred use of *lob* 'to move heavily or clumsily; to walk along with a slow lumbering movement' (OED).

1911 *Bulletin* (Sydney) 17 August p. 14: I first lobbed on to the 'far Barcoo' … years ago.

1967 *Whisper All Aussie Dictionary* in *Kings Cross Whisper* 36 p. 4: *Lob*, arrive at a scene, such as a party.

1990 V. TUPPER & R. WORTLEY *Anthology of Prison Slang in Australia* (National Library of Australia, Pandora Archive): *Lob*, to arrive. As in 'to lob at a gaol'.

1997 M.B. READ *Chopper 7: The Singing Defective* p. 207: 'I wish Tex would hurry up', complained Brian. 'What if her bloody boyfriend lobs. He's in the armed robbery squad and he won't be too thrilled at this lot'.

2006 B. MATTHEWS *Intractable ... Life inside Australia's First Super-max Prison* p. 7: A couple of weeks later I was walking the OBS yard when Ray Smith lobbed from Parramatta.

lot, the life imprisonment.
Australian Underworld and Prison Slang.
Origin: Specific use of *the lot* 'all, everything'—the maximum length of imprisonment available. In early use it often appears as *the whole lot* (OED).

1918 T. MARSHALL *Jail from Within* p. 55: Till the completion of my sentence I worked as assistant to a comrade who was 'doing the whole lot', the head gardener of Goulburn Jail.

1944 T. Hartley in G. SIMES *Dictionary of Australian Underworld Slang* (1993) p. 135: *The lot*, sentence of life imprisonment.

1950 B.K. DOYLE *Australian Police Journal* April p. 116: *The lot*, life imprisonment.

1983 E. WITHNEL *Australian Journal of Cultural Studies* 1 (May) p. 90: The names of laggings are: Twenty years, or a Life Sentence: The Lot.

1989 T. ANDERSON *Inside Outlaws: A Prison Diary* p. 150: *The Lot*, life sentence. For example, 'He's got the lot'.

1990 V. TUPPER & R. WORTLEY *Anthology of Prison Slang in Australia* (National Library of Australia, Pandora Archive): *The lot*, a life sentence.

2006 B. MATTHEWS *Intractable ... Life inside Australia's First Super-max Prison* p. 128: Jimmy was doing the lot with Ron Pilley for the underworld murder of Sydney stand-over merchant Daryl Hooker.

low jump petty sessions (court).
Australian Underworld Slang.
The term refers to the Court of Petty Sessions (later known as a magistrate's or local court). Such courts began in Britain in the late sixteenth century, and they dealt with minor offences. In contrast with the HIGH JUMP.
Origin: Because the court deals with minor matters.

1944 T. Hartley in G. SIMES *Dictionary of Australian Underworld Slang* (1993) p. 118: *The low jump*, the Low Court.

1967 *Whisper All Aussie Dictionary* in *Kings Cross Whisper* 36 p. 4: *Low jump*, a magistrate's court.

1973 *Contact: Parramatta Jail Resurgents Magazine* December p. 35: He smiled as he recalled the scene at the 'low jump' when the gun was tendered.

[**lug** *see* BLOW DOWN THEIR LUG; GOT THEIR LUG.]

lumbered taken to police station.

Australian English. Especially in Underworld Slang.

Specific use of Australian *lumber* 'to arrest, to imprison; to punish judicially' (AND). Used elsewhere, but chiefly Australian.

Origin: The original *lumber* was a variant of *Lombard* 'a native of Lombardy engaged as a banker, money-changer, or pawnbroker', and *Lombard* came to mean 'a pawnbroking establishment'. The phrase *to put to lumber* meant 'to put in pawn or pledge', and *to be in lumber* 'to be imprisoned'. The pawnbroking senses began in the seventeenth century, and the transfer to the prison senses is first recorded in Vaux' Australian dictionary (see quote 1812). Vaux is also the first evidence for the verb: 'to deposit (property) in pawn; hence, to put away privily, to imprison, arrest' (OED).

1812 J.H. Vaux *New Vocabulary of the Flash Language* in *Memoirs* (1819) II p. 188: *Lumber*, to *lumber* any property, is to deposit it at a pawnbroker's, or elsewhere for present security; to retire to any house or private place, for a short time, is called *lumbering yourself*. A man apprehended, and sent to gaol, is said to be *lumbered*, to be *in lumber*, or to be in *Lombard-street*.

1827 *Monitor* (Sydney) 2 August p. 559: He was sentenced to be lumbered for six months; i.e. to go on the tread-mill every Saturday.

1882 *Sydney Slang Dictionary* p. 6: *Lumber*, to take or carry away to the lock-up.

1944 T. Hartley in G. Simes *Dictionary of Australian Underworld Slang* (1993) p. 137: *Lumbered*, arrested.

1967 *Whisper All Aussie Dictionary* in *Kings Cross Whisper* 36 p. 4: *Lumber*, to be arrested.

1975 *Bulletin* (Sydney) 26 April p. 44 (article on underworld slang): So I get lumbered and they ask a monkey not to oppose bail. [Ed. A *monkey* is '$500'. See MONKEY.]

1981 C. Wallace-Crabbe *Splinters* p. 65: Quit it, you stupid buggers, or you'll both get lumbered! They'll be getting the cops in any time.

2003 *Age* (Melbourne) 5 January p. 20: Chief oaf got lumbered for assault and wilful damage then, with parental bankroll of medical proportions, slapped the mayor with a civil case for assault.

lunatic soup cheap potent wine.

Australian English.

The term means 'alcoholic liquor of poor quality' (AND). A British variant is *lunatic's broth*.

Origin: From the notion that such alcohol is liable to send a person mad.

1913 *Argus* (Melbourne) 15 December p. 9: One witness (Constable Dunn) said that the wine was known in the district as 'lunatic soup'. In his evidence, he said that he often watched men go into the wine hall perfectly sober and come out mad drunk in a quarter of an hour.

1956 *Bulletin* (Sydney) 28 November p. 13: Next morning in court the magistrate asked what he'd had. Told that it was 'colonial wine', he snorted, 'Lunatic soup would be a better name for it'.

1986 *Transair* March p. 9: They went about destroying themselves with the lunatic soup crippling their larynx as surely as if they'd downed an economy size tin of paint stripper.

2014 *Sunday Mail* (Sydney) 6 July p. 82: While such restrictions may be seen as a simplistic answer to a complex problem, the reality is that there would be a lot of footballers in a lot less strife if they gave the lunatic soup a fulltime swerve.

mark boy

Australian English. Often associated with *Australian Underworld and Prison Slang*.

This is an abbreviated form of *Mark Foy*, rhyming slang for 'boy'. In early use sometimes referring to a younger romantic interest or sexual partner (see quotes 1912, 1929). In some later uses the term alludes to male prostitution, and in prison contexts it often carries the implication of being a possible sexual target of older prisoners.

Origin: Rhyming slang, from the name of *Mark Foy(s)*, a former department store in Sydney, trading from 1885 to 1980. Franklyn (see quote 1960) takes the term from Baker and without justification attributes the name to a London firm, and this is repeated in Dodson & Saczek's 1972 *Dictionary of Cockney Slang and Rhyming Slang* (see quote).

1912 *Sport* (Adelaide) 13 July p. 14: They Say ... Mum caused jealousy when she left the dance with her Mark Foy. Little Bill has done his chance.

1929 *Truth* (Sydney) 3 March p. 15: When Mrs Yard admitted him to the passage, Yard came up, he went on and said, 'Ah, here's your Mark Foy is it?' 'He meant', said Ryan, 'that I was his wife's fancy boy, and I had come to see her. I said to him, I have nothing to do with Mrs. Yard. I came to see your daughter, Doris'.

1939 *Smith's Weekly* (Sydney) 11 November p. 15: To fellow confidence men and the police he is known as 'the Mark Foy', rhyming slang for 'the boy'; because when he first began to 'work the tubs' (card-sharp on passenger liners) he was remarkably youthful in appearance and he found it useful to dress as a college youth with an elderly accomplice as his 'guardian'.

1947 *Sydney Morning Herald* 8 March p. 13: 'How'd you do?' Meg asked him. 'Up the pole. I lost another hundred to-day'. She whistled. 'Jeez, are you in a bad way! What're you going to do? 'What d'you think I can do. Sing on street-corners?' 'You might go to work instead of hanging round here all the week'. 'Yeah, that'd solve everything. Know any jobs where they pay a hundred quid a week? The name's McCoy, not Mark Foy'.

1950 'Thirty-five' in G. Simes *Dictionary of Australian Underworld Slang* (1993) p. 138: *Mark Foy*, a boy (rhyming slang which gains added point in that the *mark* suggests the target of the predatory homosexual).

1954 *Argus* (Melbourne) 23 September p. 22: It was The Brain who first brought Coates—'The Mark Foy'—to my game. Coates was very elegantly dressed, smoked a big cigar. He had a very engaging personality. He talked like a high-pressure salesman, with an unlimited vocabulary. He had a real boyish face (the nickname 'Mark Foy' is Underworld slang for boy). I thought he was very well named, and liked him.

[**1961** J. Franklyn *A Dictionary of Rhyming Slang* p. 95: *Mark Foy*, boy, 20 C. Recorded by Sidney J. Baker in *A Popular Dictionary of Australian Slang*, 1943. ... The term is clearly of Cockney origin, being based on the name of a firm of cartage contractors who functioned in the London area in late 19 C. to early 20 C.]

[**1972** M. Dodson & R. Saczek *A Dictionary of Cockney Slang and Rhyming Slang* p. 33: *Mark Foy*, boy (Australian only, but of cockney origin). (Mark Foy was a London haulage contractor.)]

1983 R. Aven-Bray *Ridgey Didge Oz Jack Lang* p. 36: *Mark Foy*, boy.

1990 V. Tupper & R. Wortley *Anthology of Prison Slang in Australia* (National Library of Australia, Pandora Archive): *Mark Foy*, rhyming slang for boy.

1996 B. Thorpe *Sex and Thugs and Rock 'n' Roll* p. 263: This was Mick's variation on the way a lot of the Crossie boys, or 'Mark Foys' as they were known on the street, dressed.

1999 *Ralph* March p. 21: If someone puts it on you, it's best to stand up for yourself. Otherwise you could become someone's Mark Foy (boy). When an inmate becomes another prisoner's boy, he's subject to regular rapes until he 'comes across to the other side'.

2019 A. Kaladelfos & Y. Smaal 'Sexual Violence and Male Prisons' *Current Issues in Criminal Justice* 31 p. 353: The word 'Mark' is noteworthy given its use by supposedly rapacious homosexuals to identify and target young male inmates as possible partners.

mocker clothes.

Australian English.

The term means 'clothing, attire, dress'. The term also appears in New Zealand, with records earlier than Australia. A collection of New Zealand army sayings from a text dated 1939–45 has 'grouse mocker—Best clothes (also Groppi mokka)' and there is another record from 1947 (*Dictionary of New Zealand English*).

Origin: Of unknown origin. Perhaps from Arabic *makwa*, noun of place, from *kawa* 'to press (clothes)', associated with Egyptian clothes-pressing establishments during the First World War, and thence used by New Zealand soldiers (OED, *Dictionary of New Zealand English*). Groppi (in the New Zealand quote above) was a Cairo tea-shop and hotel.

1953 S.J. Baker *Australia Speaks* p. 106: *Mocker*, clothes in general.

1967 *Whisper All Aussie Dictionary* in *Kings Cross Whisper* 36 p. 4: *Mocker*, clothing.

1979 D.R. Stuart *Crank Back on Roller* p. 214: 'Snow is a hell to all of them if they're not clothed and fed'. ... 'Well, we're right ... we've got good mocker, good boots, the lot'.

1984 E. Withnel *Australian Journal of Cultural Studies* 2 (November) p. 62: A strong emphasis on good 'mocka' ('boob' or prison clothing) is also vital here. ... Thus the crim endeavours to 'rort' (barter, exchange, undermine the rules) new mocka: shoes made up in the prison bootshop; clothing from the tailor shop; belt from the bootshop; underwear from the laundry.

mod squad plain clothes screws who handle shanghais.
Australian Prison Slang.

The term is used to describe warders who transfer troublesome prisoners from one prison to another (see SHANGHAI). Such warders were also used to control riots.

Origin: Perhaps because these officials do not wear the warders' usual uniforms this could be an ironic reference to the American police TV show *The Mod Squad* (1968-73), where the three undercover cops wore 'hippie' clothes etc.

> **1976** *National Times* (Sydney) 19 April p. 5: Each of the four prisoners were transferred to Parramatta Jail by members of the Special Operations Division, an elite specially trained group answerable directly to Commissioner McGeechan and who are known derisively to many other officers as the Mod Squad.
>
> **1989** T. ANDERSON *Inside Outlaws: A Prison Diary* p. 150: *Mod Squad*, another name for MEU or CEU. [*Ed.* Anderson's entry for *MEU* reads: 'Malabar Emergency Unit or The Squad. Group of screws armed with mace gas, guns and batons; said to be trained to put down "disturbances"—actually a refuge for many thugs ready to seize an opportunity to brutalise and shanghai prisoners'. The entry for *CEU* reads: 'Central Emergency Unit of The Squad. Similar function to MEU but operates in Parramatta Jail and Silverwater Complex'.]

monkey $500.
General English.

The term originally meant £500, and after decimalisation in Australia (1966) it became $500.

Origin: Of unknown origin. In the 1861 quote the 'gorilla' is £1000, so perhaps the monkey is the 'smaller amount'. Even so, while there is some later evidence for this sense of 'gorilla', it is not as common as the 'monkey'.

> **1861** *Bell's Life in Victoria* 17 August p. 3: Lord Dudley, who seldom has more than one bet on the Derby, and never less than a 'monkey', offered to take three 'gorillas' about Dundee.
>
> **1889** *Dead Bird* (Sydney) 28 September p. 2: Mr Campbell Praed ... has sued Mr Graham ... for £500 damages. ... Mr Graham had to part up a 'monkey'.
>
> **1950** B.K. DOYLE *Australian Police Journal* April p. 116: Monkey, £500.
>
> **1975** *Bulletin* (Sydney) 26 April p. 44 (article on underworld slang): So I get lumbered and they ask a monkey not to oppose bail. No monkey, they say, and no way I get bail.
>
> **1990** V. TUPPER & R. WORTLEY *Anthology of Prison Slang in Australia* (National Library of Australia, Pandora Archive): *Monkey*, five hundred dollars.
>
> **2010** A. SHAND *King of Thieves* p. 15: And if a copper began to get too interested, they would just slip him 'a monkey' (500 quid).
>
> **2017** S. GREENALL *Winter Traffic* p. 29: And money. How's it work? Lap dance for a couple of hundred, head job for a monkey? What's the damage for a root?

moosh hominy (gaol breakfast).
American and Australian Prison Slang.

The term refers to 'jail food, especially porridge' (AND). It is spelt *moosh* or *mush*, and pronounced as 'mush' in the US and 'moosh' in Australia.

Origin: Probably an alteration of *mash* 'bran, meal, or the like mixed with hot water'.

1936 *Queenslander* (Brisbane) 2 July p. 4: Come, fill your mug, and in your well-swept 'peter' sing / And with your 'mush' digest this fact—you've had your fling!

1945 S.J. BAKER *Australian Language* p. 141: Jail food is *moosh*.

1950 B.K. DOYLE *Australian Police Journal* April p. 116: *Moosh*, gaol porridge.

1967 B.K. BURTON *Teach Them No More* p. 17: Moline took his plate back to his cell, where he pushed his unwilling spoon into glutinous material. The food resisted the spoon's assault. 'What's this muck?' 'That's mush', Ted explained.

1967 *Whisper All Aussie Dictionary* in *Kings Cross Whisper* 36 p. 4: *Mush*, pronounced moosh, prison porridge.

1974 R. ADAMSON & B. HANFORD *Zimmer's Essay* p. 61: The range sweeper hands you a dixie, containing boiled kibbled wheat, which is called mush. The range sweeper's offsider pours your daily ration of milk onto the mush.

1983 R. AVEN-BRAY *Ridgey Didge Oz Jack Lang* p. 36: *Moosh*, gaol porridge.

mug in tow have sucker in company.

Australian English. Especially in *Underworld Slang*.

Mug is a General Underworld Slang term for 'a dupe, a gullible person', and *in tow* is General English for 'following or going along under someone's control'. The combination of the two terms seems to be an Australian formulation.

1904 *Truth* (Perth) 23 April p. 1: If men were not bally idiots they wouldn't let spielers take them down, but that doesn't warrant the police in closing their eyes when they see a mug in tow.

1941 *Smith's Weekly* (Sydney) 22 November p. 11: It is strange some of the urging gentry are given so much rein. They are most open in their tale-telling, and straight to the point when they do pick a winner. Writer saw one the other day with a mug in tow. After a horse had won, the urger said: 'What about slipping me a couple of quid? I put you on to that winner'. The mug parted with 80/-, and the urger quickly beat it to break new ground.

1969 W. MOXHAM *The Apprentice* p. 9: Once again, it was like Scooter said: you had to put up a good front, else you'd never get a mug in tow.

1984 *Bulletin* (Sydney)19 June p. 68: 'A supplier is like a bitch on heat', he said. 'Whenever they've got the goods, they'll have a team of mugs in tow'.

mug shot police photograph.

General English.

The term means 'a photograph of a person's face, especially in police or other official records' (OED), from *mug* 'a face'. It was originally American English from the early twentieth century.

1957 *Australian Women's Weekly* (Sydney) 29 May p. 12: Television ... 'Mug shots' is the new way of saying that old-fashioned phrase 'rogues' gallery'.

1984 B. Ellem *Doing Time: The Prison Experience* p. 192: *Mug shots*, the photographs kept in police or prison files.

1990 V. Tupper & R. Wortley *Anthology of Prison Slang in Australia* (National Library of Australia, Pandora Archive): *Mug shot*, official criminal photographs kept for identification.

musical milk methylated spirits.

Australian English.

The term means 'a drink of methylated spirits and milk'.
Origin: With reference to the alcoholic effect of the drink.

1984 V. Darroch *On the Coast: Maritime Industry Life and Language* p. 118: *Musical milk*, methylated spirits diluted with other beverage including milk; such mixture, when taken internally, produces sensations of music in the head.

1987 J. Horan *Hogan: The Story of a Son of Oz* p. 34: *Musical milk*, methylated spirits.

1998 *Eyeline* (Brisbane) Autumn p. 22: In *White Angel*, MacPherson took the lowly and otherwise secret language used by methylated spirits drinkers … with names such as these—monkey's blood (metho and port), white angel (metho and white shoe polish), blue lady (metho tinted blue to prevent its consumption), goom (an aboriginal word for metho), musical milk (metho and milk) and bush champagne (metho and alka seltzer).

nephew boy who is being seated but pretends 'nice man' is his uncle.

Australian Prison Slang.

Seated in the definition means 'being the passive person in anal sex'. See SEAT. Not elsewhere recorded in the Australian evidence. There is one example of an American Underworld use of the term to describe a young boy in a sexual situation with older men (see quote).

[**1950** H.E. Goldin *Dictionary of American Underworld Lingo* p. 144: *Nephew*, a youth who is maintained by male oral sodomists and active pederasts.]

nick gaol.

General English.

This term for 'a prison' was originally Australian, although it is now used widely elsewhere. The term is also used to mean 'a police station, especially its cells' (GDS), and the evidence for this sense is mainly British.

Origin: Probably related to *nick* 'to catch, take unawares; to apprehend; (of the police) to arrest, take into custody' (OED).

1882 *Sydney Slang Dictionary* p. 9: Black Bess lumbered Mother Shooter to the Nick yesterday. She got a dream for chovy bouncing. [Translates as:] 'The prison van took Mother Shooter to Darlinghurst Jail yesterday. She got six months for shoplifting'.

1908 *Bulletin* (Sydney) 12 November p. 40: Then th' bloke what owned th' saloon starts yappin'. 'Yer ruinin' me place', he says. 'Shut yer head about yer place', we says. 'Have some sense. Can't yer see we'll all be in nick if we don't git out o' this'.

1967 *Whisper All Aussie Dictionary* in *Kings Cross Whisper* 36 p. 4: *Nick*, prison. The layout of a prison is such that the cells appear to be large nicks in the concrete.

1984 B. ELLEM *Doing Time: The Prison Experience* p. 192: *Nick*, prison.

1989 T. ANDERSON *Inside Outlaws: A Prison Diary* p. 151: *The Nick*, jail.

1995 N. IBRAHIM & M. QUINNEY *Glossary of Gaol Slang: Pentridge Gaol* (Unpublished Typescript ANDC): *The nick*, prison.

2010 *Sydney Morning Herald* 8 March (The Guide) p. 16: There have been jail terms, tolerated with stout heart. 'Takes me about a fortnight to come good in the nick. I may be locked up but my mind can go all over the place'.

nit keeper cockatoo.

Australian English.

The term means 'a person who keeps watch while an accomplice engages in an (illegal) activity' (AND). See COCKATOO.

Origin: The Australian *nit* is probably a variant of General English *nix* 'a word used as a signal that someone in authority is approaching ... Beware! Look out!' (OED). The Australian phrase *to keep nit* means 'to keep watch while an accomplice engages in an (illegal) activity'. Thus *nit keeper*: the person who keeps watch.

1893 *Coburg Leader* 8 July p. 3: Or, behind the safe cover of the friendly bathhouse he plays a sly game of draughts ... while one of the push keeps nit on the inquisitive warder, who at any moment might swoop down on the outfit and confiscate everything before booking the delinquents. But it is not the easiest matter in the world to catch them, provided the nit-keeper is a good man and well up to his business.

1953 *Advertiser* (Adelaide) 2 May p. 1: Police tonight 'kidnapped' two 'nit keepers' outside a two-up school at South Yarra.

1967 *Whisper All Aussie Dictionary* in *Kings Cross Whisper* 36 p. 4: *Nit keeper*, a watcher out for the police at a game.

1984 B. ELLEM *Doing Time: The Prison Experience* p. 193: *Nit*, someone who is strategically placed to keep a look-out and warn other members of the group if anyone is coming who could threaten whatever activity they are involved in. The person who keeps watch is known as the 'nit-keeper'.

1989 *Outrage* (Melbourne) May p. 53: In those days the rules were strict and the warders kept a sharp lookout for any homosex activities, but where there was a will there was a way. Nit-keepers were essential.

1990 V. TUPPER & R. WORTLEY *Anthology of Prison Slang in Australia* (National Library of Australia, Pandora Archive): *Nitkeeper*, a lookout.

2009 M. GATTO *I, Mick Gatto* p. 44: My first job with Kiwi Dave was at a house in Toorak that he'd been watching for a while. ... I stayed at the front door as the nit-keeper [*lookout*].

nod yer head plead guilty.

Australian Underworld Slang.

The phrase *nod the* (or *one's*) *head* means 'to plead guilty' (AND). There are many variants: *nod the nut*, *duck the scone*, etc. See also GET YER HEAD DOWN.

Origin: The 'yes' answer to the 'guilty or not' court question, indicated by the accused nodding the head.

1899 *Evening News* (Sydney) 20 April p. 4: It is the almost invariable custom of the denizens of the dock at the City Police Courts simply to nod the head when pleading guilty to an offence, which bow of obeisance is always perfectly well understood by the officer in charge of the court.

1934 *Weekly Times* (Melbourne) 3 February p. 16: How many have you against me? Get them all on at once and I will probably nod the head (plead guilty).

1968 J. ALARD *He Who Shoots Last* p. 140: Well, dey sez I done it and I wuz gonna do a stretch fer it, but I sez I ain't gonna nod me head ta dat.

1973 *Contact: Parramatta Jail Resurgents Magazine* December p. 36: Second Detective: 'We have you before a lenient judge, so nod your head. Reverse the plea and it will be a severe judge'.

2006 *Herald Sun* (Melbourne) 9 May p. 14: Faced with the choice of decades under a harsh prison regime, or something better if he 'nodded his head' and admitted guilt, John said his brother chose wisely.

nonch method used by shoplifters: concealing stolen property under coat draped casually over one shoulder.

Not otherwise recorded.

Origin: Perhaps from *nonchalant*.

not the full quid insane.

Australian English.

Occasionally in the form *the full quid* 'in full possession of one's faculties', but usually in negative contexts and constructions: 'not very intelligent, eccentric, mad'. Cf. FIVE CENTS IN THE DOLLAR.

1944 *Australian New Writing* p. 36: He'll back down; I said he wasn't the full quid, just a skite.

1973 D. FOSTER *North, South, West* p. 173: The general view ... was that he was not the full quid.

1984 J. HIBBERD *Country Quinella* p. 101: Though not the full quid, a bit sawn-off, impossible to live with.

2010 *Sydney Morning Herald* 26 June p. 7: Tolmie claims he warned Fordham and his colleagues that his uncle was 'not the full quid'.

on fire too hot to handle. Too risky.

General Underworld Slang.

The term can refer to stolen goods that are too risky to handle, or to a situation such as a potential robbery or other illegal action that is too dangerous to undertake. Not otherwise recorded in the Australian evidence.

Origin: Perhaps a variant of General English *hot* 'stolen', and therefore in some contexts 'risky to touch'. Cf. TROPICAL.

The early 1859 quote from Matsell is American, so the term probably has its origin in American Underworld Slang. Partridge in quote 1937 has clearly taken his information from Matsell.

[**1859** G.W. Matsell *Vocabulum; or, The Rogue's Lexicon* p. 32: *Fire*, danger. 'This place is all on fire; I must pad like a bull or the cops will nail me', every body is after me in this place; I must run like a locomotive or the officers will arrest me.]

[**1937** E. Partridge *Dictionary of Slang and Unconventional English* p. 277: *Fire*, danger; *on fire*, dangerous.]

on the coat ostracised.

Australian English.

The term means 'ostracised, in disfavour (with); not to be trusted; dangerous; not genuine' (AND). Also as verb *coat* 'to ostracise' (see quotes 1971 and 1973).

Origin: From the (originally underworld) signal of tugging on the lapel of one's coat with the thumb and forefinger to indicate the presence of someone not to be trusted, to stress the need for caution, etc.

1932 *Sydney Sportsman* 20 August p. 16: *Five Dock*: The razzlers are 'on the coat' this week. The mitt-slingers take complete charge, and the list of fights chalked up read goodoh. Roy Burns, hard-sockin' south-paw, has a date with Billy Cooper. [*Ed.* A *razzler* is a 'wrestler'.]

1944 T. Hartley in G. Simes *Dictionary of Australian Underworld Slang* (1993) p. 47: *On the coat*, on bad terms with someone, in coventry.—'He bunged the roast in to my sheila and I'm on the coat'. He told my girlfriend about my bad character & now she [won't] speak to me. It is derived from the signal of tugging on the lapel of one's coat with the thumb & forefinger to warn a friend or accomplice that the coast is not clear, of the need for caution. e.g. two crims are discussing a confidential matter when one of them notices a warder approaching. He simply tugs the lapel of his coat to warn his friend to shut up or change the subject.

1971 J. McNeil *The Chocolate Frog* in *The Chocolate Frog, The Old Familiar Juice: Two Plays* (1973) p. 17: Always tumbles the mugs, when yer coat 'em.

1973 *Contact: Parramatta Jail Resurgents Magazine* March n.p.: It is not for nothing that inmates regarded with contempt are put on the coat (ie. shunned) by those who still have some principles.

1973 J. McNeil *The Chocolate Frog, The Old Familiar Juice: Two Plays* p. 115 (Glossary): *Coat*, (prison slang), to ostracise. The unfavoured one is indicated to others by a tug on the lapel as he passes by.

1984 B. Ellem *Doing Time: The Prison Experience* p. 106: If caught, a peter thief will either be subjected to physical punishment from some of the other prisoners, or he will be ostracized, 'put on the coat', and left to fend for himself.

1989 T. Anderson *Inside Outlaws: A Prison Diary* p. 144: *Coated*, not spoken to, ostracised, sent to coventry. Also known as being 'on the coat'. This is usually the result of some dangerous or foolish behaviour (or because the person is not liked) which warrants a sanction, but not an extreme one.

on the grill barred door instead of steel doored cell.

Australian Prison Slang.

The phrase means '(of a cell) having a barred door, rather than a door of solid steel'.

J.S. Kerr in *Parramatta Correctional Centre: Its Past Development and Future Care* (1995) notes that both sheet iron and grilled doors were added to cells to replace the wooded doors of the original design: 'The timber cell doors proved insecure and had to be progressively sheeted in iron and rivetted. Inner iron grate doors were added to some cells' (p. 15).

on the whack entitled to a share.
General Underworld Slang.

The phrase means 'entitled to a share of the spoils'.

Origin: *Whack* is General English (recorded in Britain from the end of the eighteenth century) for 'a portion, share, allowance', appearing in such set phrases as *to get one's whack, have one's whack, take one's whack*. It is used in Australian underworld slang—see *whack* meaning 'a share of the spoils' in quote 1986. To be *in the whack* means 'to be given a share; to be part of the dividing up of the booty'. The Parramatta Glossary's phrase *on the whack* is probably a variant of *in the whack*, and both are probably shortenings of the more common *in the whack-up* and *in on the whack-up* (see quotes below, including two in square brackets from British sources). See also WHACK UP.

[**1896** G. ADE *Artie: A Story of the Streets and Town* p. 107: Jimmy says to 'em: 'Throw things my way and I'll be the Johnny-on-the-spot to see that everything's on the level. ... Well, you know what happened to Jimmy when he got down there with them Indians and begin to see easy money. He hadn't been in on the whack-up six weeks till he was wearing one o' them bicycle lamps in his neck-tie.]

[**1921** E.R. BURROUGHS *The Mucker* p. 27: There's more in this thing if it's handled right, and handled without too many men in the whack-up.]

1986 R.G. BARRETT *The Real Thing* p. 153: 'There's at least fifteen grand's worth of pot there. I'll put you in the whack'. 'I don't want to go in the whack', replied Reg, waving his arms around. 'I don't want anything to do with it'.

1993 A.S. SMITH *Neddy: The Life and Crimes of Arthur Stanley Smith* p. 254: There was only one way we could do it properly. New South Wales' finest would have to be on the whack-up. I wasted no time in contacting [*a police officer*].

2002 *Big Footy Forum* (online) 8 November: I asked him once do politicians get in with the best intent only to then get in on the whack up otherwise you won't survive? He just laughed and said 'you've got one thing wrong mate, you don't get in unless you're in the whack up!'

open go easy, anytime.
Australian English.

The term means 'an unimpeded opportunity, a free rein' (AND), 'a total lack of restriction'.

1918 *Twenty-Second's Echo: Magazine of the 22nd Battalion A.I.F.* 15 May p. 3: We did not get an open go in the way of food nor medical attention.

1945 *Border Morning Mail* (Albury) 7 July p. 2: Police have taken up the war again against cyclists who ride at night without lights. Up till recently, cyclists have had an 'open go', much to annoyance of motorists and drivers of other vehicles.

2010 *Age* (Melbourne) 6 October p. 18: Politicians seem to think that once they take office they have an open go, that they don't have to refer back to their electorates.

optic perv.

Australian English.

This is a shortened form of *optic nerve*, rhyming slang for 'a perve' i.e. a person who observes another (or others) with erotic or sexual interest; a voyeur; the act of so observing. In General English *optic*, from *optic(s)* 'eye(s)', is occasionally used to mean 'a look, a view' (see quote 2015). In Australian usage it is sometimes difficult to be certain if the sense is simply 'a look' or 'an erotic look, a perve' (see quotes 1974, 2004).

1967 *Whisper All Aussie Dictionary* in *Kings Cross Whisper* 38 p. 10: *Optic*, a pervert, from optic nerve, perve.

1974 B. Humphries *A Nice Night's Entertainment* (1981) p. 146: If you like the grouse gear, take an optic at these three big performers just come in the yard.

1983 R. Aven-Bray *Ridgey Didge Oz Jack Lang* p. 37: *Optic nerve*, perve.

2004 *Sunday Telegraph* (Sydney) 19 December p. 143: In keeping with our theme of yummy mums, we suggest you take an optic at model Grace McClure's 2005 calendar.

2015 D. Edwards *Grade Cricketer* p. 44 : 'Yeah we'll get a good optic from here', I ventured to the boys, receiving a couple of validating nods in the process.

orf have no chance.

Orf is a General English colloquial rendering of the adverb *off*, but what is meant by the definition is unclear. Given this lack of clarity, no illustrative quotations have been provided.

paper hanger passer of dud cheques.

General English.

The term was originally American English, from the early nineteenth, for 'a person who passes forged or fraudulent cheques; a forger' (OED).

Origin: *Paper* is an American term for a forged or useless cheque. With jocular allusion to the standard sense of *paperhanger* 'a person whose work is covering walls with wallpaper' (OED).

2006 B. Matthews *Intractable ... Life inside Australia's First Super-max Prison* p. 101: The professional crims—the tank men and kite flyers or paper hangers—juggled with the lifers for their position within the prison social structure.

peanut butter sandwich an honest job.

Australian Underworld Slang.

The term refers to a 'respectable' job as distinct from a criminal career. Not otherwise recorded in this specific sense, but used in Australia and elsewhere to designate honest homeliness etc.

Origin: From the perception that this is a plain but healthy kind of sandwich. Cf. American *apple pie* 'embodying traditional values (esp. motherhood and domesticity) in a positive manner; simple and wholesome, esp. in a way regarded as exemplifying particularly American ideals' (OED). The quotes, one Australian, and one American (in square brackets), show the peanut butter sandwich being used to represent a kind of solid ordinariness.

1994 *Age* (Melbourne) 12 June p. 4 (interview with Australian children's author Morris Gleitzman): 'What do you think of Enid Blyton?' 'I've read them all. When I was a kid, Enid Blyton was the bulk I consumed before I could get my hands on Richmal Crompton's "William". I think there's a bit of William in most of my characters. Enid Blyton's yarns were quite well told. But I think Enid Blyton was like a peanut butter sandwich. William was more of a salami sandwich, I guess'.

[**2013** R. ADAMS *Rubbed Out* (Google Books online ebook): 'Are you wanting something to satisfy your sweet tooth?' asked Lulu. 'Maybe some gingerbread with butter? Or homemade peppermint ice cream?' 'No', said Coco slowly, 'I want something real basic. Like a peanut butter sandwich'. 'Peanut butter and jelly?' asked Ben, sounding out the words as if trying out a foreign language. 'No jelly' said Coco, with a small sigh. 'Only peanut butter'.]

peg look.

General English (for the verb) *and Australian English* (for the noun).

This term could be a verb or a noun. The verb (also as *peg off*) is used elsewhere, but the noun is Australian.

A verb *peg* meaning 'to look at, to stare' is recorded in Britain in the middle of the nineteenth century and in the US in the first half of the twentieth century. This verbal sense continues in Australia in the second half of the twentieth century. The noun, meaning 'a look', occurs only in Australia (see quotes 1975, 1986). See also HEAVY PEG.

Origin: Figurative use of *peg* 'to fix or secure with a peg'.

1967 *Whisper All Aussie Dictionary* in *Kings Cross Whisper* 38 p. 10: *Peg*, to watch someone or something.

1968 J. ALARD *He Who Shoots Last* p. 135: I didn't like the way he was peggin' y'orf.

1970 S. JARRATT *Permissive Australia* p. 101: He's some sort of petty official with a football club. Spends half his time in the dressing room pegging off the blokes in the showers.

1972 J. MCNEIL *The Old Familiar Juice* in *The Chocolate Frog, The Old Familiar Juice: Two Plays* (1973) p. 91: I'll sit here and peg from me perch.

1975 *Bulletin* (Sydney) 26 April p. 45 (article on underworld slang): We give it a peg and decide to give the Limp another try.

1986 R.G. BARRETT *The Real Thing* p. 62: As the youth drew near Norton had a peg out of the side of his eye.

peter cell.

General English.

This term was originally Australian Prison Slang, although it is now used elsewhere, for 'a prison cell, a prison' (AND). See also BLACK PETER.

Origin: Transferred use of British Underworld Slang *peter* 'a safe or cash box; a cash register, a till'. These are all containers that are typically locked up.

1890 A. BARRÈRE & C.G. LELAND *Dictionary of Slang* II. p. 125: *Peter* ... (Australian prison), punishment cell.

1894 *Bulletin* (Sydney) 16 June p. 20: 'No. 5 Yard', said a warder to me ... on the morning after my night's rest in 'the peter'.

1919 V. MARSHALL *The World of the Living Dead* p. 85: But no more I'll scrub the peter where yer suffocates with 'eat / Or is either froze ter death with cold and damp.

1941 A.E. CLARKE *The Man Nobody Understood* p. 5: He was the one man the prison officials were constantly on their guard against ... whose 'peter' was invariably searched both by day and by night for evidence of some newly-planned villainy.

1950 B.K. DOYLE *Australian Police Journal* April p. 117: *Peter*, gaol, cell.

1971 J. MCNEIL *The Chocolate Frog* in *The Chocolate Frog, The Old Familiar Juice: Two Plays* (1973) p. 34: Every time a nit lobs in this can, they shove 'im in my peter!

1974 R. ADAMSON & B. HANFORD *Zimmer's Essay* p. 61: When the doors open, the peter has to be clean. The qualities of a clean peter are these: blankets folded atop a doubled hemp mattress, a swept floor, towels folded over the edge of the locker, bread crumbs swept from the top of the locker, and other articles, like pannikins, library books and margarine jars, stacked neatly in the locker.

1975 *Bulletin* (Sydney) 26 April p. 44 (article on underworld slang): Many other words derive from convict days. One example is interesting. A cell is called a peter, slot or tank, yet to a professional safe-breaker a peter is a safe or tank. It derives from the fact that in the convict days bank vaults were not only built in the same shape as prison cells, but constructed from the same sandstone blocks used to build the prisons.

2006 B. MATTHEWS *Intractable ... Life inside Australia's First Super-max Prison* p. 397: *Peter*, cell.

peter thief prisoner who steals from other prisoners cells. Regarded as despicable. (Not to be confused with 'tickle the peter' which means to steal from the till.)

Australian Prison Slang.

See the previous entry PETER for the earlier sense of *peter* as a 'cash register, a till'.

Origin: See PETER.

1950 'Thirty-five' in G. SIMES *Dictionary of Australian Underworld Slang* (1993) p. 153: *Peter thief*, a prisoner who steals from others' cells.

1984 B. ELLEM *Doing Time: The Prison Experience* p. 105: Because prisoners have

... generally few comforts it is considered a very serious crime for a prisoner to steal from another prisoner. The cells are left unlocked during the day and prisoners rely on mutual trust to protect the contents of their cells. ... If caught, a peter thief will either be subjected to physical punishment from some of the other prisoners, or he will be ostracized.

1989 T. Anderson *Inside Outlaws: A Prison Diary* p. 152: *Peter-thief*, person who steals from cell. Such people are not highly regarded and the traditional punishment (which screws generally leave to prisoners to enforce) is to slam the peter-thief's fingers in the cell-door, usually breaking fingers.

1998 *Illawarra Mercury* (Wollongong) 18 February p. 7: The prisoner said Morris was upset that Marsland had called him a 'Peter thief', which he explained was a prison term for an inmate who stole from other inmates.

2004 *Newcastle Herald* 2 October p. 12: Peter thieves (those who stole from cellmates) would risk being caught by fellow inmates and having the heavy steel doors slammed shut on their fingers,

piece concealable firearm.

General English.

From the sixteenth century this term was used for a variety of firing weapons, including cannons and handguns. The handgun sense became very common in the US in the early twentieth century, and this is the source of later use elsewhere.

1848 J. Syme *Nine Years in Van Diemen's Land* p. 263: Watts fell and dropped his gun, which Howe seized at the moment, and with it shot Drewe dead. Watts now dreaded a similar fate; for on asking Howe if he had killed Slambow, he replied, 'Yes; and I'll serve you the same as soon as I can load the piece'.

1989 T. Anderson *Inside Outlaws: A Prison Diary* p. 154: *Roscoe*, a gun, a shooter, a piece.

1990 V. Tupper & R. Wortley *Anthology of Prison Slang in Australia* (National Library of Australia, Pandora Archive): *Piece*, a hand gun.

1995 N. Ibrahim & M. Quinney *Glossary of Gaol Slang: Pentridge Gaol*: *Piece*, pistol.

1996 M.B. Read *Chopper 6: No Tears for a Tough Guy* p. 26: The fourth slug hit him in the upper right side of the chest and the fifth went wild. The piece only held five shots. They were all gone, but Billy wasn't. He was still coming straight at them.

pitch for it ask for trouble.

Australian Underworld and Prison Slang.

The context and significance of this phrase are unclear. In the typed-up glossary it appears in a run of terms that refer to fights and reactions. The 1990 quote gives one instance of *pitch* (but not *pitch for it*) in a prison sexual context. American English has the baseball imagery of 'pitch' and 'catch' for 'to be the active (or passive) partner in anal sex', but this is unlikely to be the source. *To pitch into* (also *to pitch into it*) is colloquial for 'attack forcibly' and *pitch* by itself can mean 'to set (one party) against another'.

1990 V. Tupper & R. Wortley *Anthology of Prison Slang in Australia* (National Library of Australia, Pandora Archive): *Pitch*, to act or strut in a homosexually provocative manner.

polish praise.

It is not clear if this is a verb or a noun. Perhaps it means that to attribute 'polish' to someone is to 'praise' them. But the context and significance of this entry are not recoverable. Given this lack of clarity, no illustrative quotations have been provided.

pony $25

General English.

Originally British for £25 or 25 guineas, first recorded in the late eighteenth century, and then used widely elsewhere. It became $25 in Australia after decimalisation (1966).

Origin: Of unknown origin. It is often suggested that as a pony is a small horse so £25 is a small amount of money—but at the end of the eighteenth century this was a considerable amount of money.

> **1843** *Satirist and Sporting Chronicle* (Sydney) 11 February p. 1: If Councillors will play at cards at the Royal Hotel, with clever fellows, they must expect to pay for their amusement. Our correspondent, we presume, had he risen a *winner* would have expected to be paid, and as a *loser* ought to pay, without raising such mean scruples about the matter as he appears to have done:—surely a wealthy Councillor cannot feel the loss of a *pony*.
>
> **1890** *Referee* (Sydney) 15 October p. 5: Best running at Botany on Monday ever seen. Betting as brisk as ever, and 'I'll bet a pony the field' reminded one of the olden times.
>
> **1932** *Referee* (Sydney) 20 January p. 24: Bob looked at the boyish, weak face of the young fellow, and said: 'Why, I'll bet a pony you will fall off the horse!' Benzon was furious. 'Make it a hundred, or, as much more as you care, Sutton', he shot back.
>
> **1950** B.K. Doyle *Australian Police Journal* April p. 117: Pony, £25.
>
> **1967** *Whisper All Aussie Dictionary* in *Kings Cross Whisper* 38 p. 10: Pony, £25 or $25.
>
> **2013** T. Peacock *The More You Bet* p. 67: '$25' was, and is, known as a 'pony', as was 25 pounds.

poof-rorter man who takes money off homosexuals.

Australian English.

Usually in the form *poofter-rorter*.

In Australian English a *poofter* (variant of the originally British term *poof*) is 'a gay man' and a *rorter* is 'a person who engages in sharp practice; a person who acts fraudulently; a con artist'. The compound *poofter rorter* is more common than *poof rorter* in Australian use, but both forms are used.

Poofter rorter has been used in a number of related ways. Baker (see quote

1943) says it means 'one who procures for a homosexual'. This is repeated as his first definition by 'Thirty-Five' (see quote 1950), but this prison-compiler had access to Baker's works, and often quotes from them. There is no other convincing evidence for this sense. Simes (see quote 1992) modifies this by suggesting the poofter-rorter might attempt to procure a partner for himself, and as a prison sense this is strongly supported by quote 1984. But this is not the Parramatta Glossary's sense. The Glossary focuses on a person who attacks and manipulates homosexuals, by physical violence and blackmail (see quotes 1938, 1950 second sense, etc.). This sense is signalled in the slightly earlier term *poof-rorting* (see quote 1938 in square brackets, although Partridge gives no indication of British and/or Australian use). This is the dominant sense.

The sense in the 1961 Patrick White quote is not entirely clear: the context is a drag performance in a suburban house; Hannah and Reen, who are in the audience, are female prostitutes, and Reen is probably accusing Hannah of 'using' the drag performer for entertainment at the party.

[**1938** E. PARTRIDGE *Dictionary of Slang and Unconventional English* (ed. 2) p. 1023: *Poof-rorting* (or *wroughting*), robbing male harlots with violence: cant: from circa 1920.]

1943 S.J. BAKER *A Popular Dictionary of Australian Slang* (ed. 3) p. 61: *Poofter*, a homosexual. Whence *poofter rorter*, one who procures for a homosexual.

1950 'Thirty-five' in G. SIMES *Dictionary of Australian Underworld Slang* (1993) p. 158: *Poofter rorter*, (i) A procurer for homosexuals. (ii) One who takes homosexuals to lonely places to bash and rob them.

1961 P. WHITE *Riders in the Chariot* p. 401: 'You are a proper pufter rorter, Hannah!' Reen had to remark, because she was a cow. 'If it wasn't for you, I wouldn't watch this, not if I was offered a good night's hay. It sends me goosey'.

1967 *Whisper All Aussie Dictionary* in *Kings Cross Whisper* 38 p. 10: *Poofter rorter*, one who preys on homosexuals.

1983 R. AVEN-BRAY *Ridgey Didge Oz Jack Lang* p. 39: *Poofter rorter*, robber of homosexuals.

1984 J. PRICE 'Homosexuality in a Victorian Male Prison' *Mental Health in Australia* July p. 8: 'Rorting' is a term commonly used to describe any ploy by which the inmate gains for himself an advantage or acquires material to which he is not normally entitled by using 'brains' or cunning as opposed to violence. To 'rort a poof' then is to 'seduce' a fellow inmate into a passive homosexual role without the use of violence. ... Just as a 'lover' gains prestige in the heterosexual world by 'seducing' (as opposed to raping) his 'conquests' so a poof-rorter directs his efforts toward sex with a boy without violence; the greater the resistance overcome by non-violent means, the greater the prestige. ... The poof-rorter 'befriends' a young inmate and 'sees him right' for the necessities and luxuries a newly arrived inmate won't have.

1992 G. Simes in R. ALDRICH & G. WOTHERSPOON *Gay Perspectives* p. 44: A *poof(ter)-rorter* is an underworld term for one who makes it his business to procure male partners for either himself or others.

1992 M.B. READ *Chopper 2: Hits and Memories* p. 176: He was involved in blackmail using both prostitutes and homosexuals, and was known in the criminal world as a '*poof rorter*'.

1994 *Meanjin* p. 360: Povey is a poof-rorter. He seduces men still in the closet and then threatens to take them public unless they pay him hush-money. But in the years he's been inside the homos have swelled up into a gay respectability that's impossible to blackmail. So he's hunting hard. Spending all his time trekking into northern Victoria, one of the last known habitats of the underground gay. I wonder how many backwoods you have to go to to make a buck as a poof-rorter these days.

[**posted** *see* LEAVE POSTED.]

pound time spent in punishment cell (without books, light, radio, tobacco).

Australian Prison Slang.

The term means 'a punishment cell in a prison; solitary confinement' (AND), 'the time spent undergoing such punishment'.

Origin: *Pound* has long been used in the sense 'an enclosure, a place for confinement', and this has often been specifically a prison. The Australian sense involves a further narrowing of meaning to a particular part of a prison that is used for punishment and solitary confinement.

1950 B.K. DOYLE *Australian Police Journal* April p. 117: *Pound*, the solitary confinement portion of a gaol.

1967 *Whisper All Aussie Dictionary* in *Kings Cross Whisper* 38 p. 10: *Pound*, punishment cells in boob.

1974 J. MCNEIL *How Does Your Garden Grow* p. 54: Yer know it's a *pinch*, I suppose? Get sprung with it and yer off tap, yer know that? ... Three days pound it's likely to get yer.

1984 G. CAREY *Just Us* p. 55: It was Manning. Manning, the screw who gave you pound for sleeping in.

1989 T. ANDERSON *Inside Outlaws: A Prison Diary* p. 153: *Pound*, solitary confinement or locked up in a cell.

2006 B. MATTHEWS *Intractable ... Life inside Australia's First Super-max Prison* p. 397: *Pound*, solitary confinement. The 'pound' was a solitary confinement cell. 'Doing pound' was doing solitary.

2018 P. KENNEDY *Long Bay* p. 111: The pound cells had no lighting. Prisoners were fed bread and water for three days.

[**press** *see* GO TO PRESS.]

pull the wrong rein make a blunder.

Australian English.

The phrase means 'to make an error, to make the wrong choice'.

Origin: From horseriding, where a horse will go in the wrong direction if the wrong rein is pulled.

1883 *Argus* (Melbourne) 29 November p. 10: It is very evident that the gentlemen who have had the reins of management in their hands have been pulling the wrong rein.

1918 *Western Star* (Toowoomba) 3 April p. 3: Mr. Jupiter Pluvius seems to very often pull the wrong rein, and sends along rain when we are not wanting it.

1947 *Daily Telegraph* (Sydney) 18 May p. 44: By the middle of the week Canterbury-Bankstown realised it had pulled 'the wrong rein'. But instead of graciously admitting the error, a clumsy attempt was made to shuffle out of the responsibility for the shenanigans.

1978 *Bulletin* (Sydney) 16 May p. 43: It could be that Gough Whitlam and Joe Riordan have pulled the wrong rein out in the Werriwa electorate. Whitlam nominated Riordan to nurse the seat during his absence abroad and this immediately gave the signal that Gough wanted Riordan to succeed him when he retires. This could result in Riordan getting rolled which would be a pity.

1989 N. Wallish *Truth Dictionary of Racing Slang* p. 65: *To pull the wrong (or right) rein*, to make any incorrect (or correct) judgement or choice.

2020 *Sydney Morning Herald* 25 April p. 51: I strongly disagree with his contention that Raelene Castle pulled the wrong rein on Israel Folau, as it is obvious to me and most that in the face of that conflagration she and the board had no choice but to react the way they did.

pull yer coat   stop what you're doing.

American and Australian English.

The phrase *pull (or tug) a person's coat*, recorded from the mid twentieth century, refers to a non-verbal way of warning someone that danger or trouble is in the offing.

The 1946 Australian citation is part of an explanation of the Australian phrase ON THE COAT, which means 'ostracised' and derives from the signal of tugging on the lapel of one's coat with the thumb and forefinger to indicate the presence of someone not to be trusted, to stress the need for caution, etc. The phrases PULL YER COAT and ON THE COAT are obviously related, but developed differences of emphasis.

1944 T. Hartley in G. Simes *Dictionary of Australian Underworld Slang* (1993) p. 47: *On the coat*, on bad terms with someone, in coventry.—'He bunged the roast in to my sheila and I'm on the coat'. He told my girlfriend about my bad character & now she [won't] speak to me. It is derived from the signal of tugging on the lapel of one's coat with the thumb & forefinger to warn a friend or accomplice that the coast is not clear, of the need for caution. e.g. two crims are discussing a confidential matter when one of them notices a warder approaching. He simply tugs the lapel of his coat to warn his friend to shut up or change the subject.

1983 R. Aven-Bray *Ridgey Didge Oz Jack Lang* p. 49: *Tug the coat*, tug the lapel to warn another of possible 'shelf'.

1984 B. Ellem *Doing Time: The Prison Experience* p. 194: *Pull his coat*, to pull someone out of trouble, or to have a talk with him and steer him in the proper direction.

pussy-footer sneak thief. (opportunist)

Australian Underworld Slang.

This is a specific use of one common meaning of *pussyfooter* (originally US): 'a person who moves quietly or stealthily; (also) someone who behaves in a sly, furtive, or underhand way' (OED).

While there are no other Australian examples for the noun *pussyfooter* in this sense, examples of the verb and an adjectival use indicate the currency of the sense (see quotes).

> **1920** *Evening News* (Sydney) 8 September p. 5: Pussyfoot Thief ... The thief had evidently sneaked in through the sleeping man's window and worked so silently that he did not wake him.

> **1930** *Truth* (Brisbane) 13 April p. 12: He went into gaol dishonest but unsophisticated. He emerged a skilled cat burglar. In that college where the professors are hardened criminals he had been taught how to pussyfoot into a bedroom without making a noise, and how to select the best places to search for hidden money and jewellery.

> **1937** *Courier-Mail* (Brisbane) 23 September p. 12: No longer, according to Mr Taylor, does the burglar go pussyfooting home in his stockinged feet, with his 'swag' slung over his shoulder after he has 'cracked a crib'. He uses a high-powered car to put as many miles as possible between himself and the long arm of the law.

put the knife through go halves with a friend.

Australian Underworld Slang.

The phrase means 'to share money, divide the spoils, etc.' Cf. WHACK UP.

> **1952** *Newcastle Morning Herald* 20 Sept p. 2: Fifty-fifty: When a bookmaker came out of a city store yesterday he opened the receipt for his purchases and a 10/ note fluttered out. Picked up by the strong wind it was soon 100 yards along Hunter-street. The bookmaker was quite prepared to let it go but a friend went after it, brought it back, and suggested jokingly: 'Put the knife through it?' The bookmaker agreed and gave him 5/. Both considered they had gained 5/.

> **1953** S.J. BAKER *Australia Speaks* p. 120: *Put a knife through money*, to split money up, a matter which the *cop out man* and his accomplices attend to after a game.

> **1955** 'Thirty-five' in G. SIMES *Dictionary of Australian Underworld Slang* (1993) p. 123: *Put a knife through it*, to divide spoils. 'Let's put a knife through it and scarper'.

> **1966** S.J. BAKER *Australian Language* (ed. 2) p. 157: Underworld vernacular ... *put a knife through it!* Said of a share-out of plunder.

put them through to brass someone.

Australian Underworld Slang.

The phrase *put (a person) through* means 'to cheat someone by not paying debts'. See BRASS. Note that quote 1967 also makes *put through* synonymous with *brass*.

Origin: Possibly an abbreviation of a longer phrase such as *put through the wringer* or (more likely) *put the cleaners through/put through the cleaners*, a variant of *to take someone to the cleaners* in the sense 'to swindle or rob someone'. Jim Ramsay was probably one of the contributors to the *Whisper All Aussie Dictionary* (see quote 1967) and in his book *Cop it Sweet* he has *put the cleaners through* (see quote 1977).

1967 *Whisper All Aussie Dictionary* in *Kings Cross Whisper* 38 p. 10: *Put through*, to cheat someone. See also brass and lash.

1977 J. Ramsay *Cop It Sweet* p. 74: *Put the cleaners through*, swindle someone completely.

put work on make sexual advances to.
Australian Prison Slang.
The term means 'to act upon someone in order to achieve an advantage', and the prison sense is a specific use.

A similar-sounding and more common Australian phrase for the sense 'make sexual advances to' is *put the word on* or *put the hard word on*. The Glossary's *put work on* feels like an awkward formulation, but its existence in a more general sense in Australian English is evidenced by the 1977 quote, and the prison-specific sense ('make sexual advances to') is evidenced by the 1984 quote.

1977 J. Ramsay *Cop It Sweet* p. 74: *Put work on,* con; flatter for gain; attempt to convince.

1984 J. Price 'Homosexuality in a Victorian Male Prison' *Mental Health in Australia* July p. 7: High social status individuals would lose respect if they participated in gang-rapes, and if they rape at all, usually only when a 'boy' they have 'put work on' 'won't come across', they do so as solo rapists.

racehorse thin gaol rolled cigarette.
Australian English.
The term means 'a thinly-rolled cigarette' (AND), 'a roll-your-own cigarette containing very little tobacco'. This is especially relevant in prison where tobacco is at a premium, controlled by weekly rations or a black market.

Origin: From the lean and sleek form of a racehorse.

1944 T. Hartley in G. Simes *Dictionary of Australian Underworld Slang* (1993) p. 168: A very thinly rolled cigarette. Thus: 'Give us a smoke mate? Go on, just a racehorse'.

1967 *Whisper All Aussie Dictionary* in *Kings Cross Whisper* 38 p. 10: *Racehorse*, a very thin cigarette. More the rule than the exception in the nick.

1989 T. Anderson *Inside Outlaws: A Prison Diary* p. 154: *Racehorse*, thinly rolled cigarette.

1994 *Canberra Times* 26 July p. 13: I delighted in the fact that I could roll a 'racehorse' (a very thin, long rollie), with one hand faster than most of the men I have ever worked with.

2006 A. Matthews *Dingo's Breakfast* p. 143: *Racehorse*, a hayburner or neddy, but also a name for a thin rollie.

ramp search.

Australian Prison Slang.

The term *ramp* as a noun means 'a search made in a jail of a prisoner's person or cell' and as a verb means 'to search (a prisoner or cell) in jail' (AND). It is not clear if the Glossary intends this as a noun or a verb or both.

Origin: Probably a specific use of *ramp* 'a swindle, a fraudulent action', originally 'the action of stealing something by violence or sudden snatching' (OED). Some have suggested an association with *rampage*, but this is unlikely.

Noun

1919 V. MARSHALL *The World of the Living Dead* p. 85: I'll toe the arrer for the ev'nin' ramp.

1944 T. Hartley in G. SIMES *Dictionary of Australian Underworld Slang* (1993) p. 168: *Ramp*, a search (by the warders, police etc.)

1968 L.H. EVERS *Fall among Thieves* p. 47: Once, a warder carrying out a 'ramp' (cell-search) reported hearing a race-broadcast.

1984 B. ELLEM *Doing Time: The Prison Experience* p. 208: Sometimes they come down here on a ramp, and search the cells.

1989 T. ANDERSON *Inside Outlaws: A Prison Diary* p. 154: *Ramp*, reckless or violent 'search', usually of a cell. This comes from 'rampage', and the term is used by both prisoners and prison officers.

2001 W. DODSON *The Sharp End* p. 86: The next time I ran into him was during a ramp in Long Bay's Central Industrial Prison.

2016 J. PHELPS *Australia's Toughest Prisons: Inmates* p. 152: We were doing ramps on cells every week and finding all sorts of shit.

Verb

1919 V. MARSHALL *The World of the Living Dead* p. 12: It would take minutes to make him secure, for he must deliver up his braces, his boots, his books, and be 'ramped' to the skin.

1944 T. Hartley in G. SIMES *Dictionary of Australian Underworld Slang* (1993) p. 168: They ramped the peters this morning.

1950 B.K. DOYLE *Australian Police Journal* April p. 117: *Ramp*, search a prisoner in gaol, as distinct from a search anywhere else.

1967 *Whisper All Aussie Dictionary* in *Kings Cross Whisper* 38 p. 10: *Ramp*, to search a person or a place.

1982 R. DENNING *Diary* p. 177: The screws ramped every cell in the jail this morning looking for Xmas brews.

2005 *Daily Telegraph* (Sydney) 15 October p. 67: While incarcerated, it was very hard to keep written documents of anything. Your cell is ramped—searched, I mean—daily and they seem to take delight in taking anything from you that gives you a link to the outside world.

[**read up** *see* BE READ UP.]

receiver of swollen goods cat.

Australian Prison Slang.

The definition applies to the specific prison context where the CAT is a young male used for passive anal sex. In other contexts, the phrase is sometimes used of a female prostitute, and the 2019 quote in square brackets is a British text referring generally to a gay man.

Origin: With jocular allusion to the standard legal phrase 'receiver of stolen goods'.

1992 G. Simes in R. ALDRICH & G. WOTHERSPOON *Gay Perspectives* p. 51: The cat may be jocularly (?) referred to as a *receiver of swollen goods*.

[**2019** G. KIRKHAM *Blues, Twos, and Baby Shoes* (online): So, Harold Clarence Spunge, my rather deceased husband, secret *Friend of Dorothy* and receiver of swollen goods, who incidentally didn't die wondering.]

red light stop, screw coming.

Australian Prison Slang.

The term means 'a prison warder; a verbal warning that a prison officer is in the vicinity'. The definition is probably to be interpreted as 'Stop! Screw coming'.

Origin: Specific use of Australian English *red light* for 'a supervisor; a manager' (AND), current in the first half of the twentieth century (see the 1925 quote for a typical example). Figurative use of *red light* 'indication of danger' (OED).

1925 *Bulletin* (Sydney) 9 April p. 24: The shed overseer or boss of the board is the 'red light'.

1944 T. Hartley in G. SIMES *Dictionary of Australian Underworld Slang* (1993) p. 168: *Red light*, a senior warder, governor, etc. Gaol discipline falls heavily on the warders as well as prisoners. While many rules are relaxed by warders they dare not countenance any refractions when 'red lights' are around. Red lights are duty bound to make a surprise inspection at irregular times so careful vigilance is kept by warders & crims. The name arises from the fact that senior officers wear red braid on their caps & also from the fact that the red light is a danger signal.

1984 B. ELLEM *Doing Time: The Prison Experience* p. 186: *Red light*, a verbal warning used when a prison officer is nearby.

1990 V. TUPPER & R. WORTLEY *Anthology of Prison Slang in Australia* (National Library of Australia, Pandora Archive): *Red light*, a warning signalling the approach of a warder or some other danger. The phrase may be said or a warning of any kind may be referred to as a red light.

remand yard hotel or club frequented by police because it's a known haunt.

Australian Underworld Slang.

The remand yard is that section of the jail where prisoners who are on remand (i.e. held in custody while awaiting trial) are allowed to exercise and socialise during part of the day. The joke here is that some hotels are frequented by so many known criminals that the place has the air of a remand yard.

2012 W. GROGAN *Terror Australis* p. 73: Kings Cross. ... As ever, the arena doesn't change, just the crowd, jettings in of jail releases and snafflings of replacements off the street. The whole joint is a remand yard, a looser wing of Long Bay Jail.

ride there for a ride back bi-sexual male.
Australian English.

This term is used of gay sexual relationships where a person is prepared to be penetrated if the other person allows reciprocal penetration. 'Bi-sexual' is an unusual term for it, but it is this reciprocal activity that the Glossary means, rather than a prisoner who has straight and gay sex. The 2007 quote shows the underlying and possibly original sense.

> **1991** *Australian Journal of Public Health* iii p. 186: My favourite in those days wasn't role playing, in so who was bitch and who was butch. My thing was that, for a ride there for a ride back, that's what I enjoyed most. ... Yeah well you'd fuck him and he'd fuck you, so that's what you would call 'a ride there for a ride back'.

> **1993** *Outrage* (Melbourne) February p. 85: Guy, 40yo ... want to meet other guys for good hot regular times, your place. Versatile preferred. A Ride There For A Ride Back.

> **2000** M.D. Davis & G.W. Dowsett in R.W. Connell *The Men and the Boys* p. 116: Homosexual sex between men allows for reciprocity, since each partner can both penetrate and be penetrated in the same way. Several of our respondents had phrases for this: 'give and take', 'a two-way street', 'tit for tat', 'a ride there for a ride back'. That is to say, the partners took turns at fucking and being fucked, or at least acknowledged a right to do so.

> **2003** *Queensland Pride* 7 November p. 27: Want to meet fit, slim man for a bike there and a ride back.

> **2007** *Herald Sun* (Melbourne) 27 July p. 15: Fraser said he had told the homicide squad detective who saw him in prison it was 'a ride there for a ride back', which meant he would do something for police if they did something for him.

ridge real.
Australian English.

The term means 'all right; genuine; dinkum' (AND).

Origin: Figurative use of *ridge* 'gold; a gold coin', a term that perhaps developed originally 'with allusion to the milled edges of certain gold coins' (OED), as something genuine and of value.

> **1938** E. Partridge *Dictionary of Slang and Unconventional English* (ed. 2) p. 1026: *Ridge*, adj., good; valuable: Australian.

> **1939** *Williamstown Chronicle* 15 April p. 2: Remember, folks, the heading of this column (They Say), and what they say in my hearing and I check up on is 'ridge' (right).

> **1950** B.K. Doyle *Australian Police Journal* April p. 117: *Ridge (or reet)*, right; or O.K.

> **1978** D. Stuart *Wedgetail View* p. 166: It seems we're off to Matta any day now. It's ridge; he reckons it's an open secret. [*Ed.* Matta is an abbreviation of 'Parramatta (Jail)'.]

right whack just deserts.
Australian English.

Origin: A *whack* is 'a portion, a share' so a *right whack* is 'a proper share; what a person deserves'. See also ON THE WHACK, WHACK UP.

1972 *Canberra Times* 22 July p. 10: A prisoner told the Pentridge jail inquiry today that the four escapers from Bendigo brought to Pentridge on the night of June 28 deserved to be bashed by prison officers. 'They got their right whack and that was it'.

1983 R. AVEN-BRAY *Ridgey Didge Oz Jack Lang* p. 41: *Right whack*, just deserts.

1991 *Age* (Melbourne) 28 February p. 15: Mr Farrell said that Macka had been acting like an uncontrollable madman. He said he knew why he was upset after being told that Macka's best friend, Graeme Jensen, had been shot by police that day. Macka had said: 'They're gonna get their right whack. They're gonna pay, the dogs'.

2016 C. MCTAGGART *Cold Gold* 4 p. 394: You're a dog, and you'll get your right whack. You owe me money, and I want it back.

rip & tear philosophy of determined thief: will not go home without scoring.

General Underworld Slang.

Probably from American adjective *rip-and-tear* 'designating or characterized by unsophisticated or violent behaviour, esp. in the commission of a crime' (OED), first recorded in 1912.

Rip and tear man is recorded in Australia as a term for 'a pickpocket' in 1953 (see quote), but the definition in the Glossary suggests a thief using physical force to achieve his ends, more than might be indicated by pickpocketing.

Origin: *Rip* meaning 'to steal' is recorded in the US from the early twentieth century. The addition of *tear* is an intensification of this, and indicates the violence that would be used if necessary.

1953 *Argus* (Melbourne) 31 October p. 9: The dip or rip and tear man (pickpocket): Years of training go into the perfection of his art. He's the complete specialist and very rarely turns his hand to anything else. ... The 'rip-and-tear man' usually works with a 'bumper-up'—someone who bumps the victim off balance and distracts his attention while the pickpocket 'lifts' the 'willy' (wallet). Most pickpockets begin as 'bumpers-up'.

Robert tongue.

Australian English.

Origin: Shortened form of *Robert Young*, rhyming slang for 'tongue'. From the name of the American film and TV actor, known especially from *Marcus Welby M.D.* (1969–76).

The quotes use the unabbreviated form.

1967 *Whisper All Aussie Dictionary* in *Kings Cross Whisper* 39 p. 4: *Robert Young*, tongue.

1983 R. AVEN-BRAY *Ridgey Didge Oz Jack Lang* p. 41: *Robert Young*, tongue.

rock spider peeping Tom.

Australian English.

Early uses of this term have the 'rock spider' spying on people in public places (especially courting couples) in order to get the opportunity to rob them, or to ogle them sexually. The current sense, 'a pedophile' (see quotes 1988 to 2017), seems to have developed from the 'peeping Tom' sense, and this development probably occurred in prison use (see quote 1990). This sense was clearly not established in Parramatta Jail in 1972. In the 1944 quote the defendant is speaking and he is saying that he did not go to the park with the intent of a thief ('tout') or peeping Tom ('rock spider'); the passage is too early for the later 'pedophile' sense.

Origin: Probably from the notion of a voyeur creeping about to spy on people, perhaps with allusion to the nursery rhyme 'Little Miss Muffet': 'Along came a spider ...'

> **1944** *Narandera Argus* 22 September p. 3: He did not go to the park to act as a park tout or a rock spider. When he put his hands on the sergeant's daughter he put them on her shoulder, and did not lean right over and pull her back on to him.
> **1950** B.K. Doyle *Australian Police Journal* April p. 117: *Rock spider*, a thief who steals from the suit-case or handbags of couples sitting or reclining in parks.
> **1980** A.S. Veitch *Run from the Morning* p. 185: 'Rock spiders', said Samms. 'I beg your pardon?' 'Blokes who perve on courting couples on the beach'.
> **1984** V. Darroch *On the Coast* p. 29: *Rock spider*, on passenger ships, persons who ogled through the passengers' cabin portholes were known as rock spiders. Such nocturnal pastime was known as rock spidering, presumably from the habit of spiders of hunting at night.
> **1988** *Courier-Mail* (Brisbane) 4 July p. 5: In prison they will be known as 'rock spiders'—the lowest of the low. Dennis Ferguson and Alexandria Brookes will spend their years behind bars unable to trust anyone but other child-sex offenders. Last week they were sentenced to 14 and 11 years respectively for kidnapping children and sexually molesting them in a Brisbane motel.
> **1990** *Canberra Times* 8 March p. 10: James Francis Murray, 40, and Frederick John Owens, 35, told him they had 'knocked' a rock spider — jail slang for a child molester.
> **2002** B. Courtenay *Matthew Flinders' Cat* p. 135: 'He thinks yiz a rock spider', Ryan said calmly, using the underworld term for a paedophile.
> **2017** *Age* (Melbourne) 8 April (Spectrum Section) p. 32: And when Simon abducts Sam after school one day, it's a shortcut to prison, and the harsh treatment a suspected 'rock spider' inevitably faces there.

rort modus operandi.

Australian English.

The term means 'a trick, a fraud, a swindle; a dishonest practice; a "lurk"' (AND), and by defining it as 'modus operandi' the Glossary is referring to a person who typically uses such tactics as his 'mode of operation'. See quote 1984 for the importance of the term in prison usage. The term is also used as a verb. The 1950 prison glossary by 'Thirty-five' (see quote below) notes that the use of the verb was 'rare' at that time, although it became common later.

Origin: From *wrought* 'worked into shape (or condition)' (OED), archaic past participle of the verb *work*. One of the American senses of *work* from the end of the nineteenth century is 'to hoax, cheat, con' (OED).

1926 'Dryblower' *Verses* p. 50: A bank-roll unto him is 'Oscar Asche', A swindle is to him a 'joke', a 'wrought'.

1938 *Argus* (Melbourne) 26 March (Supplement) p. 11: The razor sharpener wrought's a good one, too. You melts a pile of soap down in a dish, then yer mixes it with lamp-black and lets it set. Then you cuts it up into cubes about one inch square, wrap, label, and sell.

1944 T. Hartley in G. Simes *Dictionary of Australian Underworld Slang* (1993) p. 175: *Rort*, racket, shrewd 'dodge', a method of deception for getting something easy or by false pretences.

1950 'Thirty-five' in G. Simes *Dictionary of Australian Underworld Slang* (1993) p. 175: *Rort*, a trick, a cunningly devised plan ... (Rarely used as an intransitive verb, when it means to live by 'rorting'.)

1967 *Whisper All Aussie Dictionary* in *Kings Cross Whisper* 39 p. 4: *Rort*, any method of extracting money.

1984 B. Ellem *Doing Time: The Prison Experience* p. 92: Rorts are not only important for the extra unofficial comforts they bring, but also because they represent a victory over the system. They allow the prisoner some flexibility, and a belief that he is not totally institutionalized because he still has some control over his life.

1984 B. Ellem *Doing Time: The Prison Experience* p. 195: *Rort*, a perk, lurk; a devious scheme which gets around some institutional restrictions; for example, finding a way to obtain better quality food.

1990 V. Tupper & R. Wortley *Anthology of Prison Slang in Australia* (National Library of Australia, Pandora Archive): *Rort*, an advantage obtained by devious means.

1999 'How to Survive in Prison' in *Ralph* March p. 21: If you have a rort (business) don't tell anyone.

2018 J. Knight *Dictionary of Victorian Prison Slang* (online) p. 30: *Rort*, an advantage, obtained by underhand or devious means. ... To take wrongful advantage of; abuse: *to rort the system*. ... *Rorted*, to obtain by rorting. Example; 'He rorted an extra pillow for himself'.

roscoe gun.

American and Australian Underworld Slang.

Originally American for 'a handgun' (first recorded 1914).

Origin: 'It is possible that the weapon was named after a specific person, but if so, this person has not been identified' (OED).

1950 'Thirty-five' in G. Simes *Dictionary of Australian Underworld Slang* (1993) p. 175: *Roscoe*, a gun. (Have heard it said that the term comes from Roscoe, the name of a Chicago gunman).

1989 T. Anderson *Inside Outlaws: A Prison Diary* p. 154: *Roscoe*, a gun, a shooter, a piece.

1990 V. Tupper & R. Wortley *Anthology of Prison Slang in Australia* (National Library of Australia, Pandora Archive): *Roscoe/rosca*, hand gun.

1995 N. Ibrahim & M. Quinney *Glossary of Gaol Slang: Pentridge Gaol* (Unpublished Typescript ANDC): *Rosco*, pistol.

2001 *Prison & Drug Slang: NSW Corrective Services: Rosco*, pistol.

roseleaf tongue in bum.
Australian English.

The term refers to 'anilingus' (or 'rimming'). Also as *roseleafing*.

Origin: Translation of French (*faire*) *feuille de rose* '(perform) anilingus'—literally '(to do) the leaf (or petal) of the rose'.

1944 T. Hartley in G. Simes *Dictionary of Australian Underworld Slang* (1993) p. 165: Gamo, sixty-nine, daisy chain, rose leaf, ninety three etc are homosexual practises.

1972 *CAMP Ink* (Sydney) March p. 14: Sure V.D. is around but it is a disease which is very sensitive to soap and water. A more dangerous form of 'venereal disease' is hepatitis—for those on the rim of social practices. There are more than aphids to contend with in the rose-leaf. When things get out of hand and start getting tongue in cheek, keep it clean.

1980 *Libertine: Australia's Journal of Gay Affairs* 26 June p. 22: Active Greek-lover seeks warm recipients for roseleafing and intercourse.

1984 G. Knepfer *Sex in Australia* p. 147: Sex is openly talked about now—anal, Greek, oral, French, part and full and real, rosebud and roseleaf. These were known in the thirties and forties but not to us.

1996 *Meanjin* p. 17: Would you please fill out the following survey?... You may answer each question: 'Never', 'Sometimes', 'Often', 'No Response'... Now, oral-anal contact. Er, rimming—roseleafing—tonguing him out—licking his bottom!

Rudolf Vaselino one who falsely boasts of his exploits with women.
Australian Prison Slang.

This is a jocular term for a HOCK, who engages in male anal sex while in prison, though professing his heterosexual credentials.

Origin: The supposed heterosexual prowess is in the allusion to the Italian-American actor Rudolph Valentino (1895-1926), while the gay propensity is evident in the transformation of Valentino towards the lubricant 'vaseline'.

The 2007 quote is from New Zealand where the writer indicates the term *hock* was used in non-prison contexts, unlike the Australian use of the term (see HOCK).

1992 G. Simes in R. Aldrich & G. Wotherspoon *Gay Perspectives* p. 51: A notorious hock may be called ... a Rudolph Vaselino.

[**2007** W. Ings in *Public Space: The Journal of Law and Social Justice* no. 3 p. 16: A *hock* was a *straight* man who sometimes used the bogs for sex with other men. (*footnote*) The Australian term *Rudolph Vaselino* was also in evidence in New Zealand at this time and was specifically (as in Australian prisons) applied to these men.]

running feed non payment for meal in cafe.
Australian Underworld Slang.

The term refers to a person who 'does a runner' after eating a meal at a cafe (see quote). The phrase *do a runner* meaning 'to escape by running away' (see quote 2007) appears in the early 1980s (OED). The compound *running feed* is not otherwise recorded.

> **2007** L. REDHEAD *Cherry Pie* p. 181: As the guy ran past the Oyster Bar I leapt out of my seat and took off after him, ignoring the shout of the waiter who must have thought I was doing a runner.

scarper abscond on bail.
Australian Underworld Slang.

This is a specific underworld use of General English (originally British) *scarper* 'to depart hastily, run away; to escape, make one's get-away', first recorded in the 1840s. The General English sense is represented by quotes 1955 and 1967.

Origin: Ultimately from Italian *scappare* 'get away, escape'. The OED suggests that this was 'reinforced during or after the war of 1914–18 by *scapa* from Cockney rhyming slang *Scapa Flow*, to go'.

> **1945** *Tribune* (Sydney) 1 May p. 3: Underworld figures known as 'professional bailors', at a moment's notice, would provide bail as high as £500, said Mr. Cosgrove. Naturally they charged heavy interest and the need to pay this interest was a strong motive for commission of a crime during the bail period. When a criminal absconded from bail ('scarpered' was the recognised term) which had been deposited by a 'professional bailor', they usually paid back the bail before they went. The bailor would then frequently use a hard luck tale to try and get part of the original bail money returned.
>
> **1955** 'Thirty-five' in G. SIMES *Dictionary of Australian Underworld Slang* (1993) p. 123: *Put a knife through it*, to divide spoils. 'Let's put a knife through it and scarper'.
>
> **1967** *Whisper All Aussie Dictionary* in *Kings Cross Whisper* 39 p. 4: *Scarpa*, depart. Rhyming for Scarpa Flow, go.
>
> **2017** *Townsville Bulletin* 8 August p. 18: That magistrate must be terribly naive, to believe that this particular bailee will willingly front court at a later date, knowing he could go to jail, we've seen the last of him, he's going to scarper.

score twenty dollars.
British and Australian English.

This is a specific use of *score* 'twenty' for £20 and later (in Australia after decimalisation in 1966) $20.

> **1855** *Sydney Morning Herald* 12 May p. 4: Sergeant Norris deposed that about eight days since he saw prisoner walking along York-street, and watched him; at length he turned into a public house, he (witness) followed, and entered into conversation with him; he offered witness 'a score' to allow him to 'work the jug' without molestation, at the same time pointing to the Commercial Bank, within sight of which they were standing; these are thieves' slang terms, well

understood, and commonly used by them; his experience in the police had made him acquainted with their purport; it was an offer of £20 to be allowed to pick pockets at the Commercial Bank.

1946 *Singleton Argus* 24 April p. 4: According to Detective James, when he picked up the accused, Newcastle, the prisoner is alleged to have said to him: 'Listen, let us go through and I'll drop a spin your way; these things you found in my port are hot all right'. Detective James told him nothing doing. And then the confab went on again: 'Listen, there is another score in it when I see you in Sydney; don't be a — mug; take the spin now and the rest after. ... This is what he meant: The accused was offering the detective £5 (the spin) with £20 (a score) to follow if he was allowed to get away.

1967 *Whisper All Aussie Dictionary* in *Kings Cross Whisper* 39 p. 4: *Score*, the sum of $20 or £20.

1996 J. Byrell *Lairs, Urgers and Coat-Tuggers* p. 223: Needless to say, if he'd offered me a score [£20] I'd have been on top of the world.

screw prison warder.

General English.

The term was originally British, recorded from the early nineteenth century.

Origin: From *screw* 'key' (recorded late eighteenth century), thence applied to a prison warder who controlled the keys.

1894 *Truth* (Sydney) 18 March p. 4: The 'screws' (warders) are terrible dogs.

1944 T. Hartley in G. Simes *Dictionary of Australian Underworld Slang* (1993) p. 179: *Screw*, a warder.

1950 B.K. Doyle *Australian Police Journal* April p. 118: *Screw*, gaol warder.

1984 B. Ellem *Doing Time: The Prison Experience* p. 195: *Screw*, a prison officer. The word derives from the old screw key lock system.

1988 C. Galea *Slipper!* p. 86: When they let us out the screw at the gate said 'see you two back soon'. Jesus, he was right.

2006 B. Matthews *Intractable ... Life inside Australia's First Super-max Prison* p. 5: Near the shit tub some wag had written: 'Down in the dungeon, carved in rock. Three little words—screws suck cock'.

Seabreeze Hotel Long Bay Gaol.

Australian Underworld Slang.

A jocular term (not otherwise recorded) for Long Bay Gaol, situated in the coastal area between Long Bay and Botany Bay in the suburb of Malabar in the municipality of Randwick. A hotel called the Sea Breeze Hotel existed at Tom Ugly's Point on the side of Botany Bay opposite to the prison complex.

Such jocular designation of a prison as a hotel has a long history. Francis Grose in *Lexicon Balatronicum: A Dictionary of Buckish Slang, University Wit, and Pickpocket Eloquence* (London 1811) gives Newman's Hotel as a name for Newgate Prison in London. Long Bay Gaol is occasionally referred to as Long Bay Hotel in Sydney newspapers: 'Alf retired for three days rest at His Majesty's Long Bay Hotel. The Magistrate very reluctantly sent him there and begged him very hard, but in vain, to pay the small fine imposed' (*International Socialist* 27 March 1915 p. 2). Long Bay has also been known as Malabar Hilton (*Prison & Drug Slang: NSW Corrective Services*, 2001).

seat insert penis in anus.

Australian Prison Slang.

The term means 'to perform anal intercourse on a person' (AND). Cf. the definition of NEPHEW above: 'Boy who is being seated but pretends "nice man" is his uncle'.

Origin: From *seat* 'a person's buttocks'.

1950 'Thirty-five' in G. SIMES *Dictionary of Australian Underworld Slang* (1993) p. 180: *Seat*, to commit pederasty on.

1970 K. MACKEY *The Cure: Recollections of an Addict* p. 50: A tattooed teen alcho calls: Hey Horrible Horace have you ever been seated?

1992 G. Simes in R. ALDRICH & G. WOTHERSPOON *Gay Perspectives* p. 51: The cat … is also said to be *seated* (from *seat* = arse). Indulgence in arse-fucking is called the *seat*: 'He wiped the brush [women] and got on the seat'.

2001 *Prison & Drug Slang: NSW Corrective Services*: *Seat*, sodomize. *Seat something*, insert up rectum.

secko sex offender.

Australian English.

The term means 'a sexual pervert; a sex offender' (AND).

Origin: From *sex* + *-o* (a suffix added to many Australian words as a marker of colloquiality).

1949 R. PARK *Poor Man's Orange* p. 38: 'Just look at that dirty ole secko, will you?' he said disgustedly, and scooping up a stone he ran after it, yelling, 'Merv, Merv, the rotten old perv'.

1967 *Whisper All Aussie Dictionary* in *Kings Cross Whisper* 39 p. 4: *Sexos or Seckos*, prisoners sentenced for sex crimes against young persons. The most despised of all prisoners.

1984 B. ELLEM *Doing Time: The Prison Experience* p. 195: *Secco (or secko)*, someone who has been sentenced for a sexual offence; or someone who is obsessed with sex.

2006 B. MATTHEWS *Intractable … Life inside Australia's First Super-max Prison* p. 94: Lawson was a lifer and a serious secko. … In 1954 he kidnapped five models. … He raped two of them at gunpoint and sexually assaulted the others.

[seconds *see* TAKE SECONDS.**]**

seine dollar.

Australian English.

The term means 'ten shillings; a dollar'. With spelling variants such as *sein, sane, sayne*.

Origin: From German *zehn* or Yiddish *tsen* 'ten'.

Also used with reference to other amounts of ten, as a jail sentence of ten months, ten ounces of tobacco, etc.

1939 K. TENNANT *Foveaux* p. 310: I can skite if I want to. I earn the chaff. Why, if someone did a night with you and threw you a sein, you'd snatch it with both hands.

1941 S.J. BAKER *A Popular Dictionary of Australian Slang* p. 67: *Sane*, ten shillings.

1944 T. Hartley in G. SIMES *Dictionary of Australian Underworld Slang* (1993) p. 178: *Sayne*, ten shilling note.

1967 *Whisper All Aussie Dictionary* in *Kings Cross Whisper* 39 p. 4: *Seine*, ten shillings or one dollar.

serve him up give him a hiding.

Australian Underworld Slang.

To *serve (someone) up* means 'to give him a thrashing'.

Origin: As a verb, *serve* has a long history, originally in British English, meaning 'to injure, to wound' (GDS). This sense is still current, and it is likely that *serve ... up* is a variant of it. Australian English also has a noun sense of *serve* meaning 'physical abuse, a beating' (AND). The 1967 and 1984 quotes define *serve* as a verb but give the example sentence with the noun (*to give someone a serve*). Quotes 1975 and 2006 have the Australian *serve (someone) up*, which is the form that appears in the Parramatta Glossary.

1967 *Whisper All Aussie Dictionary* in *Kings Cross Whisper* 39 p. 4: *Serve*, to give a person a thrashing. 'Give the mug a serve'.

1975 *Bulletin* (Sydney) 26 April p. 46: Heaps got served up and Punchy give it to about four before some arse gave it to him with a bottle. ... To be served up is to be beaten.

1984 B. ELLEM *Doing Time: The Prison Experience* p. 196: *Serve*, to reprimand someone especially with physical force; for example, 'to give him a serve'.

2006 B. MATTHEWS *Intractable ... Life inside Australia's First Super-max Prison* p. 147: Peter was willing to fight each one separately but they four-outed him. He was badly served up when the screws threw him into the yard next to me.

set (someone) up enter into crime with someone having supplied police with prior knowledge of crime with sole purpose of having accomplices arrested in exchange for favours from police.

Australian Underworld Slang.

Origin: A variant of General English *set (someone up)* '(of police) to concoct evidence or create a situation whereby an innocent person is charged with a crime' (GDS), 'to frame (someone)'.

1984 B. ELLEM *Doing Time: The Prison Experience* p. 196: *Set up*, to frame someone; or to set up a situation in order to catch someone out.

1990 V. TUPPER & R. WORTLEY *Anthology of Prison Slang in Australia* (National Library of Australia, Pandora Archive): *Set up*, to frame someone or to organise a situation in order to catch someone out. Literally set up to knock down. May be used as a noun or verb.

1998 M.B. READ *Chopper 8: The Sicilian Defence* p. 182: I'll set Joey up today and tomorrow the fucking cops will get someone to set me up. In the end no-one wins but the fucking undertaker.

2005 J. PRING *Abo: A Treacherous Life: the Graham Henry Story* p. 289: I also know that he tried to set me up for other crimes to get himself a free ride with the cops.

shanghai sudden transfer to another gaol.
Australian Prison Slang.

The term means 'a transfer of a prisoner from one jail to another without warning'. The earlier and more common use of the term is as a verb meaning 'to transfer (a prisoner) to another jail without warning' (AND; see quote 1950). The usual reason for the transfer is to defuse a situation of strife or trouble.

Origin: From *shanghai* 'to transfer forcibly or abduct; to constrain or compel' (OED), probably from an association between the port of Shanghai and sailors kidnapped to work on ships.

1950 'Thirty-five' in G. SIMES *Dictionary of Australian Underworld Slang* (1993) p. 181: *Shanghai*, to transfer (a prisoner) from one gaol to another without warning, usually for some misdemeanour.

1967 *Whisper All Aussie Dictionary* in *Kings Cross Whisper* 39 p. 4: *Shanghai*, term used when a prisoner is transferred from one prison to another. Usually after the crim has been playing up like a bad mug.

1989 T. ANDERSON *Inside Outlaws: A Prison Diary* p. 123: The use of the shanghai—the sudden transfer of a prisoner to another jail—is a long-established tactic in NSW jails. It is especially designed to destroy prisoner organisations and to isolate those considered to be troublemakers.

2006 B. MATTHEWS *Intractable ... Life inside Australia's First Super-max Prison* p. 143: The shanghais continued. From Maitland to the Bay. From the Bay to Goulburn.

shelf informer.
Australian Underworld Slang.

The term means 'an informer; a police informer' (AND).

Origin: Of uncertain origin. Perhaps in allusion to the phrase *put on the shelf* 'put out of the way', although in the phrase the thing or person is put into 'a position or state of inactivity or uselessness' (OED).

c.1920 *Breakers of Men* (I.W.W. Prisoners Release Committee) p. 16: Unless a man is a 'shelf', that is an informer on his fellow prisoners, and prepared to fawn at the feet of officials, the chief warder in particular, he has a hard lot to contend against.

1950 F.J. HARDY *Power without Glory* p. 80: 'How do you know he's a nark?' 'Piggy recognised him. ... Says he's been a "shelf" for years'.

1967 *Whisper All Aussie Dictionary* in *Kings Cross Whisper* 39 p. 4: *Shelf*, an informer. From putting on the shelf out of harm's way.

2004 *Age* (Melbourne) 11 June (A3 Supplement) p. 2: In underworld-speak, a 'shelf' is an informer (don't ever go into a furniture store in Carlton and ask for a shelf! A stool is OK, a bed maybe—but never ever ask for a shelf) who's generally loathed by criminal types.

sheriff hock who jealously guards cat.
Australian Prison Slang.

The term means 'an older male who guards his possession of a younger passive sexual partner'. See HOCK and CAT. The use of American *sheriff* 'the chief law-enforcement officer in a county' suggests that the hock guards the cat as a sheriff guards a prisoner.

Not otherwise recorded, but Looser in her study of New Zealand prison slang describes a similar use of 'sheriff' in the gang-world outside the prison:

[**2001** D. LOOSER *Lexicon of Boobslang in the Period 1996–2000* (thesis) p. 164: *sheriff* n. 1 a gang-member who falls in love with the gang's *dirty girl* (a woman whom all the gang-members sleep with) and tries to keep her for himself, denying the other men sexual access to her. This term may also be applied to a gang-member who brings his own girlfriend to the gang quarters and refuses to let the other men sleep with her, or simply to a member who brings women to the quarters and refuses to introduce them to his fellow members. Note: if he is caught doing these things, the sheriff must wear a large badge to show that he has been seen breaking the rules. This badge must be worn at all times until he catches another person sheriffing, at which point he takes off his badge and gives it to the new sheriff. (such a person must act like a policeman (sheriff) wearing a badge and searching for signs of 'law-breaking'.)]

shirt lifter hock.
Australian Prison Slang.

In General English use this is a term for 'a gay man'. It is usually derogatory and offensive. In the prison system it has a very specific meaning, and it is used of a HOCK, a man who takes the penetrative role in male to male sex. In prison contexts, where situational homosexuality is common, the *shirt lifter* (who is called a HOCK) generally does not identify as gay, and the kind of sexual activity designated by the literal sense of the term is therefore to the fore in its application to him. See also ARSE BANDIT, DUNG PUNCHER.

Most of the early evidence for the term is Australian, but the earliest evidence is a 1958 diary entry from Britain, included in an autobiographical-like book by the historian Christopher Lee (see quote 1958 in square brackets). The Australian associations of the term were no doubt enforced by Barry Humphries' use of it.

[**1958** C. LEE (diary entry 13 January) *Eight Bells & Top Masts* (2001) p. 18: I said to Dad I thought they were really nice. Blinking shirtlifters, he said. What's that mean? You'll learn, he said.]

1966 S.J. BAKER *Australian Language* (ed. 2) p. 216: *Shirt lifter*, a sodomite.

1967 *Whisper All Aussie Dictionary* in *Kings Cross Whisper* 40 p. 4: *Shirt lifter*, a homosexual.

1979 B. Humphries *Bazza Comes into his Own*: 'You'll adore Leo! ... Now he's a top Bondi hairdresser'. ... 'Leo sounds like a flamin' shirt-lifter to me!'

1987 A. Buzo *Glancing Blows* p. 41: 'People think we're a couple of shirt-lifters', an aggrieved separated man told me after he had moved into another separated man's flat.

2013 *Northern Star* (Lismore) 8 March p. 16: Faggot! Poofter! Shirt lifter! If you find these words offensive, you are right. They are highly offensive and used to intimidate and bully. Yet every gay man has heard these abusive words hurled at them more than once in their lives.

shit kicker person of no account.

Australian English.

The term means 'an unskilled worker; a person of little consequence' (AND). In the typed-up Parramatta Glossary the entry appears immediately after TOE RAGGER and its meaning is indicated by ditto marks, making it synonymous with *toe ragger*, which is defined as 'person of no account'.

1950 'Thirty-five' in G. Simes *Dictionary of Australian Underworld Slang* (1993) p. 182: *Sh-t-kicker*, a 'short-timer' (often employed in sanitary work).

1963 'C. Rohan' *Down by the Dockside* p. 176: He was now dishonourably discharged and ambitious of becoming a big shot in the underworld, but Bluey Gleeson said, and he should know, that Clarrie would never be anything except a small-time shit kicker if he lived to be a hundred.

1985 R. Wilson *Good Talk* p. 155: 'I am the floor lady'. 'You're only the boss' shit kicker, so let's get it straight'.

1990 V. Tupper & R. Wortley *Anthology of Prison Slang in Australia* (National Library of Australia, Pandora Archive): *Shit kicker*, a junior prison officer or generally a low status person.

2014 *Daily Examiner* (Grafton) 1 January p. 4: He can sit down and yarn with the shit-kickers right through to the elite, and he still remains so humble.

shitpot talk ill of someone.

Australian English.

The term means 'to denigrate (something or someone); to rubbish'. It is synonymous with Australian *shit-can*.

1989 R.G. Barrett *Godson* p. 249: All the millionaire drug dealers were too busy building resorts and high-rises over what's left of the coastline of Australia. ... And the only thing standing in their way were the hippies and greenies—the ones trying to save the environment. The ones who the politicians, and their sycophants on certain radio stations try to shitpot all the time to cover their own smelly, slimy tracks.

2017 J. Milner *Satire and Politics* p. 41: He went on to say that since spin and hypocrisy are the staples of any government, it is naturally the job of the fourth estate to attack them for those sins. In 2013 his fellow cartoonist Bill Leake (1956-2017) was heard to put the same sentiment more colourfully during the Sydney launch of Dirt Files, a book on politics and cartooning: 'Who are we going to shitpot but those in power?'

2020 foxsports.com.au (online) 27 October: Many of their tweets are just shit potting someone because they disagree with their opinion.

shiv gaol made knife for stabbing purposes.

General English. Especially in *Underworld and Prison Slang.*

This word (also spelt *chiv*) was originally British, but is now widespread. It is first recorded at the end of the seventeenth century. It is often associated with prisons, and often appears in glossaries of prison slang worldwide.

Origin: Romany *chiv* 'knife'.

1846 *Colonial Times* (Hobart) 23 October p. 3: Witness now heard a voice from near the hut, crying out—'Ding the chiv'—that meant put away the knife.

1939 K. Tennant *Foveaux* p. 311: Down one side of his face was a long scar. 'Somebody been trying to do you up with a chivvy?' Doris asked, eyeing the scar.

1989 T. Anderson *Inside Outlaws: A Prison Diary* p. 155: *Shiv*, knife or sharp weapon, blade, can include sharpened wooden or plastic objects. Also used as a verb, eg. 'He was shivved'. A shiv may be carried for defence or to enforce threats, eg. when collecting debts.

2006 B. Matthews *Intractable ... Life inside Australia's First Super-max Prison* p. 398: *Shiv*, homemade knife.

2016 J. Phelps *Australia's Toughest Prisons: Inmates* p. 258 (Glossary): *Shiv*, a weapon made from materials found inside the prison.

short arms & deep pockets said of mean person.

General English.

Probably originally American from the 1940s (see quote 1946 in square brackets) to describe 'a person who is flush with money but keeps it hidden away and is reluctant to spend it; a stingy person'. Variants include *short arms and long pockets*.

[**1946** *Sentinel* (Milwaukee, Wisconsin) 14 September p. 2: The moderate wealthy and the comfortably usually get that way by being sound businessmen—and along the line they get into the habit of tossing the 'lettuce leaves' (dollars—ed.) around like pianos. Short arms and deep pockets!]

1976 D. Ireland *Glass Canoe* p. 65: They had to goad him. It was his shout. His pockets were long and his arms got shorter and shorter.

1991 *Tharunka* (Kensington, Sydney) 22 October p. 22: 'Look, Lizzie', I sez, 'I'd better come clean or you'll think I've got the shortest arms and the longest pockets in the state'. Long pause. 'But the fact of the matter is', I continue painfully, 'is, that, um, I am temporarily bankrupt'.

2002 *Mercury* (Hobart) 9 January p. 15: What a fine gesture by Steve Waugh and his players to donate their winnings to the NSW fire relief. What a contrast when the Queen sends her sympathy and best wishes. What a pity the lady has such short arms and deep pockets.

shorten him up cut him down to size.

Australian English.

The term can refer to a physical attack (as in the 1986 quote) or any means of making a person realise they are not as important or powerful as they think they are.

> **1986** R.G. Barrett *The Real Thing* p. 47: Norton shortened the big Wests forward up, but the referee thought it was Fred and sent him off.
>
> **2016** D.J. McTaggart *Cold Gold II* p. 398: Barry muttered, 'that fucking Slither, someone is gunna have to shorten him up, for all our sakes'. A thoughtful silence descended on the wheelhouse.

shovel room. Living quarters.

General English.

The term is recorded earliest in New Zealand (1914), but the evidence after that is primarily US.

Origin: Shortened form of *shovel and broom*, rhyming slang for 'room'.

> **1948** *Smith's Weekly* (Sydney) 25 December p. 6: The Crow's idea of high living was to pose in his shovel-and-broom with a Craven A, a crumpet, and a glass of sparkling Nell.
>
> **1950** 'Thirty-five' in G. Simes *Dictionary of Australian Underworld Slang* (1993) p. 183: *Shovel*, a house or flat (possible corruption of 'hovel'?).

show pony lair.

Australian English.

The term means 'a person who gives more attention to appearances than to performance; an ostentatious person; a show-off' (AND). Since the 1990s there is some evidence of its use in British English. The word 'lair' in the Glossary's definition is Australian English for 'a person who dresses flashily and behaves in a vulgar manner; a show-off; a larrikin' and is a back-formation from 'lairy' meaning 'flashily dressed; showy' (AND).

Origin: Figurative use of *show pony*: 'a pony which is entered in, or is of a standard suitable to be entered in, a competitive show' (OED); 'one that looks good in shows but may be less useful in practical life' (GDS).

> **1939** *Sporting Globe* (Melbourne) 6 May p. 5: They make every man do his part, and no show ponies need apply.
>
> **1964** J. Pollard *High Mark* p. 19: Don't become one of those football 'show ponies' who wear more bandages than some of those race horses we see.
>
> **1982** *Australian* (Sydney) 7 August p. 44: Admirers of Carlton's jack-in-the-box half-forward flanker, Peter Bosustow, call him 'Mr Magic' and 'Mr Wonderful'. His detractors call him a mug lair and a show pony.
>
> **1994** M.B. Read *Chopper 4: For the Term of His Unnatural Life* p. 149: I've always been a bit of a show pony with a flair for the dramatic, that's what separates criminals who are remembered from the crooks no-one ever remembers.
>
> **2006** B. Matthews *Intractable ... Life inside Australia's First Super-max Prison* p. 134: We both regarded the boast as youthful braggadocio and allayed his concerns. 'He's talking shit, Warwick. The kid wouldn't have the balls. He's just a show pony'.

2014 *Advertiser* (Adelaide) 22 February (Magazine Supplement) p. 11: At this stage I haven't quite made up my mind whether Lyons is a show-pony bogan or a brilliant politician, but he has sure got people talking about Geelong again.

silk department extra grouse.
Australian English.

The term is used to describe something that is 'the very best of its class' (AND). The definition 'extra grouse' means 'very good'. See GROUSE CIGARETTE for the meaning and origin of *grouse*.

Origin: Formerly used of a section of a department store that sold the finest and most expensive fabrics.

1941 *Benalla Ensign* 19 September p. 3: L.A.C. Clem Roberts ... and L.A.C. Frank Fitzmaurice, of Tasmania, who are attached to the Officers' Mess at Laverton, the 'Silk Department' of the Air Force, came to Benalla for the week-end to attend the ball.

1952 *Argus* (Melbourne) 8 March p. 9: I do not think there is a Melbourne apprentice who could handle Grand Monarch, so I am going for the 'silk department'. I hope Breasley will take the ride.

1992 M.B. READ *Chopper 2: Hits and Memories* p. 107: He runs a string of very physically beautiful callgirls. These are whores but they don't look like hookers. They are the silk department in the oldest profession.

1998 *Daily Telegraph* (Sydney) 15 July p. 18: Here's a new label from an old hand, Andrew Garrett, who has been better known for good value quaffers, but this one belongs in the silk department. Sourced from the cool Adelaide Hills, home of Penfolds' 'white Grange', this is rich in the French white Burgundy mould.

2017 *Australian* (Sydney) 14 August p. 27: He has arrived in the silk department of stallions with a fee hike to $110,000 for 2017.

silvertail trustee having cushy job in prison.
Australian Prison Slang.

This Australian English term originally meant 'a person who is socially prominent or who displays social aspirations; a privileged person' (AND). This sense is first recorded 1872. Later, the prison sense arises (recorded from the 1940s): 'a prisoner who receives special privileges' (AND).

The *trustee* in the Parramatta Glossary definition derives from American prison use: 'a prison inmate to whom special privileges or responsibilities are granted for good conduct' (OED).

Origin: Probably originally with reference to the wearing of dress uniforms.

1945 H.C. BREWSTER *King's Cross Calling* p. 81: The gaol barber ... always kept two razors, a sharp one for the better class prisoners who were known as 'Silver Tails' (because they were able to produce a fair amount of cash from outside sources) and the other for those who were not admitted to the select circle. Or it may be they were not 'recognized' by the 'talent' because of the pettiness of their crime.

1950 'Thirty-five' in G. SIMES *Dictionary of Australian Underworld Slang* (1993) p. 184: *Silvertail*, a prisoner who receives special privileges.

1984 B. Ellem *Doing Time: The Prison Experience* p. 196: *Silvertail*, someone who is a favourite of the authorities; for example, the writers who work in the offices are often called silvertails. Implied in this definition is the belief that they have the potential to inform because of their close relationship with the authorities and the privileges they get. Because of this they are not trusted by many prisoners.

1990 V. Tupper & R. Wortley *Anthology of Prison Slang in Australia* (National Library of Australia, Pandora Archive): *Silvertail*, a prisoner who easily obliges the authorities, and is perceived as untrustworthy by his peers.

2006 B. Matthews *Intractable ... Life inside Australia's First Super-max Prison* p. 398: *Silvertail*, elitist.

sleep prison sentence. Longer than 7 days less than 3 months.
General Underworld Slang.

The term refers to a relatively short prison term, usually ranging from three months to one year. It was first recorded in the US in 1912.

1919 V. Marshall *The World of the Living Dead* p. 85: O, no more I'll slip the toe-raggers and rag-timers the chews / Just ter brighten up their stretches, sleeps an' drags.

1967 *Whisper All Aussie Dictionary* in *Kings Cross Whisper* 40 p. 4: *Sleep*, a small prison sentence.

1989 T. Anderson *Inside Outlaws: A Prison Diary* p. 155: *A Sleep*, short sentence, say a few months or weeks. Just sleep for a while, so to speak, and you'll have done it.

2006 B. Matthews *Intractable ... Life inside Australia's First Super-max Prison* p. 398: *Sleep*, a three-month sentence.

slew & yer'll blue don't look back, keep going.
Australian Underworld Slang.

The phrase means 'if you turn your head you're likely to get into trouble; don't look back'. See also SLEW YER HEAD below.

Origin: From *slew* (also spelt *slue*) meaning 'to relax one's vigilance by looking about' (AND), from *slew* 'to turn (a thing) round upon its own axis, or without shifting it from its place; also loosely, to swing round' (OED), and in British dialect use 'to twist; to turn aside; to swerve, swing round' (*English Dialect Dictionary*) + *blue* 'make a mistake'.

In the first 1950 quote *slue* is defined as a verb but given as a noun in the illustrative sentence.

1950 'Thirty-five' in G. Simes *Dictionary of Australian Underworld Slang* (1993) p. 186: *Slue*, to turn one's head, to relax vigilance. 'One slue and you *blue*'.

1950 B.K. Doyle *Australian Police Journal* April p. 118: *Slew your blew*, 'Don't slew your blew' is to say 'keep your mouth shut and don't do your head'.

1967 *Whisper All Aussie Dictionary* in *Kings Cross Whisper* 40 p. 4: *Slew and blue*, to turn one's head when the heavies or a creditor is in range, giving him or them a full look at your features.

1973 *Contact: Parramatta Jail Resurgents Magazine* June n.p.: Now Billy, he's a real character. ... If he appears a bit shifty it's either because your smother's your best friend ... or if you slew, you blue.

1974 *Contact: Parramatta Jail Resurgents Magazine* June p. 17: The trouble was that Lot's wife, like so many other women I know, couldn't help herself. Whether it was out of sentiment or sympathy, look back she did! This is where the saying 'Slew and you Blue' originated. Because according to the Scriptures Lot's wife was suddenly transformed from a healthy woman into a pillar of salt.

1983 R. AVEN-BRAY *Ridgey Didge Oz Jack Lang* p. 14: In a flash he knew he had slued and blued. The dull light in the joint had deceived him.

1983 R. AVEN-BRAY *Ridgey Didge Oz Jack Lang* p. 45: *Slew and blue*, look round at the wrong time.

slew yer head look away.
Australian Underworld Slang.

The term means 'to turn one's head', or as *slew someone's head* 'to distract a person, especially when a crime is being committed'. The first sense is evident in the prison slang term *slug-slewer* for a man who looks at other men (literally, their *slug* i.e. penis) in the shower (see quotes 1984, 2006).

Origin: See previous entry SLEW & YER'LL BLUE.

1975 *Bulletin* (Sydney) 26 April p. 45: Anyway, we get this dead set sneak go for a willy in a supermarket. So we send in Limp to tug the tart minding the willy. Marg pussies in to slew the manager and Ratty Jack is stallin' close by waitin' to entertain the mugs with his fit bit. I was gonna take. So all right, we all move in and the Limp starts his broadcast and Marg pulls the manager into his office really givin' it to him about what an arse of a place his store really is. Ratty Jack was stallin' for me to pussy in as soon as Limp slews the tart. ... 'Slewing a head' mean(s) simply diverting someone's attention away from the scene of operations.

1984 B. ELLEM *Doing Time: The Prison Experience* p. 197: *Slug slewer*, penis watcher in the showers.

1989 T. ANDERSON *Inside Outlaws: A Prison Diary* p. 155: *Slew*, to slew means to spy, to look sideways (also to move sideways), to hang around to watch, to be a voyeur.

2006 *Sydney Morning Herald* 25 March p. 82: In the past couple of weeks he also must have picked up a fair bit of the Long Bay lexicon. ... Someone who stares at a bloke's sollicker in the shower is a slug-slewer.

slice two dollars.
Australian English.

The term was originally used for £1, and after decimalisation (1966) for $2. There was a $2 note printed from 1966 to 1987.

Origin: Figurative use of *slice* 'a thin, flat, broad piece of something'.

1946 A. GREEN *We Were (Riff) R.A.A.F.* p. 54: He played the national game until he had lifted a few 'slices' (N.T. slang for pound notes).

1950 B.K. DOYLE *Australian Police Journal* April p. 118: *Slice*, £1.

1967 *Whisper All Aussie Dictionary* in *Kings Cross Whisper* 35 p. 6: *Half a slice*, ten shillings or a dollar.

sling pay police for services rendered.

Australian English.

Sling means 'to make a gift; to pay a bribe' (AND). As a noun *sling* is 'a gift, a bribe'(AND).

Origin: Figurative use of *sling* 'to throw, cast something in some direction' (OED).

1907 C.W. CHANDLER *Darkest Adelaide* p. 5: 'Come on. Sling. ... If you don't dub up I'll punch you on the blanky jaw'. This seemed to have the desired effect, for she freely parted with two bob out of the four she had.

1950 B.K. DOYLE *Australian Police Journal* April p. 119: *Sling*, portion of the whole, or quota. But 'to sling' is to pay.

1968 J. ALARD *He Who Shoots Last* p. 219: He once told me dat da hoods dese days sling ta da coppers and shoot deir mates.

2013 T. PEACOCK *The More You Bet* p. 136: One Saturday morning he was told that the police would be raiding the joint that afternoon, but that he was not to worry, because an old bloke in a South Sydney guernsey was being slung $50 to take the rap.

slot cell.

Australian Underworld Slang.

The term means 'a prison cell; a prison' (AND).

Origin: Of uncertain origin. Cf. now British dialectal *slot* 'a bar or bolt used to secure a door, window, etc., when closed' (OED).

1947 *Pix* (Sydney) 20 September p. 15: *Peter* or *slot*, cell.

1968 J. ALARD *He Who Shoots Last* p. 196: Siddy was in the next slot to Taggy.

1984 E. WITHNEL *Australian Journal of Cultural Studies* 2 (November) p. 61: Thus at the hub of the prison are the crims' slots, their concrete tombs, solid, verifiable, three metres by two metres.

1989 T. ANDERSON *Inside Outlaws: A Prison Diary* p. 155: *Slot*, punishment cell.

2018 G. DISHER *Kill Shot* p. 47: 'Your slot okay?' Ayliffe shrugged. 'A cell's a cell, boss'. At least he wasn't sharing.

sloughed up locked in cell.

General Underworld Slang.

The verb *slough up* means 'to lock up, to imprison'. The earliest evidence for this sense is in an Australian source (see quote 1812), although its author was drawing on his knowledge of the British underworld. Other nineteenth century evidence is mainly from the US, with occasional British examples. Spelling variants for *slough* include *slour* and *slau*.

Origin: From *slough* 'to be swallowed up in a slough i.e. a swamp, an area of soft, muddy ground'.

1812 J.H. VAUX *New Vocabulary of the Flash Language* in *Memoirs* (1819) II p. 206: *Slour*, to lock, secure, or fasten ... *Slour'd* or *slour'd up*, locked, fastened.

1914 *Bulletin* (Sydney) 24 December p. 44: The door opens by inches, and a man in pyjamas has a slow peep through the crack. At length he allows them to come in, policeman and all. In silence he takes his stand behind the bar, and serves them with drinks, which are asked for in very low voices. The policeman swallows his furtively, and then says 'Good-night' and leaves. "Andy ter be in with the John Dunns', says the youth with the foxy face. The blasé man looks at him with the light of superior knowledge in his eyes and speaks for the first time. 'Drinks widger to-night, sloughs yer in ter-morrer'.

1968 J. ALARD *He Who Shoots Last* p. 151: It makes me shudder ta think of him slaued up in da Black Peter.

1984 E. WITHNEL *Australian Journal of Cultural Studies* 2 (November) p. 64: When a screw drops cigarette ash on the crim's floor, or fills the slot with smoke just prior to 'slouring up' (slamming and locking the door), particularly when the crim is a non-smoker, it can leave that crim tense and irritable for hours afterwards.

1985 T. PRIOR *A Knockabout Priest* p. 87: 'J Division in Pentridge was closed down as a Young Offenders' Group cell-block because of the pack-rapes. ... The block was set up in dormitory style, and once the YOGs were sloughed [locked up] for the night they could be necked at leisure'. Sid W explained that, in this case, 'necked' did not mean killed ... but 'taken control of'. 'It means that the persons who had "necked" him could do anything they liked to him', he said. 'In most cases, it meant they could bugger him at their leisure'.

1989 T. ANDERSON *Inside Outlaws: A Prison Diary* p. 155: *Sloughed up*, locked up in a cell, often in solitary confinement.

1995 N. IBRAHIM & M. QUINNEY *Glossary of Gaol Slang: Pentridge Gaol* (Unpublished Typescript ANDC): *Sloughed up*, locked in.

2006 B. MATTHEWS *Intractable ... Life inside Australia's First Super-max Prison* p. 106: Barrie was a lifer who got sloughed up in the tracs after they found gelignite in the library and reasoned he was going to blow his way out of jail. [*Ed.* The *tracs* refers to the section of the prison reserved for 'intractable' prisoners'.]

smack a blue be arrested and charged.
Australian Underworld Slang.

Probably a specific use of Australian English *smack a blue*, literally 'be hit with trouble/altercation' i.e. 'to run into trouble', a sense illustrated by most of the quotes below. Perhaps also alluding to *blue* as a variant of *bluey* 'a summons, thus 'be hit with a summons'.

Origin: *Blue* meaning 'a fight, an altercation' is of uncertain origin, but is perhaps related to *blue* meaning 'indecent; characterised by swearing'. *Blue* or *bluey* in the sense 'a summons' derives from the fact that early documents of this kind were printed on blue paper.

1939 K. TENNANT *Foveaux* p. 290: You can always get a bet 'cause there's sure to be some bloke wiv a life sentence an' a wireless. As long as you don't smack a bad blue, you ought to 'ave a 'appy time.

1950 'Thirty-five' in G. SIMES *Dictionary of Australian Underworld Slang* (1993) p. 16: 'He didn't have a fiddley when he smacked the blue', i.e. didn't have a pound when he got into trouble'.

1967 *Whisper All Aussie Dictionary* in *Kings Cross Whisper* 40 p. 4: *Smack a blue*, to strike trouble along life's way.

1968 J. ALARD *He Who Shoots Last* p. 24: I know the kid never had a chance. ... I did my best to stop him smacking a blue; but it wasn't enough.

1983 R. AVEN-BRAY *Ridgey Didge Oz Jack Lang* p. 45: *Smack a blue*, come undone by police.

[**smoke** *see* IN SMOKE.]

[**smother** *see* YOUR SMOTHER'S YOUR BEST FRIEND.]

smother block someone's view.

General Underworld Slang.

The term means 'to conceal a crime by blocking anyone's view of it'. It appears first as a noun in an Australian text (see quote 1915), but the earliest record of the verb is in a British text from 1930. The noun is also attested elsewhere. See YOUR SMOTHER'S YOUR BEST FRIEND for the noun.

Origin: Specific use of *smother* in the sense 'to cover up, so as to conceal' (OED).

1915 C. DREW & I.B. EVANS *The Grafter* p. 4: Look here, Mosh ... you'll have to get to work on that ticket. There's only one out. A Jay's got it, and it will be dead easy. Get some of the boys to give you a smother, and when he goes to put it in, dive on it, and see you don't miss.

1941 S.J. BAKER *A Popular Dictionary of Australian Slang* p. 68: *Smother*, to conceal (a person), to hide.

1967 *Whisper All Aussie Dictionary* in *Kings Cross Whisper* 40 p. 4: *Smother*, to cover up an act of criminal type from a man's best friend to his mother.

1975 *Bulletin* (Sydney) 26 April p. 45 (article on underworld slang): Marg and Ratty Jack was gonna smother with a big box while Limp tugged the goose behind the counter.

2006 B. MATTHEWS *Intractable ... Life inside Australia's First Super-max Prison* p. 398: *Smother*, to hide from view.

sneak go sneak theft.

Australian English.

The term is used for various kinds of secretive actions, including 'a furtive theft; a covert attempt; an unexpected assault' (AND; see quote 1992 for the 'assault' sense in a prison context).

Origin: From *sneak* 'done without warning; secret' + *go* 'an attempt'. Cf. *sneak-thief* 'one who steals or thieves by sneaking into houses through open or unfastened doors or windows; also, a pickpocket, a snatch-thief' (OED), and *go on the sneak* 'to go out working as a sneak-thief or petty pilferer' (GDS).

1950 'Thirty-five' in G. SIMES *Dictionary of Australian Underworld Slang* (1993) p. 188: 'He had a sneak go at the *peter*', i.e. robbed the till by stealth. 'He had a sneak go at the *mug*', i.e. sneaked on his victim unawares.

1975 *Bulletin* (Sydney) 26 April p. 45 (article on underworld slang): Anyway we get this dead set sneak go for a willy in the supermarket. So we send in Limp to tug the tart minding the willy.

1989 N. WALLISH *Truth Dictionary of Racing Slang* p. 33: *Sneak go*, a 'sneak go' is any action on the quiet.

1992 E.J. EASTWOOD *Focus on Faraday & Beyond* p. 221: Alex Tsakmakis developed the 'sneak go' (assault from behind, usually unprovoked) to a fine art in his violent, albeit brief, prison career. He specialised in attacking people from behind, with mop buckets.

snip ask for money.

Australian English.

The term means 'to solicit money from (someone); to cadge from' (AND). Origin: From *snip* 'to cut, to cut up or off, by or as by scissors' (OED).

1959 *Bulletin* (Sydney) 21 January p. 32: 'Can you snip Sorrowful?' 'No, he's got a death-adder in his kick'.

1967 *Whisper All Aussie Dictionary* in *Kings Cross Whisper* 40 p. 4: *Snip*, to borrow money from a person.

1989 R.G. BARRETT *Godson* p. 69: Snip your surfie mate. ... He should have plenty of money.

1990 V. TUPPER & R. WORTLEY *Anthology of Prison Slang in Australia* (National Library of Australia, Pandora Archive): *Snip*, to borrow (typically tobacco) or sometimes to cheat.

1996 M.B. READ *Chopper 6: No Tears for a Tough Guy* p. 34: 'Someone pinched all my money', said Kerry. 'Can I snip you for $500?'

2011 *Daily Telegraph* (Sydney) 21 May p. 118: And then he snipped me for $20 on the way home. I had to give it to him because I thought he'd hit me again.

snooker hiding place.

Australian English.

This noun means 'a hiding place' (AND). A verb *snooker* 'to hide' also exists in Australian English (first recorded 1968), and is more common than the noun.

Origin: From the game of snooker where a *snooker* is 'the placement of the balls in such a way that the object ball is blocked by another and cannot be struck directly by the cue ball' (OED), thereby making the ball 'hidden'.

1967 *Whisper All Aussie Dictionary* in *Kings Cross Whisper* 35 p. 6: *In smoke*, to hide out. Similar to being in snooker.

1979 L. NEWCOMBE *Inside Out* p. 8: 'It's O.K. they won't find us here'. 'We've still gotta find a better snooker than this'.

1983 R. AVEN-BRAY *Ridgey Didge Oz Jack Lang* p. 43: *Snooker (in)*, hidden.

snork child.

Australian English.

The term means 'a baby, a child, a young person'.

Origin: Transferred use of British dialect *snork* 'a young pig' (*English Dialect Dictionary*).

1941 S.J. Baker *A Popular Dictionary of Australian Slang* p. 68: *Snork*, a baby.

1944 L. Glassop *We Were the Rats* p. 273: Got a scar on his hand, but probably he's had it since he was a little snork.

1967 *Whisper All Aussie Dictionary* in *Kings Cross Whisper* 40 p. 4: *Snorks*, small children. Short for suckers of norks. [*Ed. Norks* is an Australian term for 'breasts'.]

1972 J. McNeil *The Old Familiar Juice* in *The Chocolate Frog, The Old Familiar Juice: Two Plays* (1973) p. 64: He's got his life ahead of him ... He's still only a snork.

1973 J. McNeil *The Chocolate Frog, The Old Familiar Juice: Two Plays* p. 118 (Glossary): *Snork*, (colloquial), a youth, a stripling.

1983 R. Aven-Bray *Ridgey Didge Oz Jack Lang* p. 45: *Snorks*, children.

snow dropper person who steals clothes from clothesline.
British and Australian Underworld Slang.

The term means 'a person who steals washing that is hanging out to dry'. Originally British (first recorded 1826), with Australian use from the 1860s. In later use the term narrows in sense to describe a man who steals women's underwear from clotheslines.

Origin: From *snow* 'wet white linen'.

1863 *Maitland Mercury* 8 December p. 3: Last night a quantity of linen was stolen from a line in Mrs. Tanner's. ... We wish the police would keep their eyes open, and rid us as soon as possible of these 'snow droppers'.

1927 *Cessnock Eagle* 18 March p. 10: A 'snow-dropper' was at work on Tuesday in Aberdare St., Weston, when the clothes-line in the yard of Mr Percy Jack was stripped of about £15 or £20 worth of linen and flannels.

1951 *Advertiser* (Adelaide) 11 June p. 3: With several lines of clothing to choose from, a 'snow-dropper' selected 10 pairs of briefs, worth £4 10/, belonging to Miss Nancy Eileen Caldow, of Lurline street, Mile End.

2007 ABC North West WA 14 June: A snow dropper has been nabbed by Police during the week. He was 'knocking off knickers' from the local caravan park.

solid staunch to criminal code.
American and Australian Underworld and Prison Slang.

The term means 'trustworthy, dependable, stalwart, reliable'. See quote 1931 in square brackets for earliest American evidence, and see discussion in section 4 of the introductory material.

[**1931** G. Irwin *American Tramp and Underworld Slang* p. 176: *Solid*, trustworthy; sound. To be trusted.]

1950 B.K. Doyle *Australian Police Journal* April p. 119: *Solid*, one who is firm, rigid, quite unmovable in his views, actions, and assertions; one who is firm in loyalty to a comrade.

1950 'Thirty-five' in G. Simes *Dictionary of Australian Underworld Slang* (1993) p. 191: *Solid*, staunch.

1971 J. McNeil *The Chocolate Frog* in *The Chocolate Frog, The Old Familiar Juice: Two Plays* (1973) p. 47: And yer fergettin', mate, that I've known yer as long as yer've known yerself. Don't give me all yer crap about how 'solid' yer've always been!

1973 J. McNeil *The Chocolate Frog, The Old Familiar Juice: Two Plays* p. 118 (Glossary): *Solid*, (colloquial), honest by the standard of whatever moral code is being invoked.

1978 R.J. Denning *Diary* (1982) 25 December p. 88: He has been one of the best blokes up here as he has been very solid to me.

1984 B. Ellem *Doing Time: The Prison Experience* p. 197: *Solid*, trustworthy and staunch.

1989 T. Anderson *Inside Outlaws: A Prison Diary* p. 156: *Solid*, reliable, dependable, staunch. Specifically, in jail, a person who won't talk or 'tell' is said to be solid.

1990 V. Tupper & R. Wortley *Anthology of Prison Slang in Australia* (National Library of Australia, Pandora Archive): *Solid*, good, dependable, trustworthy, staunch. A valued characteristic according to the prison code.

1991 M.B. Read *Chopper 1: From the Inside* p. 48: I guess I'm trying to say I'm sorry about Johnny. If I could wave a magic wand and fix his gimpy leg, I would. The bloke stuck solid after I shot him and said nothing to the police.

2005 J. Pring *Abo: A Treacherous Life: the Graham Henry Story* p. 95: Apart from that he was a solid crim who would never rat on you — a real old-school crim, the kind hard to come by these days. I'm not saying there are no crooks in the prison system today who are not solid like the old-school crooks, because there are plenty. It's just that these days the prisons are so full of drug addicts. Drug users have a reputation in jail for not being trustworthy.

somersault change plea of guilty to plea of not guilty.

Australian Underworld Slang.

The 'somersault' can also be from not guilty to guilty.
Origin: A specific use of *somersault* meaning 'turn over'.

1931 *Truth* (Sydney) 10 May p. 12: An accommodating type of gentleman Mr. Christie stepped into the dock at the Central Police Court last week to answer a charge of having attempted to obtain his smoking necessities by the cheap and unlawful method of breaking open one of those little kiosks that stud the broad highway of Martin Place. Edmund pleaded 'not guilty', and then discovered that as a result his case would be stood over. 'If I plead guilty, will the matter be dealt with right away?' he solicitously inquired. Gathering the impression that such would be the case, the chivalrous Mr. Christie very promptly somersaulted on his previous plea and guessed that he was guilty.

1970 *Canberra Times* 28 October p. 40: Becker said that he met Lewis in gaol in March this year when Lewis was awaiting bail in respect of the present charges. The meeting, the first of several between them, was in the trial yard shortly after Lewis arrived at Pentridge. Becker said, 'I was talking to him about racehorses, doping horses, things in general. The conversation came to King Pedro and Big Philou. I asked him how he thought he would go. He said he had a good chance of beating King Pedro but thought he would somersault over Big Philou'. [*Ed.* The phrase *beating King Pedro* refers to 'beating the charge of doping that racehorse'.]

1983 R. Aven-Bray *Ridgey Didge Oz Jack Lang* p. 45: *Somersault*, change one's plea in court.

1989 T. Anderson *Inside Outlaws: A Prison Diary* p. 156: *Somersault*, to change pleas, especially an unexpected change. You may have pleaded guilty in the magistrate's (low) court, then not guilty in the District Court. In this case, you have somersaulted and the case will have to be sent back to the low court for a hearing.

1990 V. Tupper & R. Wortley *Anthology of Prison Slang in Australia* (National Library of Australia, Pandora Archive): *Somersault*, to change a plea in court.

S.O.S. Same Old Shit. Speaking of prison meals.

General English. Australian Prison Slang in specific application to prison meals.

The term means 'the same thing as usual' (GDS), and although an alphabetism of 'Same Old Shit', it is often euphemised to 'same old story', 'same old stuff', etc. First recorded in the US in the 1920s.

1984 B. Ellem *Doing Time: The Prison Experience* p. 197: S.O.S., same old shit (for lunch or dinner).

1990 V. Tupper & R. Wortley *Anthology of Prison Slang in Australia* (National Library of Australia, Pandora Archive): S.O.S., same old shit, eg for a prison meal.

spin¹ five dollars.

Australian English.

In earlier use the term meant £5, but after decimalisation (1966) it became $5. See also BLUE BIT.

Origin: Abbreviation of *spinnaker*, with the same sense of £5, probably a figurative use of *spinnaker* 'a large sail'.

1941 *Coast to Coast* p. 225: 'How'd you go at the two-up?' I asked. 'Aw, I got a spin', said Tom. ... 'I was holdin' a score but I dropped most of it'.

1946 *Gippsland Times* (Sale) 10 January p. 4: A spin or spinnaker is a £5 note.

1975 M.B. Roberts *A King of Con Men* p. 69: He would thump the bench ... and bark, 'Fined five pound'. ... Throughout the length and breadth of Australia he was known as 'Spin McGee'—'spin' being the slang term for £5.

spin² five years.

Australian Underworld and Prison Slang.

The term means 'a five-year jail sentence' (AND).
Origin: From SPIN in the sense 'five pounds' (see previous entry).

1950 'Thirty-five' in G. Simes *Dictionary of Australian Underworld Slang* (1993) p. 191: *Spin*, five, five pounds (£5), five ounces of tobacco, five years. (As an example of how deeply the Argot is bedded in prisoners' speech, I remember a man who was for years known as 'Spin' solely because his prison number was 5.)

1983 E. WITHNEL *Australian Journal of Cultural Studies* 1 (May) p. 90: The crim learns the names of laggings, coming to think of them in terms of a chunk of time and not the carefully calibrated units of control such periods of time designate in the outside world. The names of laggings are ... Ten years: A Brick. Five years: A Spin [etc.].

1989 T. ANDERSON *Inside Outlaws: A Prison Diary* p. 156: *Spin*, a spin is a five year jail sentence. E.g. 'He's got a spin'.

2006 B. MATTHEWS *Intractable ... Life inside Australia's First Super-max Prison* p. 398: *Spin of years*, a five-year sentence.

spot $100.

Australian English.

The term means 'the sum of one hundred pounds (or dollars)' (AND).

Origin: Possibly related to the originally American suffix *-spot* (which came from describing the pips on a playing card as 'spots') to designate the value of a bank note, the number of years of imprisonment, etc., so that 'five spot = $5 or 5 years' imprisonment' etc. But if this is the case it is not clear why '100 spot' should have been the only sum abbreviated to 'spot'.

1945 S.J. BAKER *Australian Language* p. 109: £100—*spot*.

1967 *Whisper All Aussie Dictionary* in *Kings Cross Whisper* 39 p. 4: *Spot*, one hundred dollars or pounds.

1980 M. WILLIAMS *Dingo!* p. 83: 'Let us go, and we'll give you a "spot" each'. 'We couldn't do that', he said. 'Anyway, what's a spot?' 'A hundred quid!' Dave told him.

1984 B. ELLEM *Doing Time: The Prison Experience* p. 197: *Spot*, one hundred dollars.

1990 V. TUPPER & R. WORTLEY *Anthology of Prison Slang in Australia* (National Library of Australia, Pandora Archive): *Spot*, one hundred dollars.

sprung seen in the act of doing something illegal.

Australian English.

The verb *spring* means 'to discover or come upon (something or someone, usually a concealed object or someone engaged in an illicit activity)' (AND). Used in Britain, but from the end of the nineteenth century mainly Australian.

Origin: Specific use of *spring* 'cause to appear' (OED).

1842 *Geelong Advertiser* 18 April p. 2: Having received certain information and a guide, Mr Le Seouff set out about eight days since to 'spring' an illicit still, which he had been told was in full play in the tea-tree scrub at Dandenong.

1875 *Illustrated Adelaide News* ii. p. 11: It was Californian Jack, who, having unintentionally 'sprung' the lovers, was hastily 'backing out'.

1967 *Whisper All Aussie Dictionary* in *Kings Cross Whisper* 39 p. 4: *Spring*, To be sprung, one is caught in the act of doing something highly irregular.

1989 T. ANDERSON *Inside Outlaws: A Prison Diary* p. 156: *Sprung*, caught, arrested, pinched, busted, discovered.

2006 B. Matthews *Intractable … Life inside Australia's First Super-max Prison* p. 398: *Spring, sprung*, to be caught in the act of doing something illegal.

2021 *Australian* (Sydney) 11 June p. 14: Even while under lock and key for the mandatory hotel quarantine, he couldn't be contained. He was sprung by a photographer sunning himself on his balcony.

squarehead   honest citizen.
Australian English.

The term means 'an honest person; a person with no criminal convictions' (AND). The compound *squarehead* occurs occasionally in other Englishes, but the evidence is mainly Australian.

In early Australian English the term can be used to distinguish the 'virtue' of the free settler from the 'vice' of the convict and ex-convict. It is often used in contexts where an absence of a history of criminality in a person is being stressed.

Origin: From *square* 'honest or straightforward in dealing with others; honourable, upright' + *head* forming compounds 'to denote a person having a mind or head of the sort specified by the first element' (OED).

1864 J. Armour *The Diggings, the Bush, and Melbourne* p. 16: I learnt that nearly all the company had been 'Government men', as convicts style themselves. … I … got for reply a discreet hint to see as little as I could of what happened, and to keep my counsel when I did see, as being a 'square head', that is one outside of their community, I would readily be suspected were tales told out of school.

1867 *Queenslander* (Brisbane) 15 June p. 3: The old lag, too, is picked out at once by a practised eye; the 'model', or Pentonville, is easily distinguished from him again; and the free immigrant, or squarehead, is equally well spotted.

1950 B.K. Doyle *Australian Police Journal* April p. 119: *Square-head*, one who has no convictions.

1967 *Whisper All Aussie Dictionary* in *Kings Cross Whisper* 39 p. 4: *Square head*, a conformist. An unconvicted person.

1972 *Contact: Parramatta Jail Resurgents Magazine* December n.p.: The average 'square-head' is a pretty good bloke as an individual. It's only collectively that he becomes a menace to the 'crim'.

1984 B. Ellem *Doing Time: The Prison Experience* p. 9: When the police arrested me, being a 'square head' I told them what they wanted to know. I believed it when they said they wanted to help me.

1994 M.B. Read *Chopper 4: For the Term of His Unnatural Life* p. 17: I've never really mixed with squareheads and normal people, even when I was on the outside. I was surrounded by thousands of the buggers, but the only squareheads I ever really spoke to were publicans, barmen, cab drivers and bookies.

2004 *Age* (Melbourne) 20 May (Green Guide Supplement) p. 6: I think we in the squarehead (non-criminal) world live highly specialised, compartmentalised lives and we don't face death very often, we don't know how to deal with it.

2006 B. Matthews *Intractable … Life inside Australia's First Super-max Prison* p. 398: *Squarehead*, a John citizen, somebody without a criminal record.

square off apologise.

Australian English.

This is a specific use of Australian *square off*, which has a range of meanings including 'to set matters right; to settle a difference; to conciliate (a person); to placate' (AND).

Origin: From General English *square* 'to conciliate, satisfy' (OED).

1926 'J. Doone' *Timely Tips for New Australians*: To 'square off', to smooth over the resentment of another.

1941 S.J. Baker *A Popular Dictionary of Australian Slang* p. 70: *Square off*, to apologise for one's self, to set matters right in a case of misunderstanding.

1968 S. Gore *Holy Smoke* p. 56: So what about givin' a man another go, now he's squared off with you?

1977 J. Ramsay *Cop It Sweet* p. 85: *Square off*, make amends; apologize.

2000 G. Allen *Outlaws of the Kimberley Underworld* p. 205: You don't have to square off for him Lester, but thanks.

stall clear out.

Australian English.

The term means 'to clear out, get out, shoot through'.

Origin: It derives from, and is closely related in sense, to British *stall* (or *stall off*) meaning 'to walk off', but the Australian sense usually has emphasis on escaping from a difficult situation, and with a degree of urgency.

1946 *Singleton Argus* 24 April p. 4: 'Stall out of town', said the detective, meant letting them leave the town; in effect, the same as 'going through'.

1968 J. Alard *He Who Shoots Last* p. 2: 'But if I stand here talking ta you much longer I'll have a change of heart. Anyhow, I'd better stall'.

1985 R.G. Barrett *You Wouldn't Be Dead for Quids* p. 108: They had another couple of beers. ... 'One more and we'll stall'.

1990 V. Tupper & R. Wortley *Anthology of Prison Slang in Australia* (National Library of Australia, Pandora Archive): *Stall*, run off.

starter substitute for vaseline (margarine or any such thing)

General English.

The term means 'a lubricant used for anal sex'.

Starters is recorded in P. Baker's British *Fantabulosa: A Dictionary of Polari and Gay Slang* (2002), as an example of Polari. Polari was 'a form of slang incorporating Italianate words, rhyming slang, cant terms, and other elements of vocabulary, which originated in England in the 18th and 19th centuries as a kind of secret language within various groups, including sailors, vagrants, circus people, entertainers, etc. In the mid 20th cent. a form of the language was taken up by some homosexuals, esp. in London' (OED). It is possible that this is the origin, although the Parramatta use and other Australian evidence may represent independent formulations.

1967 B.K. Burton *Teach Them No More* p. 141: I've brought a starter with me today, so there's no need to be scared. I got some peanut oil from the kitchen, so you've got to give it to me. God, I love you, baby.

1990 V. Tupper & R. Wortley *Anthology of Prison Slang in Australia* (National Library of Australia, Pandora Archive): *Starter*, oil or lubricant which is utilised in prison for sodomic practices or masturbation.

stiff uncensored letter smuggled out of prison.
General Underworld and Prison Slang.

The term refers to a letter that is smuggled into or out of prison, thus avoiding the censorship of the authorities. It was originally British (mid nineteenth century), but is now widespread.

Origin: Of uncertain origin. The earliest uses (from the 1820s on) are for paper documents such 'a promissory note or bill of exchange' (OED), and perhaps 'stiff' refers to the stiffness of the paper in such documents. The term then narrows in meaning to a particular kind of letter, and this is now the predominant sense.

1893 *Herald* (Melbourne) 14 December p. 1: The searching of the prisoners and their cells at Pentridge has been resumed this morning, but nothing of a startling nature has yet been discovered. One of the reasons for the search is said to be the finding of what is known in prison slang as a 'stiff', viz. a letter from a recently discharged prisoner announcing his intention of planting a 'swag' near the prison. How the 'stiff' got into Pentridge and was left lying about is one of those as yet unsolved mysteries of the prison signalling code. An old dodge was for discharged prisoners to get as near the prison boundary walls as possible, and then send up a kite with a message written on it. As soon as this was flying over the quarries the string was cut, and down the kite fell for Bill Sykes and mates to peruse. Nothing of this kind has, however, been observed lately, and yet somehow these letters get in.

1894 *Truth* (Sydney) 6 May p. 3: There has been no small stir in Darlinghurst Gaol over the discovery of the fact that some warders have been in the habit of regularly communicating with prisoners' friends outside the gaol, and bringing back 'stiffs' or letters to the man in the 'Stone Jug'.

1919 V. Marshall *The World of the Living Dead* p. 86: I remembers well the stiff I got a year ago wot said / 'When yer time's up, come back 'ome—we wants yer Jim'.

1950 'Thirty-five' in G. Simes *Dictionary of Australian Underworld Slang* (1993) p. 197: *Stiff*, a letter sent in or out of prison illicitly.

1967 K. Tennant *Tell Morning This* p. 44: 'You know what Julie's like'. 'Do I not? Every time she smuggles out a stiff. It begins: "Rene, if I find you have been wearing my clothes, I'll smash your face in". And she would too'.

1967 *Whisper All Aussie Dictionary* in *Kings Cross Whisper* 39 p. 4: *Stiff*, an illegal letter smuggled from the nick.

1984 B. Ellem *Doing Time: The Prison Experience* p. 50: Censorship is a lot of rot, really, because if you're gonna put something they don't like in a letter you send out a stiff. So what's the use of censorship? You can beat it with stiffs.

1989 T. Anderson *Inside Outlaws: A Prison Diary* p. 157: *Stiff*, illegal letter, letter smuggled through searches. These were more common when mail was more heavily censored and more restricted. However, mail between jails is still heavily restricted, so stiffs still pass between jails by various means.

2001 *Prison & Drug Slang: NSW Corrective Services: Stiff*, letter or note smuggled out of a prison.

stink fight.

Australian English.

The term means 'a strong or violent disagreement, a fight'.

Origin: Intensification of General English *stink*. One of the General English senses of *stink* is 'a row or fuss; a furore' (especially as in 'kick up a stink') (OED), recorded from the early nineteenth century. This sense is certainly common in Australia, but it has existed alongside a 'stronger' sense of *stink*, often with suggestions of physical violence. The distinction between the two senses is often a fine one—for example, in the 1921 quote the sense is simply 'a disagreement, a row', whereas in the 1928 quote there is more violence than would usually be associated with the term *stink* in General English.

> **1921** *Telegraph* (Brisbane) 13 December p. 8: Defendant replied, 'No. Payne is just out, and he wouldn't sell anything to me. I had a stink with him about 12 months ago'.
>
> **1928** *Daily Standard* (Brisbane) 30 October p. 7: Blood saturated everything. There was a large pool of it on the bedroom floor. A sheet on the bed showed a blood stain which gave the appearance of having been put there by a person wiping a razor or some such instrument. … In a back room there was a pair of wet trousers with blood stains on the braces. … Defendant said: 'The joker and I had a "stink"'. … Asked how he accounted for the bloodstains defendant said that he did not know how they got there. Witness said to defendant: 'You can see that the blade has been wiped, and here is where it was wiped', pointing to the mark on the bed clothes. Defendant said, 'Yes, it looks like it'. Asked how the shirt came by its stains defendant said, 'In the "stink", I suppose, I was wearing it then'. He also said that the cause of the trousers being wet was that the other 'joker' had thrown them over him during the 'stink'.
>
> **1944** L. Glassop *We Were the Rats* p. 65: I was in the last stink and, take it from me, your paybook's your Bible.
>
> **1985** R.G. Barrett *You Wouldn't Be Dead for Quids* p. 98: They'd had a bit of a stink … with a bunch of yobbos from the Western Suburbs out on a bucks' night just looking for trouble. … Les decked five. Billy got three.
>
> **1993** A.S. Smith & T. Noble *Neddy: The Life and Crimes of Arthur Stanley Smith* p. 148: The nights always ended in a stink, with me having to do the fighting. He couldn't hold his hands up.
>
> **2016** R. Vaculik *Bra Boy* p. 61: I was the typical waxhead kid, but I had this big afro at the time, this big ball of hair that I was pretty stoked with. I'd been told by the older guys down the beach, 'You better be careful with that hair, Rich. You get into a stink and someone's going to get a hold of it and gearstick ya'.

stir gaol.

General English.

This term was originally British (first recorded 1835), and later used more widely.

Origin: Probably from Romany *sturabin* 'prison'.

1940 *Sunday Times* (Perth) 11 February p. 24: The professor doesn't think it's very decent / To smother all our lingo up with slang ... And no doubt he'd turn a sickly shade of pale / If he heard referred to once as 'stir' or 'chokey' / The place he knows as prison or as gaol.

1950 B.K. DOYLE *Australian Police Journal* April p. 118: *Stir*, gaol.

1989 T. ANDERSON *Inside Outlaws: A Prison Diary* p. 157: *Stir*, jail, the nick.

stir-crazy institutionalized.

General English.

The term means 'suffering a psychosis caused by imprisonment in jail'. It first appeared in the 1920s. It is now used more widely for various kinds of psychological disturbance (see quote 2022). See also BOOB HAPPY.

1984 B. ELLEM *Doing Time: The Prison Experience* p. 198: *Stir crazy*, a person who is considered to be a bit dippy or emotionally unbalanced.

1986 *Canberra Times* 30 December p. 8: Solicitors speak of clients who are depressed and 'stir-crazy'.

2001 *Prison & Drug Slang: NSW Corrective Services*: *Stir crazy*, prison delirium syndrome.

2022 *Advertiser* (Adelaide) 8 January (Year 12 Supplement) p. 18: It is important for people to take breaks from study and do different things, otherwise you will go stir crazy.

straw bail bail papers signed by sugar bag on worthless surety.

General Underworld Slang.

The term means 'bail that is given on sureties that are worthless'. The implication in the Glossary's reference to the SUGAR BAG (a police officer who takes bribes) is that the authorities know that the bail monies are not sound and are 'on the take'.

Origin: The underlying notion is that the surety for the bail is unsound, either 'made of straw' or put up by 'straw men'. See the two quotes from British and American sources in square brackets (1853, 1859). Note that the 1846 Australian example is the earliest. The OED evidence has not been recently updated.

1846 *Melbourne Argus* 8 December p. 2: In consequence of the facilities which the law gives of binding parties to the peace, and the reckless manner in which they are made available, the Bench have arrived at the determination of requiring good bail in all such cases, considering that the system of receiving straw bail had gone to too great an extent.

[**1853** *Notes & Queries* 1st Ser. 7 86: Straw bail is, I believe, a term still used by attorneys to distinguish insufficient bail from 'justifiable' or sufficient bail.]

[**1859** J. R. BARTLETT *Dictionary of Americanisms* (ed. 2) 455: *Straw bail*, worthless bail; bail given by 'men of straw', i.e. persons who pretend to the possession of property, but have none.]

1937 *Advocate* (Burnie) 27 August p. 5: Melbourne ... Amending legislation to prevent 'straw bail' by demanding the deposit of a surety or security by anyone who appealed to the Court of General Sessions against a decision of the Court of Petty Sessions passed all stages in the Legislative Assembly today.

1967 *Whisper All Aussie Dictionary* in *Kings Cross Whisper* 40 p. 4: *Straw bail*, the system of someone going surety for bail of someone unlucky enough to be caught out in a misdemeanour.

1977 J. Ramsay *Cop It Sweet* p. 86: *Straw bail*, surety for bail.

1983 R. Aven-Bray *Ridgey Didge Oz Jack Lang* p. 45: *Straw bail*, bail on property (House of Straw).

suck his brain see what he knows.

General English.

This idiom first appears in the *Lexicon Balatronicum: A Dictionary of Buckish Slang, University Wit, and Pickpocket Eloquence* (London 1811): 'To suck. To pump. To draw from a man all he knows'. The dictionary then gives an illustrative sentence *The file sucked the noodles's brains* and translates it: 'the deep one drew out of the fool all he knew'. Cf. the idiom *to pick someone's brains*, first recorded in the late eighteenth century.

1870 *South Australian Chronicle* (Adelaide) 4 June p. 11: We make bold to state that a better Governor's speech, or one containing more useful ideas, was never delivered in South Australia than the one we have just listened to; Mr. Strangways need not be ashamed of his programme, and whoever may succeed him will have to do what Mr. Bright deprecated—'suck his brains'. We mean the Attorney-General's—not Mr. Bright's. Whoever may succeed the present Government, the policy of the present Government will be carried out in the main, for it is what the country needs and must have.

2013 *Advertiser* (Adelaide) 8 December p. 76: When I trained at Port a few years ago I'd heard that Kane was one of the most professional blokes going around so I sucked his brain and tried to get as much information as possible.

sugar bag policeman who accepts bribes.

Australian English.

The term means 'a person who accepts bribes or "sweeteners"' (AND). Outside the prison this is usually a police officer; inside the prison it is a warder.

1877 *Vagabond Papers* 3rd Series p. 139: The warder who overlooks these little things, and who will make presents of tobacco, or traffic, is called a 'sugarbag'. I expect I was about the sweetest sugarbag they have had in Pentridge for a long time.

1928 *News* (Adelaide) 28 February p. 1: After having been charged defendant said to the constables, 'You have been in the "sugar bag" for years, and I am going to get you if it costs me £100'. ... Mr Rollison (cross-examining witness)—You know what being in the sugar bag means? Witness—Yes, I do. — It means that you are being constantly bribed? —Yes. —You know that there have been persistent rumors about you and Worrall accepting bribes?

1968 L.H. Evers *Fall Among Thieves* p. 68: She knows that the copper who's number one is a sugar-bag so she talks to him half-cunning about a little something in his hand.

1972 P. Berman & K. Childs *Why Isn't She Dead!* p. 66: If a policeman is called a 'sugarbag' by other police or the underworld he is on the take, the sugar merely sweetens or lightens any offence.

sunk no chance of acquittal.
Australian Underworld Slang.
Specific use of General English *sunk* meaning 'in a hopeless position; finished, ruined, done for' (OED).

1990 V. Tupper & R. Wortley *Anthology of Prison Slang in Australia* (National Library of Australia, Pandora Archive): *Sunk*, found guilty.

1993 M.B. Read *Chopper 3: How to Shoot Friends and Influence People* p. 193: I didn't shoot Sid Collins. It would have been the lime funeral, not a hospital bed if I had. Margaret and I were planning to get married in June, so even I wouldn't be shooting people in May. I don't know why they decided to set me up with the crime ... I don't know. Sunk by nitwits for the only one I didn't do. Then again, for the ones I've got away with I'm still well in front. What a twisted comedy.

2020 *Sydney Morning Herald* 12 December p. 4: 'I'm speechless and in a state of disbelief, I have been sunk on murder when I am innocent of organising this murder', Abu-Mahmoud wrote from a holding cell at the Supreme Court.

swy¹ two years.
Australian Underworld and Prison Slang.
The term means 'a prison sentence of two years'.
Origin: From German *zwei* 'two'.
In 1898 an article in the *Bulletin* newspaper says that a slang term in Western Queensland for a florin ('two shillings') is *swideener*. *Deener* was a common slang term for a shilling, so a *swi-deener* is 'two shillings'. The shortened form *swy* became an Australian term for a 'two-shilling coin' from the 1920s, and later in Prison Slang *swy* meant a 'two-year prison sentence' and 'two ounces of tobacco'. The term *swy-up* first appeared in 1911 as a synonym for *two-up*.

1941 S.J. Baker *A Popular Dictionary of Australian Slang* p. 75: *Swy*, the game of two-up. (2) A sentence of two years' gaol. (3) A florin.

1946 *Singleton Argus* 14 April p. 4: The 'swy' was a couple of years in gaol.

1975 *Bulletin* (Sydney) 26 April p. 44 (article on underworld slang): So the low creeps got me a swy with a one. [*Ed*. The phrase *a swy with a one* means 'two years' imprisonment with a minimum of one'.]

1983 E. Withnel *Australian Journal of Cultural Studies* 1 (May) p. 90: The names of laggings are: Two years: A Swy.

2006 B. Matthews *Intractable ... Life inside Australia's First Super-max Prison* p. 399: *Swy of years*, a two-year sentence.

swy² two ounces of tobacco.

Australian Prison Slang.
>See also DOUBLE.
>Origin: See previous entry swy¹.

>**1950** 'Thirty-five' in G. SIMES *Dictionary of Australian Underworld Slang* (1993) p. 199: *Swy*, two, two shillings, two pounds (£2), two ounces of tobacco, two years, the game of two-up.
>
>**1984** B. ELLEM *Doing Time: The Prison Experience* p. 198: *Swy*, two years, or two ounces of tobacco.
>
>**1989** T. ANDERSON *Inside Outlaws: A Prison Diary* p. 157: *Swy*, packet of tobacco. ... A swy has long been used as a form of currency in jail, as a unit of gambling.
>
>**1995** N. IBRAHIM & M. QUINNEY *Glossary of Gaol Slang: Pentridge Gaol* (Unpublished Typescript ANDC): *Swy*, tobacco.
>
>**2010** *Northern Territory News* 16 September p. 11: Christian Bible paper has been the cigarette paper of choice in the gaol population of Australia for yonks; for biggest mob time. It makes the 'swy' that much sweeter (a 'swy' is gaol-speak for a 'two ounce' packet a tobacco).

[**tail** *see* BACK A TAIL.]

take it to the toe run, try to escape.

Australian English.
The phrase means 'to depart, to leave quickly, to escape'. The formulation HIT THE TOE is more common. Other variants are *take to the toe, get on the toe*. The evidence is for *take to the toe* rather than *take it to the toe*.

>**1929** *Advertiser* (Adelaide) 8 June p. 18: When asked why he ran away the accused said, 'I always take to the toe when the coppers are about'.
>
>**1950** 'Thirty-five' in G. SIMES *Dictionary of Australian Underworld Slang* (1993) p. 203: *Take to the toe*, to run away.

take seconds think again.

British and Australian Underworld Slang.
The term is not well attested, and the examples below are British. Not otherwise recorded in the Australian evidence.
Origin: Probably related to the phrase *take the seconds* (see quotes), perhaps an abbreviation of *take the second thoughts*.

>[**1930** D. MACKENZIE *Hell's Kitchen: The Story of London's Underworld* p. 307: I settled down to go straight when I got out of prison four months ago. As the Underworld puts it, I decided to 'swallow the anchor' or to 'take the seconds'.]
>
>[**1950** E. PARTRIDGE *A Dictionary of the Underworld* p. 712: *Take the seconds*, to abandon a projected crime, on second thoughts.]

take the knock cheat someone of his share, in part or whole.

Australian English.

The phrase means 'to fail to pay a debt, especially a gambling debt'.

Origin: This is a specific use of the General English phrase *to take the knock* 'to sustain a severe financial or emotional blow, to suffer a setback' from *knock* 'a misfortune, a rebuff, a blow' (OED). The phrase can mean 'to suffer financial losses, often in gambling' (GDS). The Australian sense develops from this, referring to a situation where the person welshes on a deal, especially by not paying gambling debts.

The 1888 evidence is from an Australian writer in an Australian newspaper, but reporting on an incident that took place in Britain.

1888 *Sportsman* (Melbourne) 18 April p. 1 (in the quote Sutton is a bookmaker): Sutton's luck took a turn, and Sutton 'took the knock', which, being interpreted, means that he was temporarily unable to meet his engagements. This, by the way, happened more than once in Australia, but he invariably paid up honorably the moment he got on his legs.

1924 G.H. Lawson *Dictionary of Australian Words and Terms* p. 28: *Taking the knock*, to avoid payment.

1930 *Referee* (Sydney) 14 May p. 1: A junior member of a prominent Sydney business, who is also a member of Tattersall's Club, Sydney, failed to liquidate betting liabilities amounting to several thousands incurred at Randwick on Easter Saturday and Easter Monday. In a nutshell this punter 'took the knock' on settling day for £3000.

1950 *Smith's Weekly* (Sydney) 14 October p. 15: Sydney firm has an employee on its staff whom it can't sack for the next three years—not without going out of business, anyway. He was under notice of dismissal when he 'took the knock' on a fair-sized wad of stake money given him by other members of the staff to punt on their behalf at Randwick. The horses nominated won, and the amount he should have returned ran into a nice three-figure sum. At the end of the week, when his notice expired, the employees held a stop-work meeting at which the boss was told bluntly that not only was the no-hoper not to be sacked, but that he would continue on in his job until the punters had recovered their money from him.

1968 J. Alard *He Who Shoots Last* p. 58: 'Dey say crime don't pay', was Porky's conversational contribution. Lefty was quick to pick him up 'Neither does dat bookie ya had here last week. I heard Treacle Teeth saying he took da knock on Crafty Wilson and Erskinville Ernie'.

1983 R. Aven-Bray *Ridgey Didge Oz Jack Lang* p. 31: *Take the knock*, refuse to pay a debt.

tank a safe.

Australian Underworld Slang.

Origin: Specific or transferred use of *tank* 'an artificial receptacle, usually rectangular or cylindrical and often of plate-iron, used for storing water, oil, or other liquids in large quantities' (OED).

1901 W.S. Walker *In the Blood* p. 143: To 'open tank' I yearn, 'screw in' or 'make a turn'.

1941 S.J. Baker *A Popular Dictionary of Australian Slang* p. 11: *Blow a tank*, to open a safe by means of explosive.

1948 *Sunday Times* (Perth) 30 May p. 3: For the want of a better name permit me to call my tank-bursting instructor Jack. For your benefit a tank is any safe, ranging from the Commonwealth's to baby's money box.

1950 B.K. Doyle *Australian Police Journal* April p. 119: *Tank*, a safe.

1967 *Whisper All Aussie Dictionary* in *Kings Cross Whisper* 41 p. 4: *Tank*, a safe. People who specialise in robbing banks are usually described as tank men.

1981 *Sydney Morning Herald* 2 March p. 1: Dugan claimed that more than 30 years ago a friend had been arrested, convicted and sentenced for a Sydney tank robbery—a safe cracking—which he had not done. Dugan said he knew this because he had done the job himself.

1984 B. Ellem *Doing Time: The Prison Experience* p. 198: *Tank*, a money safe.

tankman person who specializes in stealing from safes.
Australian Underworld Slang.
  The term means 'a safe-breaker' (AND).
  Origin: See previous entry TANK.

1953 *Argus* (Melbourne) 31 October p. 9: The 'Tank Man', the aristocrat of criminals, whose skill and patience can open the door to wealth, or a few office records. He needs years of training to 'bust' a safe, seldom dies wealthy.

1967 *Whisper All Aussie Dictionary* in *Kings Cross Whisper* 41 p. 4: *Tank*, a safe. People who specialise in robbing banks are usually described as tank men.

1974 C. Paton *I Was a Prison Parson* p. 40: As a 'tank' man (safe-blower) Harry had seen a lot of gaol.

1977 J. Ramsay *Cop It Sweet* p. 88: *Tank-man*, one who robs safes.

1984 B. Ellem *Doing Time: The Prison Experience* p. 198: *Tank man*, someone who is good at opening safes.

2006 B. Matthews *Intractable ... Life inside Australia's First Super-max Prison* p. 99: Tex Lawson, the gangling tank man and escape artist.

2010 A. Shand *King of Thieves* p. 6: Like most criminal activities, thieving is a vocation, a specialised trade even. A tank man cannot be a hoister, no more than a dip (pickpocket) can be a gunnie or a bust man (burglar). [*Ed.* A *hoister* is a 'shoplifter'. See HOISTER.]

ted vagina.
Australian English.
  Also in the form *Theodore* (see quotes 1996, 1998).
  Origin: Of unknown origin.

1981 *Tracks* April p. 3: As for kicking anybody up the arse it sounds to me like you need a good kick up your woofy ted.

1989 R.G. Barrett *Godson* p. 27: He could feel the bristle of her ted, warm and moist through her knickers.

1996 B. Thorpe *Sex and Thugs and Rock 'n' Roll* p. 227: Yeah, he's always after some Theodore.

1998 B. Thorpe *Most People I Know* p. 115: He winked, shaking his lapel. 'Ted' or 'Theodore' was street slang for pussy.

2002 R.G. Barrett *Mystery Bay Blues* p. 169: Grace crushed her mouth onto Norton's as he stroked the beautiful, wet tenderness of her ted.

throw off camouflage the truth.

Australian Underworld Slang.

The term means 'to use misdirection or disguise to cover up the truth'.

Origin: Related to the General English senses of *throw off*. As a verb, *throw off* can mean 'to shake off or elude (a pursuer, a fellow competitor in a race, etc.)', related to the longer phrase *to throw off the scent*. The derived noun *throw-off* often has a stronger emphasis on the means of doing this, as 'deceit; an illusion, a disguise'. These senses get us closer to the specific Australian sense listed in the Glossary—'camouflage the truth'.

The 1971 quote, also from Parramatta Jail, is a noun, but it demonstrates the emphasis on disguise, camouflage, and misdirection. The 2018 quote gives a verbal definition for sense 1 but uses the noun in the illustrative sentence.

1971 *Contact: Parramatta Jail Resurgents Magazine* August n.p.: S.S. — Sir, what is your real name? — Actually, Brown is my real name. It's what you call a throw-off.

1990 V. Tupper & R. Wortley *Anthology of Prison Slang in Australia* (National Library of Australia, Pandora Archive): *Throw off*, to avoid the issue. For example a prison officer would be accused of throwing off where he refused to make a decision about a request. Alternatively a prisoner may feign ignorance when confronted about an issue. Sometimes just throw.

1997 *Sydney Morning Herald* 1 May (Supplement) p. 2: The royal commission revealed that the corrupt other world of police and criminals has its own language. ... *Throwing off*, telling a lie.

2018 J. Knight *Dictionary of Victorian Prison Slang* (online) p. 36: *Throw-off*, 1. vb To direct attention away from something. Example: 'He left that empty pouch lying around as a throw-off'. 2. n An excuse, usually a false one. Example: 'That's just a throw-off!' *Throw-off pouch* A near empty pouch of tobacco that could be displayed when another prisoner asked for a 'plug' or a 'snip' so that the prisoner could claim he could not spare any tobacco because he hardly had any left.

[**toe** *see* TAKE IT TO THE TOE.]

toe ragger person of no account.

Australian English.

The term means 'a tramp, a down-and-out', and is also used as a general term of abuse (AND). When the term first appeared in the 1880s it was very much a class term, with the *toe-ragger* sometimes literally revealing his poverty by wearing toe rags instead of socks, and figuratively bearing the scorn of his social superiors. From very early on in the history of the word, it was used in prisons, and there also marked the lowest in the prison hierarchy (see quotes 1880, 1881, 1886). Since the lowest in the prison hierarchy were often short-termers, this explains why *toe-ragger* came to be used of a short-term prisoner (see quotes 1884, 1918, 1950, 1962, 1977).

Origin: From *toe-rag* 'a strip of cloth wrapped round the foot and worn inside a boot, in place of a sock. Also ... as an emblem of poverty or disreputableness' (AND).

1878 *Pilgrim* (Sydney) 2nd Series iii. p. 11: They were a motley crowd. 'Toe-raggers' was an appropriate name for them. There was not a pair of socks, with the exception of mine own, in the whole community.

1880 *Evening News* (Sydney) 10 April p. 7: The 'toe-ragger' (so called from the habit his class have of wrapping their feet in old rags in default of boots) who has come in possibly on a charge of drunkenness, or under that truly absurd and most supremely British enactment, the Vagrant Act, is treated even by the prisoners with contumely, scorn, and contempt.

1881 *Bulletin* (Sydney) 5 November p. 5: In prison, as well as out of it, society divides itself into certain sections where the idiosyncrasy of the individuals who compose them are distinctly felt. There is a prison aristocracy as well as a common mob, and 'toe-raggers' (men living on 'a spud a-day'), and there is quite as much arrogance occasionally displayed as I witness daily on the part of those who roll in their carriages towards the humble menial who opens the door.

1884 *Queensland Figaro* (Brisbane) 26 July p. 126: 'Short-timers' or those unfortunate prisoners whose stay will not exceed a period of six months, and who are known also under this distinguishing term of 'toe-raggers', have not the opportunities of becoming on good terms with the warders that longer-sentenced men have.

1886 *Sydney Morning Herald* 6 August p. 4: One individual is what is called in the gaol a 'toe-ragger', or one of those wretched looking creatures whose clothes are in rags and thickly bespattered with evil smelling loathsomeness, whose feet are chiefly enveloped in a rotten covering, half socks and half rags, and whose attenuated body is scored all over with the blood marks which are caused by the finger nails in their never ending scratching to obtain relief from the tormenting presence of vermin.

1888 *Queensland Figaro* (Brisbane) 21 January p. 119: At a congregation of bushmen in a bush township, as may be known, the bosses and 'silvertails' occupy different hotels to those which the 'toe-raggers' and rouseabouts patronise.

1918 T. MARSHALL *Jail from Within* p. 45: Christ Orlmighty, some o' you toeraggers (short-timers) take the cake.

1941 S.J. BAKER *A Popular Dictionary of Australian Slang* p. 77: *Toeragger*, a person of no position, wealth or attainments.

1950 'Thirty-five' in G. SIMES *Dictionary of Australian Underworld Slang* (1993) p. 203: *Toe-ragger*, a prisoner serving a short sentence.

1962 D. McLEAN *The World Turned Upside Down* p. 114: He's only a 'toe-ragger', that's what they call a short-term prisoner.

1977 J. RAMSAY *Cop It Sweet* p. 90: *Toe-ragger*, short-term prisoner.

1990 V. TUPPER & R. WORTLEY *Anthology of Prison Slang in Australia* (National Library of Australia, Pandora Archive): *Toe ragger*, someone who is at nadir of social acceptance in prison or anywhere else. Often applied to an informer.

toey anxious.

Australian English.

The term means 'restive, touchy; ill-at-ease, nervous, anxious; keen to begin (a race etc.)' (AND). The earliest evidence refers to racehorses keen to begin a race. Another sense 'randy; eager for sex' appears in the 1980s.

Origin: From the movements of an anxious racehorse at the start of a race.

1929 *Brisbane Courier* 12 February p. 4: When the horse entered the enclosure he seemed to him to 'be a bit toey and sweaty'.

1950 'Thirty-five' in G. Simes *Dictionary of Australian Underworld Slang* (1993) p. 203: *Toey*, anxious to be gone; restless (especially of a prisoner who anticipates early release or transfer to a prison camp).

1959 *Overland* xiv. p. 20: The other umpire a bit toey out there at square leg.

1967 *Whisper All Aussie Dictionary* in *Kings Cross Whisper* 41 p. 4: *Toey*, to be nervous.

1990 V. Tupper & R. Wortley *Anthology of Prison Slang in Australia* (National Library of Australia, Pandora Archive): *Toey*, agitated or unsettled. There is a clear inference that a toey prisoner is a potential escapee.

2021 *Canberra Times* 20 May p. 44: It's fair to say Melbourne is, right now, as close as it's been to a 13th premiership as at any stage of the long run of outs. And long-suffering Demon fans are quite rightly starting to get a little toey about the prospect.

tom jewellery.

General English.

From the 1930s in the full form *tomfoolery*, and from the 1950s in the abbreviated form *tom*.

Origin: Abbreviated form of *tomfoolery*, rhyming slang for 'jewellery'.

1983 R. Aven-Bray *Ridgey Didge Oz Jack Lang* p. 47: *Tom foolery*, jewellery.

2010 A. Shand *King of Thieves* p. 85: The 'tom' (short for tomfoolery, rhyming slang for jewellery) had fetched more than £20 000.

track screw who brings contraband for prisoners in exchange for fee.

Australian Prison Slang.

The term means 'a prison warder who traffics in illegal goods for prisoners' (AND).

Origin: From *track* 'to deal in something, esp. illegally', or a figurative use of *track* 'to follow a path'. Note the early use of a variant *track-in* in quote 1939.

1939 K. Tennant *Foveaux* p. 290: Yer brother Freddy says there's usually a track-in, some screw who's willin' to do his job warderin', to smuggle snout to the men so you won't go short of a smoke.

1950 'Thirty-five' in G. Simes *Dictionary of Australian Underworld Slang* (1993) p. 205: *Track*, a prison warder who will carry contraband messages or goods out of or into a prison for a prisoner.

1967 *Whisper All Aussie Dictionary* in *Kings Cross Whisper* 41 p. 4: *Track*, a person, usually a screw, who will take the odds of being sacked to make things a little easier for the prisoners by trafficking in goods in exchange for coin of the realm.

1990 V. Tupper & R. Wortley *Anthology of Prison Slang in Australia* (National Library of Australia, Pandora Archive): *Track*, a prison worker who engages in trafficking with inmates.

2001 *Prison & Drug Slang: NSW Corrective Services*: *Track*, a prison warder who will carry contraband.

trick cyclist psychiatrist.

General English.

Originally British military slang from the 1940s, then used more widely.

Origin: Jocular modification of *psychiatrist*, modelled on the *trick cyclist* who perform tricks on a bicycle.

1964 C. Barrett *Address: Kings Cross* p. 126: He handed me a professional card across the table, and waited to see my reaction, The card was that of the psychiatrist, Byron Lords. 'So now you think I need a trick cyclist?' I asked bitterly.

1984 E. Withnel *Australian Journal of Cultural Studies* 2 (November) p. 69: The screws aim for the flesh, the 'trickcyclists' aim for the mind.

2020 *Herald Sun* (Melbourne) 31 October (Lifestyle Section) p. 12: My father adored roaring at the television and when asked if it was really necessary to berate whoever was on the screen by one of his daughters, he rather sportingly said: 'It's therapeutic and a lot cheaper than a trick cyclist' (psychiatrist).

tropical very risky.

Australian Underworld Slang.

The term means '(of goods) stolen; (of actions) highly illegal, highly dangerous' (AND). Cf. General English *hot* 'stolen'. See also ON FIRE.

1950 'Thirty-five' in G. Simes *Dictionary of Australian Underworld Slang* (1993) p. 206: *Tropical*, hot.

1967 *Whisper All Aussie Dictionary* in *Kings Cross Whisper* 41 p. 4: *Tropical*, any goods not paid for by the possessor can be classified as tropical. How tropical, depends on what sort of fuss goes on to generate heat.

1977 J. Ramsay *Cop It Sweet* p. 91: *Tropical*, description for stolen goods or unpaid-for merchandise.

1983 R. Aven-Bray *Ridgey Didge Oz Jack Lang* p. 47: *Tropical*, something stolen (hot).

1991 M.B. Read *Chopper 1: From the Inside* p. 66: [The Governor of Pentridge] explained to me that for every dozen or so bashings and attacks the Overcoat Gang did, only one would get a mention on any report, and none, if any, on my personal records. It was getting a bit tropical and I had to ease it up for a while.

2001 *Prison & Drug Slang: NSW Corrective Services*: *Tropical*, police interest or trouble.

tug his head distract his gaze.

Australian Underworld Slang.

The phrase means 'to distract a person while a crime is being committed'. Not widely attested. In the quote below the phrase is abbreviated to 'tug'.

1975 *Bulletin* (Sydney) 26 April p. 45: Anyway, we get this dead set sneak go for a willy in a supermarket. So we send in Limp to tug the tart minding the willy. It was this woman who was guarding the willy (money) and the success of the operation rested on the Limp distracting her.

tumble lose temper.

Australian Underworld Slang.

The term means 'to be thrown off balance, to be provoked'.

Origin: Probably related to General English sense of *tumble* 'to fall; esp. to fall in a helpless way, as from stumbling or violence' (OED).

1971 J. McNeil *The Chocolate Frog* in *The Chocolate Frog, The Old Familiar Juice: Two Plays* (1973) p. 35: Kevin: (*taking offence at last*) Look, will you stop calling me names??? Or at least settle on *one*? I've had a dozen so far ... whatever they might mean. Tosser: (*grinning with delight*) ... We've tumbled 'im at last.

1973 J. McNeil *The Chocolate Frog, The Old Familiar Juice: Two Plays* p. 119 (Glossary): *Tumble*, (colloquial), to confuse, to upset the balance.

1984 B. Ellem *Doing Time: The Prison Experience* p. 199: *Tumble*, to react when being deliberately provoked or stirred. To let someone get under your guard.

1990 V. Tupper & R. Wortley *Anthology of Prison Slang in Australia* (National Library of Australia, Pandora Archive): *Tumble*, to allow oneself to be easily provoked.

1995 N. Ibrahim & M. Quinney *Glossary of Gaol Slang: Pentridge Gaol* (Unpublished Typescript ANDC): *Tumble*, react to deliberate provocation.

tune in listen to other people's conversation.

General English.

Originally *tune in* referred to the process of tuning 'a radio or television to a particular station or transmission, or a particular frequency' (OED). It can also mean 'to listen', with the extra emphasis of gathering information: 'to become mentally receptive to, or aware of; to comprehend' (OED).

1950 *Daily Telegraph* (Sydney) 23 July p. 27: He looked at Sarah, who had been pretending to read a paper at the counter but had been tuned in on our conversation.

2005 I. Evans *Odd Socks* p. 345: I lean back and glance casually over towards the other table so I can tune in on the conversation there.

turn it up give crime away.

Australian Underworld Slang.

This is a specific use of General English *turn up* 'to give up, renounce, abandon, cast off, discard' (OED).

1812 J.H. Vaux *New Vocabulary of the Flash Language* in *Memoirs* (1819) II p. 221: *Turn up*, to desist from, or relinquish, any particular habit or mode of life, or the further pursuit of any object you had in view, is called *turning it up*.

1967 *Whisper All Aussie Dictionary* in *Kings Cross Whisper* 41 p. 4: *Turn it up*, to desist at doing something.

turn (someone) up give evidence to bring about accused person's acquittal.

Australian Underworld Slang.

This sense probably developed from British *turn up* 'to set free, turn loose; to discharge or release (a prisoner)'. The releasing of a prisoner sense is first recorded in Vaux' Australian dictionary (see quote 1812). In this use, the acquittal or 'turning up' is done by a jury or magistrate; in the later Australian underworld use the acquittal is achieved by a witness manipulating the evidence or 'taking the rap' himself.

1812 J.H. VAUX *New Vocabulary of the Flash Language* in *Memoirs* (1819) II p. 221: *Turned up*, a person acquitted by a jury, or discharged by a magistrate for want of evidence, etc., is said to be *turned up*.

1967 *Whisper All Aussie Dictionary* in *Kings Cross Whisper* 41 p. 4: *Turn up*, to be turned up as for a partner in any crime to take the full blame, allowing his buddy to go free.

1971 J. MCNEIL *The Chocolate Frog* in *The Chocolate Frog, The Old Familiar Juice: Two Plays* (1973) p. 23: Why didn't yer help him beat it, hey? Yer dog of a thing! Why *didn't* yer turn 'im up?

1989 T. ANDERSON *Inside Outlaws: A Prison Diary* p. 159: *Turn up*, apart from the ordinary meaning of appearing at, fronting, or arriving, this means: to plead guilty to protect an accomplice. For instance, you may plead guilty to a robbery and then say that no other person ... was involved. You may even plead guilty to a crime you did not commit, so as to turn up a friend.

twine to hoodwink.

Australian Underworld Slang.

The term means 'to trick, deceive, con'.

Origin: Of uncertain origin. A verb *twine* with a similar sense appears in a passage in an 1869 British text *Six Years in the Prisons of England* by 'A Merchant', printed in the *Temple Bar Magazine*:

'Harry', I asked, 'what's that "bloke" here for, who occupies the end bed?' 'Twineing'. 'Twineing! What's that?' 'Don't you know that yet? why you must be a greenhorn not to know that. Well! I'll tell you. Suppose you start in the morning with a good sovereign and a 'snyde' half-sovereign in your pocket; you go into some place or other, and ask for change of the sovereign, or you order some beer and give the sovereign in payment; it's likely you will get half-a-sovereign and silver back in change. Then is the time to 'twine'. You change your mind, after you have 'rung' your snyde half 'quid' with the good one, and throwing down the 'snyde' half, say you prefer silver; the landlord or landlady, or whoever it is, will pick up the snyde half-quid, thinking of course it is the same one they had given you!' [*Ed.* The term *snyde* means 'counterfeit', and *rung* means 'substituted'.]

In this example, 'to twine' is to make the counterfeit substitution, and this probably derives from *twine* in the sense 'to twist'. It is possible that this is the ancestor of the Australian term, although there is a large time gap.

1967 *Whisper All Aussie Dictionary* in *Kings Cross Whisper* 41 p. 4: *Twine*, a con trick.

1984 B. ELLEM *Doing Time: The Prison Experience* p. 199: *Twine*, to con someone.

1990 V. TUPPER & R. WORTLEY *Anthology of Prison Slang in Australia* (National Library of Australia, Pandora Archive): *Twine*, to deliberately mislead.

1995 N. IBRAHIM & M. QUINNEY *Glossary of Gaol Slang: Pentridge Gaol* (Unpublished Typescript ANDC): *Twine*, to con some-one.

twist, the being declared an habitual criminal.
Australian Underworld Slang.

See KEY for the possible sentencing consequences of being declared a habitual criminal.

Origin: Since it is synonymous with KEY perhaps it alludes to a turn of the key.

1941 S.J. BAKER *A Popular Dictionary of Australian Slang* p. 79: *Twist*, an habitual criminal.

1946 *Singleton Argus* 14 April p. 4: The 'key' is a well-known underworld description for an habitual criminal (other fancy underworld terms for the same thing are 'the twirl', and 'the gate', and 'the twist').

1950 B.K. DOYLE *Australian Police Journal* April p. 120: *The twist*, to be declared an habitual criminal.

1967 *Whisper All Aussie Dictionary* in *Kings Cross Whisper* 41 p. 4: *Twist*, same as key man.

1968 J. ALARD *He Who Shoots Last* p. 197: 'Did you hear how long Siddy got?' 'I understand he got the twist', informed the killer. 'That's highly probable. With a record like his they often get the key. Still, it is not as bad now as previously. It used to be an indeterminant sentence'.

1990 V. TUPPER & R. WORTLEY *Anthology of Prison Slang in Australia* (National Library of Australia, Pandora Archive): *Twist*, an habitual prisoner.

[under *see* GO UNDER.**]**

under a cloud under suspicion of being a dog.
Australian Prison Slang.

The term means 'suspected of being an informer'.

This is a specific use of the General English meaning of the phrase (first recorded in Britain in the seventeenth century) 'in trouble or difficulties; out of favour; with a slur on one's character'. A DOG in the prison system is 'an informer', the lowest on the social hierarchy.

2007 M.B. READ *Chopper 11: Last Man Standing* p. 59: Caine entered Pentridge under a cloud of suspicion along with a storm of laughter.

under the lap secretive.

Australian English.

The phrase means '*(adjective)* secret, clandestine; *(adverb)* secretly, clandestinely' (AND). Quote 1971 is adjectival, but the others are adverbial.

Origin: Probably a variant of such idioms as *under the counter*, *under the table*, referring to clandestine activities.

> **1897** *Ballarat Star* 19 March p. 4: I have heard under the lap that they intend to play up £25,000, and if it comes off with them they will not be back for Caulfield. One fielder who has been backing against the lucky pair said to me on the day they left, 'I don't wish them any harm, but if they don't come back for 10 years so much the better for me'.
>
> **1910** *West Australian* (Perth) 28 April p. 6: The bookmaker will always be with us, and, therefore, I think it is far better to license him for the courses than have him betting 'under the lap', as surely would be done.
>
> **1941** S.J. BAKER *A Popular Dictionary of Australian Slang* p. 79: *Under the lap*, confidentially, between you and me.
>
> **1966** J. WATEN *Season of Youth* p. 129: 'Gentlemen. The law demands you leave'. ... But there was plenty to be had under the lap. The tried and trusted were ... given the OK to go upstairs and drink in the dining room without having to buy a meal. It was quite illegal.
>
> **1971** J. MCNEIL *The Chocolate Frog* in *The Chocolate Frog, The Old Familiar Juice: Two Plays* (1973) p. 47: An' listen: if you're some kind of under-the-lap dog, then you just sit up on yer tucker-box.
>
> **2014** *Leader Messenger* (Adelaide) 5 November p. 7: There are also tax implications if committee members are aware of and participating in paying players under the lap or the old brown paper bags.

under the lights questioned at C.I.B.

General Underworld Slang.

A reference to a method of wearing a suspect down by interviewing under bright lights and with sleep deprivation. The 1950 quote suggests an American origin. In the Parramatta Glossary there is specific reference to the Criminal Investigation Branch (C.I.B.), made up mainly of plainclothes detectives.

> [**1950** H.E. GOLDIN *Dictionary of American Underworld Lingo* p. 231: *Under the light*, undergoing police questioning, often under third degree coercion.]

[undone *see* BRING UNDONE; COME UNDONE.]

vag charged with vagrancy.

American and Australian English.

Vag as an abbreviation of *vagrant* or *vagrancy* originated in the US in the second half of the nineteenth century, and soon after appeared in Australia. The phrase *on the vag* meaning 'on a charge of vagrancy' and the verb *to vag* meaning 'to charge someone with the crime of vagrancy' similarly begin in the US but soon appear in Australia. In the Glossary, *vag* is defined as 'charged with vagrancy', and this could be an abbreviation of the phrase *on the vag*, or a form of the past participle/adjective *vagged*. A noun *vag* also appears in Australia meaning '(on) a charge of vagrancy' (see quote 1896).

1865 *Bendigo Advertiser* 2 October p. 3: He met Detective O'Neil who told him that if he was not off in twenty-four hours, he (O'Neil), would 'vag' him i.e. bring him up under the Vagrant Act.

1876 *Gippsland Times* (Sale) 25 May p. 4: Many young larrikins are brought up 'on the vag'.

1896 *Bulletin* (Sydney) 11 April p. 17: A layer and a backer were run in at a Perth (W.A.) rural meeting, though everybody else was betting all day. ... Under W.A.'s precious law if they again offend they are liable to 12 months 'vag'.

1901 *Daily News* (Perth) 2 April p. 3: 'Vagged' ... Wm. Simpson was charged with being a person without any lawful visible means of support.

1922 D. COLLINS *Stolen or Strayed* p. 49: The offence alleged against Tim Hanson on the charge-sheet was that he had 'no visible means of support', otherwise he was 'vagged'.

1968 J. ALARD *He Who Shoots Last* p. 83: The Earl clarified his monetary status: 'I'm as broke as the ten commandments'. 'It's serious, ya knows. If I wuz picked up, dey could vag a man' ... was Ruff's summary of his predicament.

1977 J. MCNEIL *Jack* in *Collected Plays* (1987) p. 228: I was often pinched for Vag.

1984 P. READ *Down There With Me On Cowra Mission* p. 57: I walked into town ... and I got vagged ... Got ten days out of it.

1990 V. TUPPER & R. WORTLEY *Anthology of Prison Slang in Australia* (National Library of Australia, Pandora Archive): *Vagged*, arrested for vagrancy.

verballed be mispresented by lies.

British and Australian Underworld Slang.

The term *to verbal* means 'Of a police officer, detective, etc.: to allege, esp. dishonestly, that (a person accused or suspected of criminal activity) made a verbal confession or said something incriminating; to fabricate (a verbal confession or incriminating statement by a suspected criminal)' (OED). The earliest evidence is for the noun in the 1967 Australian quote listed below. The earliest evidence for the verb is in a 1972 British text, along with this 1972 Parramatta Glossary.

1967 *Whisper All Aussie Dictionary* in *Kings Cross Whisper* 43 p. 11: *Verbal*, uncorroborated evidence given by police.

1974 J. MCNEIL *How Does Your Garden Grow* p. 39: But I do think it's a bit rough, the ways yer planted that wire on me. Yer know it's almost as bad as the way yer verballed me about not facing the wall.

1989 T. ANDERSON *Inside Outlaws: A Prison Diary* p. 9: Fabricated confessions (verbals) were commonplace and virtually all the detectives involved in our case had verballed people in other cases.

1995 N. IBRAHIM & M. QUINNEY *Glossary of Gaol Slang: Pentridge Gaol* (Unpublished Typescript ANDC): *Verbal*, to fabricate admission or confession.

2006 B. Matthews *Intractable ... Life inside Australia's First Super-max Prison* p. 399: *Verbal, verballed*, a fabrication or lie, something false or untrue, fabricated evidence used by police to gain a conviction in criminal trials. To be 'verballed' is to be the victim of untrue confessional evidence.

virgin derogatory term, pure cunt (no good person).

Word play on *pure cunt* meaning 'an absolute bastard' and 'a chaste vagina'. Not otherwise recorded.

walk up start there for the taking.

Australian English.

The term refers to 'something that is easily achieved; someone who is very capable of achieving a result, doing well at a sport, etc.; a pushover; a certainty'.

Origin: From horseracing, where a walk-up start at the beginning of a race might be preferred over a standing start (see quotes 1895, 1927), and where a horse that is granted a walk-up start may have an advantage.

1895 *Australasian* (Melbourne) 6 April p. 14: Most men who know anything about a horse will allow that the natural and reasonable way of starting is by walking the horses up, and having a man with a flag in front to drop his when he sees the starter drop his flag. There can then be no false starts, or any left at the post, excepting by accident, which will always occur in all things human. ... All this will be obviated with a walk-up start.

1927 *Sydney Sportsman* 6 September p. 8: Are our starters ever going to give the walk-up start a trial? ... Something like 16,000 people went up to Warwick Farm to see the meeting of the four great horses Limerick, Commendation, Amounis, and Valicare. It promised to be the race of a century, but when the horses lined up for the start Commendation resolutely refused to stand flatfooted at the barrier. He reared and backed away from the tapes, and for a while it looked as though the race was going to be spoilt. Then the starter so far compromised with his principles as to let Commendation walk up to the tapes while the others were standing still. Naturally he was first out and got an advantage over everything else in the race. If the lot had been allowed to walk up there would have been no trouble, no delay, and fair play to all.

1952 *Mudgee Guardian* 15 September p. 1: The Mudgee Amateur Swimming Club has certainly got away to a 'walk up' start, its annual meeting being the most successful held in its history.

1965 *Tribune* (Sydney) 3 March p. 12: The ACTU has seriously erred in thinking its claim was a walk-up start . . . that it was purely a matter of checking on the Prices Index Movement. 'This is poor leadership. The essential mass campaign has not been organised'.

1987 *Australian Jewish News* (Melbourne) 21 August p. 59: Rookie golfer Steve Rubinstein quickly learned that being a pennant lawn bowler is no walk up start to being a good putter, even though similarities include having a good eye, fine touch and steady nerves.

2021 *The Land* (North Richmond) 23 September p. 100: He said barriers to entry into the sector had been extraordinarily high for young people. ... 'Already you're looking at half-a-million dollars in cattle before anything else. There are not many young people that get a walk-up start'.

wallopers uniformed police.

Australian English.

A *walloper* is 'a police officer' (AND).

Origin: Ultimately from *wallop* (verb) 'to beat soundly, belabour, thrash' (OED). *Walloper* was used earlier in British English for a person who beats others with a stick or cudgel.

1904 *Sunday Times* (Perth) 26 June p. 9: Wellington-st. Walloper. All those who walk Wellington-street, / This uniformed person will meet / Who chases the dogs / From the carpets and togs, / With his well-wielded whip and his feet.

1939 *Daily News* (Perth) 8 April p. 27: Another man, as cries of 'police', 'cops' and 'wallopers' went up from the stampeding players, snatched a pound note from the two-up ring and leapt through the window.

1950 B.K. Doyle *Australian Police Journal* April p. 120: *Wallopers*, police.

1983 A.F. Howells *Against the Stream* p. 25: The two wallopers dragged him to his feet and tried to frog-march him off.

1990 V. Tupper & R. Wortley *Anthology of Prison Slang in Australia* (National Library of Australia, Pandora Archive): *Walloper*, a police officer. The reference is to the use of a police cudgel or baton.

2013 *Australian* (Sydney) 25 October p. 9: A hearty 'get well' to Richie Benaud, who's a bit the worse for wear after his 1963 Sunbeam Alpine had an altercation with a nature strip and a brick wall. Benaud is spending a couple of days in hospital with chest and shoulder injuries, his jolly mood no doubt buoyed by the knowledge the wallopers aren't pressing charges.

warb shabbily dressed person.

Australian English.

The term means 'an idle, unkempt, dirty, or disreputable person' (AND).

Origin: Probably from *warble* 'the gadfly or its larva which produces "warbles"' (OED), which are small tumours or swellings on the back of cattle etc.

1933 Les Robinson in W. Murdoch & H. Drake-Brockman *Australian Short Stories* (1951) p. 215: We were both of us what, in the back country, are called 'warbs', meaning confirmed and irredeemable loafers.

1950 'Thirty-five' in G. Simes *Dictionary of Australian Underworld Slang* (1993) p. 211: *Warb*, a dirty or untidy person.

1956 R. Park & D. Niland *The Drums Go Bang* p. 126: Alongside this masterpiece he felt the warbiest of the warbs, the shabbiest of the shabs.

1967 *Whisper All Aussie Dictionary* in *Kings Cross Whisper* 43 p. 11: *Warb*, a very grubby person.

1972 J. McNeil *The Old Familiar Juice* in *The Chocolate Frog, The Old Familiar Juice: Two Plays* (1973) p. 111: Yer a warb ... a chat ... a wino ... yer a vagrant ... And that's a thief in this town, mate!

1973 J. McNeil *The Chocolate Frog, The Old Familiar Juice: Two Plays* p. 119

(Glossary): *Warb*, (colloquial), a dirty or untidy person.

1981 P. Barton *Bastards I Have Known* p. 53: Together with a couple of warbs (homeless alcoholics) and a few other social misfits.

2010 *West Australian* (Perth) 16 January (Agenda Section) p. 23: Our main job earlier in the evening shift was to go around arresting warbs—homeless drunks—and park drinkers.

Warwicks arms.

Australian English.

A *Warwick* is 'an arm'.

Origin: Abbreviated form of *Warwick Farm*, rhyming slang for 'arm'. Warwick Farm is the name of a racecourse in Sydney. Quotes 1944 and 2007 illustrate the complete Warwick Farm form.

1944 *Biscuit Bomber Weekly: Magazine 1st Australian Air Maintenance Co.* 4 November p. 2: So I put my Warwick-Farm around her bushel-and-peck and kissed her on the North-and-South.

1962 D. McLean *The World Turned Upside Down* p. 40: I don't want to get elephants. I just want a drop of dad 'n' mum to loosen up me warwicks.

1983 J. Byrell *Up the Cross* p. 10: He got holda one drop kick by the left warwick and yanked him inta the whisper and stamped on his loaf with his right plate.

1989 E.A. Wallish *Truth Dictionary Of Racing Slang* p. 86: *Warwicks*, rhyming slang for arms—Warwick Farm. Warwick Farm is a metropolitan racecourse on the outskirts of Sydney. On a hot day a strapper might complain of being 'a bit hot (or Len Lott) under the Warwicks'.

2007 *Courier-Mail* (Brisbane) 8 September (Cars Guide Section) p. 4: I had the 'Warwick Farms' (arms) hanging out the window. I just loved it.

[**water** see GO TO WATER.]

weed tobacco.

General English.

The term was originally British, appearing in the seventeenth century. It appears in Australia in the second half of the nineteenth century. In the Australian prison context *weed* often refers to the inferior tobacco issued as part of weekly rations.

1950 'Thirty-five' in G. Simes *Dictionary of Australian Underworld Slang* (1993) p. 211: *Weed*, tobacco. ... Tobacco is the jail currency. Half a pound of butter is worth a swy (2 oz); a tube of toothpaste or shaving cream, about the same; a tin of syrup or plum jam, one ounce; more expensive jam, two ounces. In jail, every service, favour and commodity, is as readily reducible to price in tobacco as it is to money in civil life.

1967 B.K. Burton *Teach Them No More* p. 45: 'Like some weed?' Harry said, offering a mottled red packet of prison issue tobacco.

1972 *Contact: Parramatta Jail Resurgents Magazine* December n.p.: Tobacco in prison is wealth, it is currency, it is a balm and a curse just like money outside the walls. Prisoners trade everything from false teeth to shoe laces for it, if they need it; some will steal it if they can, in fact a full weed pouch is as much a status symbol as a full pocket of money outside.

1977 J. Ramsay *Cop It Sweet* p. 95: *Weed*, tobacco.

1984 B. Ellem *Doing Time: The Prison Experience* p. 199: *Weed*, tobacco.

1990 V. Tupper & R. Wortley *Anthology of Prison Slang in Australia* (National Library of Australia, Pandora Archive): *Weed*, marijuana or tobacco.

[**whack** *see* ON THE WHACK, WHACK UP.]

whack up divide into shares.

General English.

The verb *whack* or *whack up* meaning 'to divide, to share' appeared at the end of the nineteenth century, and especially in American contexts could mean to divide up loot, and that is the implication of the term in the Glossary.

Origin: From *whack* (recorded in Britain from the end of the eighteenth century) meaning 'a portion, share, allowance', appearing in such set phrases as *to get one's whack, have one's whack, take one's whack*. See ON THE WHACK.

1812 J.H. Vaux *New Vocabulary of the Flash Language* in *Memoirs* (1819) II p. 223: *Wack*, to share or divide any thing equally, as *wack the blunt*, divide the money.

1888 'R. Boldrewood' *Robbery Under Arms* III. p. 196: We hadn't much trouble dividing the gold, and what cash there was we could whack easy enough.

1907 *Sunday Times* (Perth) 6 October p. 2: He had arranged to snavel no less than 55 per cent. of the gross takings of the house, and left 45 to be whacked up between the wrestlers.

1973 J. McNeil *The Chocolate Frog, The Old Familiar Juice: Two Plays* p. 119 (Glossary): *Whack up*, to share.

1977 J. Ramsay *Cop It Sweet* p. 96: *Whack up*, divide the spoils.

1989 T. Anderson *Inside Outlaws: A Prison Diary* p. 160: *Whack Up*, share. If someone has a share, he/she is 'in whack'. If someone is being called on to share, he/she's asked to whack up.

1994 M.B. Read *Chopper 4: For the Term of His Unnatural Life* p. 160: The very best of friends will gather to whack up the booty, and each man will sit at the table with his hand on his gun butt as the pie gets cut up.

2010 A. Shand *King of Thieves* p. 41: What amazed the Kid even more was the fact that when they whacked up the proceeds, everyone got the same share. There was no hierarchy in this team, every member was as crucial as the next to its success.

wheelman driver of get away car.

General English. Especially in Underworld Slang.

The term has been used from the 1940s for an expert police or criminal driver. It was originally used in the US (from the end of the nineteenth century) for 'a cyclist'.

2006 B. Matthews *Intractable ... Life inside Australia's First Super-max Prison* p.

17: He was a brilliant wheel man; despite a motorbike accident that had fucked his foot he could still drive like a bat out of hell.

2021 *Sydney Morning Herald* 17 December p. 8: 'I'm driver', Munshizada replied. He would be the driver in all three murders, viewed as the most competent wheelman in the crew.

whippy wallet.

Australian English.

The term means 'a place in which money is kept, such as a wallet; the money in such a place; a supply of money' (AND).

Origin: Of unknown origin, but perhaps related to *whip* (verb) 'to move (something) in some way suddenly or briskly; to take, put, pull, push, strike, cut, flourish, etc. with a sudden vigorous movement or action' (OED). There is another, and perhaps related, sense of *whippy* in Australian English. From the early twentieth century it was used as the name of the base in a children's hide-and-seek game.

1967 *Whisper All Aussie Dictionary* in *Kings Cross Whisper* 43 p. 11: *Whippy*, pocket. Sometimes whip your kick, or willy, same as wallet.

1973 *Kings Cross Whisper* 44 p. 16: I've never yet met a Kiwi who didn't cry poor mouth while he snipped you bone dry and all the time had a secret whippy tucked away somewhere you didn't know about.

1980 *Sun-Herald* (Sydney) 27 January p. 66: Fair dinkum, if a man had enough in the willy, I mean whippy, I'd get myself a charlie … and shout her seven or so ounces of sheer joy.

1983 R. AVEN-BRAY *Ridgey Didge Oz Jack Lang* p. 10: The vanilla fudge had hit him up for fifty Oxford scholars. It was a hefty blow on his whippy at that time. [*Ed. Vanilla fudge* is rhyming slang for 'judge', and *Oxford scholar* is rhyming slang for 'dollar'.]

1983 J. BYRELL *Up the Cross* p. 162: 'Are you sure that's all he's got on him, Harold?' 'Yeah, Scholar', said Heavy Harold, slowly lowering Fruity Orchard to the pavement. 'Apart from these twelve quids and some small change from his hip whippy'.

1997 *Australian* (Sydney) 9 July p. 7: The NSW Wood royal commission into police corruption showed the practice was well entrenched in that State, where it was referred to in police jargon as a whippy—'money found during the execution of a search warrant which is retained and divided among police'.

2013 *Northern Daily Leader* (Tamworth) 20 September p. 40: If Todd has any Blue Ginger winnings left, they might go into his whippy to pay for a fast-approaching six-week trip to the USA.

wild duck won't settle debts.

Australian English.

The term means 'a person who defaults on a debt and is unlikely to repay it'.

Origin: Of unknown origin. Perhaps with a punning allusion to wild ducks not settling on the water (see quote 1981 for an explanation along these lines).

1981 *Queensland Hansard, Legislative Assembly*, 10 November, p. 3334: I instance John Hannay of Mackay. He is a shonky hotelier of the worst order. He is better known in Brisbane as the proprietor of the Whisky Au-Go-Go Night Club that was burnt down in 1973. ... I hear that he is once more in the news for being robbed—or so he says—of $40,000 from a locked safe in the Oriental Hotel in Mackay. It would be interesting to know how many times Hannay has been burgled or robbed—no doubt for the purpose of insurance and as an excuse to defer showdowns with his creditors. In liquor, circles his nickname is 'The Wild Duck' because he never settles. ... I point out that not so long ago this shadowy businessman, who does not pay his debts ... big-noted himself shouting members of his staff a free trip to the United States of America.

1985 *Courier-Mail* (Brisbane) 20 October p. 60: The political 'wild duck' we wrote about last week finally settled long enough to pay his debts—some two years old.

1989 E.A. WALLISH *Truth Dictionary Of Racing Slang* p. 88: *Wild duck*, a person who has failed to settle a financial commitment, and of whom a doubt is expressed about him or her ever settling.

1990 V. TUPPER & R. WORTLEY *Anthology of Prison Slang in Australia* (National Library of Australia, Pandora Archive): *Wild duck*, an inmate who does not pay his debts.

willy wallet.

Australian English.

The term means 'the amount of money at one's disposal, esp. for betting; money, a sum of money' (see quotes 1949, 1975); 'a wallet; a pocket' (see quote 1950).

Origin: Unexplained use of a form of the name *William*.

1949 L. GLASSOP *Lucky Palmer* p. 36: Two quid? Break it down. That's me willie. That's all I got.

1950 'Thirty-five' in G. SIMES *Dictionary of Australian Underworld Slang* (1993) p. 213: *Willie*, a pocket.

1953 *Argus* (Melbourne) 31 October p. 9: The pickpocket 'lifts' the 'willy' (wallet).

1967 *Whisper All Aussie Dictionary* in *Kings Cross Whisper* 43 p. 11: *Willy*, a wallet.

1975 *Bulletin* (Sydney) 26 April p. 45: Anyway, we get this dead set sneak go for a willy in a supermarket. So we send in Limp to tug the tart minding the willy. It was this woman who was guarding the willy (money) and the success of the operation rested on the Limp distracting her.

1983 R. AVEN-BRAY *Ridgey Didge Oz Jack Lang* p. 9: He wasted no time in diving into his burrow and extracting his willy.

Woodpeckers' Day Friday reserved for sentencing guilty pleas.

Australian Underworld Slang.

Not otherwise recorded.

Origin: Perhaps from the notion that the guilty nods proceeded as quickly and regularly as a woodpecker taps its beak against the wood of a tree.

worker prostitute.
Australian English.
Cf. General English *working girl* 'prostitute' (GDS from the 1920s). The term *sex worker* first appears in the US in 1971.

1971 J. McNeil *The Chocolate Frog* in *The Chocolate Frog, The Old Familiar Juice: Two Plays* (1973) p. 49: I never even knew she was a worker ... not when I first got on with her.

1973 J. McNeil *The Chocolate Frog, The Old Familiar Juice: Two Plays* p. 119 (Glossary): *Worker,* (colloquial), prostitute.

1990 V. Tupper & R. Wortley *Anthology of Prison Slang in Australia* (National Library of Australia, Pandora Archive): *Worker,* a prostitute.

yarra mad.
Australian English.
The term means 'insane, stupid' (AND).
Origin: From the name of a psychiatric hospital at *Yarra* Bend on the Yarra River in Melbourne, Victoria (cf. General English *round the bend*). See quote 1869 for an early reference to the place.

1869 *The Telegraph, St Kilda, Prahran and South Yarra Guardian* 24 July p. 7: But, an' you love me, Mr. Editor, don't tempt me again in a similar manner, or you'll drive me to Yarra Bend.

1943 S.J. Baker *A Popular Dictionary of Australian Slang* (ed. 3) p. 89: *Yarra,* stupid, crazy.

1968 J. Alard *He Who Shoots Last* p. 126: Da foist week I wuz here, I cracked it fer a load of da Sandy McNabs (*footnote*: load of crabs, little biting insects which can be acquired in public conveniences and in various other places); dey nearly drove me yarra.

1971 J. McNeil *The Chocolate Frog* in *The Chocolate Frog, The Old Familiar Juice: Two Plays* (1973) p. 50: What'ser matter? You gone yarra, or somethin'?

1980 *Sydney Morning Herald* 20 October p. 26: Kingston Town is a good horse ... but in my opinion he would not have lived with Phar Lap. I know a lot of people will say I'm 'Yarra'; but that's my belief.

2007 *Sunday Mail* (Brisbane) 30 September p. 100: Now I'd be more than happy to harbour a grudge against Lyon for no other reason than he plays for Manly, but the fact that he ripped the heart out of Parramatta a few years ago makes it very hard. I mean anyone who can drive 50,000 Parras yarra can't be all bad.

your smother's your best friend common saying among thieves.
Australian Underworld Slang.
The Glossary defines smother as 'block someone's view', and it is Underworld Slang meaning 'to conceal a crime by blocking anyone's view of it'. The phrase therefore means 'your best friend is a thing or person that conceals the crime you have committed or are committing'. Probably with jocular allusion to 'mother' ('your mother's your best friend').

Not otherwise recorded, but the noun *smother* meaning 'a stratagem to obscure the committing of a crime' is illustrated in the Australian (1915, 2010) and British (1943) quotes below. In British slang *smother* could mean 'an overcoat, a wrap' (GDS, with evidence from 1900 to 2003).

1915 C. Drew & I.B. Evans *The Grafter* p. 4: Look here, Mosh ... you'll have to get to work on that ticket. There's only one out. A Jay's got it, and it will be dead easy. Get some of the boys to give you a smother, and when he goes to put it in, dive on it, and see you don't miss.

[**1943** *Police Journal* (Chichester, West Sussex) p. 70: *Smother*, something used by pickpockets to cover their activities, usually an overcoat, newspaper, or parcel.]

1973 *Contact: Parramatta Jail Resurgents Magazine* June n.p.: Now Billy, he's a real character. ... If he appears a bit shifty it's either because your smother's your best friend ... or if you slew, you blue.

2010 A. Shand *King of Thieves* p. 64: When everyone was getting set for their individual tasks, pulling heads, stealing keys, providing smothers or blocks, getting ready for the take, the minder kept an eye on everyone in the shop.

zack six months.
Australian Underworld and Prison Slang.

The term for 'a prison sentence of six years or six months' (AND). The main use of this word *zack* has been for 'sixpence'.

Origin: Probably from Scottish dialect *sax pence* (sixpence), although cf. German *sechs* (pronounced *zeks*) 'six'.

1919 V. Marshall *The World of the Living Dead* p. 84: Done the zac I got fer cattle duffin' up Gilgandra way, / A zac's hard labour—wot I had ter do.

1941 S.J. Baker *A Popular Dictionary of Australian Slang* p. 84: *Zack*, six months' gaol.

1971 J. McNeil *Chocolate Frog* in *The Chocolate Frog, The Old Familiar Juice: Two Plays* (1973) p. 20: Tosser: How long are yer doin'? Kevin: Six months ... down at the Petty Sessions... Shirker: Why'd yer get the zac?

1983 E. Withnel *Australian Journal of Cultural Studies* 1 (May) p. 91: The names of laggings are: Six months: A Zac.

2006 B. Matthews *Intractable ... Life inside Australia's First Super-max Prison* p. 399: *Zac*, six-month sentence.

APPENDIX A

TWO PAGES FROM THE MANUSCRIPT

APPENDIX A

(I)

Squarehead:	Honest Citizen.
Crim:	Professional thief. This term only applies to those who uphold criminal code. It is a mistake to think that anyone in gaol automatically qualifies.
Rort:	Modus Operandi.
Tank:	A Safe.
Tankman:	Person who specializes in stealing from safes.
Bust:	Breaking & Entering. (commercial premises)
Bustman:	One who specializes in busts.
Barber:	One who steals from residential premises without forcing entry.
Pussy-footer:	Sneak thief. (opportunist)
Hoister:	Shoplifter.
Head-Puller:	A person who directs shop assisant's attention elsewhere while accomplice steals.
Tug his head:	Distract his gaze.
Nonch:	Method used by shoplifters. Concealing stolen property under coat draped casually over one shoulder.
Clout:	Method used by shoplifters. Concealing stolen property under topcoat while being worn.
Smother:	Block someones view.
Your smother's your best friend:	Common saying among thieves.
Dip:	Pickpocket.
Willy:	Wallet.
Whippy:	Wallet.
Bumper:	Dip's accomplice. Bumps into victim while dip removes Whippy.
Dudder:	Person who sells inferior quality goods and presents them as high grade merchandise.
Wheelman:	Driver of get away car.
A Drop:	A Fence. Reciever of stolen goods.
Paper Hanger:	Passer of dud cheques.
Bouncer:	Dud cheque.
Fly a Kite:	Pass dud cheque.
Flap:	Blank cheque leaf.
Snow Dropper:	Person who steals clothes from clothesline.
Worker:	Prostitute.
Kupie:	Prostitute.
Hoon:	Man who lives off worker.
Poof-rorter:	Man who takes money off homosexuals.

APPENDIX A

(9)

Show Pony:	Liar.
Rudolf Vaselino:	One who falsely boasts of his exploits with women.
In & Out Like a honeymoon Prick:	Said of short termer who repeatedly comes to gaol.
Kate Lee:	Tea.
Dook:	Pass something secretly.
Carve Him Up:	Pull all his money off him.
Silk Department:	Extra Grouse.
Secko:	Sex Offender.
Healy:	Trick to it.
Tune in:	Listen to other peoples conversation.
Come out of the woodwork:	Appear from nowhere.
Drop from the ceiling:	Suddenly appear beside you.
On the Coat:	Ostracised.
Toe Ragger:	Person of no account.
Shit Kicker:	" " " "
Blonk:	Idiot.
Dubbo:	Imbecile.
Snip:	Ask for money.
Lob:	Arrive.
Mocker:	Clothes.
Remand Yard:	Hotel or Club frequented by police because its a known haunt.
Seine:	Dollar.
Slice:	Two Dollars.
Spin (Or Blue Bit):	Five Dollars.
Brick:	Ten Dollars.
Score:	Twenty Dollars.
Pony.	$25
Half Spot:	$50
Spot:	$100
Monkey:	$500
Grand:	$1000.
Not the Full Quid:	Insane.
Five cents in the dollar:	Insane.
Yarra:	Mad.
Warricks:	Arms.

APPENDIX B

TRANSCRIPTION OF GLOSSARY,
WITH CORRECTIONS AND EMENDATIONS
INDICATED IN FOOTNOTES.

TRANSCRIPTION OF GLOSSARY, WITH CORRECTIONS AND EMENDATIONS INDICATED IN FOOTNOTES.

The footnotes indicate the corrections and emendations to be made.
The manuscript's page numbers are given in round brackets.

(Page 1)

Squarehead:[1] Honest Citizen.
Crim: Professional thief. This term only applies to those who uphold criminal code. It is a mistake to think that anyone in gaol automatically qualifies.
Rort: Modus Operandi.
Tank: A Safe.
Tankman: Person who specializes in stealing from safes.
Bust: Breaking & Entering.[2] (commercial premises)
Bustman: One who specializes in busts.
Barber: One who steals from residential premises without forcing entry.
Pussy-footer: Sneak thief. (opportunist)
Hoister: Shoplifter.
Head-puller: A person who directs shop assistant's attention elsewhere while accomplice steals.
Tug his head: Distract his gaze.
Nonch:[3] Method used by shoplifters. Concealing stolen property under coat draped casually over one shoulder.
Clout: Method used by shoplifters.[4] Concealing stolen property under topcoat while being worn.
Smother: Block someones[5] view.
Your smother's your best friend: Common saying among thieves.
Dip: Pickpocket.
Willy: Wallet.
Whippy: Wallet.
Bumper: Dip's accomplice. Bumps into victim while dip removes Whippy.
Dudder: Person who sells inferior quality goods and presents them as high grade merchandise.
Wheelman: Driver of get away car.

---

[1] Remove colons from all entries and make headwords bold
[2] Remove full stop
[3] Replace stop with colon
[4] Replace stop with colon
[5] Correct to: someone's

A Drop: A fence.[6] Reciever[7] of stolen goods.
Paper hanger: Passer of dud cheques.
Bouncer: Dud cheque.
Fly a Kite: Pass dud cheque.
Flap: Blank cheque leaf.
Snow Dropper: Person who steals clothes from clothesline.
Worker: Prostitute.
Kupie: Prostitute.
Hoon: Man who lives off worker.
Poof-rorter: Man who takes money off homosexuals.

(Page 2)

Block: Wristwatch.
Cockatoo: Lookout.
Nit Keeper: Cockatoo.
A Go: Right time to strike.
Sneak go: Sneak Theft.
Open Go: Easy, anytime.
Walk Up Start: There for the taking.
Case: Get layout of premises for prospective robbery.
Bugged: Alarmed.
Rip & Tear: Philosophy of determined thief.[8] Will not go home without scoring.
Earn: Proceeds of robbery.
Crack It: Have an earn.
Kick A Goal: Be successful.
Kick On: Better yourself financially.
Whack Up: Divide into shares.
On the Whack: Entitled to a share.
Take the knock: Cheat someone of his share, in part or whole.
Brass: Not pay your debts.
Lash: To take the knock.
Put Them Through: To Brass someone.
Twine: To Hoodwink.
Bad Trot: Lean Time.
Going Bad: Not having any success.
Can't Fire: No ability.
Can't aim up: No ability.
Cannon: Concealable firearm.

---

[6] Change to semicolon: fence;
[7] Correct to: receiver
[8] Replace stop with colon

Joint:[9] " " "
Piece:[10] " " "
Shovel: Room. Living quarters.
Gig: Witness[11] someone who is watching.
Don't be A Gig: Mind your own business.
Lamping: Watching.
Tropical: Very risky.
On Fire: Too hot to handle. Too risky.
Sprung: Seen in the act of doing something illegal.
Peg: Look.

(Page 3)

Heavy Peg: Close scrutiny.
Pull yer Coat: Stop what your[12] doing.
Haste: Stop immediately or you'll be sprung.
Red Light: Stop[13] Screw coming.
Drop off: Quit what your[14] doing or else.
Easy Mark: Soft touch.
Mug in Tow: Have sucker in company.
Captain: Person who foots the bill.
Handle: Con someone.
Handrush: Bustle someone into decision.
Lift: Steal.
Knock: Murder.
Jacks: Detectives.
Heavies: Detectives.
Wallopers: Uniformed Police.
Dog Squad: Undercover Police.
Bun Wagon: Police Paddy Wagon.
Darbies: Handcuffs.
Mug Shot: Police photograph.
Get Buckled: Be Arrested.
Come Undone: Be foiund[15] out.
Smack A Blue: Be arrested and charged.
Dead to Rights: Caught red handed.

---

[9] Take definition from previous entry: concealable firearm.
[10] Take definition from previous entry: concealable firearm.
[11] Add semicolon to clarify sense
[12] Correct to: you're
[13] Add comma: stop, screw coming
[14] Correct to: you're
[15] Correct to: found

Half inched: Stolen.
Orf: Have no chance.
Hit the Toe: Run[16] try to escape.
Take it to the toe: Same as above[17].
Stall: Clear out.
Scarper: Abscond on bail.
Lumbered: Taken to Police Station.
Bodgie: False.
Give a Bodgie: Give an alias.
Bodgie address: False address.
Under the Lights: Questioned at C.I.B.
Being Grilled: Being interrogated.
Come nothing: Make no admissions.
Come yer Guts: Confess.

(Page 4)

Go to Press: Write statement incriminating self or others.
Go to Water: Weaken under pressure.
Give (someone) Up: Inform on someone.
Dropped: Informed on.
Shelf: Informer.
Lag: Give someone up.
Finger: Point out, accuse.
Clean the books up: Confess to numerous unsolved crimes.
Do A Deal: Plead guilty for pre-arranged sentence.
Sling: Pay Police for services rendered.
Sugar Bag: Policeman who accepts bribes.
Set (someone) Up: Enter into crime with someone having supplied police with prior knowledge of crime with sole purpose of having accomplices arrested in exchange for favours from police.
Ginger Ale: Bail.
Straw Bail: Bail papers signed by Sugar Bag on worthless surety.
Front: Appear in court.
In smoke: Hiding from police.
Low Jump: Petty sessions (Court)
High Jump: Quarter Sessions.
Beak: Magistrate.
Nod Yer Head: Plead Guilty.
Get Yer Head Down: Plead Guilty.

---

[16] Punctuation added: run,
[17] Take definition from previous entry: run, try to escape.

APPENDIX B

Woodpeckers' Day: Friday reserved for sentencing guilty pleas.
Somersault: Change plea of guilty to plea of not guilty.
Hand Up Brief: Open and shut case.
Go Under: Be found guilty by jury.
Fitted: Found Guilty.
Sunk: No chance of acquittal.
History: In Dire straits.
Beat It: Be acquitted.
Get Up:[18] "   "   "
Be Read Up: Have criminal record read aloud in court.
Jump the Box: Give sworn evidence.
Turn (Someone) Up: Give evidence to bring about accused person's acquittal.
Cop The Blue: Take the blame.
Loaded: Framed.

(Page 5)

Verballed: Be mispresented by lies.
Dollied: Loaded with false material evidence.
Cold: Innocent of charge laid against you.
Laggin': Prison sentence.
Hoist The Flag: Appeal against conviction or severity of sentence.
Bed & Breakfast: Seven days imprisonment.
A Sleep: Prison sentence. Longer than 7 days less than 3 Months.
A Drag: Three Months.
A Zack: Six Months.
A Clock: Twelve Months.
A Swy: Two Years.
A Spin: Five Years.
A Brick: Ten Years.
The Key: Being declared an Habitual Criminal.
The Twist: Same as above.[19]
The Lot: Life Imprisonment.
Boob: Gaol.
Nick: Gaol.
Stir: Gaol.
Can: Gaol.
Seabreeze Hotel: Long Bay Gaol.
Kick along with it: Not going to appeal.
Box on with it: Contest court case.

---

[18] Take definition from previous entry: be acquitted.
[19] Take definition from previous entry: being declared an habitual criminal.

Do It on Yer Head: Serve sentence as easy as possible.
Do It on the shit tub:[20] "   "   "   "   "
Do It Tough: Let sentence get you down.
Do It Hard:[21] "   "   "   "   "
Boob Happy: Eccentric. Divorced from reality. Brought about by the strain of gaol routine. Similar to battle fatigue.
Stir-Crazy: Institutionalized.
Weed: Tobacco.
Boob Tobacco: Low grade gaol issued tobacco.
Grouse Weed: Outside tobacco high quality.
Grouse Cigarette: Tailor made.
A Double: two ounces of tobacco.
A Swy:[22] "   "   "   "
Shiv: Gaol made knife for stabbing purposes.

(Page 6)

Jigger: Gaol made crystal set (illegal).
Boil Up: Make illegal cup of tea in cell.
Fat Wick: Strip of sheeting or like material spread with fat, rolled up, and lit for purposes of boiling up.
Peter: Cell.
Peter Thief: Prisoner who steals from other prisoners cells. Regarded as despicable (Not to be confused with "Tickle the Peter" which means to steal from the till.)
Slot: Cell.
Sloughed Up: Locked in cell.
Black Peter: Punishment Cell devoid of light and furniture.
Pound: Time spent in punishment cell (without books, light, radio, tobacco.)
Go-Slow: Punishment Cell.
On the Grill: Barred door instead of steel doored cell.
Knock Up: Bang loudly on Cell door when in need of medical attention.
Screw: Prison Warder.
Brasco: Shithouse. (Toilet)
Moosh: Hominy (Gaol breakfast)
Burgoo:[23] "   "   "
Dry: Unmade Tea(leaves)
Boob Tea: Weak gaol made tea.

---

[20] Take definition from previous entry: serve sentence as easy as possible.
[21] Take definition from previous entry: let sentence get you down.
[22] Take definition from previous entry: two ounces of tobacco.
[23] Take definition from previous entry: hominy (gaol breakfast)

Kite: Newspaper.
Dodger: Bread.
Hock: Active Homosexual.
Cat: Passive Homosexual.
Dung Puncher: Another name for a Hock.
Arse Bandit: Person prepared to rape a male if need be.
Shirt Lifter: Hock.
Ballarat: Cat.
Reciever[24] of Swollen Goods: Cat.
A Ride There For A Ride Back: Bi-sexual Male.
Sherriff:[25] Hock who jealously guards Cat.
Put Work On: Make sexual advances to.
Seat: Insert penis in anus.
Roseleaf: Tongue In Bum.
Kyber: Arse.

(Page 7)

Blot: Anus.
Freckle: Anus.
Lemon:[26] "
Mark: boy
Starter: Substitute for vaseline (Margarine or any such thing).
Shanghai: Sudden transfer to another gaol.
Mod Squad: Plain Clothes screws who handle shanghais.
Ramp: Search.
Track: Screw who brings contraband for prisoners in exchange for fee.
Snooker: Hiding place.
Hotpoint: Put something over someone.
Dog: Informer.
Left Handed Drop: Giving information to a Dog knowing full well the authorities will be told thereby reducing the chance of blame.
Under The Lap: Secretive.
Under A Cloud: Under suspicion of being a dog.
Pull The wrong Rein: Make a blunder.
Slew Yer Head: Look away.
Slew & Yer'll Blue: Don't look back[27] keep going.
Stink: Fight.

---

[24] Correct to: receiver
[25] Correct to: sheriff
[26] Take definition from previous entry: anus.
[27] Add comma.

Back Up: Seek Revenge.
Back Stop: Someine[28] prepared to support you on[29] fight.
Tumble: Lose Temper.
Pitch for it: Ask for trouble.
Shorten Him Up: Cut Him down to size.
Serve Him Up: Give him a hiding.
Square Off: Apologise.
Cop It Sweet: Don't retaliate
Backdown: Decline to fight.
Dog It: Squib It.
Left For Dead: Abandoned by friends.
Leave Posted: Stand someone up. Also not bail friend out.
Get Over: Intimidate someone.
Suck His Brain: See what he knows.
Got Their Lug: Have someone listening to you.
Blow down their lug: Ear Bash.
Can't Be Educated: Won't be told.

(Page 8)

Lamp: Look
African.[30]: Cigarette.
Racehorse: Thin gaol rolled cigarette.
Silvertail: Trustee having cushy job in prison.
Roscoe: Gun.
Jerry: Realize.
Stiff: Uncensored letter smuggled out of prison.
Right Whack: Just Deserts.
Put the knife through: Go halves with a friend.
Snork: Child
Take Seconds: Think again;
Ridge: Real.
Arsey: Lucky
Flum: Fluke It.
Trick Cyclist: Psychiatrist.
Half Pie: Half hearted.
Turn It Up: Give Crime away.
Peanut Butter Sandwich: An Honest Job.
Toey: Anxious.

---

[28] Correct to: someone
[29] Correct or emend to: in
[30] Remove stop

Barley: Cut It out.[31] Stop It.
Cut It Out: Do gaol rather than pay fine.
Bung It: Pass contraband on to someone else to avoid being buckled with it.
Solid: Staunch to criminal code.
Tom: Jewellary.[32]
Vag: Charged with vagrancy.
Crusted:[33] " " "
Doing The Crust: Serving a sentence for vagrancy.
Shitpot: Talk ill of someone.
Go Off The Tub: Commit suicide by hanging.
Go Off The Bars:[34] " " " " "
Robert: Tongue.
Boy In The Boat: Clitoris.
Ted: Vagina.
Bridge: Exposing sensuous parts of body.
Optic: Perv.
Dear John: Goodbye letter from lover.

(Page 9)

Show Pony: Lair.
Rudolf Vaselino: One who falsely boasts of his exploits with women.
In & Out Like a honeymoon Prick: Said of short termer who repeatedly comes to gaol.
Kate Lee: Tea.
Dook: Pass something secretly.
Carve Him Up: Pull all his money off him.
Silk Department: Extra Grouse.
Secko: Sex Offender.
Healy: Trick to it.
Tune in: Listen to other peoples[35] conversation.
Come out of the woodwork: Appear from nowhere.
Drop from the ceiling: Suddenly appear beside you.
On the Coat: Ostracised.
Toe Ragger: Person of no account.
Shit Kicker:[36] " " " "
Blonk: Idiot.

[31] Change stop to semicolon: cut it out; stop it.
[32] Correct to: jewellery.
[33] Take definition from previous entry: charged with vagrancy.
[34] Take definition from previous entry: commit suicide by hanging.
[35] Add apostrophe: people's
[36] Take definition from previous entry: person of no account.

Dubbo: Imbecile.
Snip: Ask for money.
Lob: Arrive.
Mocker: Clothes.
Remand Yard: Hotel or Club frequented by police because its[37] a known haunt.
Seine: Dollar.
Slice: Two Dollars.
Spin (or Blue Bit):[38] Five Dollars.
Brick: Ten Dollars.
Score: Twenty Dollars.
Pony: $25
Half Spot: $50
Spot: $100
Monkey: $500
Grand: $1000.
Not the Full Quid: Insane.
Five cents in the dollar: Insane.
Yarra: Mad.
Warrwicks:[39] Arms.

(Page 10)

Bin: Pocket.
Kick: Pocket.
Cunning Kick: Undeclared Money.
Short Arms & Deep Pockets: Said of mean person.
A Leg Up: Assistance
S.O.S.: Same Old Shit. Speaking of Prison meals.
Chew & Spew: Prison stew.
Cliner: Dud.
Bad Mug: Person who makes mountain out of molehill.
Air Raider: Nagging Shiela.[40]
Howya Travellin'?: How are you fixed for money.
Hit Yer Kick: Your Turn to Shout.
Keep Yer guard up: Be Careful.
Deadset: No doubt.
Virgin: Derogatory term, Pure Cunt (No good person)
Cunt Starver: In gaol for maintenance. (not supporting wife)

---

[37] Correct to: it's
[38] Make separate entry for 'blue bit'
[39] Correct to: Warwick
[40] Correct to: sheila.

Warb: Shabbily dressed person.
Bat Material: Pornographic material. (Masturbation)
Cruel: Ruin Chances.
Crab: Impede progress.
Bring Undone: Cause someone to be found out.
Butter Up: Use flattery as means to exploit.
Bunch Up: Put someone in impossible position.
Clacker: Arsehole.
A Break: An Excuse.
Flat: Grouse Tobacco.
Leg-Opener: Alcohol supplied to Woman.
Throw Off: Camouflage the truth.
Drack: Ugly
A Barrel: Benefit night, proceeds going toward payment of bail or defence Counsel of Crim arrested.
Kentucky: Collection taken up for same reason as above[41].
Rock Spider: Peeping Tom.
Polish: Praise.
Chaff: Money.
Nephew: Boy who is being seated but pretends 'nice man' is his Uncle.

(Page 11)

Back A Tail: Follow after someone else in sexual intercourse.
Wild Duck: Won't settle debts.
Musical Milk: Methylated spirits.
Lunatic Soup: Cheap potent wine.
Form: Criminal record.
Jump: Shop-Counter.
Cold Bite: Ask a stranger for money.
Running Feed: Non payment for meal in cafe.
He's Elephants: He's Drunk.
Lice Ladders: Sideburns.

---

[41] Change to: collection taken up, proceeds going toward payment of bail or defence counsel of crim arrested.

APPENDIX C

ALPHABETISED GLOSSARY,
WITH CORRECTIONS AND
EMENDATIONS INCLUDED.

ALPHABETISED GLOSSARY, WITH CORRECTIONS AND EMENDATIONS INCLUDED.

African: cigarette.
air raider: nagging sheila.
arse bandit: person prepared to rape a male if need be.
arsey: lucky.

back a tail: follow after someone else in sexual intercourse.
backdown: decline to fight.
back stop: someone prepared to support you in fight.
back up: seek revenge.
bad mug: person who makes mountain out of molehill.
bad trot: lean time.
Ballarat: cat.
barber: one who steals from residential premises without forcing entry.
barley: cut it out; stop it.
barrel: benefit night, proceeds going toward payment of bail or defence counsel of crim arrested.
bat material: pornographic material. (Masturbation)
beak: magistrate.
beat it: be acquitted.
bed & breakfast: seven days imprisonment.
being grilled: being interrogated.
be read up: have criminal record read aloud in court.
bin: pocket.
black peter: punishment cell devoid of light and furniture.
block: wristwatch.
blonk: idiot.
blot: anus.
blow down their lug: ear bash.
blue bit: five dollars.
bodgie: false.
bodgie address: false address.
boil up: make illegal cup of tea in cell.
boob: gaol.
boob happy: eccentric. Divorced from reality. Brought about by the strain of gaol routine. Similar to battle fatigue.
boob tea: weak gaol made tea.
boob tobacco: low grade gaol issued tobacco.
bouncer: dud cheque.

box on with it: contest court case.
boy in the boat: clitoris.
brasco: shithouse. (toilet)
brass: not pay your debts.
break: an excuse.
brick¹: ten dollars.
brick²: ten years.
bridge: exposing sensuous parts of body.
bring undone: cause someone to be found out.
bugged: alarmed.
bumper: dip's accomplice. Bumps into victim while dip removes whippy.
bunch up: put someone in impossible position.
bung it: pass contraband on to someone else to avoid being buckled with it.
bun wagon: police paddy wagon.
burgoo: hominy (gaol breakfast).
bust: breaking & entering (commercial premises).
bustman: one who specializes in busts.
butter up: use flattery as means to exploit.

can: gaol.
cannon: concealable firearm.
can't aim up: no ability.
can't be educated: won't be told.
can't fire: no ability.
captain: person who foots the bill.
carve him up: pull all his money off him.
case: get layout of premises for prospective robbery.
cat: passive homosexual.
chaff: money.
chew & spew: prison stew.
clacker: arsehole.
clean the books up: confess to numerous unsolved crimes.
cliner: dud.
clock: twelve months.
clout: method used by shoplifters: concealing stolen property under topcoat while being worn.
cockatoo: lookout.
cold: innocent of charge laid against you.
cold bite: ask a stranger for money.
come nothing: make no admissions.
come out of the woodwork: appear from nowhere.
come undone: be found out.

come yer guts: confess.
cop it sweet: don't retaliate.
cop the blue: take the blame.
crab: impede progress.
crack it: have an earn.
crim: professional thief. This term only applies to those who uphold criminal code. It is a mistake to think that anyone in gaol automatically qualifies.
cruel: ruin chances.
crusted: charged with vagrancy.
cunning kick: undeclared money.
cunt starver: in gaol for maintenance. (not supporting wife)
cut it out: do gaol rather than pay fine.

darbies: handcuffs.
deadset: no doubt.
dead to rights: caught red handed.
Dear John: goodbye letter from lover.
dip: pickpocket.
do a deal: plead guilty for pre-arranged sentence.
dodger: bread.
dog: informer.
dog it: squib it.
dog squad: undercover police.
doing the crust: serving a sentence for vagrancy.
do it hard: let sentence get you down.
do it on the shit tub: serve sentence as easy as possible.
do it on yer head: serve sentence as easy as possible.
do it tough: let sentence get you down.
dollied: loaded with false material evidence.
don't be a gig: mind your own business.
dook: pass something secretly.
double. two ounces of tobacco.
drack: ugly.
drag: three months.
drop: a fence; receiver of stolen goods.
drop from the ceiling: suddenly appear beside you.
drop off: quit what you're doing or else.
dropped: informed on.
dry: unmade tea(leaves).
dubbo: imbecile.
dudder: person who sells inferior quality goods and presents them as high grade merchandise.

dung puncher: another name for a hock.

earn: proceeds of robbery.
easy mark: soft touch.

fat wick: strip of sheeting or like material spread with fat, rolled up, and lit for purposes of boiling up.
finger: point out, accuse.
fitted: found guilty.
five cents in the dollar: insane.
flap: blank cheque leaf.
flat: grouse tobacco.
flum: fluke it.
fly a kite: pass dud cheque.
form: criminal record.
freckle: anus.
front: appear in court.

get buckled: be arrested.
get over: intimidate someone.
get up: be acquitted.
get yer head down: plead guilty.
gig: witness; someone who is watching.
ginger ale: bail.
give a bodgie: give an alias.
give (someone) up: inform on someone.
go: right time to strike.
going bad: not having any success.
go off the bars: commit suicide by hanging.
go off the tub: commit suicide by hanging.
go-slow: punishment cell.
go to press: write statement incriminating self or others.
go to water: weaken under pressure.
got their lug: have someone listening to you.
go under: be found guilty by jury.
grand: $1000.
grouse cigarette: tailor made.
grouse weed: outside tobacco high quality.

half inched: stolen.
half pie: half hearted.
half spot: $50.

handle: con someone.
handrush: bustle someone into decision.
hand up brief: open and shut case.
haste: stop immediately or you'll be sprung.
head-puller: a person who directs shop assistant's attention elsewhere while accomplice steals.
healy: trick to it.
heavies: detectives.
heavy peg: close scrutiny.
he's elephants: he's drunk.
high jump: Quarter Sessions.
history: in dire straits.
hit the toe: run, try to escape.
hit yer kick: your turn to shout.
hock: active homosexual.
hoister: shoplifter.
hoist the flag: appeal against conviction or severity of sentence.
hoon: man who lives off worker.
hotpoint: put something over someone.
howya travellin'?: how are you fixed for money.

in & out like a honeymoon prick: said of short termer who repeatedly comes to gaol.
in smoke: hiding from police.

jacks: detectives.
jerry: realize.
jigger: gaol made crystal set (illegal).
joint: concealable firearm.
jump: shop-counter.
jump the box: give sworn evidence.

Kate Lee: tea.
keep yer guard up: be careful.
Kentucky: collection taken up, proceeds going toward payment of bail or defence counsel of crim arrested.
key, the: being declared an habitual criminal.
kick: pocket.
kick a goal: be successful.
kick along with it: not going to appeal.
kick on: better yourself financially.
kite: newspaper.

knock: murder.
knock up: bang loudly on cell door when in need of medical attention.
kupie: prostitute.
kyber: arse.

lag: give someone up.
laggin': prison sentence.
lamp: look.
lamping: watching.
lash: to take the knock.
leave posted: stand someone up. Also not bail friend out.
left for dead: abandoned by friends.
left handed drop: giving information to a dog knowing full well the authorities will be told thereby reducing the chance of blame.
leg-opener: alcohol supplied to woman.
leg up: assistance.
lemon: anus.
lice ladders: sideburns.
lift: steal.
loaded: framed.
lob: arrive.
lot, the: life imprisonment.
low jump: petty sessions (court).
lumbered: taken to police station.
lunatic soup: cheap potent wine.

mark: boy.
mocker: clothes.
mod squad: plain clothes screws who handle shanghais.
monkey: $500.
moosh: hominy (gaol breakfast).
mug in tow: have sucker in company.
mug shot: police photograph.
musical milk: methylated spirits.

nephew: boy who is being seated but pretends 'nice man' is his uncle.
nick: gaol.
nit keeper: cockatoo.
nod yer head: plead guilty.
nonch: method used by shoplifters: concealing stolen property under coat draped casually over one shoulder.
not the full quid: insane.

on fire: too hot to handle. Too risky.
on the coat: ostracised.
on the grill: barred door instead of steel doored cell.
on the whack: entitled to a share.
open go: easy, anytime.
optic: perv.
orf: have no chance.

paper hanger: passer of dud cheques.
peanut butter sandwich: an honest job.
peg: look.
peter: cell.
peter thief: prisoner who steals from other prisoners cells. Regarded as despicable (not to be confused with "tickle the peter" which means to steal from the till).
piece: concealable firearm.
pitch for it: ask for trouble.
polish: praise.
pony: $25.
poof-rorter: man who takes money off homosexuals.
pound: time spent in punishment cell (without books, light, radio, tobacco).
pull the wrong rein: make a blunder.
pull yer coat: stop what you're doing.
pussy-footer: sneak thief. (opportunist)
put the knife through: go halves with a friend.
put them through: to brass someone.
put work on: make sexual advances to.

racehorse: thin gaol rolled cigarette.
ramp: search.
receiver of swollen goods: cat.
red light: stop, screw coming.
remand yard: hotel or club frequented by police because it's a known haunt.
ride there for a ride back: bi-sexual male.
ridge: real.
right whack: just deserts.
rip & tear: philosophy of determined thief: will not go home without scoring.
Robert: tongue.
rock spider: peeping Tom.
rort: modus operandi.
roscoe: gun.
roseleaf: tongue in bum.

Rudolf Vaselino: one who falsely boasts of his exploits with women.
running feed: non payment for meal in cafe.

scarper: abscond on bail.
score: twenty dollars.
screw: prison warder.
Seabreeze Hotel: Long Bay Gaol.
seat: insert penis in anus.
secko: sex offender.
seine: dollar.
serve him up: give him a hiding.
set (someone) up: enter into crime with someone having supplied police with prior knowledge of crime with sole purpose of having accomplices arrested in exchange for favours from police.
shanghai: sudden transfer to another gaol.
shelf: informer.
sheriff: hock who jealously guards cat.
shirt lifter: hock.
shit kicker: person of no account.
shitpot: talk ill of someone.
shiv: gaol made knife for stabbing purposes.
short arms & deep pockets: said of mean person.
shorten him up: cut him down to size.
shovel: room. Living quarters.
show pony: lair.
silk department: extra grouse.
silvertail: trustee having cushy job in prison.
sleep: prison sentence. Longer than 7 days less than 3 months.
slew & yer'll blue: don't look back, keep going.
slew yer head: look away.
slice: two dollars.
sling: pay police for services rendered.
slot: cell.
sloughed up: locked in cell.
smack a blue: be arrested and charged.
smother: block someone's view.
sneak go: sneak theft.
snip: ask for money.
snooker: hiding place.
snork: child.
snow dropper: person who steals clothes from clothesline.
solid: staunch to criminal code.

somersault: change plea of guilty to plea of not guilty.
S.O.S.: Same Old Shit. Speaking of prison meals.
spin¹: five dollars.
spin²: five years.
spot: $100.
sprung: seen in the act of doing something illegal.
squarehead: honest citizen.
square off: apologise.
stall: clear out.
starter: substitute for vaseline (margarine or any such thing).
stiff: uncensored letter smuggled out of prison.
stink: fight.
stir: gaol.
stir-crazy: institutionalized.
straw bail: bail papers signed by sugar bag on worthless surety.
suck his brain: see what he knows.
sugar bag: policeman who accepts bribes.
sunk: no chance of acquittal.
swy¹: two years.
swy²: two ounces of tobacco.

take it to the toe: run, try to escape.
take seconds: think again.
take the knock: cheat someone of his share, in part or whole.
tank: a safe.
tankman: person who specializes in stealing from safes.
ted: vagina.
throw off: camouflage the truth.
toe ragger: person of no account.
toey: anxious.
tom: jewellery.
track: screw who brings contraband for prisoners in exchange for fee.
trick cyclist: psychiatrist.
tropical: very risky.
tug his head: distract his gaze.
tumble: lose temper.
tune in: listen to other people's conversation.
turn it up: give crime away.
turn (someone) up: give evidence to bring about accused person's acquittal.
twine: to hoodwink.
twist, the: being declared an habitual criminal.

under a cloud: under suspicion of being a dog.
under the lap: secretive.
under the lights: questioned at C.I.B.

vag: charged with vagrancy.
verballed: be mispresented by lies.
virgin: derogatory term, pure cunt (no good person)

walk up start: there for the taking.
wallopers: uniformed police.
warb: shabbily dressed person.
Warwicks: arms.
weed: tobacco.
whack up: divide into shares.
wheelman: driver of get away car.
whippy: wallet.
wild duck: won't settle debts.
willy: wallet.
Woodpeckers' Day: Friday reserved for sentencing guilty pleas.
worker: prostitute.

yarra: mad.
your smother's your best friend: common saying among thieves.

zack: six months.

www.ingramcontent.com/pod-product-compliance
Lightning Source LLC
Chambersburg PA
CBHW020318010526
44107CB00054B/1894